ROMANESQUE SCULPTURE

OF THE PILGRIMAGE ROADS

ROMANESQUE SCULPTURE
OF THE PILGRIMAGE ROADS

BY

A. KINGSLEY PORTER

IN TEN VOLUMES

VOLUME I

TEXT

REPRINTED BY

HACKER ART BOOKS

NEW YORK

1966

FIRST PUBLISHED
1 9 2 3

Printed in the United States of America

CONTENTS

PART II: PILGRIMAGE SCULPTURE

LIST OF DATED MONUMENTS[1]

604. Venasque, Notre-Dame-de-Vic. Tomb of Boethius.
670. Bewcastle cross.
740. Hexham cross, now in Durham Library.
848. Naranco, Santa Maria.
848. Naranco, San Miguel de Linio.
893. Val de Dios, consecrated.
1002. Sagra S. Michele. Coro vecchio, Foresteria.
1002–1118. Dijon. Rotunda of St.-Bénigne.
1005. Piacenza, S. Savino. Campanile.
1006. Torino, S. Solutore. Church now buried.
1006. Sant Pere de Casserres.
1007. Beaulieu-les-Loches. Oldest portions.
1007–1026. St.-Martin-de-Canigou.
1008. Torcello, Cattedrale. Nave and apse mosaic.
1008. Vigolo Marchese. S. Giovanni.
1010. Maillezais, Abbaye, consecrated.
1012. Sant Cugat de Salon.
c. 1012–1020. Angers, St.-Martin. Carved plaque and core of nave.
1013. Bernay, Abbaye. Core of nave piers and south side-aisle wall.
1015. Hildesheim, Dom. Bronze doors completed (begun after 1107).
1016. Thiers, St.-Genès. Capitals of apse, north absidiole and eastern respond of southern side aisle.
1019–1025. Aquileia, Cattedrale. (Rebuilt in 1348.)
1019–1040. Sant Vincenç de Cardona.
1020. St.-Genis-des-Fontaines. Lintel (Ill. 513).
1020. St.-Michel-de-Cuxa, campanile.
1020. Carpignano near Otranto, grotto. Frescoed Christ.

[1] In this list are included only monuments, the dates of which can be determined by documentary evidence, and which are of significance for the chronological problems of the XI and XII centuries discussed in the following pages. The list makes no pretense of being complete; I hope, however, it may supply a somewhat broader basis for study than has hitherto been available. A few desultory dates before 1000 and after 1200 are included for purposes of comparison.

1060. Sculptures of the Mauritskirche, Münster, now in West-fälischen Landesmuseum.

Before 1061. Bouzemont.

1062. Sant Miguel de Cruelles.

1062. Caen, Abbaye-aux-Dames, begun. The crypt and the lower parts of walls belong to church finished before 1083.

1063. Crucifix of San Isidoro of Léon, now in Museo Arqueológico, Madrid (Ill. 654, 655).

1063. Ivory arca of S. Isidoro of Léon, fragments of which survive in box now in Museo Arqueológico, Madrid (Ill. 651–653).

1063 (begun)–1095 (consecrated). Venice, S. Marco.

1063. Pomposa, Campanile, begun.

1063–1118. Pisa, Cattedrale.

1064. Souvigny, consecrated. The remains of the narthex belonged to this church.

1064. Sant Lorenç del Munt.

1064. Caen, Abbaye-aux-Hommes. Façade and lower parts of nave belong to church begun in this year.

1065. Amalfi, Cattedrale. Bronze doors.

1065. Verona, S. Fermo Maggiore. Romanesque basilica begun.

1066. Monte Cassino, bronze doors.

1068–1097. Nevers, St.-Etienne.

1069. Santa Maria de Mur, consecrated (frescos now in Boston are later).

1069. Port-à-Binson.

Before 1070. Lesterps. Vaults of nave, part of clocher and exterior walls.

1070. Rome, S. Paolo f. l. m. Bronze doors.

1070–1103. Aix-en-Provence, Cathédrale St.-Sauveur, southern aisle.

1071–1130. St.-Benoît-sur-Loire. Damaged by fire in 1095 (Ill. 1414–1422).

1072. Zara, S. Maria, consecrated.

1072. Taranto, Cattedrale, begun. (Nearly completed in 1084).

1073. Ste.-Croix of Quimperlé, consecrated.

1073. Verona, S. Trinità. Southern absidiole.

1073. Léon. Romanesque cathedral, of which the foundations have been excavated.

1073–1076. Santo Domingo de Silos, cloister in construction (Ill. 666–673).

1093–1133. Durham, Cathedral. Choir vaulted 1104.

1094. San Juan de la Peña, consecrated.

1094. Charlieu, Abbaye, consecrated (Ill. 4).

1095–1130. St.-Jouin-de-Marne (Ill. 946–950).

1095. Milan, Chiesa d'Aurona. Fragments, group "D" now in Museo Archeologico.

1095. Pontida. Fragments of tomb of S. Alberto.

1095. Alet, Cathédrale, consecrated.

1096. Poiters, Montierneuf. Core of church consecrated. Begun soon after 1078. Body of the duke Guillaume translated into the church in 1087.

1096. Charroux, Abbaye, consecrated.

1096. Carcassonne, St.-Nazaire. Nave in construction.

1096. Huesca, San Pedro el Viejo, begun (Ill. 529–534).

1097. Verona, Cattedrale. S. Maria Matricolare.

1098. Bari, S. Niccola. Throne (Ill. 152–155).

1098. Cruas. Mosaic of apse.

1098. Trani, Cattedrale begun.

c. 1099. Rivolta d'Adda.

1099. S. Benedetto di Portesana.

1099–1106. Modena, Cattedrale. Façade sculptures, Porta della Pescheria and crypt, but the two latter subsequently altered.

c. 1100. Head of King Oistein, Bergen museum.

1100. Moissac cloister (Ill. 262–273).

1100. Milan, S. Sepolcro. Transept ends.

1100. Airvault, consecrated (Ill. 898–902).

1101. Nonantola, S. Michele.

1101. Canosa, consecrated.

1101–1128. Angoulême, Cathédrale (Ill. 929–940).

1102. Abbazia di Sesto Calende, S. Vincenzo.

1103–1113. Sessa Aurunca, Cattedrale.

1104. Roffeno-Musiolo.

1104. Vézelay. Destroyed choir consecrated. Existing nave immediately begun (Ill. 28–46).

After 1105. Secqueville-en-Bessin.

c. 1106. Padova, S. Sofia. Parts of eastern half of edifice.

1106. Avallon, St.-Lazare. Choir.

1106–c. 1165. Modena, Cattedrale. Nave.

1107. Lyon, St.-Martin-d'Ainay, consecrated.

1120. Thiers, St.-Genès.

1120–1130. Mainz, Dom, vaults.

c. 1120–1132–1146. Autun, Cathédrale (Ill. 67–81).

1120. Verona, S. Zeno. Campanile above podium.

1121. Nevers, Notre-Dame.

1121f. Nonantola. Western portal, southern side-aisle wall, western bays of northern side aisle, piers of nave and crypt vaults.

1122. Marseille, Cathédrale Ancienne. Altar-frontal (Ill. 1283, 1284).

1122. Lucca, San Michele di Scheto, consecrated.

c. 1122. Ganogobie. Mosaic pavement.

1122–1132. Piacenza, Cattedrale. Interior of choir, crossing up to triforium level, façade sculptures.

c. 1123. Padova, S. Sofia. Parts of western half of edifice.

1123. Verona, S. Giovanni in Fonte.

1123. Sant Climent de Tahull (frescos now in Barcelona museum).

1123. Santa Maria de Tahull (frescos, I understand, either have been, or are to be, transferred to Barcelona Museum).

1124. Senones, St.-Pierre, consecrated.

1125. Barcelona, S. Pablo al Campo, consecrated (Ill. 550).

1125. Bellefontaine, begun.

1125. St.-Amand-de-Boixe. Transepts and eastern bay of nave consecrated (Ill. 941–945).

1125–1149. Angers, Cathédrale. Nave (except vaults), façade, and base of towers.

1127. Troia, Cattedrale. Southern bronze doors.

1129. Freckenhorst, Stiftskirche. Baptismal font.

1129. Milan, S. Giorgio in Palazzo.

c. 1130–1150. Parma, Cattedrale. Body of edifice up to vaulting capitals.

1130–1154. Angers, St.-Aubin. Tower.

1131. Auvers, Absidiole.

1131–1148. Cefalù, Cattedrale.

1132. Santa Maria in Cellis, near Carsoli. Wooden doors.

1132. Pavia, S. Pietro in Ciel d'Oro, consecrated.

1132. Vézelay. Narthex consecrated (Ill. 47–51).

Before 1133. Moûtiers-St.-Jean. Capitals now in Fogg Museum, Cambridge, Mass. (Ill. 62–66).

1133. Foligno, Cattedrale. Romanesque remains.

1133. Romans, begun (Ill. 1334–1338).

1162. Pistoia, S. Giovanni Fuorcivitas. Portal (Ill. 199).

1162. Parma, Cattedrale. Vaults.

1162–1182. Reims, St.-Remi. Reconstruction including sculptures of consoles.

1163. Paris, St.-Germain-des-Prés, consecrated. Western portal dated from this period.

1163. Assisi, S. Maria Maggiore. Rose-window.

1163. Paris, Cathédrale, begun. Consecration in 1182.

1164. Verona, S. Giovanni in Valle.

1164. Vercelli, S. Bernardo.

1164. Jazeneuil. Choir finished.

1164. Sens, Cathédrale, consecrated. At this time finished up to three western bays of nave.

1165. Louvain, St.-Michel.

1165. St.-Guilhem-le-Désert. Narthex.

1165. Monterappoli, portal.

1166. Pistoia, S. Andrea. Portal (Ill. 191–193).

1166. Braunschweig, Lion of Herzog Heinrich.

1166. Cúgnoli. Ambo.

1166. Rocamadour, Crypte St.-Amadour and Basilique St.-Sauveur.

1166–1189. Monreale, Duomo.

1166–1199. Poitiers, Cathédrale. Choir.

1167. Villanova.

1167. Pistoia, S. Bartolommeo in Pantano. Portal.

1167–1184. Modena, Cattedrale. Campanile (subsequently altered).

c. 1168. Mozac. Châsse de Saint Calmin.

1169. Périgueux, St.-Etienne. Tomb of the bishop Jean.

1169. Troia, Cattedrale. Pulpit.

1170. St.-Amant-de-Boixe. Nave, except eastern bay and lantern finished (Ill. 1135).

1171. S. Maria di Ronzano.

1171. Milan, S. Simpliciano. Western portal and responds of narthex.

1171. Piacenza, S. Antonino. Northern portal and sculptures.

1171. St.-Pons-de-Thòmières. Later capitals of cloister (Ill. 1265–1274).

1171. Milan, Porta Romana.

1171–1172. S. Lorenzo de Carboeiro.

1173. Pisa, Campanile, begun.

1220. Amiens, Cathédrale, begun.
1220–1231. Altamura, Cattedrale.
1224. Narbonne, St.-Paul. Vaults.
1221. Burgos, Catedral, begun.
1225–1230. S. Giovanni in Venere. Western Portal.
1226. Laon, Cathédrale. North portal in façade tower.
1227. Longpont (Aisne), consecrated.
1229. Bitonto, Cattedrale. Ambo (Ill. 244, 245).
1233. Milan, Palazzo della Ragione. Equestrian statue of Oldrado da Tresseno.
1234. Auxerre, Cathédrale. Choir finished.
1237. Bamberg, Dom, consecrated.
1238. Cellole, Cattedrale, completed.
1238. Bazzano, S. Giusta.
1238. Provins, St.-Quiriace. Transept in construction.
1239. Cambronne. South side aisle and chevet.
1240. Prata Ausidonia. Ambo.
1240. Traù, Duomo. Portal.
1247. Paris, Sainte Chapelle, finished.
1247. Beauvais, Cathédrale, begun.
1253. Sculptures from choir-screen of Wessobrunn now in the Munich museum.
Between 1255 and 1266. Carcassonne, St.-Nazaire. Chapel of Bishop Randulphe.
1259. Brioude, St.-Julien. Vaults.
1262. Troyes, St.-Urbain, begun.
1265. Narbonne, St.-Paul. Choir finished.
After 1266. Carcassonne, St.-Nazaire. Tomb of Bishop Randulphe.
1267. Curcumello. Ambo.
1269. Carcassonne, St.-Nazaire. Nave and transepts begun.
1270. Matera, Cattedrale, finished.
1272. Narbonne, Cathédrale, begun.
1278. Rouen, Cathédrale. Portail de la Librairie begun.
1283. Giovinazzo, Cattedrale, consecrated.
1295. Bisceglie, Cattedrale, consecrated.
After 1316. Altamura, Cattedrale. Portal.

ROMANESQUE SCULPTURE OF THE PILGRIMAGE ROADS

CLUNY

I

THE CHRONOLOGICAL PROBLEM

My own conception of Romanesque chronology was originally that which critical opinion in general still follows. This system of dating I found to be accepted, and there appeared to be no reason to question its accuracy.

In studying the Romanesque art of Lombardy, I found a great number of documents which established for this region, at the end of the XI and early XII century, a chronology notably earlier than that admitted for the rest of Europe. The fact seemed singular, but I explained it on the ground that Lombardy at this period was in advance of the North.

Returning to the study of French art, and re-reading the literature, I was struck by the number of monuments, the style of which is said not to correspond with the documentary evidence for date. The phrase that such and such a monument must be later than the literary sources would lead us to believe, is repeated so frequently that it becomes a stereotyped formula. We are told that Ste.-Croix of Quimperlé is really not of 1083, but of the XII century; that the apse of St.-Guilhem-le-Désert is not of 1076, but of the XII century. The crypt of St.-Eutrope of Saintes is given to the XII century in spite of the clearest and most circumstantial evidence that it was consecrated in 1096; the vaults of the tower of St.-Hilaire of Poitiers are believed to be not of the end of the XI century, but of the XII century; Bellefontaine is considered to date not from 1125, but from later; the capitals of Cluny (Ill. 5–10) are ascribed not to 1088–1095 as the documents indicate, but to the XII century; those of Autun (Ill. 67–79) are assigned not to c. 1120–1132 as documented, but to 1150–1160; the obviously contemporary ones of Vézelay (Ill. 28–46), a church the narthex of which was consecrated in 1132, are similarly ascribed to some twenty years later; the façade of Angoulême (Ill. 929–940) is called not of 1128, but of the second half of the XII century; the inner tympanum of Charlieu (a church consecrated in 1094), clearly much earlier than the porch of c. 1140, is called not of 1094, but of the XII century (Ill. 4); the transepts of St.-Amand-de-Boixe (Ill. 941–945) are ascribed not to 1125 but to 1170; Chadennac (Ill. 1034–1040) is called not of 1140, but of 1170; Fontevrault not of 1119 but of the second quarter of the XII century; the Bayeux embroidery not of from shortly after 1066 but of the XII century;[1] the tympanum of Moissac (Ill. 339-342) documented as before 1115 has been ascribed to 1130. From France this same system of setting aside documents has been extended to other lands: the tomb of S. Alberto at Pontida, dated 1095, has been assigned to after 1214; the façade sculptures of Modena dated 1099–1106 by a contemporary chronicle and an inscription, are said really to have been executed after 1140; the Porta della Pescheria at Modena, also dated 1099–1106, is ascribed to the end of the XII century; the northern portal of Borgo S. Donnino, dated 1106, is also assigned to the XIII century; the reliefs of Cremona dated 1107–1117 are called "un peu antérieurs au milieu du XIIe siècle"; the Ferrara portal, dated 1135 by an inscription, is said nevertheless to be "guère avant 1150"; the portal of the cathedral of Verona, dated 1139, is, notwithstanding, assigned to the middle of the century; the sculptures of the baptistry of Parma, begun in 1196 according to a contemporary inscription, still "ne sauraient être antérieures à 1220"; the cloister of S. Orso of Aosta, dated 1133 by an inscription, must really

---

[1] Mr. Roger Loomis has definitively proved that the Bayeux embroidery dates from soon after 1066.

be some years later; the cloister sculptures of Santo Domingo de Silos are considered not of 1073-1076 as documented, but of *c.* 1130.

There are two stock explanations for the existence of these supposedly misleading documents. The first, and most used, assumes that the construction of Romanesque buildings proceeded very slowly, and with many delays; that the actual building might take place years after the date given in the documents for the beginning of the construction, or the consecration [1] of the church or even its completion.

This theory possibly holds true of certain Gothic monuments, but I know of no good reason for extending its application as a general rule to the Romanesque age. The step from saying that the construction might have taken place years after, to saying that it must have taken place years after, was a short one. What had been found to be possibly true of certain Gothic monuments, came to be considered necessarily true of all Romanesque monuments.

The second explanation for the existence of these misleading documents is to suppose that in each case the building in question was subsequently reconstructed. In any one instance this hypothesis might carry conviction, although it is always intrinsically improbable that a second rebuilding should have taken place so soon after the first; but in such a number of instances it becomes untenable. It was certainly not the custom in the Middle Ages to pull down a new church as soon as it was finished.

It would seem that the setting aside of so many documents could be justified only if the style of the monuments in question had been found to be inconsistent with that of other and more numerous monuments of better authenticated date. But I found that such was far from being the case. Indeed, the penury of dated monuments of this period in France is a commonplace.

[1] In the XII century, the consecration normally took place either when the entire church, or some considerable portion, such as the choir, had been completed. Often a first consecration marked the completion of the choir, a second the completion of the entire church. Very exceptionally, for special reasons, the consecration was hastened or postponed. But to argue from such exceptional cases — I do not know of a single one in the XII century which can be proved — that all consecration dates are misleading, is illogical and unwarranted.

This penury, it is true, exists especially in the Ile-de-France. In the neighbouring regions a few monuments of accepted date can be found. These are:

1077.	Bayeux cathedral, crypt.
c. 1083–1093.	Caen, St.-Nicolas.
1083–1099.	Poitiers, Ste.-Radegonde. Choir and west end.
1088–1119.	Angers, Eglise du Ronceray.
1095–1130.	St.-Jouin-de-Marne.
1096.	Poitiers, Montierneuf, consecrated.
1096.	Charroux, consecrated.
1097.	St.-Etienne of Nevers, consecrated.
1100.	Airvault, consecrated.
1107.	Lyon, St.-Martin d'Ainay, consecrated.

I confess that the more I studied this list, and compared it with the list of rejected dates, the greater became my perplexity. Not only was the list of accepted dates singularly meager in comparison with those that were rejected, so that, supposing the two to be incompatible it was difficult to see why the former should have been preferred; but the fact of incompatibility between the two seemed to me far from obvious. Why, for example, if the choir of Montierneuf at Poitiers is admitted as of 1096, should the crypt of St.-Eutrope of Saintes be considered later? Furthermore, I remarked that the monuments, the dates of which were admitted, lay without exception either in Normandy, in Poitou or in Auvergne — that is to say in provinces which might *a priori* be expected to be *retardataire*. It seemed to me very significant that in cultured Burgundy, notwithstanding the great profusion of documents, there was not a single monument of accepted date.

In fact, the more I studied the literature, the more evident it became to me that, as a rule, in determining the age of any given work, less weight had been attached to comparison with dated monuments or to documents than to archaeological theory. The date assigned was really fixed according to a pre-conception of the development of style, which enabled the scholar to judge on internal evidence the age of any monument. It is in reliance upon this archaeological system that scholars have disregarded a large proportion of the documentary evidence for French buildings.

In fact, the unquestioning confidence placed in this chronological theory, not only by scholars of France, but by those of the world, is evident on almost every page of archaeological writing. The premise is universally accepted as a firm basis from which to draw conclusions, although its truth seems never to have been really tested.

Yet my own faith, I confess, was further shaken by observing certain proven errors into which this theory had led some even of its most eminent exponents. Thus in the same work, M. André Michel's *Histoire de l'Art*, on one page M. Enlart states that the reliefs of S. Isidoro of Léon are of the XI century,[1] while on another,[2] M. Bertaux dates the same reliefs to 1147. Therefore an archaeological theory which is preferred to authentic documents, must nevertheless have led one or the other of these distinguished scholars into a chronological error of a century.

Nor does this instance stand alone. Comte de Lasteyrie, relying on the theory, held that St.-Front of Périgueux was reconstructed after the fire of 1120; but from the researches of Chanoine Roux it now seems probable that the church consecrated in 1047 still stands. The vaulted basilicas of Lombardy were thought to be of the XIII century; but it is now admitted that they are of the XI century. It was considered axiomatic that no basilicas were vaulted in Europe before the XI century; but numerous examples some two centuries earlier have been found in Spain. The crosses of Hexham and Bewcastle were pronounced works of the XII century;[3] whereas it transpires that they are authentically dated by inscriptions 740 and 670 respectively.[4] Zimmermann assigned the apostles of Milan cathedral to the end of the XIII or beginning of the XIV century[5] — " das

[1] I, 2, 564.   [2] II, 1, 250.
[3] Enlart in Michel's *Histoire de l'Art*, I, 2, 520–521.
[4] Enlart in Michel's *Histoire de l'Art*, II, 1, 199–200.
[5] 197.

Werk kann frühestens aus dem Ende des 13. oder gar erst Anfang des 14. Jahrhunderts stammen " —; but Gall has shown that they were executed in 1186. M. Bertaux assigned the pulpit at Canosa to the end of the XI century [1] — " fin du XIᵉ siècle " —; but the ink was hardly dry on his pages, when Wackernagel [2] discovered an inscription proving that the pulpit is anterior to 1041. Comte de Lasteyrie assigned the frieze of St.-Gilles to the end of the XII century; but it is certain that it is contemporary with the great statues, and executed about 1140. Comte de Lasteyrie assigned the façade of St.-Trophîme of Arles to 1180; it was, however, erected in 1152. The sculptures of Conques have been ascribed to the second half or end of the XII century; but they were executed by sculptors who worked at Santiago before 1124. The Cagliari pulpit has, by the greatest Italian critic, not only been dated 1260, but judged a work by the hand of Fra Guglielmo, the well-known assistant of Niccola Pisano; however, the investigations of Scanno have proved that it is a century older, and more precisely that it was begun in 1158 and finished in 1162. The tomb of Widukind at Enger near Herford has been assigned to the middle of the XII century; but the investigation of Creutz [3] leaves no doubt that it is on the contrary of the early years of the XII century. The cathedral of Conversano in Apulia (Ill. 179) was believed to be a surely dated monument of 1369–1373; but it now appears that the inscription was misread, and that the church really dates from 1159–1174. Nor can I claim to have been myself less mislead than others. Relying on theory I assigned to the XII century the S. Ambrogio altar, which, however, I now see, is as the inscription indicates, essentially of the IX century.

Such chronological errors, showing in every case underdating on the part of the archaeologists who had followed orthodox theory, led me to suspect that that theory, far from being an infallible guide, might be founded on the supposition that the mediaeval styles developed later and more consistently than was actually the case. This suspicion deepened when I noted that archaeological writers, even

[1] 445.   [2] 4 f.   [3] 56.

when forced by the strength of the evidence to accept the documented date for works of the late XI or early XII century, do so in many cases with the utmost reluctance, and are obviously troubled by a discrepancy between the style displayed by the given object, and that which archaeological theory had led them to expect at the date in question. Thus M. Bertaux studies the throne at Bari (Ill. 152–155) which is dated 1098, and marvels over its advanced style: " Si l'oeuvre n'était pas datée de manière irrécusable par l'inscription et par une chronique contemporaine, on la croirait postérieure d'un siècle à l'archevêque Hélie." [1] M. Louis Serbat writes of St.-Etienne of Nevers, which he accepts as of the documented dates, but adds: "Quand on veut tenir compte à la fois et des textes et des faits, l'étude de St.-Etienne de Nevers ne va-t-elle pas sans être quelque peu déconcertante." [2] Yet St.-Etienne of Nevers, when compared with the closely related and contemporary cathedral of Santiago, is seen to be singularly *retardataire*. A great German scholar, after having assigned to 1118 the pulpit of Canosa, now known to be some eighty years earlier, studies the pulpit of S. Basilio at Troia, dated 1158 by an inscription. He is amazed at the advanced style: "Hätte man diese Inschrift nicht, so könnte man versucht sein, die Kanzel in's XIII Jahrh. herab zu rücken." [3] M. André Michel illustrates and describes the Externstein of the Teutoburger Forest, dated, as he remarks, 1115. But he goes on to observe: "C'est bien plus avant dans le XII⁰ siècle qu'on serait tenté de placer un morceau de cette envergure." [4]

In the light of these facts, I became conscious of an inconsistency running through the mediaeval archaeology of the Romanesque period; on the one side are the documents, consistently (for the accepted dates are by no means irreconcilable with the rejected) indicating an earlier date, on the other the theory setting all these dates some years later. The consistency of the documents between

[1] 446.
[2] *Cong. Arch.*, 1913, 352.
[3] In order to explain the marvel, he supposes the pulpit to have been executed in Sicily.
[4] *Histoire de l'Art*, II, 2, 741.

themselves, and their inconsistency with the theory, seem to have passed unobserved.

In view of the grave indictment of the archaeological theory by the documents, it becomes incumbent to study upon what evidence this theory is based, and to trace the steps by which it has taken form.

The science of mediaeval archaeology may be considered to have been initiated by De Caumont, who studied especially the monuments of Normandy. His labours found a quick echo in England. Knowledge of the monuments of these two regions far to the north, inaccessible to the artistic centres of the South, gave from the beginning an impression of slow and late development for Romanesque.

From Normandy, the centre of archaeological research was soon transferred to Paris. The new school displayed from the start an admirable spirit of critical scepticism. In fact early writers had too often loved the glory of their native land with greater fervour than was compatible with impartial judgment. Monuments of the author's country had been ascribed to fabulous antiquity; any documentary evidence, especially if it tended to establish great age for the local antiquities, had been accepted without criticism of style. Under De Caumont a more scientific spirit had already begun to reign. The new school regarded all with doubt, no date which could be questioned was accepted. Monuments were carefully and minutely compared and correlated. With a fine scorn for the chauvinism of the earlier generation, this school tended to accept the latest, rather than the earliest, date possible.

The leader of the new movement was M. Lefèvre-Pontalis. His *Architecture Religieuse dans l'ancien Diocese de Soissons*, overthrew the chronology of Fleury, and became the foundation-stone of the modern science of mediaeval archaeology.

The basis of departure for the chronological study in this book was narrow — the author confined himself to the Soissonnais, a district characterized by a singular penury of documents. The *terminus ad quem* was the abbey of St.-Denis, 1137–1140; he found an earlier point of support in the priory of Bellefontaine, the construction of which was authorized in 1125; by a masterly study of the internal evidence, he arrived at the conclusion that the ambulatory of Morienval must date from the early years of the XII century. This was a modification of the same author's earlier, and it seems to me sounder, opinion, that the ambulatory of Morienval was built in the last quarter of the XI century.[1]

There ensued a controversy. Moved by the spirit of reaction against the excessively early dating of the previous generation, scholars rushed to the attack of this dating of Morienval. Into the discussion there entered comparison only with the undated churches of the Ile-de-France. M. Lefèvre-Pontalis again yielded; it was conceded that the ambulatory of Morienval was built only after 1122 when relics were translated.

This solution of the controversy, like so many solutions of archaeological discussions, was a politic compromise, the truth of which was never in any absolute fashion proved. I can not help feeling that M. Lefèvre-Pontalis' first position was probably nearer right than his later one, and that if he had held fast to it, we should have less rejected documents for which to account. Morienval must be much older than Bellefontaine, which the documents discovered by M. Lefèvre-Pontalis give reason to believe was begun in 1125. Therefore to assume the ambulatory of Morienval as a dated monument of after 1122, was opening the door to the possibility of grave error.

Nevertheless, the question was considered as closed, and the chronology of the Ile-de-France as definitely settled. Studies were extended to the rest of France and to foreign countries. Monument after monument was examined separately, and its date determined by comparison with the edifices of the Ile-de-France or with other buildings, of which the chronology had by similar means been established. Any documents inconsistent with the archaeological system that thus grew up were simply set aside. This seems to be the explanation of the formidable list of disregarded documents that we have enumerated.

[1] Lefèvre-Pontalis, *Arch. Rel.*, I, 74.

From time to time investigators in the provinces of France, or in Spain or Italy, by studying the monuments and documents of a local region, arrived at a somewhat earlier chronology. Such scholars, however, seldom affected the archaeological opinion of the world. Any chronology, inconsistent with the orthodox chronology, was *a priori* rejected. The only dissenting voice given serious consideration, was that of M. Marignan, who proposed to move the entire chronological chain a half century *later!*

Indeed, the scholars of the last half century, while always keenly on the alert against the danger of assigning too early a date, seem to have been singularly oblivious of the converse danger of assigning a date too late. The possibility that any given monument may actually be earlier than it can be demonstrated to be, has been lost from sight. It has become a received maxim of archaeology that a thing may be later, but can not be earlier, than it can be proved to be. One feels throughout this literature, that the writers are keenly on their guard against dating too early. Reproaches are addressed to those scholars who have not sufficiently weighed the possibility that a monument may be later than the documents indicate. The writers seem to pride themselves upon being too clever to have fallen into such a trap. But they show no caution against the danger of dating too late. Such archaeologists are constantly asking themselves in regard to any monument: " may it not be later ? ", and unless positive proof is forthcoming, are very apt to conclude that it is. They have an air of virtue in selecting the latest possible date, as if a temptation had been victoriously overcome. It seems to have been forgotten that, by the law of averages, it is safer, in cases of latitude, to assume the middle, rather than the latest possible date. By always choosing, in cases of doubt, the latest date, a generation of archaeologists has inch by inch edged Romanesque chronology down.

Moreover, archaeological method has assumed for the Ile-de-France the same artistic hegemony over Europe before 1140 that the region manifestly possessed afterwards. Yet it is certain that before the XII century the art of the Ile-de-France was distinctly *retarda-*

taire. The rib-vaulted nave of Durham cathedral, in the north of England, where art was certainly not precocious, was projected in 1093, although a parallel stage of development does not seem to have been reached in the Ile-de-France until thirty years later. No figure sculpture in stone worthy of the name, appears to have existed in the neighbourhood of Paris until nearly 1140, although such was executed in Lombardy, in Languedoc, in Burgundy and in Spain forty years before. No building, at least so far as we know, comparable to Santiago, or St.-Sernin, or S. Ambrogio, or Cluny, or St. Mark's, or the cathedral of Pisa was erected in the Ile-de-France before St.-Denis. Capitals with naturalistic leafage are found at Santiago in Spain forty years before they appear in northern France. However much one may — and must — admire the rural architecture of the Ile-de-France, the fact is certain that until 1140 it was distinctly *retardataire* in comparison with the more southern districts of France, with Italy and with Spain.

The danger of an archaeological method which dated the architecture of all Europe on the basis of that of Paris seems therefore manifest.

In the hope of throwing light upon the problem raised by the conflict between the unanimous opinion of the archaeologists on the one hand, and the nearly unanimous evidence of the documents on the other, I have set at the beginning of this volume a list of the dated monuments of the period in question. While this makes no pretense of being complete, it is, I think, sufficient to reveal the fact that the documentary evidence for Romanesque chronology is far more abundant than has hitherto been suspected. The list includes not only monuments in France, but a certain number in Italy, Spain and other lands, the art of which shows stylistic affiliation with that of France during the Romanesque period.

This chart makes it clear that the Romanesque art of Europe before 1140 was far from presenting that uniform and logical development which characterized the Ile-de-France after that date. The idea of evolution, combined with a vicious tradition of criticism inherited from Vasari, appears to have led the archaeological world into a false conception of the history of mediaeval art. The smooth and orderly progress that actually did exist in certain arts, such as transitional architecture, or Italian painting of the Quattrocento, has been assumed to hold in all periods and all styles. The history of art has been viewed as a gradual and continuous unfolding from crude beginnings towards ultimate perfection. Periods of decline have of course been recognized, but have not been allowed to disturb belief in evolutionary principles.

It is, however, a very open question to what extent the facts in the history of art correspond with the theory of evolution as expounded in the biological sciences. The modern war monuments in Périgord are certainly quite different from the pre-historic cave-paintings,[1] but how much actual progress they display might well be disputed. The truth seems to be that the earliest art of which we have record is about as good as any which the human race has succeeded in producing during some forty thousand years of nearly unceasing endeavour. More careful study of the painting of the XI and XII centuries has revealed the fact that many of what had been thought to be discoveries of the Quattrocento painters had been anticipated by their Romanesque predecessors. From the tombs of Venasque, Bobbio and Pavia we learn that the VII and VIII centuries, instead of being an age of the utmost artistic degeneration, were capable of producing subtle and thoughtful carved decoration in stone of the finest execution.

The history of art, considered in its broad outlines, seems to show, not a continuous evolution from lower to higher forms, but a number of recurrences of the cycle archaic, classic, decadent, each of which ends approximately where it began.[2] It would, however, be easy to exaggerate the regularity and persistence of these cycles. Whole arts,

---

[1] The paintings in the cave at Altamira in the Asturias, discovered by a Spaniard in 1879, sneered at by the orthodox, finally won official recognition from the French Academy in 1906. It took twenty-seven years for an evident truth to permeate the bars of prejudice raised by the theory of evolution.

[2] It is worthy of remark that archaic art tends to be religious, decadent art, secular.

like Byzantine painting, can not be pigeon-holed in such categories, and any movement which they display can only be characterized as aimless drifting. Now Romanesque figure art appears to be of this type. We find in it, as a rule, change, but not necessarily advance. Only in the transition to Gothic does the style become, in any true sense of the word, archaic.

The orthodox chronology of Romanesque has assumed a constant progression from lower to higher forms which did not in fact exist. It is easy to say that any work which is crude is early, and any work which is fine is late. This facile formula may satisfy those who seek generalities, and shun the sifting of complicated evidence. Its fallacy has, however, always been tacitly admitted. No serious archaeologist would question that the extremely crude sculptures of Chambon (Ill. 1250) are of the XII century; whereas the much finer sculptures of the cloister at Moissac (Ill. 262–273) are admitted to be of 1100. A glance at the chart will reveal a great number of similar anomalies. Polished Santiago was being built at the same moment as rough St.-Nicolas of Caen. The technically advanced sculptures of the throne of S. Niccola at Bari (Ill. 152–155) were carved in 1098; while the far more primitive work at Rutigliano (Ill. 163–165) is of 1108. Technically and stylistically the lintel of St.-Genis-des-Fontaines (Ill. 513) dated 1020 or still more that of St.-André-de-Sorrède (Ill. 514–515) and the lunette of the cathedral of Troia (Ill. 172) which was executed about 1119, would seem to be related; instead, however, of being works of the same school, they are separated geographically by half of Europe, and chronologically by a century.[1] The cathedral of

---

[1] M. Bertaux, 664–665, ascribes the tympanum of Troia to *c.* 1200. "Le groupement des figures et le travail des draperies rappellent d'une manière frappante le relief du portail de Monte S. Angelo qui est daté de 1198." In this I confess that I am unable to follow the eminent archaeologist. His reasoning is indeed a typical example of that partiality for late dating of which we have been complaining. The bronze doors below the tympanum of the portal of Troia were executed in 1119; consequently the portal which holds them must be earlier. The style of the Troia tympanum is entirely in accord with this documentary evidence. In placing the tympanum of Troia (Ill. 172) beside that of S. Maria of Monte S. Angelo (Ill. 231), I am struck not by the resemblances of which M. Bertaux speaks, but by the complete difference. It is only necessary to compare the faces to be persuaded that the Troia relief is three quarters of a century earlier, and indeed dates from precisely the time the documentary evidence would lead us to believe.

Foggia, begun in 1179, is a copy, practically without advance, of the cathedral of Troia, begun in 1093. The cathedral of Bitonto reproduced, a century later, S. Niccola of Bari. The font of St.-Barthélemy of Liège, dated 1112, is of a far more developed style than the other font, now in the museum at Brussels, and dated 1149. The Arca Santa of Oviedo (Ill. 656–660) dated 1075, seems closely related to, but less advanced than, the doors of Hildesheim, dated 1015. These Hildesheim doors of 1015 appear much more advanced than the lintel of St.-Genis-des-Fontaines of 1020 (Ill. 513).

In Auvergne there were executed in the XII century, and even at an advanced period of the XII century, buildings in which the ornamental sculpture was exceedingly crude. There is no contemporary structure in England, nor in Apulia, nor in Lombardy, nor in Spain, nor in France to rival in technical finish St. Mark's of Venice or the cathedral of Pisa. Consider the gulf which separates either of these structures from the cathedral of Durham, which was not begun until 1093!

Indeed, archaeological controversies give proof of the lack of progress characteristic at times of the art of the Middle Ages. It is still disputed whether the golden altar of S. Ambrogio be of the IX or of the XII century; whether the sculptures of Cividale be of the VIII or of the XII; whether the baptistry at Florence be of the VI or of the XII; whether the Hexham and Bewcastle crosses be of the XII or the VII; whether S. Miniato be of the XI or of the XII. Such differences of opinion force us to recognize that the lapse of even six centuries brought on occasion a change of style so slight that we are unable to detect it, if it exist at all. No one has yet been able to date mediaeval frescos on their style. Ivories of one century show the same characteristics as sculptures of another. The greatest difference of opinion still reigns among scholars as to the dating of certain miniatures.

From all this, we can only conclude that Romanesque art was singularly uneven in its production. Nor is it my new chronology, I hasten to add, that introduces this chaos. It has always existed, flagrantly existed, in the orthodox system, although the fact has been passed over in silence. It was the fashion to assume that Romanesque art displayed the same orderly progression which is characteristic of French transitional architecture. Why should troubling discrepancies be insisted upon?

Although Romanesque art is not, broadly speaking, evolutionary, it is still not without change, nor without certain tendencies which it is entirely possible to trace. Thus from an inspection of the chart it appears that in general the South was in advance over the North; Italy and Spain abreast of southern France, southern France in advance over northern France, northern France over England, Belgium [1] and Germany. While this is true of the general state of the art, individual motives travelled with amazing rapidity from one end of Europe to the other. And in the same region we may find productions of the utmost divergence, executed side by side, contemporaneously.

This vital fact should be borne in mind in considering the chronology of the monuments, the documented date of which has been rejected by orthodox archaeology. These dates do not fall outside the broad frame of Romanesque development, as indicated by the documentary evidence assembled in the chart. There is, I think, no feature in any one of the monuments of which the dates have been set aside, which can not be paralleled in some contemporary and dated monument.

I am therefore persuaded that orthodox archaeology is in error in rejecting the dates furnished by the documents for this group of monuments. In the following chapters it will appear that the documents and the monuments are in reality in perfect agreement; and the history of Romanesque art will be seen in a light less dramatic, less Darwinistic, but I think more convincing, than that hitherto imagined.

[1] See Lemaire, 307–308.

II

THE ELEVENTH CENTURY

MODERN art may be considered to have begun with the Byzantine renaissance of the X century. This outburst of artistic activity seems to have spread from the East over Europe. Before the year 1000 renewed artistic activity appears sporadically in several widely separated regions of the West. In Spain architecture rose during the X century to extraordinary heights; capitals were carved with surprising skill in the Rhone valley, as in the crypt of Cruas or the baptistry of Venasque; while in Germany the Othonian miniatures and ivories developed types of such beauty, that they impressed indelibly the memory of the XII century sculptors of France, and still serve as models to artists of to-day. By the XI century, the renaissance had enflamed the entire continent of Europe.

In the East, figure sculpture was applied to the exterior of churches apparently as early as the VII century, certainly from the time of the X century renaissance. The church of Achthamar in Armenia, a dated monument of 915–921 is adorned with sculptures which seem to indicate an Eastern derivation for many of the later developments in the West.[1] Not only is the fact of monumental sculpture in stone foreshadowed, but here are found numerous details which have become characteristic of occidental sculpture of the XII century. The draperies of Guglielmo [2] and Santiago (Ill. 681–684), the medallions of Angoulême (Ill. 929–931), the adossed reliefs of Moissac (Ill. 262–273) and St.-Michel-de-Cuxa (Ill. 558, 559), the gestures of Chartres and Arles (Ill. 1369, 1371, 1373, 1374, 1376), a myriad other features of occidental sculptures are anticipated.

[1] The church at Achthamar has been published by Strzygowski, *Armenier*, 289 f.
[2] See Porter, *Lomb. Arch.*, IV, Plate 83, Fig. 8; Plate 142, Fig. 2, 3; Plate 143, Fig. 1; Plate 144, Fig. 1, 2; Plate 145, Fig. 1, 3. Also, Porter, *Les Débuts de la Sculpture Romane*, 51, and Monteverdi, 23, 13, 14, 48.

One of the oldest extant monuments of western sculpture is preserved in a remote village of the eastern Pyrenees. It is precisely in such regions that archaeology has taught us to expect *retardataire* art; and, indeed, no one who had an archaeological reputation to lose, or still less to win, would ever have dared assign the lintel of St.-Genis-des-Fontaines (Ill. 513) to an earlier period than the latter part of the XI century, were it not for a unique chance. The lintel is dated between 1020 and 1021 by an inscription of unquestionable authenticity.[1] This rare good fortune furnishes us with a conspicuous landmark to guide our course over the uncharted waters of the early XI century.

St.-Genis-des-Fontaines does not stand alone. In the tympanum of the not very distant church of Arles-sur-Tech is incorporated a relief (Ill. 518) obviously of the same school, but of finer and more advanced execution. This relief also happens to be dated; the church was consecrated in 1046.[2] We can, therefore, see the progress that has been scored in a quarter of a century. The same rate of develop-

[1] ✠ ANNO VIDESIMO QVARTO RENNATE RO'BERTO REGE VVILIELMVS GRA DEI ABA | ISTA OPERA FIERI IVSSI' IN ONORE SCI' GENESII CENOBII CVE VOCANT FONTANAS.

[2] Brutails, 57; *Cong. Arch.*, 1906, 131. The relationship of the *Christ* of Arles-sur-Tech (Ill. 518) to that of St.-Genis (Ill. 513) hardly needs demonstration. The same bead ornament occurs on the border of the garment of the *Christ* at Arles, and on those of the angels at St.-Genis. The position of the two Christs is identical, even to the detail that in each case the book is grasped in the left hand about its upper outer corner. Both have the same peculiar top-shaped head. The beard in both cases is pointed, and indicated by the same convention of parallel incised lines. The convention of parallel folds on the right sleeve is in both cases the same. The pattern on the books is very similar, and the border identical. In each case the draperies form a circle over the right knee. In each case the hair is parted in the middle, and indicated by parallel incisions. The eyes in each case are indicated by double incised ovals. In both cases the drapery falls over the feet in similar folds.

On the other hand I entirely fail to see any close relationship between the *Christ* of Arles-sur-Tech and the sculptures at St.-Michel-de-Cuxa (Ill. 556–559), Corneilla-de-Conflent (Ill. 528), St.-Jean-le-Vieux at Perpignan (Ill. 618–620) or the tombs at Elne (Ill. 623–627). When Comte de Lasteyrie (638) suggests such a comparison, especially with the last two monuments, I can not believe that he really meant to say, as his words imply, that the style of these monuments of the XI and of the XIII centuries is similar. The eminent archaeologist was, I take it, merely perplexed and exasperated to find that these surely dated monuments failed to show that evolutionary progress towards more developed forms which orthodox theory had led him to expect. It is indeed singular that this, and so many similar, examples of contradiction between the monuments and documents on the one hand, and the theory on the other, should never have raised the suspicion that the difficulty might lie with the theory, and not with the monuments and documents.

ment, if maintained, might easily arrive in another half century at the perfection of the capitals of Cluny (Ill. 5–10).[1]

The sculptor of Arles-sur-Tech doubtless knew the earlier work at St.-Genis-des-Fontaines; but that was not the only source of his inspiration. If we compare his facial types, the folds and borders of his draperies, the drawing of the feet, the ornamental patterns with the bible of Roda,[2] a Catalonian manuscript of the X century, we shall be convinced that he studied miniatures as well.

Another monument belongs to this same group of sculptures. In the lintel of St.-André-de-Sorrède (Ill. 514–515), which is the next village to St.-Genis-des-Fontaines, are sculptures so similar that one is almost tempted to call them the work of the same hand. St.-André is, however, evidently slightly later than St.-Genis; if we compare the heads of the three Christs (Ill. 513, 515, 518) we shall perceive without difficulty that they fall in the order St.-Genis, St.-André, Arles-sur-Tech. The relief of St.-André may be assigned to *c.* 1030 without fear of serious error.

In the interior of the church at St.-André has been preserved a fragment of relief (Ill. 517), mutilated almost beyond recognition. It represents a haloed figure, possibly an apostle, holding an object broken away, perhaps a book. The interest of this sculpture for our study lies in the circumstance that the legs are crossed.

This mannerism, which became a characteristic motive of the Spanish and Aquitanian schools of the XII century, is of very ancient origin. It is found, for example, in stone sculpture, in a Roman relief of the museum of Arles (Ill. 516), and in the spandrel figures of Zwartnotz in Armenia,[3] a monument which dates from 641–661. The latter instance is of especial interest, because the legs are placed

[1] In point of fact, the school of the Pyrenees had not at this date, at least in so far as it is possible to judge from the extant monuments, advanced beyond the point of the tympanum of St.-Féliu-d'Amond (Ill. 548). Here the right wing of the left angel is still executed with the same convention used for the left wing of the St. Matthew at Arles-sur-Tech (Ill. 518). In other respects, however, the style at St.-Féliu is strikingly different from that of Arles. The St.-Féliu tympanum should be compared with the tympanum at Mzchet, illustrated by Strzygowski, *Armenier*, 602.

[2] Paris, Bib. Nat., Cod. lat. 6, illustrated by Clemen, 335–336.

[3] Published by Strzygowski, *Armenier*, 427.

in precisely the "x" position generally associated with the XII century work of Toulouse. The motive of crossed legs was also widely diffused among ivories and miniatures in the East and West. It is impossible to determine from which among the many possible sources our sculptor borrowed the motive.[1]

It should not, of course, be assumed that St.-Genis was the first architectural sculpture in stone in the West after the Romans. It is, on the contrary, certain that sculpture in stone never ceased to be executed in Europe. In England the crosses of Bewcastle (670) and

[1] I am tempted to risk the conjecture that the motive of crossed legs probably originated in Greek Asiatic monuments, like the Heroön at Tyrsa. It was certainly widely diffused in the art both of the East and of the West during the first ten centuries. It is found, for example, in a Roman relief in the museum at Cairo, illustrated by Strzygowski, *Cairo Cat.*, 21; also in four bone-carvings of the III–IV centuries, *ibid.*, 184–185, and Tafel XV. It is also found in an ivory book-cover of the V, VI or VII century preserved in the archaeological museum at Ravenna, and illustrated by Pelka, 39; in an Irish manuscript of very early date, Dublin, Kells Gospel, Trinity College, A. I. 6 (58), illustrated by Zimmermann, 169; in a south Anglo-Saxon gospel of the IX century, Rome, Vat. Barb. Lat. 570, fol. 9 b, illustrated by Zimmermann, 314; in a miniature of an Apocalypse of 975, in the cathedral of Gerona, Mas phot. C 27699 — in this case the legs are in the "x" position; in the frescos of the XI century at S. Angelo in Formis, near Capua; in the Register of New Minster, Winchester, of *c.* 1030, British Museum, Stowe manuscript 960, illustrated by Bond, Thompson and Warner, II, 17; in a miniature of the Bible of Charles the Bald at the Bibliothèque Nationale, illustrated by Venturi, II, 281; in a psalter of the same library dating from the X century, illustrated by Diehl, 569; in a miniature of a Bible of S. Paolo f. l. m. at Rome, dating from the third quarter of the IX century, illustrated by Boinet, Pl. CXXIV; in a St. Gallen manuscript of the last half of the X century at the Universitätsbibliothek at Basel, No. B IV. 26, f. 68, illustrated by Escher, VIII; in the Bamberg Apocalypse of the X century, illustrated by Wölfflin, 38; in a X century Fulda miniature of the Universitätsbibliothek at Basel, No. A. N. IV. 18, f. 31, ed. Escher, 34; in a manuscript of the XI or XII century, illustrated by Diehl, 576; in a manuscript of the Winchester school, early XI century, British Museum, Stowe 944, illustrated by Herbert, Pl. XIII; in a psalter of St. Swithun's Priory, school of Winchester, XII century, British Museum, Cotton MS., Nero C IV, f. 39; in the miniatures of a *ménologe grec* of the XI century, executed at Mount Athos, Moscow, Bibliothèque Synodale, No. 183, illustrated by Treneff; in the mosaics of the Church of the Nativity at Bethlehem, assigned to the XII century; in the mosaics of Kief, dating from soon after 1037, illustrated by Diehl, 482, and by Millet in André Michel, I, 2, 192, etc. Crossed legs are also characteristic of the school of miniature painting of Salzburg — see for example the *Perikopenbuch von St.-Erentrud*, München, Kgl. Hof- und Stiftsbibliothek, Clm. 15903, c. p. 52 or the *Gebhardsbibel* in the Stiftsbibliothek of Admont, Cod. 511, illustrated by Swarzenski, taf. XXVIII, XXIX, XXX. I strongly suspect, however, that this group of manuscripts was influenced by the sculptures of the South-west. Thence seem to come the attenuation, the revealing draperies, the heads tipped up, the movement, all characteristic of these miniatures. The armour is of precisely the same type as in the cloister reliefs of Santo Domingo de Silos (Ill. 670). There is, indeed, nearly formal proof that the manuscripts were inspired by the sculptures. The initials of the *Perikopenbuch aus Passau*, Munich, Clm. 16002, illustrated by Swarzenski, 300, have adossed figures evidently derived from jamb sculptures.

Hexham (740) seem satisfactorily authenticated;[1] Messrs. Prior and Gardner ascribe numerous other works to the centuries preceding the year 1000.[2] At Mainz the sculptured tomb-stone of the archbishop Hatto (†913) is still extant.[3] In France there is documentary evidence that stone sculptures were made before the year 1000.[4] There are indeed extant examples which may be dated with considerable confidence to this period. The relief at Charlieu (Ill. 1) is combined with decorative carving of an unmistakably Carlovingian character.[5] The figures over the window of the Basse-Oeuvre at Beauvais (Ill. 1411) were doubtless, like all mediaeval sculpture, carved before they were placed, but form an integral part of the cathedral built by Hervé (987–998).[6]

Other sculptures have been assigned on the basis of their style to a date before 1000. In the exterior of the apse of St.-Paul near Dax are embedded a series of reliefs (Ill. 327–332). These show two distinct manners. To one group belong the reliefs representing grotesques (Ill. 329),[7] the Maries at the Tomb (Ill. 327),[7] a griffin and Heaven (Ill. 328); to the other those depicting three apostles (Ill. 332), the Last Supper (Ill. 331), the Betrayal (Ill. 330), the Crucifixion (Ill. 330) and a single figure (Ill. 228). Comte de Lasteyrie,[8] without distinguishing between the two sharply differentiated styles, ascribes the sculptures to the X century, and asserts that they are ancient fragments, re-employed in the XII century reconstruction of the apse.

I think the eminent archaeologist has again been led astray by the

---

[1] Prof. A. S. Cook believes that the English crosses are of the XII century. See his letter on *The Ruthwell and Bewcastle Crosses* in the London *Times* Literary Supplement, June 30, 1921, p. 420, with bibliographical references.

[2] 109–144.   [3] Dehio, 173.

[4] De Lasteyrie, 635. There is no reason for assuming that such sculptures were crude. The English crosses of Bewcastle (670) and Hexham (740) are technically as competent as performances of the XII century, for which they have been mistaken. Ivory-carvings, miniatures and reliefs in metal show entire mastery of plastic form on the part of Carlovingian artists. To assign sculptures to the X century simply because they are crude is uncritical.

[5] It should be compared with a plaque in the museum of Carpentras.

[6] The statement that the façade is not of 987–998, but of the XI century (*Cong. Arch.*, 1905, LXXIII, 3) seems to be based solely on the theory that all mediaeval buildings must be later than the documents indicate.

[7] Restored.   [8] 154.

orthodox dogma that crude sculptures must be early. In regard to the date of the first group, at least, we need not remain long in doubt. A comparison of the angel to the left of the tomb in the Dax relief of the Three Maries (Ill. 327) with the angel at the right of the tympanum at Toulouse (Ill. 309) will satisfy us that we have here to do with works of the first quarter of the XII century.

But may not Comte de Lasteyrie's dating be correct for the other set of reliefs?

The question deserves careful investigation. Let us compare these reliefs (Ill. 330–332) with those of the Basse-Oeuvre (Ill. 1411), which we have seen are authentic works of the X century. The two show no points of contact; the styles are entirely different. Similarly when we compare Dax (Ill. 330–332) with Azay-le-Rideau[1] (Ill. 896), we note that while the heads are set on the bodies in the same awkward way, and certain draperies have a distant similarity, the two styles are essentially far apart. Nor are analogies apparent with the relief (Ill. 897) which forms part of that church of St.-Mesme at Chinon which was under construction in 1025.[2] Nor except in the beaded ornament of the borders of the garments (Ill. 332), also characteristic of the early Catalan school, do the sculptures of Dax show points of contact with St.-Genis (Ill. 513) and its derivatives. It is rather to monuments of the end of the XI or the early XII century that our reliefs are analogous.

Thus the motive of a sculptured frieze belongs to the XII century. The earliest extant example is Guglielmo's at the cathedral of Modena.

[1] The style of this façade is that which by most archaeologists is associated with the X century. Yet no explanation has ever been offered why monuments of this period should be so abundant in the lower Loire basin, and so rare elsewhere in France. The sculptures of Azay-le-Rideau (Ill. 896) are not without analogy with two of the figures now enwalled in the gable of the north transept of St.-Hilaire-le-Grand of Poitiers (Ill. 912). Now the canons of St.-Hilaire returned from their exile of nearly a century at Le Puy about the middle of the X century; and it is tempting to see in the figures in question fragments of the works of embellishment executed at St.-Hilaire about this time. The style of the capitals and of the ornament over the arcades seems clearly to be that of the second half of the X century. There is therefore some reason to believe that the sculptures of Azay-le-Rideau are really of this period. The other two figures of St.-Hilaire are of an advanced period of the XII century (Ill. 914).

[2] De Lasteyrie, 152.

The application of such a frieze to the exterior of an apse recurs elsewhere only at Selles-sur-Cher (Ill. 1077–1082). It will be necessary, even at the expense of a considerable digression, to establish the chronology of Selles and a group of related monuments before proceeding further with the discussion of Dax.

The upper frieze at Selles (Ill. 1082) is a dated monument of 1145.[1]

The lower frieze at Selles, as well as the reliefs flanking the window, are by a different hand, but in my opinion not very much earlier.[2] This artist shows a close relationship stylistically with a bone box in the Kaiser Friederich Museum at Berlin. The box[3] is called by Prof. Goldschmidt a Franconian production of c. 1100. He recognizes through the internal evidence that it must be the work of two very unequal artists working in collaboration; the better laid out the general lines of the composition and finished in part the cover; the inferior completed the work. Now it is this second, or inferior, artist who shows close points of contact with the sculptor of the Selles frieze. The eyes in the two works are done in the same extraordinary manner; the hair is similarly rendered; the draperies are very alike; the drawing of the beards and the noses is the same; the scene of the Betrayal at Selles shows a Christ and Judas, precisely like the Christ and Judas on the box. The staffs carried by the executioners in the scene of the Betrayal of the box, are like the staffs carried by the same characters in the same scene of the frieze. The development of a long series of scenes in the two works is similar. In both there is the same *outré* iconography. These analogies are indeed so striking that I even wonder whether the sculptor of the frieze

---

[1] Orthodox archaeology, as usual, disregards the documentary evidence, and places the upper frieze in the early years of the XII century. To me, however, it seems clear that the sculptures in question are really of the date indicated by the document. The style (Ill. 1082) is closely analogous to that of the east window of Aulnay (Ill. 981), a monument admitted to date from the fourth decade of the XII century.

[2] Only a few fragments, like the Visitation of the north wall (Ill. 1076), analogous to the reliefs of Ste.-Radegonde of Poitiers (Ill. 907, 908) have the appearance of dating from the early XII century. We are, however, always too apt to forget that a sculptor who learned his style in the early years of the XII century, might easily still be active in 1145.

[3] Published by Goldschmidt, II, No. 173.

at Selles was not the same artist who completed the Berlin box.[1]

If we accept Prof. Goldschmidt's attribution of the box to the school of Franconia, we must conclude that the sculptor of Selles was a German. That, however, does not seem to me to be proven. The closest precedent for his style which I know is the tympanum of La Lande de Fronzac (Ill. 917). May it not be that this crude and backward artist was formed in the West of France?

The same hand can be recognized in a capital from the Eglise du Ronceray (Ill. 922) now in the Musée Archéologique at Angers. Here again is represented one of the scenes from the Passion which seem to have formed part of the stock in trade of our artist. This capital at Angers gives us a point of chronological support; the church was consecrated in 1119, so the capital presumably is earlier than that year.

The lower frieze at Selles (Ill. 1077–1081) is, as we have seen, by this same artist who worked at Angers before 1119; but there are reasons for believing that it is a much later work. The scenes from the Passion which it represents (Ill. 1079–1081) belong to the Santiago-Beaucaire-St.-Gilles cycle. The seated Pilate is a reversal of the seated Christ in the Santiago Crowning with Thorns (Ill. 680). The composition of the group of executioners haling Christ before Pilate, repeats that of the St.-Gilles frieze (Ill. 1321); two farther apart drag Christ from in front, two close together push Him from behind; Christ's hands are in each case in the same position, and in both works the foremost executioner calls Herod's attention with the same gesture. The Washing of the Feet (Ill. 1079) repeats, line for line, the composition of Beaucaire (Ill. 1292, 1293) and St.-Gilles (Ill. 1318). Now since the Selles frieze copies the St.-Gilles frieze, and

---

[1] This suggestion may seem startling to the reader, but will, I trust, appear somewhat less so, if he have the patience to read this volume to the end. He will find that Romanesque sculptors changed their manner, and their geographical position, with extraordinary, and hitherto unexpected facility and frequency. He will also find how isolated and individual these works are, and that their similarities can not be explained by saying that both are merely crude. It is true that I do not know of any other example of a sculptor in stone who also worked in bone or ivory. There is, however, no reason why the same artist might not have used both mediums.

since the St.-Gilles frieze is not earlier than about 1140, it is evident that the lower frieze at Selles, as well as the upper, must be later than 1140. We may then with considerable confidence conclude that both were executed for the church rebuilt after 1145. Once again the documents seem more reliable than archaeological theory.

But it will be objected that the uppermost figure to the left of the window above at Selles (Ill. 1074) recalls the mysterious reliefs of La Celle-Bruère (Ill. 1469, 1470); and these are considered by orthodox archaeology to be older fragments re-employed in the construction of the church about the middle of the XII century, hence much earlier in date.

Here again, however, archaeological theory seems to have led a great scholar into error. The reliefs of La Celle-Bruère are not older than the façade in which they are employed. If we compare the facial types in the finished relief (Ill. 1469) with that of the Cain in the Nîmes frieze (Ill. 1383), we shall be convinced that the two are not only contemporary, but very closely related. La Celle-Bruère seems, in fact, an evident copy. Now the frieze of Nîmes can not be earlier than about 1150. The relief of La Celle-Bruère may be slightly later. It was doubtless executed for the new church which, as M. Lefèvre-Pontalis has so beautifully shown, was erected at precisely this time.

The resemblance of the reliefs at Selles to those of La Celle-Bruère is therefore only one more proof that the sculptures of Selles date from the fourth decade of the XII century.

Let us now return to the study of the sculptures of Dax, with the certainty that Selles is a monument of about the middle of the XII century. The analogy we have remarked between these two series of reliefs, representing scenes from the Passion, and inserted in the exterior of the apse, would therefore argue a late date for Dax.

Another indication in the same direction is afforded by the fact that the facial types of the Dax reliefs (Ill. 330–332) show the closest analogy with those of Santo Domingo de Silos (Ill. 667–673) which we shall find date from the last quarter of the XI century. Moreover, the folds of the tablecloth in the Dax Last Supper (Ill. 331) are very like those of the skirts of the *Christ* at St.-Amour (Ill. 106), a work which is certainly of the XII century.

There is, however, even more conclusive proof. In the apse of St.-Paul of Dax, below the frieze, are sculptured capitals, obviously not second-hand material, but made for the position they now occupy. Now in one of these capitals we recognize the hand of the sculptor who made the reliefs we have been studying. Doubt is no longer possible. The artist who carved the second set of reliefs (Ill. 330–332) worked upon the architecture of the apse, which is obviously and admittedly a monument of the first third of the XII century. The reliefs are not older fragments re-employed, but were made for their present position. Although so different in style, the two sets, like the analogous reliefs at Selles, are contemporary with each other as well as with the building which they adorn.

Moreover, we notice that the capitals, one of which is by the sculptor of the second set of reliefs, are similar to, and obviously contemporary with, those of La Sauve Majeure (Ill. 333, 334). Now La Sauve Majeure was not founded until 1079,[1] and the existing ruins are of the second quarter of the XII century.

From all this we may safely conclude that the sculptures of St.-Paul near Dax, far from being fragments of the X century re-employed, were made for their present position about 1120.

Now that the ground is cleared of these monuments of the XII century, which have been masquerading as pre-Romanesque, let us return to the study of St.-Genis, and attempt to trace the drift of artistic currents in this surely dated monument of 1020.

The most striking, and on the whole probably most significant group of analogies offered by St.-Genis are with the art of the Orient. In the top-shaped head, the low and flat relief, the work at St.-Genis recalls Achthamar.[2] The upper wings of the seraphim are crossed in the two sculptures in precisely the same manner. The acanthus

---

[1] Mortet, 258.
[2] Illustrated by Strzygowski, *Armenier*, 289.

leaves of St.-Genis (Ill. 513) and St.-André (Ill. 515) are obviously of Byzantine type.[1]

On the other hand, St.-Genis shows points of contact with monuments of the West. Some of these are themselves already under Byzantine tradition, so that the possibility presents itself that the Eastern elements of St.-Genis may not have come directly from the East, but through some intermediary in the Occident. M. André Michel has remarked that the draperies and the drawing of certain heads at St.-Genis recall the pax of Duca Orso at Cividale.[2] In the drawing of the eyes and head, and in the types of the angels, the St.-Genis relief resembles the lintel from S. Lorenzo of Zara, now at S. Donato.[3] We have already spoken of the analogies between St.-Genis (Ill. 513) and the lunette of the cathedral of Troia (Ill. 172). There also appears to be relationship between St.-Genis and certain ivories of the Ada group. The draperies of St.-Genis, especially the sleeves, recall an ivory-carving of the VII century, representing a beardless Christ surrounded by the evangelists, now in the Fitzwilliam Museum at Cambridge.[4] Even more interesting are the points of contact with an ivory book-cover, dating from the IX or X century, and also belonging to the Ada group.[5] This ivory is now preserved in the cathedral of Narbonne, but as it came there from a private collection in 1850, it is not certain how long it has been in Catalonia. The peculiar double aureole[6] of St.-Genis occurs in ivories of the Ada group[7] as well as elsewhere.[8] In fact there are many indi-

---

[1] In this connection, it is interesting to remark that the tympanum from Egmond, in the Ryksmuseum at Amsterdam, the most primitive extant Romanesque sculpture in Holland, has a Greek inscription (Illustration in Ligtenberg, Tafel I).

[2] Illustration in Fogolari, 51.

[3] Illustrated by Gurlitt, 70.

[4] Illustrated by Goldschmidt, I, No. 7.   [5] *Ibid.*, No. 31.

[6] This motive perhaps originated, as Mr. Walter S. Cook has suggested, in the sphere upon which Christ is often seated in early iconographic representations, as *e.g.* the mosaic at S. Lorenzo f. l. m. at Rome. This sphere seems to have been enlarged to form a lower lobe in outline to the aureole; then this two lobed outline was retained when the sphere was omitted.

[7] See the *Majestas Domini* of the Kaiser Friederich Museum at Berlin, illustrated by Goldschmidt, I, No. 23, a work assigned to the IX or X century.

[8] *E.g.* an ivory of the Hessisches Landmuseum, Darmstadt, of the school of Cologne, *c.* 1000, illustrated by Goldschmidt, II, No. 72; in one of the second half of the XI century in the Brit-

cations that the early art of Catalonia underwent a strong German influence. The draperies of Catalan manuscripts, such as, for example the X century Bible of Roda,[1] are thoroughly German — compare the book-cover of Kaiser Arnulf (887–899) at Munich.[2] It is evident that Catalan frescos and panel paintings of the XII century were strongly influenced by Othonian miniatures. It is not surprising therefore that German influence should be traceable at St.-Genis. It is less easy to account for the fact that the drawing of the eye, and the facial types of St.-Genis recall the frescos of the X century at Grotta dei Santi near Calvi.[3]

In addition to these semi-Byzantine influences, it seems probable that purely Western tradition entered to a considerable extent into the style of the St.-Genis lintel. The analogies to which we have already called attention between the Bible of Roda and the sculptures of Arles-sur-Tech would give reason to believe that the early sculpture of the Pyrenees is rooted in the local art of Catalonia. The horseshoe arches of the lintel are a clear trace of this influence at St.-Genis. I note moreover a certain resemblance between the lintel of St.-Genis (Ill. 513) and the Carlovingian sculpture at Charlieu (Ill. 1). This it is true is more apparent than real, and upon close study narrows down to a similar sleeve convention, and the use of beading. Much more unexpected is the analogy shown by certain of the larva-like figures standing under the niches at St.-Genis, with those carved more than a century later in the cloisters of S. Orso at Aosta.[4] The strangeness of the proportions, the peculiar working of the hair and eyes, the use of beadings, the similar management of the draperies in

ish Museum of London, illustrated by Goldschmidt, II, No. 119; in the Evangelaire de Noailles, of the second half of the IX century, Paris, Bib. Nat. lat., 323, illustrated by Boinet, Pl. CXXXV; in the bible of St.-Aubin of Angers, in the Bibliothèque de la Ville at Angiers, No. 4, X century, illustrated by Boinet, Pl. CLII; in the Bible of S. Callisto of the IX century, illustrated by Clemen, 63. The motive early became characteristic of Catalan art; it is already found in the X century Bible of Roda, Paris, Bib. Nat. lat. 6, illustrated by Clemen, 335.

[1] Paris, Bib. Nat. lat. 6, illustrated by Clemen, 335–336.
[2] Illustrated by Dehio, II, ab. 304.
[3] Illustrated by Bertaux, 245. There is probably a common Byzantine influence behind all these works.
[4] Illustrated by Porter, Lomb. Arch., IV, Plate 15, Fig. 3.

these two works can hardly be due to chance, and are the more puzzling that the two mountain monasteries are so widely separated geographically, as well as chronologically.

Whatever the explanation of this analogy may be, it seems clear that the style of St.-Genis shows a local tradition strongly under the influence of Byzantine monuments, and probably also affected by some such German ivory as that which now exists in the cathedral of Narbonne.

It is worthy of remark that the three monuments which represent for us the school of the first half of the XI century in the eastern Pyrenees are all in the churches of Benedictine abbeys. It was only at a later period that Arles-sur-Tech, with which St.-André was united, was given to Moissac, and thus became Cluniac. In the first half of the XI century all three monasteries were of the pure Benedictine order, and thus in close ecclesiastical relationship, as well as geographical proximity.

Since Cluny was the child of the Benedictine order, it is not surprising to find that important characteristics of Burgundian sculpture are foreshadowed at St.-Genis. The motive of angels holding an aureole with the figure of Christ was assuredly not new in sculpture; it is found for example in the *paliotto* of Pemmore at Cividale.[1] It was, nevertheless, destined to become a favourite theme of the Cluniac school. The violent movement of the angels of St.-Genis foreshadows the superb angels supporting the aureoles of Burgundian tympana like Charlieu (Ill. 4). The draperies of St.-Genis in their simple overlapping broad folds, cut like those of Chinese statues of the Tang dynasty, and in their mannered spirals and whirls are strangely like the types of drapery consecrated by the Burgundian style. The motive of a lintel decorated with figures standing under the arches of a blind arcade became characteristically Burgundian. From all this we gather another proof, were any needed, of how closely Cluniac art depends upon Benedictine art.[2]

By far the most significant fact about the XI century sculptures of

[1] Illustration in Fogolari, 47.   [2] See below, p. 87.

the eastern Pyrenees is, however, their existence. Was it only in a remote mountain valley that sculpture flourished at this period in Europe?

Such is no doubt the impression given by the histories of mediaeval sculpture. A little reflection, however, suffices to bring conviction that the case was far otherwise.

Wackernagel has made a most valuable study of certain pulpits in Apulia. That at Canosa, signed by Acceptus, had long been known, and assigned on its style to the end of the XI century. Wackernagel discovered fragments of other pulpits, obviously by the same hand, at Siponto and Monte S. Angelo. The Siponto pulpit bore an inscription with the name of Leo, doubtless the archbishop of Siponto, who is known to have flourished about 1040; and the Monte S. Angelo pulpit bore the signature of Acceptus and the date 1041. Doubt is therefore not possible: in this remarkable series of works we have authentic monuments of the second quarter of the XI century.

Now these pulpits of Acceptus are all executed with the utmost delicacy, refinement and precision of technique. The crudeness which orthodox theory would lead us to expect is totally lacking. The later centuries produced in Apulia an art that was different, but never an art which was more beautiful.

Especially is this true of the sculptured human head beneath the eagle at Monte S. Angelo.[1] This already possesses the classic quality which we associate with the time of Frederic II. The modelling is highly naturalistic; the proportions are carefully studied, much more so than in, for example, the reliefs of the ambulatory at St.-Sernin (Ill. 296–305). The hair and beard are executed with an effectiveness that would do credit to a Greek artist of the V century B.C. If the planes are reduced to the lowest terms, they are still used effectively, and with an understanding of light and shade. The head is individualized, and full of character.

The eagles of Acceptus[2] give us an equally high idea of his art.

[1] Illustrated by Wackernagel, Tafel II, d.
[2] *Ibid.*, Tafel I, b: Tafel II, d.

Like everything which he does, they are extremely *voulus*. He produces the effect he desires with unerring sureness of touch. The characterful heads almost make us think of the "Pien Luan" of the Freer Collection; the heraldic outlines, the splendidly mannered convention for the feathers are emotional. Even such a detail as the claws, in the Monte S. Angelo pulpit, is carved with a feeling for values not unworthy of Rodin.

The work of Acceptus shows then, none of the crudeness of St.-Genis. It is even much finer than the contemporary sculpture at Arles-sur-Tech. Nor is it surprising that the rich plain of Italy should produce a more refined art than a valley of the Pyrenees.

Apulia lies, however, far to the south, in a region peculiarly exposed to Byzantine influences. Did stone sculpture in northern Europe attain at this period the same high merit?

Fortunately it is easy to give an answer. In the museum of Marseille is preserved the tomb of St. Isarne (Ill. 1278), which comes from the crypt[1] of the abbey of St.-Victor, of which it is known that the church was consecrated in 1040.[2] From the epitaph we learn that St. Isarne died in 1048.[3] His tomb-stone (Ill. 1278) which was cer-

---

[1] Laurin, 25.

[2] *Ibid.*, 34. The existing church is not all of one period, but has been, nevertheless, dated too late. This is not the place to enter into the long technical discussion involved by consideration of this question. I shall only observe that a capital of the crypt of St.-Lazare, conceded to date from 1040, is sculptured with a superbly expressive head.

[3] + OBIIT ANNO MXLVIII INDIC . . . . . AEPACTA . . . . .
XP SACRA VIRI CLARI SVNT HIC SITA PATRIS ISARNI:
MĒBRA SVIS STVDIIS GLORIFICATA PIIS:
QVAE FELIX VEGETANS ANIMA PROVEXIT AD ALTA:
MORIB' EGREGIIS PACIFICISQ' ANIMIS:
NĀ REDIMITVS ERAT HIC VIRTVTIS SPECIEBVS:
VIR DNĪ CVNCTIS P[RO] QVIB' EST HILARIS:
QVAE FECIT DOCVIT ABBAS PIVS ATQ' BEATVS:
DISCIPVLOSQ' SVOS COMPVLIT ESSE PIOS:
SIC VIVENS TENVIT REGIM̄ SED CLAVDERE LIM̄:
COMPVLSVS VITE EST ACRITER MISERE:
REXIT BIS DENIS 'SEPTEMQ' FIDELIT̄ ANNIS:
CŌMISSV̄Q' SIBI DVLCE GREGEM DNĪ:
RESPVIT OCTOBRIS TRAS OCTAVO KALENDAS:
ET CEPIT RVTILI REGNA SVBIRE POLI:
CERNE P[RAE] COR QVE LEX HOMINI NOXA P(RO)TOPLASTI
+ IN ME DEFVNCTO LECTOR INEST MISERO
SICQ' GEMENS CORDE + DIC DIC DEVS HVIC MISERE AM:

tainly sculptured soon afterwards shows the qualities that we are already coming to recognize as characteristic of the XI century. The face is exceedingly realistic, and finely modelled. It impresses one as an accurate and highly expressive portrait of the deceased. The long, drooping cheeks, the strong nose, the eyes stern even in death are full of character. If the draperies about the shoulders are executed in a somewhat schematized fashion, those about the feet are finely expressive. The feet themselves are sensitively modelled. The monument possesses a character of austerity and grandeur far surpassing the attainments of the XIII century, and which it would be difficult to parallel in the XII century.

The same mastery of form, the same sense of beauty is shown in other stone sculptures of the XI century. The reliefs of the portal of St. Emmeran at Regensburg (Ratisbon) in Germany (Ill. 1279–1282) are dated between 1049–1064 by an inscription.[1] Again we have stone sculptures full of dignity and power. The long face and the curls of the St. Emmeran recall those of St. Isarne, but the hair convention of the Christ is more akin to that of Acceptus' head at Monte S. Angelo. The draperies are adequately rendered, sometimes by parallel fine lines which seem copied from a miniature, but also by heavy plastic folds, showing already quite the character of the XII century. We are here far from the painter's technique of Arles-sur-Tech (Ill. 518); the *St. Emmeran* (Ill. 1281) shows a strong feeling for the third dimension that fairly foreshadows Giotto in its use of the background arch to throw the figure into sharper relief. When the two representations of the Deity at Regensburg and at Arles are compared (Ill. 1279 and Ill. 518) we notice a certain general similarity of type and posture, extending even to the thrones and the position of the legs, but the Regensburg *Christ* seems much more accomplished. This is perhaps less due to a somewhat later date than to closer proximity to the centres of civilization.

Of the tomb of St.-Front at Périgueux, sculptured in 1077 by a certain Guinamundus, a Cluniac monk of La Chaise Dieu, nothing

[1] ABBA REGINVVARDVS HOC FORE IVSSIT OPVS

remains; we have only the brief description in the Pilgrims' Guide: *Cuius sepulchrum cum nullis aliis Sanctorum sepulchris consimile est, rotundum tamen, ut Dominicum sepulchrum, studiosissime fit, et cuncta caeterorum Sanctorum sepulchra pulchritudine miri operis excellit.* When we consider the high merit of monuments like Santiago and Moissac seen by the author of this description, we can only conclude from his praise that this tomb of 1077 was far from crude.

It has been the custom of archaeologists, in dealing with the history of mediaeval sculpture at this period, to separate works in stone from works in metal, and consider the latter a "minor art" which may conveniently be left out of consideration. Such an arbitrary division has made it possible to keep alive a little longer the dogma that early sculpture is crude. It does not, however, seem conducive to forming an accurate conception of XI century art. Sculpture in metal is not essentially different from sculpture in stone. There is no reason to suppose that a knowledge of form which could be expressed in one medium could not be expressed also in the other. We have already found abundant evidence that the XI century was master of its chisel. Works in metal can therefore be most instructive in informing us of the taste and artistic accomplishment of the time.

The bronze doors of Hildesheim are familiar to everyone. They are indeed a supreme masterpiece. The composition is satisfying; the drawing masterly; the execution impeccable. In the long list of bronze doors made throughout Germany and Italy in the centuries that followed, there is, with the single exception of Monte S. Angelo — also a work of the XI century — none comparable. Now these bronze doors are dated 1015 by an inscription.[1] The appearance of so perfect a work at this period has startled historians of art, even though the matter was toned down by classing the doors as "minor art." Yet there is nothing in these monuments, splendid as they are, which is not in entire accord with the time in which they were produced. They are merely the translation into bronze of forms long

[1] AN DŌM INC MXV B EP DIVE MEM HAS VALVAS FVSILES
IN FACIE ANGELICI TEPLI OB MONIMT SVI FEC SVSPENDI

familiar to German artists. The composition must be inspired by some miniatured Bible, like that of Bamberg.[1] The technical execution — by which I mean the drawing, facial types, drapery folds — recalls the golden book-cover of Kaiser Arnulf (887–899),[2] now in the Munich library, but coming from St. Emmeran at Regensburg.

The bronze column of Hildesheim was executed before 1022.[3] It served as a paschal candelabrum; and there can be little doubt that it was inspired neither by the spiral columns of Trajan and Marcus Aurelius at Rome, nor yet by those others of Theodosius and Arcadius that once existed at Constantinople,[4] but by one of the destroyed metal paschal candelabra of the Roman churches. The style is, however, purely German, and closely related to that of the bronze doors.

It is not only at Hildesheim that are found admirable works in metal executed in the XI century. The altar (983–1002) and ambo (1002–1024) at Aachen, the statue of Ste. Foy at Conques (anterior to 1010) all bear witness to the perfection of this art.[5]

The Arca Santa of Oviedo, although unknown, or nearly so, to historians of art, is in some ways as epoch-marking a monument as the doors of Hildesheim. Like the doors, the Arca (Ill. 656–660) enjoys the advantage of being surely dated. An inscription, partly destroyed it is true, but the meaning of which can still be deciphered, states that the Arca was the gift of King Alfonso, who can only be the sixth of that name (1072–1109). In the inscription the name of the king's "sister Urraca" also occurs.[6] Now we know from a contemporary document that this monarch and his sister Urraca were

---

[1] Bamberg, Hofbib., A. I. 5. Illustrated by Boinet, Pl. XXIX. Compare especially the scenes of God reproaching Adam and Eve, and of God giving Eve to Adam. This manuscript dates from the second quarter of the IX century.

[2] Illustrated by Dehio, ab. 304.

[3] For a study of the date, see the admirable monograph by Dibelius, 103 f.

[4] Erected in 386 and 403 respectively. See Fondation Piot, 1895, II, 99.

[5] Cf. this text: Fecit (Gauzlin, abbot of Fleury c. 1026) et analogium hispanico metallo compactum, diebus utendum feriarum, fusoria industria solidatam, quatuor vallaverat leunculorum pulchritudine; desuper columnam, trium cubitorum habentem altitudinem, fusili arte fabricatam, atque undique vario opere politam, in cujus centro volantis aquilae radiabat similitudo (Vie de Gauzlin, ed. Delisle, 39–40). Compare also the descriptions of the altar-frontals of St.-Gilles and Santiago in the *Pilgrims' Guide* (ed. Fita).

[6] Vigil, 15.

present at the invention of the relics in 1075.[1] We can only conclude that this invention was the occasion for the gift of the Arca.

The Arca is unquestionably of Spanish workmanship — the many analogies, especially of the cover with the Arca of San Millán de la Cogolla (Ill. 638–649) are obvious. However, the reliefs show another and very different influence. It is that of the bronze doors of Hildesheim, or of some of the works of the German goldsmiths, with which these are related. German Othonian models left an indelible impress upon the sculpture of Europe during the XI and XII centuries.

The engraved cover of the Arca Santa is derived from a southern French or Spanish manuscript. The Crucifixion[2] is very close to that of an XI century manuscript of Limoges.[3]

These monuments of the first three quarters of the XI century which we have examined are doubtless few in number, but still sufficient to enable us to perceive, first that the plastic art of the XI century was different from that of the XII century, but not necessarily inferior either in conception or in execution; and secondly that the modern archaeological dogma, that the sculpture of the XI century was crude and barbarous, is a serious and fundamental error.

[1] Vigil, 76.   [2] Mas photograph, C. 25255.
[3] Bib. Nat. latin 11550. Compare also the Oviedo silver book-cover. Mas photograph, C. 25261.

III

EARLY SPANISH IVORIES

THE school of ivory-carving which grew up in Spain during the XI century throws unexpected light upon the knowledge of form possessed by artists in this period which modern archaeologists and historians of art have so strangely neglected. Although the literature dealing with early Spanish ivories is considerable, the historical significance of this art does not appear to have been appreciated.

One of the oldest and most important monuments extant is assuredly the Arca of San Millán de la Cogolla (Ill. 638-649). I have not been able to obtain access to the jealously secreted ivories themselves, but the photographs [1] give a sufficient idea of their character.

The relics of San Millán were discovered in 1030. It is an ancient tradition that they were translated in 1033 in the presence of Don Sancho el Mayor, king of Navarre, and that the Arca which still in part survives was given by that king on that occasion.[2] Don Emmanuel Gómez-Moreno [3] and Señor Sentenach, however, refer the Arca to a translation by García Sánchez in 1053.[4] In any event it may safely be considered a monument at least as early as the third quarter of the XI century.

Compared with the crucifix of San Isidoro of Léon, now in the Madrid Museo Arqueológico (Ill. 654, 655), and which is a surely dated monument of 1063, the ivories of San Millán appear much cruder and more primitive; it is tempting to consider them earlier. They impress one, too, as being earlier than the book-cover of Jaca, now in the Metropolitan Museum at New York (Ill. 519), and which was given by the queen Felicia, who died in 1085.

---

[1] I owe these photographs to the kindness of Don Emmanuel Gómez-Moreno.
[2] Debenga, 296.   [3] 295.
[4] Don Emmanuel Gómez-Moreno thinks the Arca may have been executed as late as *c.* 1076.

The Arca of San Millán was in part destroyed by the French under Napoleon. Among the portions lost at this time was an inscription recording the names of the artists who executed the ivories. These were a certain Enel . . . and Rodolphus, his son. This name Rodolphus suggests a Germanic origin.

The style of the ivories also seems to show German influence. So much is this the case, that no less an authority than Graeven[1] has ascribed the panel at Florence (Ill. 650) which (although the fact appears never to have been recognized) is certainly of the same school as the San Millán Arca, indeed, even by the same hand or hands, to the Rhenish school of the XI or XII century. The ascription is without doubt erroneous, the panel in question must be Spanish; but that so great a connoisseur should have mistaken it for a German work is eloquent proof of the German influences which are shown by the style. Goldschmidt[2] has recognized the German character of the New York crucifix (Ill. 710) which is a later work of this same school. A comparison between the figure to the left within the house in the San Millán relief of the Devil exorcised from the House of Parpalinense (Ill. 644), and the Christ of the Doubting Thomas in the Figdor collection at Vienna, the latter a work of the Echternach master of about 990,[3] will leave us in no doubt of the Teutonic derivation of the San Millán ivories.

The influences between Spain and Germany did not flow in only one direction. It is certain that German ivories of the XII century show imitation of the art of the pilgrimages.

While the San Millán Arca shows German influence, it is nevertheless a work essentially Spanish in character. The execution is quite different from that of the German ivories. The horse-shoe and trefoiled arches are a markedly Spanish (ultimately Moorish) characteristic.

A series of ivory reliefs in the Museo Arqueológico at Madrid show evident affinity of style with the San Millán Arca. Together with

[1] *Ital.*, No. 31. [2] II, No. 27.
[3] Illustrated by Goldschmidt, II, No. 24.

fragments from Arab boxes — one of which bears an inscription datable 1043–1077 — they have been mounted to form a casket (Ill. 651–653); the whole comes from San Isidoro of Léon. It is natural to conjecture that these reliefs, representing the Beatitudes, originally formed one of the six ivory boxes given to San Isidoro by Don Fernando I (1037–1065).[1]

Related in style to the San Millán Arca, but inferior in quality, is a little relief in the Metropolitan Museum at New York.[2]

On the other hand, a very different, and much more finished style appears in the great crucifix (Ill. 654, 655), which also comes from San Isidoro of Léon, and which is now also in the Museo Arqueológico at Madrid. This crucifix has the advantage of being incontestably dated: at the foot of the cross is the inscription FERDINANDVS REX SANCIA REGINA; it is therefore beyond any question the very crucifix which it is known was presented by these sovereigns to San Isidoro in 1063.[3] The style of this remarkable work singularly anticipates the stone sculpture of the XII century. On the other hand it differs notably from that of the group of ivories we have just been studying. So sharp indeed is the change of manner that I can detect but one peculiarity common to both — it is the custom, later taken over by the sculptors in stone, of hollowing out the pupil of the eye, and inlaying it with another material. I can not agree with those authors who think that the figure of Christ in the Madrid crucifix is inferior in execution to the ornamental work upon the cross. This face seems to me indeed to be one of the notable achievements of mediaeval art. I should not, however, be surprised if it were by a different hand from the one that executed the cross, and perhaps the body of the Christ. The hand of this artist reappears, Mr. Breck believes, in the book-cover of the Metropolitan Museum in New York (Ill. 665). The ornamental carving, the draperies, the hands and the feet are certainly identical in the two

[1] José Amador, in *Museo*, II, 545. The arches with spiral colonnettes of this ivory are like those on the pilasters of the west façade of Chartres.

[2] Illustrated by Breck, 218. Accession number 17.190.142.

[3] *España Sagrada*, XXXVI, Appendix, p. clxxxix.

works. The faces of the New York book-cover are, however, very inferior to those of the Madrid Christ; nor is the quality of even the decorative parts so fine.

The excellent technique of the Madrid crucifix, as well as several motives of decoration [1] are derived from Saracenic models. There can be little doubt that the superlative excellence at times displayed by Spanish art during the Romanesque period is due to the inspiration of the highly finished and technically accomplished productions of the Moors. It is Mussulman influence which raised Mozarabic architecture, the sculptures of Santo Domingo de Silos, and the ivories we have just been studying to a level equal with, if not superior to, that of the best contemporary work in Europe.

The Moors were accomplished ivory-carvers, and seem to have anticipated the Christian Spaniards in the field. At least I know of no Christian Spanish ivory as early as the celebrated casket of the cathedral at Pamplona, dated 1005 by an inscription.[2] This box already stands on an extremely high level of technical excellence; the ornamental work is even better than the figures, a fact easily explained since Mohammedan artists were rarely allowed to practise making representations of the human form. The same skilful execution is characteristic of other Moorish boxes, like the one of the Burgos Museum, dated 1026, or that from Palencia, dated 1049,[3] which is now in the Museo Arqueológico at Madrid.

Another crucifix now at San Marcos of Léon, but coming from the same stupendous treasure of San Isidoro (Ill. 703) is closely related to the Madrid carving. The head is superior to those of the New York ivory, but inferior to that of the Madrid crucifix. The ancient cross of the San Marcos crucifix is lost. It is known from literary descriptions [4] that there existed in the treasure of San Isidoro an ivory crucifix, with an image and inscription referring to Doña

---

[1] See for a study of this question the Boletín de la Sociedad Española de Excursiones, XIV, 1906, 14.

[2] This casket has been published many times — among others, by Bertaux, *Exp. Ret.*, 205.

[3] Vives, 36.

[4] Manuel de Assas in *Museo*, I, 209.

Urraca (1032–1101). It is tempting to conjecture that the Christ of San Marcos is a part of this crucifix.

Another work closely related to this group is the ivory-carving (Ill. 519) incorporated in a book-cover of silver filigree work now in the Metropolitan Museum of New York.[1] The book-cover formerly belonged to the cathedral at Jaca.[2] At the base of the cross is the inscription FELICIA REGINA; the ivory must therefore have been given by the wife of Sancho Ramirez; and she is known to have died in 1085. The crucifix must consequently have been executed before this date.

In style the crucifix is related to the group that we have just been studying, most closely perhaps to the crucifix at San Marcos (Ill. 703), although it is by no means without points of contact with the Madrid ivory (Ill. 654, 655).

At San Millán de la Cogolla is preserved a second ivory reliquary (Ill. 661–664), known as the Arca of S. Felices.[3] The style is not without relationship to that of the Arca of San Millán; so much so that Señor Sentenach made one Arca out of the two.[4] The style is however distinctly different. The San Felices Arca appears to be more advanced; the facial types show points of contact with those of the New York book-cover. It may very likely date from the last quarter of the XI century.[5]

A crucifix now in the Metropolitan Museum in New York shows obvious relationship with this group of ivories (Ill. 710). The cross is modern, and the Christ has lost His right arm since the photograph published by Prof. Goldschmidt[6] was made. The style of this figure shows analogies especially with that of the New York book-cover (Ill. 519), but it is coarser and more advanced. Prof. Gold-

[1] It has been published by Mr. Breck in his illuminating paper on Spanish Ivories in the Morgan Collection — a work which is fundamental for the intelligent study of Spanish sculpture, and indeed the only comprehensive survey of the subject which exists.

[2] De Leguina, 247.

[3] I am indebted to Don Emmanuel Gómez-Moreno also for the photographs of this inaccessible monument.

[4] Gómez-Moreno, 295.

[5] The assertion that it dates from the XIII century is unsupported by the slightest evidence.

[6] II, No. 27.

schmidt dated it about 1200; Mr. Breck put it back fifty years to
1150; perhaps a date about 1125 would be still more probable.

A further stylistic development along the same lines is shown in
another relief of the Metropolitan Museum at New York, representing the Journey to Emmaus and the *Noli me tangere* (Ill. 709). A
comparison of this ivory with the stone reliefs of apostles by Gilbert's
assistant from St.-Etienne of Toulouse reveals striking similarity.
The hair convention of the middle figure in the Journey to Emmaus
(Ill. 709) is similar to that of one of the Toulouse apostles (Ill. 439,
right-hand figure); that of the figure to the left in the Journey to
Emmaus (Ill. 709) and of Christ in the *Noli me tangere* are similar
to that of another of the apostles (Ill. 436). The raised right hand of
the figure to the right of the Journey to Emmaus (Ill. 709) is strikingly like that of one of the Toulouse apostles (Ill. 439, central
figure). The draperies of the Mary Magdalen (Ill. 709) are undeni-
ably similar to those of the beardless apostle (Ill. 439). The facial
types are essentially the same (Ill. 709 and Ill. 437). Most vital of
all, however, is the similarity of feeling that runs through the two
works. Such coarseness, such vulgarity, such diabolic cynicism could
not have been twice invented.

We shall find reason to believe that the Toulouse apostles were
executed in the fifth decade of the XII century. The question arises
whether the ivory is a prototype or a derivative. I am inclined to
believe the former. While there are many provable examples of
sculptures copied from ivories at this period, I know of none of ivories
copied from sculptures. The ivory seems throughout more vigorous,
more archaic. The costume is of an earlier type. The XI century
neck-slit appears in two out of the four figures in the ivory, while
in the reliefs it has entirely disappeared, except in one figure (Ill.
436), where it appears in very modified form. The parted hair convention, while very similar in the two works (Ill. 709 and Ill. 437) is
at Toulouse distinctly more naturalistic and advanced than in the
ivory.

It therefore seems to me probable that the ivory is earlier than the relief. Mr. Breck assigned the former to about the middle of the XII century; I should be inclined to place it before 1140.

Mr. Breck took the ivory to be Spanish. The analogies with the Toulouse apostles might seem to give reason to question whether it might not rather have been made in Toulouse. This supposition is, however, not necessary. The same plastic style prevailed at Toulouse and in northern Spain. Our ivory closely resembles in style the New York crucifix (Ill. 710) which seems to be certainly Spanish. The composition of the Journey to Emmaus (Ill. 709) recalls that of the same subject at Santo Domingo de Silos (Ill. 667). Moreover, we have seen that there were certainly several ateliers of ivory-carving in Spain during the Romanesque period, while I know of no proof that such existed in Toulouse. The hypothesis that the ivory is Spanish seems therefore tenable.

IV

SANTO DOMINGO DE SILOS

THE older portion of the cloister of Santo Domingo de Silos is a dated monument of the XI century.

The abbot Santo Domingo died in 1073,[1] and was buried in the cloister, the construction of which he had begun. In 1076 the body was moved, but the epitaph on a capital (Ill. 666) remained, and still remains. A cenotaph was subsequently erected to mark the place where the body first rested.

From this it follows, as an inevitable consequence,[2] that the capital with the inscription (Ill. 666) dates from between 1073 and 1076. Indeed, graver, and hitherto unsuspected, conclusions follow. The study of the internal evidence of the cloister itself proves, whatever has been said to the contrary, that the north and east galleries and the north bay of the west gallery are all substantially contemporary with each other, with the capital, with the inscription and with the six reliefs of earlier style (Ill. 666-673).[3]

Whoever will compare the ear of the harpy in the dated capital (Ill. 666) with the ear of the Christ in the Deposition (Ill. 669), or the hair conventions in the capital (Ill. 666) with those in the reliefs (Ill. 667, 669-673), will be convinced that the two are not only of the same period, but by the same hand. The lettering of the inscription of 1073-1076 (Ill. 666) is exactly like that of the reliefs (Ill. 667, 669-673). The sculptured capital of the cloister representing the four and twenty elders (Ill. 668) is obviously by the same hand as the reliefs on one side, and the dated capital on the other. It is incredible that such similar works should be separated by a period of eighty years as asserted by orthodox archaeology.

[1] Rodrigo, 26.
[2] This was first recognized by M. Bertaux in André Michel, II, 1, 223.
[3] Roulin has published numerous photographs of the capitals.

It may, indeed, well be that the reliefs are slightly later than 1073–1076. After the cloister had been begun, building activity appears to have been transferred to the church. This was consecrated in 1088.[1] Although an inscription implies that the cloister, too, was dedicated at this time, it is conceivable that the reliefs may have been executed after this date. This would bring them into the last fifteen years of the XI century.

The style of the reliefs is in entire agreement with the documentary evidence for date.

A striking peculiarity of these sculptures is that the reliefs are placed under arches. In the relief of the Doubting Thomas (Ill. 671), which is perhaps the latest of the series, the arch is surmounted by a sort of canopy, sculptured with architectural motives, and with human figures playing upon musical instruments.

At first one might be tempted to suppose that such a canopy would indicate a date later than the XI century; but it will be remembered that canopies were used in ivories and miniatures of the X century.[2] They are also characteristic of the ivories of the XI century in Spain. We find them in the Arca of San Millán (Ill. 638), in that of San Felices (Ill. 661) and in the Beatitudes from San Isidoro of Léon (Ill. 651–653). In stone sculpture the motive appears in the reliefs of St. Emmeran at Regensburg (Ill. 1279, 1281, 1282) which as we have seen are dated 1049–1064. Its presence at Santo Domingo de Silos in the late XI century is therefore entirely to be expected. The only innovation is the introduction of human figures into the architecture.

---

[1] Férotin, 72.

[2] See for example the book-cover of the Kaiser Friederich Museum in Berlin, illustrated by Goldschmidt, II, No. 52, 53. Canopied arches are characteristic of miniatures of the school of Winchester, with which the Santo Domingo reliefs may be suspected of being connected. Thus in the Benedictional of St. Aethelwold at Chatsworth, there appear over the arches framing the miniatures on folios 3 and 100 canopies adorned with the representations of two cities, very like the Jerusalem and Bethlehem of Roman mosaics (illustrated by Warner and Wilson). The motive is somewhat simplified in the Benedictional of Paris, folio 43r, illustrated by Homburger, Tafel IX. It may have originated in the ornaments placed either side of arches in Carolingian manuscripts, such as the late IX century Gospel of Morienval, preserved at Noyon (it was saved by evacuation in the war), and illustrated by Boinet, Pl. LXXXI.

The placing of reliefs in arches is also characteristic of the period. This motive is of very ancient origin,[1] and became widely diffused through its use on Early Christian sarcophagi.[2] From sculpture in stone it passed into miniatures[3] and frescos,[4] and became especially characteristic of the school of Winchester.[5] It was taken over in ivory-carvings — we find it for example in the Echternach ivory at the Cluny Museum,[6] in the Ada group ivory of the X century in the Bibliothèque Nationale,[7] in an ivory of the X century at the Bargello.[8] In the XI century its use in ivory carvings became especially frequent — we find it in a Byzantine ivory of the Kaiser Friederich Museum at Berlin,[9] in another of the British Museum,[10] and in Spain in the Arca of San Millán (Ill. 639, 640, 643, 644, 648), in that of San Felices (Ill. 664) in the Florence fragment (Ill. 650) and in the reliefs of the Beatitudes (Ill. 651–653) from San Isidoro at Léon. It is also found in the Arca Santa of Oviedo of 1075 (Ill. 658). The motive was therefore very much at home in Spain in the XI century. In stone sculpture the idea is found at St.-Pierre de la Citadelle at Metz[11] — in this case the arch is triangular — at Azay-

---

[1] It is found on a Roman relief in the Museum of Sens.

[2] This motive found its way into the Far East — there is an example of it in a stone stupa of the Henry H. Getty collection illustrated by A. Getty (*The Gods of Northern Buddhism*, Oxford, Clarendon Press, 1914. 4to), Pl. XIII c. It is also found on a Coptic relief of the Cairo Museum, illustrated by Bauer und Strzygowski, 159, and in wooden panels in the same museum, dating from the III to the IV century (Strzygowski, *Cairo Cat.* Taf. VII). Two wooden consoles from Bawit in the Cairo Museum (illustrated by Strzygowski, *Cairo Cat.*, Taf. VII) are decorated with figures of saints in niches, strongly recalling the cloister sculptures of Moissac.

[3] It is found in the Gospels, called of Charlemagne, at Abbeville, illustrated by Boinet, Pl. X; in the Gospels of the British Museum, Hart. 2788, of the early IX century, illustrated by Boinet, Pl. XIII; in the Gospels of Lorsch, at Rome, Vatican, Pal. lat. 50, illustrated by Boinet, Pl. XVII; in the Gospels of St.-Médard of Soissons, Paris, Bib. Nat., lat. 8850, illustrated by Boinet, Pl. XXI–XXII; in the Gospels of Ada, at Trèves, illustrated by Boinet, Pl. VIII.

[4] In the ruins of Arab-Djami at Constantinople (Ebersolt, Pl. XXXIV).

[5] See the miniatures cited above, and the Benedictional of St. Aethelwold, *passim*, illustrated by Warner and Wilson.

[6] Illustrated by Goldschmidt, II, No. 25.

[7] Illustrated *ibid.*, No. 36.

[8] Illustrated by Graeven, 36.

[9] Illustrated by Millet, *Iconographie*, 24.

[10] Illustrated by Graeven, I, 54.

[11] Illustrated by de Lasteyrie, 42.

le-Rideau (Ill. 896), in a relief of St.-Mark's, assigned by Grabelentz to the XI century,[1] at St.-Mesme of Chinon (Ill. 897) — a dated monument of 1025, — at St. Emmeran of Regensburg (Ill. 1279, 1281, 1282) — 1049–1064, and in the tomb from Santa Cruz de la Serós (Ill. 527). The motive is therefore characteristic of stone sculpture of the XI century.

On the other hand its use became rare after the year 1100. The cloisters of Moissac (Ill. 262–273), dated 1100, may be taken as marking the end of the tradition.[2] After that date the arch is commonly retained only in lintels, or in friezes, where similar figures are repeated under a series of arches.[3] In this particular, therefore, the sculptures of Santo Domingo de Silos clearly show the style of the XI century.[4]

The motive of the hand raised, with the palm turned outward, which occurs at Santo Domingo in the reliefs of Doubting Thomas (Ill. 671) and the Ascension (Ill. 672) is also consistent with an XI century date. This motive, too, is of ancient, and apparently of Eastern origin, since it is found on two wooden consoles of the V century from Bawit in the Cairo Museum.[5] In the Far East it is of frequent occurrence from a very early period, and is familiar to students of Oriental iconography. It is found, for example, to cite one instance among many, in a gilt bronze image of before 781 belonging to the Imperial Household, and exhibited in the Kyoto

---

[1] Illustrated by Ongania, Pl. 279.

[2] Except that for the sake of unity the arch was repeated from the earlier in the later reliefs of Santo Domingo de Silos (Ill. 721).

[3] See what is said below, p. 133 f., of the history of the arched lintel. It is from lintels like those of Nicolò that are derived the reliefs under arcades of the baptismal font of Hulla (illustrated by Roosval, Taf. XII).

[4] There are a few examples of the survival of the arch motive into the XII century, as in a capital at Autun (Ill. 79), in a capital of St.-Benoît-sur-Loire (Ill. 1416), in the sculptures of La Daurade at Toulouse (Ill. 471), at S. Vicente of Avila (Ill. 850–851), in the cloister of Ripoll, at St.-Gilles (Ill. 1325), etc. In miniatures we find it in a Syriac Gospel of the XII or XIII century, illustrated by Omont, *Fond. Piot*, XIX, Pl. IV–IX. It is also in a Beatus Manuscript of the late XII century, published by Sentenach, 215. It is often used in enamel work, but always with a row of similar figures, as in the altar-frontal from Santo Domingo de Silos, now in the Burgos Museum, or the reliquary by Rogkerus von Helmershausen, of 1100, illustrated by Creutz, 19.

[5] Illustrated by Strzygowski, *Cairo Cat.*, Taf. VII.

Exposition.[1] In the IX century the motive appears in the Occident, in a fresco of the lower church at S. Clemente of Rome and in the chapel of S. Lorenzo ai Sorgenti di Volturno.[2] In the X century we find the motive in a book-cover of S. Marco at Venice;[3] then it appears in miniatures of the school of Winchester [4] with which the Santo Domingo sculptures show so many affinities. But it is in the XI century that the motive becomes common. We find it in a Byzantine plaque of steatite in the museum of Berlin,[5] in the mosaics of St. Luke at Phokis,[6] in a mosaic of Mt. Athos,[7] in an ivory casket of the XI–XII century at the Bargello, in Florence,[8] in a Byzantine ivory plaque of the XI–XII century in the treasure of the cathedral at Trèves,[9] and in a cameo of the XI century in the Schatz-Kammer of Vienna.[10] The motive is constant in Spanish ivories of the XI century. It is found in the Arcas of San Millán (Ill. 639, 641, 643, 644, 648, 649) and San Felices (Ill. 661–664), and in the Jaca book-cover (Ill. 519). It is also found on the Oviedo Arca Santa (Ill. 656, 659). In stone sculpture the motive appears in the Carlovingian relief found at St.-Pierre de la Citadelle at Metz; [11] it is prominent in the sculptures of 1060 from the Mauritzkirche, now in the West-fälischen Landesmuseum at Münster and in the reliefs of 1049–1064 at St. Emmeran of Regensburg (Ill. 1281). Its presence at Santo Domingo de Silos at the end of the XI century is therefore entirely normal. The motive continued to be popular in the XII century, especially in the Pilgrimage school of sculpture. In the XII century, however, the hands are apt to be large and coarse, while in the XI they are generally small and refined. This difference will be readily

[1] This statue is illustrated in the catalogue of the Exposition.
[2] Illustrated by Bertaux, Pl. III, 100.
[3] Illustrated by Venturi, II, 656.
[4] See the Benedictional of St. Aethelwold, *passim*, illustrated by Warner and Wilson. Also the Besançon Gospels, illustrated by Homburger, Pl. XI.
[5] Illustrated by Schlumberger, II, 85.
[6] Illustrated *ibid.*, II, 93.
[7] Illustrated *ibid.*, II, 141.
[8] Illustrated *ibid.*, III, 69.
[9] Illustrated *ibid.*, III, 565.
[10] Illustrated *ibid.*, III, 593.
[11] Illustrated by de Lasteyrie, 42.

appreciated upon comparing the New York ivory (Ill. 709) with the mosaics of St. Luke at Phokis.[1] Now the Santo Domingo hands are distinctly of the XI century type.

The little capitals under the arches of the Santo Domingo reliefs at first sight seem almost Gothic in character, and to suggest a date at an advanced period of the XII century. Similar capitals are, however, found in the choir of the cathedral at Santiago, which dates from 1078–1102. Much has been written of the imitation of nature by the stone-carvers of the XII century in the Ile-de-France, and of the appearance about 1140 of local flora in Gothic capitals. The inspiration seems, in fact, to have come less from "the tender forms of the budding spring," than from the capitals that had been executed at Santiago some sixty years before. Certain ones of the cathedral of Noyon, for example, seem almost like direct reproductions of those in the Santiago triforium. These Gothic-like capitals are perhaps derived from Carlovingian manuscripts. Those of Santo Domingo de Silos, for example, might easily have been inspired by some such miniature as that of the Gospels of Ada at Trèves,[2] dating from the VIII or IX century. We have found many other indications of the influence of Germany upon the art of Spain, and indeed of Europe, in the XI century.

M. Bertaux[3] seems to have been deterred from dating the sculpture of Santo Domingo de Silos to the XI century by the form of the shields, which are pointed (Ill. 670), whereas he seems to be under the impression that round shields were used in the XI century. This is an error. Pointed shields were regularly used in the last quarter of the XI century[4] although round ones occasionally persisted until

---

[1] Illustrated by Schlumberger, II, 93.

[2] Illustrated by Boinet, Pl. VIII.

[3] In André Michel, II, 1, 227.

[4] Examples may be found as early as the middle of the XI century in a miniature illustrated by Lefebvre des Noëttes, 216 (Bib. Nat. MS. lat. 6), and in the Arca of San Millán (Ill. 647). There are numerous examples of the last quarter of the XI century. Thus we find them on a capital of the church at Airvault (Ill. 899), a monument consecrated in 1100; in a manuscript illustrated by Quicherat, 135; in the Gospels of the Countess Matilda, Morgan Library, New York, dated 1098–1099, illustrated by Warner, XII; in a miniature of the "Histoire de Skylitzès," a manuscript of the XI century in the national library of Madrid, illustrated by Schlumberger,

an advanced period of the XII century.[1] The absence of a nasal piece in the armour at Santo Domingo (Ill. 670) is an indication of date in the XI century.[2]

M. Bertaux[3] in studying the relief of the Deposition (Ill. 669) remarks the curious flame-shaped pebbles at the foot of the cross, and observes that they are similar to those on a capital of St.-Etienne of Toulouse.[4] He concludes that Santo Domingo de Silos is derived from Toulouse,[5] and consequently later in date. The truth seems to be, however, that the relationship was the other way about. These flame-shaped pebbles are an ancient Spanish motive. They are found in precisely the same form in an early miniature of the Crucifixion in a missal of San Millán de la Cogolla,[6] now in the Biblioteca of the Academia de Historia. The same motive reappears in the Arca of San Felices (Ill. 662) and something like it in the Arca of San Millán (Ill. 640, 644). It seems, therefore, certain that it originated in Spain, and that it was there known in the XI century, and indeed much before.[7]

II, 388 and III, 112 (here the Saracens have round shields); in the Bayeux tapestry (where a very few round shields also occur); in a miniature of the XI century, Bib. Nat., lat. 8878, illustrated by Lefebvre des Noëttes, Fig. 24; in an ivory-carving of the XI century at the Bargello in Florence, illustrated by Graeven, *Ital.*, No. 30; in the sculptures of the Mauritzkirche, now in the Westfälischen Landesmuseum at Münster, dated 1060 and illustrated by Creutz, Pl. II; and in a miniature of the *Gebhardsbibel* at the Stiftsbibliothek of Admont, Cod. 511, illustrated by Swarzenski, Taf. XXXI, and apparently dating from the 1070's.

[1] They are found on a capital of the middle of the XII century at St.-Maurice of Vienne, illustrated by Bégule, 118; with pointed ones in the sculptures of Ripoll (Ill. 570, 588); in the Bede of St.-Feliú of Gerona, illustrated by Sacs; and in the destroyed pavement of Brindisi, a dated monument of 1178 (Bertaux, 494).

[2] See Lefebvre des Noëttes, 230.   [3] In André Michel, II, 1, 226.

[4] The motive also appears on a capital of St.-Nectaire representing the Three Maries at the Tomb (Ill. 1190), and on a capital of the southern side aisle of Notre-Dame-du-Port of Clermont-Ferrand (Ill. 1184) representing the Temptation. Both these works are of the second half of the XII century, and belong to a school formed, as we shall see (p. 234 f.), under the influence of Spanish sculpture.

[5] The only other example of the motive that I know in France is in the frescos of Vicq. These also present many analogies with Spanish work. Mr. Cook calls attention to the similarities of the draperies to Catalan frescos. The composition of the Last Supper is like that of the same subject on the Arca of San Felices (Ill. 661).

[6] Illustrated by Godoy Alcántara in *Museo*, III, 65. Something very like this motive is in several panels of the Hildesheim doors, *e.g.*, scene of the Adoration of the Magi, illustrated by Dibelius, Taf. 8.

[7] Could it have been derived from a misunderstanding of the cloud swirls of some such min-

In the eyes of M. Bertaux, the crossed legs of the Santo Domingo reliefs (Ill. 667–673) were also an indication of derivation from Toulouse and of late date. We have already traced the history of this motive,[1] and have seen how ancient is its origin, and how wide its diffusion. There is not the slightest reason to suppose that it came into Spain from Toulouse. It was already acclimated in the peninsula in 1075, for we find it in that year in the Arca Santa at Oviedo (Ill. 657).

A peculiarity of the costumes in the Santo Domingo reliefs (Ill. 667–673) is the presence of a vertical slit in the front of the neck of the under-garment. This is found in other works of the XI century — in the Gospels of the Countess Matilda in the Morgan Library at New York,[2] a dated work of 1098–1099; in the Arcas of San Millán (Ill. 638–649) and San Felices (Ill. 663, 664); in the Bayeux tapestry; in the reliefs of the Beatitudes from San Isidoro of Léon (Ill. 651–653); in a capital of Jaca (Ill. 520) and in the throne of San Niccola of Bari (Ill. 154), a dated monument of 1098. The motive occasionally persisted in the XII century, as we have seen,[3] but its presence at Santo Domingo tends to confirm the dating to the XI century.

A peculiarity of the armour at Santo Domingo (Ill. 670) is the chain mail covering the chin. Armour of precisely this same type is found in the Arca of San Millán (Ill. 647).

Another peculiarity of the style of the Santo Domingo sculptures is the drawing of the arms. Take for example the extended arm of Christ in the Doubting Thomas (Ill. 671). The member seems to be made of wood; there is no joint at the elbow; the upper arm is disproportionately short, the biceps are not indicated. The fingers of the hand are drawn like parallel sticks, the thumb along side of the

iature as that representing the Second Coming of Christ in the Benedictional of St. Aethelwold at Chatsworth, folio 10, illustrated by Warner and Wilson?

[1] See above, p. 21.

[2] Illustrated by Warner.

[3] See above, p. 42. It also occurs in one of the reliefs of Angoulême (Ill. 932), in a sculpture from Ebreuil (Ill. 1255), in an apostle of St.-Gilles (Ill. 1310), in a capital of Clermont-Ferrand (Ill. 1174), in the relief of the Shepherds from Parthenay (Ill. 1054), in the Queen of Sheba of the Pórtico della Gloria (Ill. 839), at La Lande de Fronzac (Ill. 917).

others. This primitive modelling of one member in a style in many ways so accomplished is striking. Now in the S. Isidoro crucifix of 1063 (Ill. 654) we find arms that are modelled in precisely the same manner, even to the most minute particulars; and here again this primitive anatomy contrasts with a technique in other ways remarkably perfect. This peculiar manner of drawing the arms is characteristic of the XI century; in the XII century the treatment was entirely different, as may for example be seen in the New York ivory (Ill. 710).

It has been supposed that the movement of the figures in the Santo Domingo reliefs (Ill. 667–673) indicates a date in the XII century. However, a little reflection suffices to bring the conviction that precisely such movement was characteristic of the last quarter of the XI century. There is assuredly no lack of movement in the Oviedo Arca Santa of 1075 (Ill. 657). We find it also in the minor figures of the Madrid crucifix of 1063 (Ill. 654, 655). Nor is it absent in the frescos representing the life of St. Alexius in the lower church of S. Clemente at Rome, works executed between 1073 and 1084. Precisely such thin wiggly figures as those of Santo Domingo (Ill. 672) are found on the Jaca book-cover, which was carved before 1085 (Ill. 519). The movement of Silos is, moreover, completely paralleled in the capitals of Cluny (Ill. 5–10), which date from 1088–1095.

The clinging draperies of Santo Domingo (Ill. 667–673) are closely analogous to those of the Jaca book-cover of before 1085 (Ill. 519). They also resemble those of Cluny (1089–1095), falling in the same folds over the legs, or hanging down in the same zig-zag edges (Ill. 5–10). When we compare the draperies of Silos with those of the *Christ* at St. Emmeran of Regensburg (1049–1064), we notice not only that they are of the same clinging type, with similar broad flat folds, but we find the same convention of indicating the modelling by two parallel lines (Ill. 1279, 1280).

The hair and beard convention used at Santo Domingo de Silos (Ill. 667–673) consists of a division into strands each of which is incised with a number of parallel lines. Now the hair is executed in precisely this same way in the *Christ* of St. Emmeran of Regensburg (Ill. 1279, 1280), which is a dated monument of 1049–1064.[1]

The skilful handling of groups of figures at Silos (Ill. 671–673) recalls the frescos of the life of St. Alexius in the lower church of S. Clemente at Rome (1073–1084). A similar treatment of masses, and heads tipped in the same way recur in the Gospels of the Countess Matilda, in the Morgan Library, a dated work of 1098–1099.[2]

The harpies of the Silos capital (Ill. 666) are very similar to the sphinxes sculptured on the right side of the throne at Canosa, just above the elephant. Now this throne is a dated monument of 1078–1089.[3]

The mastery of line and delicacy of technique characteristic of Silos (Ill. 667–673) are paralleled in the frescos of the life of St. Alexius in the lower church of S. Clemente at Rome (1073–1084). Even a closer analogy is to be found in the capitals of Cluny (1088–1095). The faces at Cluny though of different type are like those of Silos in being archaic and conventionalized (Ill. 5–9).

When we compare the sculptures of Silos (Ill. 667–673) with those of Moissac cloisters (Ill. 262–287), which are dated 1100, we are at once struck by the many points of contact.[4] These are so evident, and have been so much insisted upon, that it is unnecessary to de-

---

[1] The motive must be of very ancient origin, since it runs through the art of the Far East. The hair of a statue of Shindatsura-Taisho, for example, in the temple Kofuku-ji at Nara, a work of the early Fujiwara period (888–1068 A.D.) — illustration published by the Nara Imperial Museum — has hair executed according to this convention and flaming upward, very like the hair of the demons on the capitals of Vézelay (Ill. 42). The convention, indeed, persisted in the sculpture of the XII century, being found at Souillac (Ill. 346), Moissac (Ill. 365) and in the Externstein of the Teutoberger Forest, a dated monument of 1115 (illustrated by Creutz, Taf. V), in a relief of the Nikolauskapelle of the Münster at Freiburg (illustrated by Weise, abb. 3) and elsewhere. The Externstein should be compared with the Santo Domingo Deposition (Ill. 669) for other details as well.

[2] Illustrated by Warner. A Catalan antependium of the Barcelona Museum, No. 2, called to my attention by Mr. Cook, shows analogous grouping, and heads similarly tipped. This painting, however, is inspired by the sculptures. The draperies are like those of the Moissac cloister reliefs.

[3] Photograph by Alinari, No. 35224.

[4] Note that the scale ornament so characteristic of Moissac (Ill. 267) is found at Silos (Ill. 671).

scribe them in detail; for our purpose the points of difference are more significant. It is obvious that Moissac is coarser, Silos more refined. Compare for example the hands at Moissac (Ill. 266) with the hands at Cluny (Ill. 5) and at Silos (Ill. 671). It is clear at once that Moissac conforms to what we have learned to recognize as the XII century type, whereas Cluny and Silos are of the earlier, XI century tradition. There is the same difference throughout the sculptures — at Moissac we feel everywhere the settling down of the coarse and brutal manner which was to culminate in such works as the Toulouse apostles (Ill. 437–443). When we compare the New York ivory (Ill. 710) with the Madrid crucifix (Ill. 654) we feel precisely the same difference that we find between the Moissac cloisters (Ill. 262–273) and those of Silos (Ill. 667–673). It is the difference between the XII and the XI century. Fatigati considered the cloisters of Silos later than those of Moissac, because they are better. He was right that they are better, but this fact should rather be considered an argument for their being earlier.

When we look closely at the sculptures of the Moissac cloister (Ill. 262–273), we notice that the faces are more individualized and better characterized than those of Silos or Cluny. The hair conventions also are more naturalistic and more varied. The hat of the St. John at Moissac (Ill. 269) seems obviously more advanced than that of the Silos Christ at Emmaus (Ill. 667). The hair of the St. James at Moissac (Ill. 265) is evidently more developed than the hair at Silos (Ill. 667). The ornamental borders to the garments of St. Durand (Ill. 262, 264) and St. James (Ill. 265) at Moissac have no counterpart at Silos (Ill. 667–673). The cross of St. Andrew at Silos (Ill. 673) seems more primitive than that of the seraph of the St.-Sernin ambulatory (Ill. 298). The letters of the inscriptions at Santo Domingo (Ill. 667–673) are more archaic than those of Moissac (Ill. 262–273).

We look through the entire field of XII century sculpture without finding a single parallel for the style of Santo Domingo. The reader will only have to compare the photographs of monuments like Ripoll

(Ill. 561–593) or Leire (Ill. 712–716) to be convinced of the wide gulf which separates such works from Silos.

We may, therefore, I think, conclude that the sculptures of Santo Domingo de Silos were executed, precisely as the documentary evidence indicates, in the last third of the XI century.

The question whence this art was derived remains. It can perhaps never be fully answered. We have seen that the Silos reliefs present numerous points of contact with earlier and contemporary ivory-carvings of Spain. Certainly local tradition must be credited with having contributed fundamentally to the formation of the style.

It may be suspected that the Benedictine style of Monte Cassino influenced the development of this sculpture. Santo Domingo was, we know, during his entire life in close touch with Monte Cassino.[1] It is perhaps this common Benedictine influence that explains the points of contact between Santo Domingo with Cluny on the one hand and S. Clemente of Rome on the other. The church of San Marcello of Capua contains a southern portal (Ill. 166) which shows analogies both with Cluny and with Santo Domingo. Now this church depended directly upon Monte Cassino.[2]

The similarities between Santo Domingo and the sculptures of St. Emmeran of Regensburg are probably to be accounted for by the German influence which we have seen was exerted upon Spanish ivories.

Another and unexpected analogy with the Santo Domingo sculptures is not so easily explained. There is an obvious similarity with the reliefs of Chichester cathedral in England.[3] These are believed by Messrs. Prior and Gardner to date from as early as c. 1000. We have already remarked numerous similarities between the sculptures of Silos and manuscripts of the school of Winchester. Even more

---

[1] Fategati, 27.

[2] Inscriptions connect the church with the abbot Alferius, who is mentioned in 1113 (Schulz, II, 165). One of these placed over the western portal reads:

✚ DA[T] XPO BALVAS: ABBAS ALFERIVS ALBAS
VT CAELI REGNVM: VALEAT PENETRARE SUPERNVM

[3] Illustrated by Prior and Gardner, 138.

striking are the points of contact with an English Latin Gospel of the XI century.[1] In this we find the Silos feeling for line and delicacy. But most striking of all is the similarity of Silos to an English manuscript of the first half of the XII century from Bury St. Edmunds.[2] The Christ of the Silos Journey to Emmaus (Ill. 667) in facial type, cap, attenuation, and movement of lines is strikingly similar to the protagonist in a miracle of St. Edmund; the grouping of the crowd in the miniature recalls the relief of Doubting Thomas (Ill. 671), although it is somewhat less rhythmic. A New Testament written at Bury St. Edmunds in the first half of the XII century[3] is similar in style to the Miracles of St. Edmund, and also presents analogies with the work at Silos. I can only suppose that the same work of art, perhaps an English miniature, served as prototype for both the Silos reliefs and these manuscripts of the XII century.[4]

It is a singular fact that a Beatus manuscript of 1109, written for the abbey of Santo Domingo, shows no affinity with the sculptures, but similarity to Irish miniatures.[5]

From the aesthetic point of view, the reliefs of Santo Domingo represent a notable achievement. The formal and archaic composition is founded upon a subtle appreciation of the significance of opposed lines and masses. How satisfactory, for example, is the grouping of the guards about the tomb of Christ (Ill. 670); how exquisite the two end figures, lunging strongly outward from the central group, as in a Pontormo drawing. There is the perfection of balance in the Nicodemus and the Joseph of Arimathea bending

---

[1] Illustrated in the Burlington Catalogue, Pl. 21, No. 21.

[2] Illustrated in the Burlington Catalogue, Pl. 23, No. 18. I owe this observation to Mr. Cook.

[3] Illustrated in the Burlington Catalogue, Pl. 28, No. 23.

[4] This might also account for the similarities between Silos and Cluny, for Cluny as we shall see was under the strong influence of manuscripts of the school of Winchester. What is puzzling is that the Bury St. Edmunds Testament seems to show evidence of having itself fallen under the influence of sculpture. The draperies of the Christ in the upper part of the miniature to which we have referred look as if they had been inspired by the Virgin of the Annunciation of the Moissac porch (Ill. 376).

[5] British Museum, Add. MS. 11, 695. Illustrated by Bond and Thompson, I, 48–49. The Ryerson Beatus, of the end of the XII century on the other hand, resembles the Silos sculptures in the rigid rows of figures, and in the hands raised, palm outwards.

over the dead Christ; and the diagonal line formed by the lid of the sarcophagus is singularly happy. We shall have to journey far before we encounter again composition as original and as successful. And can even the proudest moment of the Italian Renaissance show a relief to equal the Pentecost (Ill. 673) — apparently the earliest, and certainly the finest of the series — with the twelve apostles, like candle-flames, swirling towards the Day-Spring from on high?

The historical importance of Santo Domingo de Silos is very great. Its direct influence may be traced in such monuments as the cloister at Moissac (Ill. 262–287), the porch at Souillac (Ill. 343–352), and the cloisters at Arles (Ill. 1344–1365) and St.-Guilhem-le-Désert (Ill. 1397–1399). From such centres as these, its message could be carried to well-nigh every sculptor of the XII century in Europe.

There is one other monument which should be studied before we turn away from the XI century in Spain. This is the grand Virgin (Ill. 770) now in the Madrid Museo Arqueológico, and coming from Sahagún. Sahagún, a focal point on the road of St. James, was the most important Cluniac possession in Spain. The statue [1] lacks the delicacy of technique characteristic of Santo Domingo, but in compensation possesses something of the aloofness and impassivity of Mr. Berenson's Bodhisattva which it so unexpectedly resembles, even in technical detail. The folds of the drapery are doubtless derived from Cluny; something in the shape of the group with two symmetrical and strongly empathic curves, reaching their widest point at the hips, recalls the tympanum of Charlieu (Ill. 4), which is dated 1094. The zig-zag drapery edges are also like Charlieu. This way of treating the drapery edge is, however, very ancient in Spain, being found in an Iberian statue of the Madrid Museum (Ill. 637).[2] Evidently the Virgin of Sahagún is a product of the last years of the XI century; in fact, there can be no doubt that it belonged to

[1] It was found placed "al centro de una ventana tapiada de la iglesia de San Tirso, para cuyo punto indudablemente no habia sido hecha" (Juan de Dios, in *Museo*, VII, 289). Thence it went to Léon, and to Madrid in 1869.

[2] For the history of the motive, see below, p. 72.

the church of Sahagún begun in 1080[1] and consecrated in 1099.[2]

The Virgin is seated on a chair, the legs of which are carved at the ends to represent animals' claws. This is the earliest example I know of a motive destined to win great popularity in the XII century.

[1] Lampérez, I, 692.   [2] Escalona, 88.

V

THE BARI THRONE

The throne at S. Niccola of Bari (Ill. 152–155) is dated 1098 by an inscription [1] and by a contemporary chronicle.[2]

The archivolt of the ancient portal of the cathedral at Monopoli (Ill. 158–162), a building begun in 1107,[3] is, as Wackernagel has recognized,[4] by the same hand.[5]

Now, what is extraordinary, is that certain sculptures at St.-Gilles in Provence show close analogies with the style of this sculptor who worked in Apulia at the end of the XI and the beginning of the XII century. The lioness of remarkable realism beneath the Bari throne (Ill. 155) is exceedingly like the animals in procession below the St.-Gilles frieze (Ill. 1316). The lioness just below the Flagellation (Ill. 1322), for example, has the same head, the same ears, the same eyes, the same nose, the same body, the same legs, the same claws, the same lank proportions. This resemblance is the

[1] ✠ INCLITVS ATQ. BONVS SEDET HAC IN SEDE PATRONVS
PRESVL BARINVS HELIAS ET CANVSINVS

[2] MLXXXXVIIII. Ind. VII. Tertia die intrante mense Octubr. vênit Papa Urbanus cum plures Archiepiscopi, et Episcopi, Abbatibus, et Commitibus, intraverunt in Bari, et suscepti sunt cum magna reverentia, et praeparavit Domino Helia nostro Archiepiscopo mirificam sedem intus in Ecclesia Beatissimi Nicolay confessoris Christi. Et fecit ibi Synodum per unam ebdomada. Post completis dies octo perrexit in pace; et in mense Julii obiit ipse Papa Urbanus, et surrexit Pascalis Papa. (Anonymi Barensis *Chronicon*, ed. Muratori, *Rerum Italicarum Scriptores*, V, 155).

[3] The archivolt bears the inscription:
† MILLENIS ANNIS CENTENIS ATQ; P[ER]ACTIS SEPTENIS.
NAT' DEI XPS VENTVS IN ORBĒ: HOC P̄SVL TEP̄LV IVSSIT FIERI
ROMOALDVS: ANNIS T̄ DENIS PLENIS SIBI PONTIFICATV; TEMPORE SVB
COMITIS MAGNI DÑI Q' ROBERT' AVXILIO CVIVS TĒPLI LABOR EDITVS
HVIVS.

[4] 44.

[5] It is unnecessary to repeat here what has already been said by Wackernagel, and never questioned. The intelligent reader may indeed easily convince himself that the Monopoli archivolt and the Bari throne are works of the same artist by comparing the photographs (Ill. 152–155 and Ill. 158–162). On the other hand the archivolt at Acerenza is inferior in quality, and the work of a copyist.

more striking that such naturalistic animal sculptures are exceptional in Romanesque art. These animals would indeed make us
think of Barye rather than of the XI or XII century. Nor do I
know of any other representation of a lioness in Romanesque
sculpture.

The heads of the angels of the Monopoli archivolt are very similar to the heads below the frieze and on the capitals of St.-Gilles.
Compare with the heads of Monopoli (Ill. 158–162) the head just
below the Flagellation (Ill. 1322) or on the capital beneath (Ill.
1322). In both there is the same round proportion, the same low
forehead, the same broad, flat nose, the same line from the nose to
the corners of the mouth, the same arched eye-brows, the same incised pupils, the same execution of the eye-lids, the same round
flabby chin, the same dimple between the chin and the mouth. The
head in the lioness' mouth at Bari (Ill. 155) is very like the head beneath the Money Changers at St.-Gilles (Ill. 1316). The man in the
mouth of the lion under *St. Peter* at St.-Gilles (Ill. 1325 a) has
draperies of precisely the same peculiar type as those of the supporting figures of the Bari throne (Ill. 152). The lions beneath the
foot-stool of the Bari throne (Ill. 152) are similar to those beneath
the great statues at St.-Gilles (Ill. 1325 a, 1325 b); the motive of
supporting lions is essentially Italian; three of the lions at St.-
Gilles have manes executed according to the same peculiar and
characteristic convention as that of the right-hand lion under the
Bari throne (Ill. 152).

I can only account for such analogies by supposing that the animals and heads below the St.-Gilles frieze, numerous capitals, and
the four lions beneath the statues flanking the central portal in the
same church are by a sculptor from Apulia, and probably by the very
master of the Bari throne. We shall later find reason to believe that
these portions of the St.-Gilles façade were in construction about
1140. They are therefore some forty years later than the Bari
throne. In fact the style of the work at St.-Gilles is unmistakably
more mature and advanced.

The question arises whether the Bari master may have also collaborated in the production of the celebrated frieze of St.-Gilles (Ill. 1315–1322) which bears indubitable traces of being the work of more than one hand. The scene of the Betrayal (Ill. 1319, 1320) notably differs from the other portions of the frieze; and it should be observed that the hair of Judas is executed according to the same striking and peculiar convention used in one of the supporting figures of the Bari throne (Ill. 154). This convention is again repeated in the Peter and the executioner behind Judas in the same scene. The latter wears a peculiar conical casque, very like the one of the supporting figure of the Bari throne (Ill. 154).[1]

The origin of this sculptor whose activity covers the first half of the XII century, and who wandered from Apulia to Provence becomes a matter of considerable interest. Unfortunately the evidence is insufficient to make possible a definite solution of the problem.

His earliest work known to us is in Apulia. We have seen that a school of sculpture of high merit existed in that province as early as the second quarter of the XI century. Are we on the basis of these facts to award Apulia the same hegemony in Romanesque sculpture that has been claimed for her in that of the Renaissance?

Only one monument of Lombard sculpture is earlier than the Bari throne, and that is the tomb of S. Alberto at Pontida, executed presumably immediately after the death of the saint in 1095. The similarity of the Bari throne to this work is evident, although not strikingly close. The animals in both are good; although the horse of the Pontida St. James[2] is far from rivalling the superlative excellence of the lioness of the Bari throne. The mane at Pontida is indicated by a convention not dissimilar to that used for the manes at Bari. The faces of the supporting figures at Bari and of the Pontida St. James are of the same heavy type, with massive jaw.

[1] Caps of the same type are found on two capitals of Vézelay (Ill. 31).
[2] The tomb of S. Alberto at Pontida is illustrated in Porter, *Lombard Architecture*, IV, Plate 189, Fig. 1, 2.

The Pontida reliefs are more closely related to the Porta dei Leoni of S. Niccola at Bari (Ill. 156). The archivolt of this portal is obviously a more ancient fragment re-employed in the present doorway; its evident similarities of style with the throne [1] make it certain that it belonged to that church of S. Niccola which was begun in 1087,[2] which two contemporary documents state was in construction in 1089,[3] of which the crypt was built in 1090,[4] which was sufficiently advanced in 1098 to accommodate a papal council [5] which was consecrated in 1105,[6] of which the steps of the ciborium were executed after the death of Elia in 1105 [7] and before that of Eustachio in 1123,[8] and which two contemporary inscriptions explicitly state was built by Elia (1089–1105), and which, an inscription tells us, was adorned by Eustachio (1105–1123). The archivolt may therefore be considered as certainly anterior to 1105.

When we compare this archivolt [9] with the Pontida St. James we are at once struck by the similarity of the horses. The movement of the legs is the same, also the drawing of the eyes and ears. We notice, too, that the same curious little convention of hollow circles

---

[1] The conical casque of the central supporting figure of the throne reappears in the right-hand horseman of the archivolt; the facial types are very similar; the right leg of the figure to the right of the centre in the archivolt reproduces, line for line, the right leg of the central supporting figure; there is the same comprehension of plastic form; the same mastery of anatomy.

[2] Wackernagel, 59.

[3] *Cod. Dip. Bar.*, V, 23, 25.

[4] Mill. LXXXX Ind. XIII. Mense Sept. intravit Urbanus Papa in civitate Bari, et consecravit Helias Archiepiscopus in civitate Bari prid. Octubr. Et in Kal. Octubr. edificavit confessionem Sancti Nicolai. (Anonymi Barensis *Chronicon*, ed. Muratori, *Rerum Italicarum Scriptores*, V, 154.) Elia was in fact consecrated not in 1090 but in 1089.

[5] See above, p. 59.

[6] Wackernagel, 2.

[7] They bear the inscription:

✠ HIS GRADIBVS TVMIDIS ASCENSVS AD ALTA IECATVR
HIS GRADIBVS BLANDIS QVERERE CELSA DATVR
ERGO NE TVMEAS QVI SVRSVM SCANDERE QVERIS
SIS HVMILIS SVPPLEX PLANVS ET ATVS ERIS
VT PATER HELAS HOC TEMPLVM Q PRIVS EGIT
QVOD PATER EVSTASIVS SIC DECORANDO REGIT

[8] Bertaux, 450 f., concedes this date for the steps, but places the ciborium 1139–1154 because of the enamel plaque representing St. Nicolas crowning King Roger. This plaque, however, might easily be later than the ciborium, just as the portrait of Victor Emmanuel III in the choir might easily be later than the empty chair beneath it.

[9] See especially the large-size details published by Wackernagel, Tafel XXVII d and e.

is used to indicate the mail of the knights at Bari, and to decorate the saddle-strap of the horse at Pontida. The facial types and hair conventions are very similar.

An even closer analogy with the Bari archivolt is, however, offered by the Porta della Pescheria at Modena.[1] In the two is represented the same strange iconographical subject — the inscriptions at Modena make it certain that we are dealing with a lost episode of the Arthurian cycle. In both knights on horse-back approach from either side a central stronghold, which is defended by other warriors. The horses are very analogous; the knights are dressed in similar armour, with coat of mail reaching to their knees, pointed shields, lances with pennants, and conical casques. At Modena the casques have nose-pieces, at Bari they have not; and at Modena the mail covers the throats and chin, which at Bari are left exposed.[2] This is the armour which was in use in the last years of the XI or early years of the XII century and analogous to that which we have found at Santo Domingo de Silos (Ill. 670). The saddles and bridles are of the same type except that at Bari there is a strap passing underneath the horses' tails, which is lacking at Modena.

An archivolt of the cathedral of Angoulême (Ill. 939) executed as we shall see[3] between 1110 and 1128 should be compared with the two archivolts of Bari and Modena. It also represents a combat of cavaliers before a walled town. The horses are more poorly drawn than either those of Bari or of Modena, but are of essentially the same type, and the movement of the legs is the same. At Angoulême the shields are round, instead of pointed; the saddles have sometimes a tail strap as at Bari; the lances are without pennants;[4]

---

[1] For a detailed study of these sculptures see my *Lombard Architecture*, III, 44 f.

[2] These two peculiarities would seem to indicate a somewhat later date for Modena than for Bari. In chronological questions it is, however, dangerous to place too much reliance upon details of costume.

[3] P. 307.

[4] This is the more singular that the *Church* at Vézelay a dated sculpture of 1120 (illustrated by Porée, 17) holds a lance with pennant; one also is attached to the lance in the Externstein of the Teutoberger Forest, dated 1115 (illustrated by Dehio, abb. 412).

three of the knights have conical casques, like those of Bari and Modena, but a peculiarity is that from one of these casques and from the crown of King Arthur, there seems to flutter a sort of veil. The mail falls in a skirt to the knees, as at both Modena and Bari, but covers the chin as at Bari, but not at Modena. At Modena and Bari the saddles have only one girth, whereas at Angoulême they have two — this is an indication that Angoulême is later than the other two. The straps of the harness at Angoulême are ornamented with little circles like those of the *St. James* at Pontida.

By this comparison of the details, the reader will doubtless have been convinced of the close relationship of the three reliefs, but he will have seen that the indications for priority are contradictory and confusing. On the whole, Angoulême seems distinctly the latest of the three, and it appears more closely affiliated with Bari than with Modena. Between Bari and Modena, the latter seems more restful and abler, and is therefore presumably earlier. If the archivolt of Modena was sculptured soon after work was begun on the cathedral in 1099, it is possible that it might have been copied at Bari before 1105, and that Bari might have been copied at Angoulême in the second decade of the XII century.

The motive of cavaliers jousting is by no means confined to the three reliefs which we have been studying. We find it in a manuscript of St. Albans, earlier than 1146, and preserved at Hildesheim.[1] Here it is explained that what is seen *corporaliter* must be understood *spiritualiter;* these warriors who fight should recall to us the spiritual combats we must wage against evil. Evidently a pious cleric is inventing an edifying sermon upon an artistic motive that originated with a very different and purely secular meaning which had, perhaps, already been forgotten.

That the motive did not develop from the reliefs of the Arthurian cycle which we have been studying is indicated by the fact that it is found on the ivory box of the cathedral of Pamplona, dated 1005.[2]

[1] Illustrated by Goldschmidt, *Albanipsalter*, 46 f.
[2] Illustrated by Bertaux, *Exp. Ret.*, 205.

It enjoyed considerable popularity in Spain, being found in a Spanish manuscript,[1] on a capital of the chapter-house of Santa Cruz de Rivas (Palencia), on the ablution-basin of Játiva (Valencia),[2] on a capital of the Catedral Vieja at Salamanca (Ill. 736) and on a capital of the Eremita de Revenga (Segóvia).[3]

It was in Italy, however, that the motive was most widely diffused. We find it sculptured upon a relief of c. 1120 walled into the campanile of S. Stefano of Pavia,[4] and in another of the Palazzo Municipale of Narni.[5] It also occurs on capitals of Sta. Sofia of Benevento, S. Giovanni in Borgo of Pavia and S. Agata dei Goti.[6] In Dalmatia it is found in a sculpture now in the Museo S. Donato at Zara.[7]

In France I know only three examples of the motive: a sculpture in the Musée Ochier at Cluny (Ill. 27), a relief in the apse of St.-Gildas-de-Rhuis and a relief flanking the portal of the priory at Anzy-le-Duc.

The motive, therefore, appears to be at home in Italy or in Spain rather than in the North.

The one monument of the North which does offer close analogies with the archivolts of Modena and Bari and the architrave of Angoulême is the Bayeux "tapestry." When we compare the warriors here with those of the Porta della Pescheria we notice great similarity in the armour. The embroidery shows the same pointed shields (although a few round ones are introduced) some plain, some with devices; the same conical casques with nose-pieces; spears of the same type with identical banners; in both some of the cavaliers are in armour and helmeted, others without armour and bare-headed. The one essential difference is that the Modena warriors in armour have a coat of mail with skirts, while those of the Bayeux

---

[1] Illustrated in Museo Español de Antigüedades, IX, unnumbered plate.
[2] Illustrated by Fatigati, 11.
[3] Illustrated in the Boletín de la Sociedad Española de Excursiones, 1895, 111, 52.
[4] Illustrated in my Lombard Architecture, IV, Plate 179, Fig. 1.
[5] Illustrated ibid., Plate 179, Fig. 3.
[6] Bertaux, Ital. Mér., 476.
[7] Illustrated by Gurlitt, 74.

embroidery wear tight-fitting trousers. The "tapestry" which as Mr. Roger Loomis has shown certainly dates from not long after 1066, resembles Modena more closely than Bari or Angoulême; the chronological order appears to be Bayeux, Modena, Bari, Angoulême.[1]

We therefore conclude that the atelier of Modena influenced that of Bari. But there are also other indications that the atelier of Bari influenced that of Modena.

The Bari throne was carved in 1098; the cathedral of Modena was not begun until 1099. There is consequently no doubt that the throne is earlier than the sculptures by Guglielmo at Modena.[2] But these sculptures resemble the throne so closely that it would seem they must have been thence inspired.

Motives characteristic of the art of Guglielmo, and apparently from him passed on to later sculpture, are supporting lions and supporting human figures. Now both of these are found in the throne of Bari (Ill. 152). Nor do the resemblances end here. The curious wire hair of the supporting figure to the left of the Bari throne (Ill. 153) reappears constantly in Guglielmo's work, for example, in the figure to the left, next to the ark, in the relief of Noah and his three sons. One of Guglielmo's most striking peculiarities is the indicating of the folds of the drapery by two parallel incised lines; now this occurs also on the Bari throne (Ill. 154). Another ear-mark of his style is the wave-like pattern formed by the lower edges of his garments. This also is found in the central supporting figure at Bari (Ill. 154). The facial types, with low forehead, bulging cheeks and heavy chin are the same at Bari and at Modena. In both the figures are of the same stodgy proportions, with heads too big for their bodies. In both there is the same vigorous and plastic, but not over-refined, attack. The anatomy and drawing of the nude shows in both the same power and the same ignoring of physical facts. The

---

[1] The armour portrayed on the portable altar of the school of Cologne, now in the Louvre (illustrated by Creutz, 15) seems to be of a type later than that of Bari, and perhaps also later than Angoulême.

[2] See Porter, *Lombard Architecture*, III, 35 f; IV, Plates 142, 143, 144, 145.

supporting figure under the Deity at Modena bends his legs in the
same curves, and carries his load on the back of his bowed neck, precisely as do the supporting figures at Bari (Ill. 154). Such similarities are not due to chance. The Bari throne is by a master distinct
from, I think, Guglielmo, but surely closely related to him.

A strange piece of evidence bearing upon this question has been
discovered by Mr. Roger Loomis. He has observed that the name
Wiligelmus signed on the Modena façade is very like Wilgelmus,
which is one of the forms of the name used upon the Bayeux embroidery. From this he concludes that the sculptor of Modena was
a Norman. Now nothing in the art of Guglielmo would lead us to
suppose that he came from sculpture-less Normandy. If his name
be Norman, it must be that he was a Norman of Apulia, with the
art of which region, we have seen, his style shows close affinities.

There is reason to suspect that the architecture of the cathedral
of Modena, begun in 1099, was influenced by that of Bari, begun in
1087. At Modena we find a sharp turning away from the vaulted
type of church which had been in use up to that date in Lombardy.
The introduction of a wooden roof at Modena, the design of the
false triforium gallery, the columns of the intermediate piers — all
features hitherto unaccounted for — must be ascribed to the influence of S. Niccola.[1]

On the other hand, there is every reason to suppose that the architecture of S. Niccola was influenced by Lombardy. The arched
corbel-tables must have been thence derived. The porches are later
than, and presumably copied from, those of Guglielmo at Modena.[2]
The developed crypt is a Lombard feature.

There are other analogies between the art of Apulia and that of
Lombardy which must be taken into consideration. If we compare
the capital in the crypt of S. Niccola at Bari representing lions
(Ill. 151), the two bodies of which are united by a single head placed
in the angle, with the same motive on the pulpit of S. Ambrogio at

[1] See my article in *Studies in Art*, Vol. 1, No. 1.
[2] I owe to one of my students, Mr. H. R. Hitchcock, Jr., the observation that the motive of
supporting the columns on corbels is derived from the palace at Spalato.

Milan (Ill. 175), we shall at once be struck by the similarity. The motive itself is peculiar and thoroughly Lombard. Furthermore, we notice that the mane is executed according to the same convention, the tail is twisted about the legs in the same way, the eyes and nose are similar. Such close resemblances are not due to chance; the two works belong to the same art.

We note, moreover, a marked analogy between the supporting figures of the Bari throne (Ill. 152) and the supporting figure at the angle of the S. Ambrogio pulpit (Ill. 175).[1] The lions of the Bari throne (Ill. 152) are very analogous to the one above a capital of the S. Ambrogio pulpit (Ill. 174). Both crouch in the same peculiarly flattened position, with the body not quite touching the ground; in both the tail twists around the hind leg; in both the body is very long; and the mane of the S. Ambrogio lion is executed by the same convention as that of the lion on the Bari capital (Ill. 151). Finally we notice that the faces of the Milan pulpit are precisely the same as those of the Bari throne.

In this case the weight of evidence seems to show that Lombardy derived from Apulia; for the lions of S. Ambrogio and Bari are analogous to the lions under the throne of Monte S. Angelo, a monument believed to date from the XI century.[2] Indeed the indications are that the idea of using sculptured animals for supports and also that of using sculptured human beings for the same purpose developed in Apulia earlier than in Lombardy.

It is, however, probably idle to debate whether Lombardy anticipated Apulia, or Apulia Lombardy. What seems certain is that between Lombardy and Apulia, and especially between Modena and Bari we have an interlocking relationship such as we shall presently discover between Toulouse and Santiago. There were influences back and forth in both directions. The art of the two regions, so widely separated geographically, was the same.

[1] In the much later capital of Mozac, in Auvergne (Ill. 1224), the position of the arms is still the same.
[2] Bertaux, *Ital. Mér.*, 449.

Nor is it at all clear whence this Lombard-Apulian art is derived. It seems to appear suddenly, without preparation, in both regions.

Like so much Western art, it was undoubtedly influenced by Byzantium. It is, I suppose, from the East that the motive of supporting figures, so prominent in Lombardy and Apulia, is ultimately derived. This motive is found as early as the IX century in the Utrecht Psalter,[1] to which Graeven[2] believes that it came from a Byzantine original. A supporting figure with crossed legs, quite Lombard-Apulian in character, and labelled TERRA is at the foot of a Crucifixion on a book-cover with portraits of Otto III and his mother Theophano (hence dating from the end of the X century).[3] Schlumberger believes that this book-cover is of Byzantine workmanship; it was certainly strongly influenced by Byzantine models. There is a supporting figure at the base of the Madrid crucifix of 1063 (Ill. 654); here again I can only suppose that the motive is due to Byzantine influence.[4]

The peculiar convention for the treatment of the manes of the lions and horses to which we have already called attention in Lombard-Apulian works I suppose also to have been derived from some lost or unknown Byzantine model. It is found in Spain at a very early period. We notice it, for example, on the capitals of San Pedro de la Nave, a church which has been called Visigothic, but which is more probably a Mozarabic construction of the IX century. The same manes recur on the Pamplona ivory box of 1005, and on the S. Millán Arca (Ill. 638–649).

The lioness of the Bari throne (Ill. 155) and the life-like animals of the St.-Gilles frieze (Ill. 1316) recall the animals depicted in the mosaics of Kief, which date from 1040[5] and the naturalistic tigers on an ivory book-cover of the British Museum,[6] executed for the

---

[1] Folio 57.   [2] 33–34.

[3] Illustrated by Schlumberger, I, 440.

[4] A supporting figure is found in a miniature of the Gospels of Countess Matilda, a dated manuscript of 1098–1099 in the Morgan Library, illustrated by Warner XXII. But this manuscript seems to have copied sculpture — at least the draperies are derived from the Grado throne.

[5] Illustrated by Schlumberger, III, 409.

[6] Egerton MS. 1139, illustrated by Dalton, Pl. XVI.

Angevin court in Jerusalem presumably between 1118 and 1131, and showing strong Byzantine and Plantagenet influences. Nor is it probable that the motive of lions used as supports originated in the Lombard-Apulian school. The sarcophagus of Pelayo at Covadonga is carried on two crouching lions.

The peculiar spiral curls of the Bari master also seem to be derived from Byzantine precedents. Something very like them is found in a Coptic relief of St. Menas from Thekla [1] dating from the V or VI century, as well as in several panels of ivory from the Grado throne [2] also, it appears, a Coptic work of the V or VI century.

The peculiar square shape of the wings of the angels at Monopoli (Ill. 158–162) recurs on capitals of the cloister at Moissac (Ill. 282) and at St.-Sernin of Toulouse (Ill. 300). Are we here again to suppose a common Byzantine prototype? [3]

In any event the busts of angels in the voussures of the portal at St.-Trophime of Arles (Ill. 1372) must be of Apulian origin. They are dissimilar to any voussure sculptures in France, but like those of the Monopoli archivolt (Ill. 158–162),except that they are placed parallel to the voussures, instead of radiating.

[1] Illustrated by Kaufmann, 65.

[2] Published by Maclagen, 187.

[3] The number of parallels between Monopoli and Spain and Aquitaine is certainly striking. The Christ of the Deposition in the architrave of Monopoli (Ill. 157) — by a different hand from the archivolt — is exceedingly like the Christ of the Léon crucifix (Ill. 703) and that of New York (Ill. 710).

VI

CLUNY

THE church of the abbey of Charlieu was consecrated in 1094. Of this building there still exists the western portal (Ill. 4). About 1140 the celebrated outer porch (Ill. 108–110) was added. A comparison of the two works makes it obvious that the inner porch is in style much more primitive than the outer. It is therefore entirely natural to conclude that the inner portal is a dated monument of 1094.

However, as in so many other cases, modern archaeological opinion has set aside the documents, and concluded that the style of the inner portal is so advanced that it must have been executed after the consecration of 1094.

I confess that I can see in the style nothing which is inconsistent with the date of 1094 indicated by the documents. The capitals which still survive in the eastern bays of the ruined nave of Charlieu are precisely like those still in place on the exterior of the absidial chapels of Cluny. Cluny begun in 1088 was consecrated in 1095. The absidial chapels, the first part to be erected, must therefore certainly date from 1088–1095. Charlieu, consecrated in 1094, would be contemporary, and in fact the style of the capitals is identical. The agreement of the external and internal evidence is complete. It would indeed be a strange chance if both documents were unreliable, and both churches reconstructed exactly the same number of years after their consecration.

Moreover, the style of the older tympanum at Charlieu (Ill. 4) is precisely the style of the last decade of the XI century. Compare the Christ in an aureole with the same subject in the Arca Santa at Oviedo (Ill. 657), a dated monument of 1075. Notwithstanding the obvious differences, easily comprehensible in monuments separated by many hundreds of kilometres, it is clear at a glance that the two works present striking analogies. The draperies fall in the same zig-zag edges.[1] Above the feet of the Christs, the draperies in the two works flare out in precisely the same manner. There is the same ropy feeling in the folds. The position of the two Christs with spread-apart knees and raised right hand is identical. The conception of an aureole held by angels is the same, and the wings of the upper angels at Oviedo are spread out to fill the space, just as are those of the Charlieu angels to fill a slightly different space. I can see nothing in the Charlieu relief inconsistent with the style of the last decade of the XI century as shown by the Oviedo Arca Santa. In fact, the Oviedo work would seem if anything rather later. The lower angels in contorted positions recall those which we shall find in Burgundian sculpture of the XII century.

The draperies of the tympanum of Charlieu are very analogous to those of the Salerno altar-frontal of 1084.

When the Christ of Charlieu (Ill. 4) is compared with that of Arles-sur-Tech (Ill. 518), a dated monument of 1046, it is seen that the two are strikingly similar in composition. This is evidently the type of the XI century. If at Charlieu the draperies are somewhat more naturalistically rendered, that is easily accounted for by the half century which separates the two works.

When we compare the Christ of Charlieu (Ill. 4) with that of Regensburg (Ill. 1279), dated 1049–1064, we find an even more patent analogy. Here the draperies are rendered by a convention which is different from that of Charlieu, but which is hardly less realistic. The attitude is again the same, with spread-apart knees, book held in the left hand, and the right hand raised in benediction.

---

[1] This convention, which we have seen, can be traced as far back as Iberian times in Spain (Ill. 637), was also characteristic of archaic and archaistic classical sculpture. It occurs, for example, in the statue of Minerva found in 1902, and now in the museum of Poitiers. Something very like it is found in ivory book-covers of the Ada group in the Brussels Museum (illustrated by Pelka, 91), and in the vision of Ezekiel in the XI century Bible of S. Callisto (illustrated by Clemen, 63). It also occurs in two ivories of the X century in the British Museum illustrated by Dalton, Pl. XXIV, 46. It is found, as we have seen, p. 57, in the Virgin of Sahagún of 1099, and, as we shall see, in the works of Guglielmo at Modena and Cremona, and at St.-Sernin of Toulouse (Ill. 319).

The throne is even decorated with similar little openings, which are also characteristic of the throne of the Christ of the Oviedo Arca Santa (Ill. 657). In view of the fact that the Regensburg *Christ* is known to date from the fifth or sixth decade of the XI century, it seems a bold assertion to say that the style of the Charlieu tympanum is such that it must have been executed in the XII century.

Similarly, when we place the Charlieu Christ (Ill. 4) beside the Christ of the ambulatory of St.-Sernin of Toulouse (Ill. 296), a monument which really does date from the early years of the XII century, we perceive that Charlieu is earlier. The draperies are simpler and more primitive; the modelling is less elaborate; the throne is rendered in less detail, and is less ornamented.

I have therefore no hesitation in setting down the Charlieu tympanum as an authentically dated monument of 1094, and in using it as a foundation-stone for the study of the chronology of Romanesque sculpture.

The question arises whether the lintel of Charlieu is contemporary with the tympanum. The style is certainly different, and it must be admitted that the two are not by the same hand. I do not think, however, that it is necessary to suppose that the lintel was a fragment brought from an earlier church. A marked difference of style in contemporary works is one of the characteristics of Burgundian sculpture, and need in no way disquiet us. The lintel is less skilfully executed than the tympanum, but the style does not appear to be essentially more archaic. It seems probable that the two were sculptured about the same time, and for the position which they still occupy, but by different masters.

The style of the Charlieu tympanum shows analogies with the art of Lombardy and with that of Aquitaine. The two angels holding the mandorla are similar to the Enoch and Elijah of Guglielmo holding the inscriptions of Modena and Cremona.[1] The gestures are the same, the draperies have the same zig-zag. The faces of Charlieu have without exception been mutilated, but in the fragments that

[1] See my article in the Gazette des Beaux Arts, LXI, 1919, 50-51.

survive one seems to feel, or perhaps rather guess, a Guglielmo-esque character. The draperies have Guglielmo's heaviness and simplicity and the same rope-like treatment occurs. The lintel with arches recalls the lintels of Piacenza, Ferrara and Verona.[1] Below the lintel at Charlieu are two very Guglielmo-like supporting figures.

On the other hand, a relationship with Aquitaine is also probable. The lintel with apostles foreshadows that of St.-Sernin (Ill. 308). The type of Christ we have already seen is analogous to that of the St.-Sernin ambulatory, and the zig-zag drapery edges, as has been remarked, recur at Toulouse (Ill. 319).

These similarities perhaps justify the inference that Charlieu, an elder daughter of Cluny, may have exerted considerable artistic influence, through the pilgrimages, along the roads to Rome and Compostela.

The tympanum of Charlieu is the earliest example I know in the West of the motive of two angels holding an aureole with the figure of Christ, sculptured in stone, in the tympanum of a church. The theme became a favourite one in Burgundian sculpture, and spread thence all over Europe. It undoubtedly came to Charlieu from the Orient.

In sculpture, we find the motive in the Coptic tympanum of Daschlut,[2] at Mzchet in the VII century,[3] and at Achthamar in Armenia[4] in the early X century. A Byzantine stone relief of the X–XI centuries, representing the twelve festivals, now in the treasure of the cathedral of Toledo, has a rounded top in which Christ is represented between two angels and two cherubim. The composition approaches that of Charlieu, except that there is no aureole, and Christ holds His hands down, not raised in blessing. Finally the lintels of St.-Genis (Ill. 513) and St.-André (Ill. 514), both as we have

[1] A propos of the relationship of Guglielmo with France, it is interesting to compare the Enoch and Elijah reliefs of Modena and Cremona with the mosaic representing the same prophets at Cruas (illustrated by Révoil, III, Pl. LXXVIII–LXXIX). The Cruas mosaic is dated 1098, and is therefore slightly earlier than the reliefs.

[2] Illustrated by Strzygowski, *Hell. und Kopt. Kunst*, 22.

[3] Illustrated by Strzygowksi, *Armen.*, 433.

[4] *Ibid.*, 602.

seen executed under Byzantine influence, offer evident analogies with the Charlieu composition.

Among ivories we find the motive of Christ in an aureole supported by angels in the Barberini ivory of the Louvre, an Alexandrine work of the IV–VI centuries.[1] With this should be compared the Murano ivory of the same period in the Ravenna museum.[2] The Ascension of the Metz group in the Louvre [3] vaguely foreshadows lintels and tympana like Montceaux-l'Etoile (Ill. 104). The aureole with the Deity supported by two angels is of frequent occurrence in ivories of the Ada group, which are admitted to be strongly influenced by Byzantine models.[4] Angels supporting the aureole of Christ are found in a Metz group ivory of Veste Coburg [5] of the X century, in another of the same period at St.-Paul in Kärnthen [6] in one of the first half of the XI century in the Kunstgewerbe Museum of Cologne,[7] in another of the same period in the museum of Rouen,[8] in the *Evangelier* of the Äbtissen Theophanu, in the Stiftskirche of Essen,[9] in an ivory box of the first half of the XI century at Osnabruck,[10] and in an ivory box of the late XI century at Darmstadt.[11]

A Mesopotamian manuscript of 586 gives reason to believe that the motive may have originated in the scene of the Ascension.[12] Christ in an aureole is a theme which constantly occurs in the Utrecht Psalter; He is often accompanied by angels, who occasionally even hold the aureole.[13] A similar composition is found in the Chatsworth Benedictional of St.-Aethelwold, of the school of Winchester dating from *c.* 980.[14] St. Stephen is seen in an aureole sustained by two angels, and placed under an arch.

Among frescos we find the motive in Coptic work of the VI century,[15] and at S. Angelo in Formis near Capua at the end of the XI

[1] Diehl, 274
[2] *Ibid.*, 283.
[3] Goldschmidt, I, No. 87.
[4] *Ibid.*, I, Tafel VIII–IX.
[5] *Ibid.*, I, No. 87.
[6] *Ibid.*, No. 90.
[7] *Ibid.*, II, No. 47.
[8] *Ibid.*, II, No. 50.
[9] *Ibid.*, II, No. 29.
[10] *Ibid.*, II, No. 102 e.
[11] *Ibid.*, II, No. 103 e.
[12] Diehl, 235.
[13] Folio 53 b.
[14] Illustrated by Wilson and Warner, folio 18.
[15] Diehl, 67.

century. The latter instance is especially illuminating because the fresco is in a lunette over the portal, and hence very closely analogous to, as well as contemporary with, the Charlieu sculptures. The Byzantine influence in the S. Angelo frescos may have been exaggerated, but is admitted.

In view of all this, the fact of Byzantine influence at Charlieu seems certain. It should also be observed in this connection that there are traces of Byzantine influence in later works of the Burgundian school. The movement and fluttering draperies characteristic of its productions are anticipated in the frescos of S. Vincenzo at Volturno [1] which are dated 820–843. The spirit of such works seems to have found its way into ivories as well as sculptures — see, for example, the book-cover called Franconian of about 1100 in the Kaiser Friederich Museum at Berlin.[2]

The Cluniac [3] priory of Mont-St.-Vincent has a sculptured tympanum (Ill. 3) which appears to be more primitive in style than that of Charlieu (Ill. 4). The two evidently have relationship,[4] and those who believe that cruder works are necessarily earlier, will see in Mont-St.-Vincent the prototype, in Charlieu the development. It must be remembered, however, that Mont-St.-Vincent is placed on the summit of a picturesque but inaccessible mountain. In the Middle Ages, mountain art seems generally to have been retarded art. We shall find in the XII century that mountainous Auvergne followed far behind advanced Burgundy, just as the Pyrenees lagged behind the plains of Toulouse and Spain, and the Apennines behind Tuscany and Lombardy. It may therefore very well be that in Mont-St.-Vincent we have sculpture which is merely a crude and

---

[1] Illustrated by Rizzo e Toesca, III, 410. I presume that these most important frescos still exist *in situ*. In April, 1921, I made the long and fatiguing journey to see them, but having reached the crypt, found it locked, and all access denied. It was said that the keys had been carried off to Naples by the proprietor. Apparently no one had visited the crypt since 1912. The frescos have been photographed by the Italian government.

[2] Goldschmidt, II, No. 173.

[3] Marrier, 1706, 1711.

[4] One of the capitals of Mont-Saint-Vincent is exactly like a capital of Charlieu. Beneath the lintel there is also a console with supporting figure.

retarded echo of earlier models, rather than an art which is genuinely archaic.

Châteauneuf, on the other hand, lies in a region where there is no reason to expect *retardataire* forms. The lintel (Ill. 2) is extraordinarily uncouth; if we grant, as I think we must, that it is earlier than Charlieu, fifteen years is the least that we could allow for such an amount of progress. This would bring the Châteauneuf lintel to 1080 or earlier. The analogy with the lintel of Charlieu (Ill. 4) is obvious and striking; this, indeed, seems to be the earliest extant example of this type of lintel, in which a series of figures, usually apostles, are placed in a row, often under arches. The motive which may well be ultimately derived from Early Christian sarcophagi became a standard one in Burgundian art, and spread thence to Languedoc, to Spain, to Lombardy, to Tuscany, to Apulia and to northern France.

We are now face to face with the most thorny, and also the most delightful, problem offered by the history of Burgundian art — the capitals of Cluny. These admirable sculptures have been much praised from an aesthetic standpoint, but they will never be praised sufficiently. They are, indeed, one of the masterpieces of art of all time. The extraordinary delicacy of the technique, the mastery of line, the sureness of touch are unsurpassed, even by the paintings of Simone Martini or of Botticelli. In comparison the portals of Chartres seem to lack finesse (Ill. 5–9).

The capitals of Cluny are a striking example of the quality that Mr. Berenson has named "illustration." Among all the representations that plastic art has consecrated to music, where shall we find another which has so caught the very spirit of song? It is clear that the monks of this abbey loved the arts. In early times the reform of Cluny did not perhaps lack that austerity, almost puritanical, which later made the Cistercians enemies of beauty. A taste for art is commonly the first step on the road to Avernus. Happily, the monks who constructed the abbey of Cluny had already journeyed some distance along this rose-embowered path. There is no doubt of their enthusiasm for art.

This, indeed, I suspect, is expressed in the capitals. Cluniac icon-ography was always highly complicated, and generally offers inten-tionally something of an intellectual puzzle. That it should, was entirely in accordance with the love of subtlety characteristic of the order. The complete meaning of the Cluny capitals has never been unravelled, and may perhaps long await a complete solution. The older archaeologists saw in certain of these enigmatic figures the arts of metal-work, miniature-painting and sculpture. This identifica-tion, indeed, is supported by no very convincing proofs,[1] but none more satisfactory has yet been proposed.

However it may be in regard to the other fine arts, there is no doubt that the sculptor of Cluny has represented Music. Indeed, he dedicated to this subject eight reliefs. A smaller number would not have sufficed to express the multiple and changing character of melody. For mediaeval music, of which the sculptor of Cluny has so profoundly understood and expressed the charm, was essentially melodic. A heritage from the Greeks, it still preserved its sim-plicity and freshness; its wings had not yet been cut by the addition of complex harmonies. Mediaeval music, like the Greek, was founded on modes, each of which possessed a peculiar char-acter. The sculptor of Cluny has represented music in its eight different modes.

Compared with this conception of music, all other representations that I know seem flat and unprofitable. I shall not speak of modern works — that would be an unwarranted cruelty to an age that has already too much lost faith in itself; it is enough to turn to the figures of music on the French cathedrals of the XIII century. The merit of these sculptures is universally conceded; yet how utterly such cold, lifeless and correct virgins striking little bells fail to express, like the capitals of Cluny, the essence of the art! It is only in India that we find representations of the art of music in any way comparable to those of Cluny. The Hindu artists also loved to paint the eight

---

[1] Such a subject hardly recurs in mediaeval art until Giotto's campanile at Florence: yet at Cluny all was unique.

modes. They have left us drawings of great inspiration. But the genius of the sculptor of Cluny is far superior.[1]

The fact that the eight modes of music were placed in the choir of the abbey of Cluny, in parallel with the four rivers of Paradise, the four Virtues, the four Winds, and beside the story of Adam and Eve, is to be explained not only upon symbolic grounds; such were, as M. Mâle has recognized, without doubt present in the sculptor's mind; but more than this, we are justified in seeing in the subject a proof of the high esteem in which the art of music was held by the Cluniac monks. It is known that St. Odon wrote a dialogue on music; and to him other treatises on the same subject have also been, although probably erroneously, attributed.[2] There is, however, even a personal touch to be traced in the music capitals of Cluny. In the life of St. Hugh by Gilon[3] we read that the initiative in the construction of the new abbey church was taken by Gunzo, whose life was for this miraculously prolonged seven years, from 1088 to 1095. Now these seven years, in which Gunzo was the active instigator of the works of construction, were precisely the ones, as we shall see, in which the ambulatory was built. But, this Gunzo, we are told by Gilon, was an accomplished musician — *psalmista precipuus*. We easily gather that it was Gunzo who inspired the glorification of the divine art in the choir of the abbey of Cluny.

The other capitals of Cluny are no less fine than those representing the modes of music. The Four Rivers of Paradise (Ill. 5) are full of the spirit of water. The lines flow with the smoothness of a swirling stream. Compared with these figures, the river-gods of Rome seem coarse, and the symbolic figures in Christian mosaics inexpressive.

---

[1] To appreciate the exceedingly fine quality of the Cluny capitals, we can not do better than to compare the face of the Third Tone (Ill. 7) with the very inferior copy on the column from Coulombs, now at the Louvre (Ill. 1472).

[2] A manuscript, containing a treatise on music which seems to have relationship to the Cluniac monasteries of Burgundy, is preserved in the imperial library at Vienna (it has been illustrated by the Soc. Fr. Rep. Min. Peint., 1913, Pl. XIX). The subject of the miniatures recalls the capitals of Cluny, but the style is rather analogous to Autun.

[3] Mortet, 272.

The delights of the terrestrial paradise are suggested by a foliage of incomparable beauty.

It is under this same leafage, watered by the morning dew, fragrant with the perfume of the fig and olive, that is set the drama of Adam and Eve. It is an incomparable rendering of this theme so ancient, but for the artist always new. The yielding to temptation of the fascinated, yet terrified couple; their wistful spying from the bushes when, in the cool of the evening, God walks in the garden; each act of the tragedy is portrayed with subtle and profound psychology. The nudes are drawn with the tenderness of Masolino, but the understanding of character suggests rather Sassetta.

But the greatest glory of the capitals of Cluny is a quality that has been considered a defect. They are admirably mannered. Mediaeval art can show nothing comparable. In an age of manner, these are the supreme examples.[1]

The troubled question of the date of these masterpieces must now be considered.

St. Hugh began to build a new abbey church at Cluny in 1088.[2] Seven years later, in 1095, advantage was taken of the presence of the pope Urban II in the monastery to celebrate the consecration of the high altar.[3] This ceremony is represented in a miniature of a manuscript of 1188 formerly belonging to St.-Martin-des-Champs. Here the choir at least of the church is shown as completed.[4]

Gilon's life of St. Hugh states that that abbot built the church in twenty years, and that it would have been astounding if an emperor

---

[1] I shall return to this subject elsewhere.

[2] Plancher, I, 302; Mortet, 271.

[3] Praeterea [Urbanus II, 1905] rogatus à domno Hugone ipsius monasterii venerabili Abbate altare majus novae basilicae, astantibus plurimis Episcopis, monachis, clericis quoque, ac plebe innumerabili, in honore resurrectionis Domini nostri Jesu Christi et beatae semper virginis Mariae sanctorumque Apostolorum Petri et Pauli ac protomartyris Stephani devotissimè consecravit VIII. Kal. Novembris, indictione IIII. et praecepit ut in ipso die eadem basilica oportuno tempore dedicaretur. (Baluze, VI, 474). A forced and unjustifiable interpretation of the last phrase has led to the conclusion that in 1095 nothing but the foundations had been built. The consecration of 1095 was also recorded in a lost inscription of the choir, published by Virey in *Millénaire*, II, 247.

[4] This miniature is reproduced by Haseloff, in Michel, II, 1, 307.

had constructed so great an edifice in so short a time.[1] This text can only be interpreted to mean that the church was practically finished when St. Hugh died in 1109. Mabillon, who saw the archives while they were still intact, says that the church was built in twenty years.[2] Dom Plancher states that the church was actually finished in 1112.[3] An inscription in the choir, now destroyed, but a copy of which has been published by Virey[4] states the construction lasted twenty-five years (1088–1113).

St. Hugh in 1109 was buried in the choir of the church which he had constructed.[5]

In 1124 St. Bernard delivered his celebrated harangue against the *luxe* of church-buildings.[6] This sermon seems to have been aimed especially against the newly constructed church of Cluny.

The church was certainly entirely finished before 1125, for in that year the vaults fell. Obviously they could not have fallen had they not been built. Besides, the text which tells us of this catastrophe, explicitly mentions that the church had recently been erected.[7]

Six years later, the damage had been repaired, and the completed church was consecrated[8] by the pope Innocent II. Although the building has been destroyed almost entirely, it is still easy to trace the alterations made 1125–1131. The original vaults had been semicircular. Until the XIX century, these still existed in the choir.[9] They were replaced by the pointed vaults which may yet be seen in

---

[1] Incepit, et Deo juvante, talem basilicam levavit intra viginti annos, qualem si tam brevi construxisset imperator, dignum admiratione putaretur. (Mortet, 273).

[2] Tanta basilica . . . opus est annorum viginti. (Mabillon, V, 235).

[3] I, 512.

[4] *Millénaire*, II, 246. Major ecclesia est opus anno XXV constructore sancto Hugone.

[5] Ex utraque chori parte cernitur ambo unus, in quo lectiones olim recitabantur. . . . Sub altari matutinali St. Hugonis abbatis, immensi que istius aedificii auctoris, tumulus visitur ab haereticis violatus. (Mabillon, reprinted by Virey, in *Millénaire*, II, 234).

[6] Mortet, 366.

[7] (1125). Ipsa die terribile prodigium illic contigit. Ingens basilicae navis, quae nuper edita fuerat, corruit; sed. protegente Deo, neminem laesit. Sic pius Dominus omnes pro temeraria invasione inspirata ruina terruit, sua tamen omnes immensa benignitate salvavit. (Oderici Vitalis, *Ecclesiasticae Historiae*, XII, XXX, ed. A. le Prevost, IV., 426).

[8] Virey, in *Cong. Arch.*, LXXX, 73; lost inscription in the choir, published by Virey in *Millénaire*, II, 246.

[9] See the lithograph of Sagot, reproduced in the *Millénaire de Cluny*, II, Pl. III.

the transept. It is certain that the ambulatory was not rebuilt in 1125–1131, for had it been, pointed arches would surely have been introduced, as in the rest of the edifice; but Sagot's lithograph distinctly shows that all the arches of the chevet, including that of the nave vault, were semicircular.

The church was damaged in the Revolution, but was not destroyed until the XIX century.[1]

The documents therefore are clear and unequivocal: the choir begun in 1088 had been built in 1095 when the high altar was consecrated; and the entire building was finished within a few years after the death of St. Hugh in 1109, that is, in 1112 or 1113.

These dates show that the church of Cluny was built with extraordinary speed. Until the construction of the modern St. Peter's at Rome Cluny was the largest church in Europe. Yet it is by no means impossible that it should have been constructed in twenty-five years, or that the choir should have been built in seven years. If Cluny was the largest church-building in Europe, the abbey also disposed of unparalleled resources. Gilon expressly says that the building of so

---

[1] En 1811, bien que la main des utilitaires eut déjà dispersé et vendu les pierres du temple, bien qu'un grand chemin coupât déjà par la moitié l'immensité de la basilique, cependant trois énormes clochers, couverts en ardoises, et brillant de loin au soleil; le grand portail surmonté de sa rose et encadré entre deux grosses tours carrées; quelques arceaux de la grande nef suspendus dans l'air et interrompant la vue du ciel d'espace en espace: les colonnes du choeur encore debout; l'abside presque intacte avec ses vielles peintures, et quelques chapelles des bas-côtés, témoignaient assez de la splendeur et de la mesure du colossal édifice. . . . Au fond du vestibule se présentait le portail véritable et primitif de la basilique; ce portail, devenu intérieur, avait 20 pieds de hauteur et 16 de largeur. Ses jambages étaient décorés de huit colonnes, quatre de chaque côté, dont les intervalles étaient remplis par des ornemens riches et variés; trois étaient d'un seul bloc. . . . Les battans de la porte avait été recouverts de peintures. (The lintel, he goes on to state, contained twenty-three — recte 24? — figures, doubtless representing elders). Dans le tympan du portail dominait une majestueuse figure assise, tenant un livre de la main gauche, et de la droite donnant sa bénédiction. A ses côtés étaient représentés les figures symboliques des quatre évangélistes, et quatre anges, portés sur des nuages, embrassant et comme supportant le médaillon ovale dans lequel le trône du Christ était enfermé. La première archivolte qui couronnait le bas-relief se composait d'une suite de petits cintres, sous chacun desquels était des anges en adoration, hors dans celui du milieu qu'occupait le Père Eternel. Deux autres archivoltes concentriques à la précédente présentaient, la première, des feuillages, et la seconde, des médaillons d'où sortaient des têtes toutes variées d'expression. . . . Sur la muraille, comprise entre cette galerie supérieure et les cintres du portail, on avait sculpté en bas-relief quatre statues d'apôtres d'environ cinq pieds de grandeur (Lorain, writing in 1839). See the lithograph of the portal by Sagot, reproduced in the Millénaire, II, Pl. II.

great a church in so short a time was a feat which no emperor would have been able to accomplish. In point of fact, however, the speed was not greater than in other contemporary buildings. We are too apt to assume in Romanesque constructions the interminable delays which became characteristic of building in the Gothic period. But the complicated mouldings, the ubiquitous decoration, the general complication which made building slow in the XIII and following centuries, had in the XI not yet been invented. And in fact even great churches were erected at this time with astonishing speed. The basilica of Monte Cassino, one of the most important churches of Europe, was erected in the space of five years, 1066–1071. In this time, not only was the church constructed, but the site was prepared, by planing down the jagged mountain-top. Materials had to be carried 500 metres up a steep mountain side. Columns were brought from Rome for this construction, as they were for Cluny.[1] Three years after the main church had been consecrated, the secondary church at Monte Cassino, S. Bartolommeo, was dedicated.[2]

St. Mark's at Venice, begun in 1063, was eight years later sufficiently advanced so that it could be used for services. The abbey of St. Albans in England, a church of immense size, 275 feet long, was built in eleven years, from 1077–1088.[3] The choir of Vézelay was built in eight years, 1096–1104. The choir of St.-Denis was erected in four years, from 1140–1144.

What generally delayed mediaeval constructions was not the slowness of the workmen, but lack of funds. In the case of an establishment like Cluny that disposed of unlimited resources, work could be pushed through promptly. It became a matter of pride that it should be.

We note, moreover, that the two statements that the choir of Cluny was built in seven years, and the entire church was built in twenty-five are entirely consistent with each other. From the accu-

---

[1] In the early XI century columns had been brought from Rome for St.-Benoît-sur-Loire. (Mortet, 34). Later Suger planned to bring some for St.-Denis.
[2] Bertaux, *Ital. Mér.*, 158.
[3] Perkins.

rate plan published by M. Virey,[1] we learn that the choir was almost exactly one-fourth the length of the entire church. Supposing the same rate of building to have been maintained throughout the edifice, it would consequently have required one-fourth of twenty-five years, or a little more than six to construct the choir. This is not very different from the seven which the documents tell us actually were taken.

The documentary evidence that the choir of Cluny was built between 1088 and 1095 is therefore intrinsically credible.

It has nevertheless been set aside by orthodox archaeology.

The reason for doing so is that the style of the capitals of the ancient ambulatory now preserved in the Musée Ochier (Ill. 5–9), is said to show that they are of the XII century.

The matter has been very little discussed, and no one seems to have felt it worth while to show why the style could not be that of the XI century. In general the capitals have been quickly passed by with the mere statement that they are of the XII century. This vague dating at least possesses the advantage of a certain generosity. It gives a lee-way of a hundred years. Prudent scholars must have felt confidence that there would be latitude for all eventualities. One can not, however, help feeling a certain astonishment that one of the most important monuments of French Romanesque art should have been left in this indeterminate position, and that those who have set aside the documents indicating a date in the XI century have never stated why they have done so, nor placed the capitals of Cluny in relation with the monuments of the XII century with which they are said to be contemporary.

Let us suppose that the orthodox archaeologists are right, and that the capitals of Cluny date from the XII century. Where in that century, a little more precisely, may we place them?

Is it rather to the first or to the second half of the century that these capitals are to be ascribed? Their delicacy might make us at first think of monuments of about 1180. We should perhaps have no

[1] In the *Millénaire*, II, 230.

great difficulty in believing them part of that wave of delicacy in technique that spread over the architecture of France in the last half of the XII century, and culminated in the south transept of Soissons. However, we search northern figure sculpture in vain for work analogous to the capitals of Cluny. The Cluny artist remains different and apart. Whether we compare Cluny with the Toulouse Annunciation (Ill. 480–485) in the South, or with Senlis (Ill. 1505–1513) in the North, or with the tomb of St.-Lazare at Autun in Burgundy (Ill. 147–149), we perceive that the spirit is not that of the second half of the XII century as we know it elsewhere. In fact, after the construction of the western portal of Chartres in the fifth decade of the XII century, figure sculpture abandoned the ideal of delicacy. The draperies tend to become ever more substantial, the folds heavier, the figures more ponderous. It is the Cistercian frost blighting the dainty wild flowers of the Cluniac spring. If the ideal of delicacy touched for a moment the mouldings and capitals, it was a late back-draft, without real analogy to the sculptures of Cluny.

The ascription to the second half of the XII century must therefore be abandoned.

M. Vitry, who is I think the only orthodox archaeologist who has ventured to propose a definite date for the capitals of Cluny, ascribes them to the middle of the XII century.

Since no specific grounds for this attribution are vouchsafed, we can only test its accuracy by comparing the capitals of Cluny with surely dated monuments of the period in question. Happily we need not seek far to find such. The church of St.-André-le-Bas of Vienne preserves two capitals dated 1152 by an inscription. Since Vienne is geographically not very far separated from Cluny, we have here an excellent opportunity for comparison.

Put the Vienne capital representing Job (Ill. 1218) beside the Cluny capital representing the Third Tone (Ill. 7). In each we have the figure of a bearded man in a somewhat similar posture. But what a vast gulf separates the two works! Compare the naif and schematised working of the eye at Cluny with the elaborate and conscious

execution at Vienne; the archaic hair and beard at Cluny with the
deeply undercut and naturalistic hair and beard at Vienne; the un-
modelled face of Cluny with the wrinkles and detailed realism of the
face at Vienne; the simple draperies of Cluny with the elaborate and
deeply undercut folds of Vienne; the schematised ear at Cluny with
the naturalistic ear at Vienne. Or compare the modelling of the nude
as shown in the bare leg of the Vienne Job (Ill. 1218) with that of the
Cluny Rivers of Paradise (Ill. 5). In the one we have an almost exaggerated articulation of the muscles, a realistic rendering of the
cords and even veins, in the other no attempt to reproduce the details
of anatomy. See how much more realistic are the hands and feet at
Vienne than at Cluny. We notice, too, that the capital at Vienne
is full of plastic feeling; it is essentially conceived in the round;
while that of Cluny is essentially flat, a translated drawing. It is
evident that Vienne represents the end, Cluny the beginning, of a
tradition.

The capitals of Cluny are therefore not of the middle of the XII
century, but earlier.

Shall we then ascribe them to the second quarter of the XII century? The naturalistic foliage makes the attribution tempting. It
will be remembered that the Gothic artists of the Ile-de-France began about 1135 to introduce the leaves of plants into their capitals,
and thus inaugurated the Gothic decorative style. It is natural to
suppose that the capitals of Cluny reflect this same movement.
However, as we compare more closely the Cluniac foliage with that
of the Ile-de-France, the analogy which we had believed to find evap-
orates. The Gothic foliage of the XII century is strictly architectural
and highly conventionalized. It is derived from the ornamentation
(perhaps chance) of the uncarved leaves of a Corinthian or Corin-
thianesque capital and from capitals of the XI century like those at
Santiago de Compostela. The Cluny capitals on the other hand
show the close imitation of actual leaves and fruit, represented not
conventionally, but realistically. Even the purely naturalistic carving of the Flamboyant period can hardly show such exact observa-

tion of nature; and plant forms of equal beauty were hardly attained again until Giotto painted the Arena chapel.

To find a real analogy for the naturalistic foliage of the Cluny capitals we have to go back to that XI century with the style of which they have been called incompatible. We find leaf forms and animals very like those of the Cluny capitals on a sculptured column in the museum of Tschinili-Kiosk at Constantinople.[1] This is certainly anterior to 1100, and indeed may well be much older. There is leafage similar to that of the capitals of Cluny on a capital of the crypt of the church of S. Niccola at Bari,[2] dating from 1090. The study of natural forms is one of the striking characteristics of the Benedictine art of Monte Cassino in the second half of the XI century.[3] From Monte Cassino this characteristic came to the frescos of the lower church of S. Clemente at Rome executed between 1073 and 1084. Here the birds and fruit of the dado, and the fish swimming about the submerged chapel are among the most realistic achievements of mediaeval art, in spirit entirely similar to the capitals of Cluny. In view of the many bonds between Cluny and Rome it is hardly surprising that this motive should have been borrowed at Cluny from Italy. From the capitals of Cluny it found its way to a few other French monuments of the early XII century; to the cloisters of Moissac of 1100 (Ill. 279), to Vézelay (1104-1120) — Ill. 32 — and to Saulieu (consecrated in 1119) — Ill. 53.

Among the monuments of the second quarter of the XII century there is therefore none which shows analogy with the capitals of Cluny. But when we come down to the first quarter of the century, we begin to find similarities.

It is in fact not only in the foliage that the capitals of Saulieu are like those of Cluny. The two series are obviously related in many particulars.

[1] Illustrated by Strzygowski, *Byz. Plas. der Blut.*, Taf. I, II.

[2] Illustrated by Wackernagel, Taf. XVI b.

[3] Les peintres du Mont Cassin acquirent une virtuosité qui tenait du prodige. En quelques années de travail discipliné ils apprirent non seulement à copier, mais à regarder; ils mêlèrent aux imitations des figures byzantines de véritables études d'après nature. (Bertaux, *Ital. Mér.*, 273).

However, when we compare with attention the capitals of Cluny
(Ill. 5–9) with those of Saulieu (Ill. 52–61) we can not but be convinced that Cluny is much earlier. The foliage of the Saulieu capital
of the Temptation (Ill. 53), for example, is executed with an insistence upon meticulous detail which makes that of the Cluny Rivers
of Paradise (Ill. 5) seem very primitive. The Saulieu capitals are
much more plastic, and use many more planes. The faces are far
more naturalistically rendered. Compare, for instance, the face of
the angel behind Christ in the Saulieu Temptation (Ill. 53) with that
of the River of Paradise at Cluny (Ill. 5). Or compare the Balaam
at Saulieu (Ill. 56) with the Third Tone at Cluny (Ill. 7). It is clear
that the Saulieu sculptor thinks in the round, in three dimensions;
while the Cluny master thinks only in two; that the Saulieu sculptor
is stronger and more vigorous, while the Cluny Master is more subtle
and delicate; that the Saulieu Master is more naturalistic, the Cluny
sculptor more archaic. The many resemblances abundantly prove
that Saulieu must be directly or indirectly a derivative from Cluny.
In view of all this it seems certain that Cluny is earlier, and notably
earlier than Saulieu. The nave of the latter, which is the only part
that has come down to us, was presumably begun immediately after
the consecration of the choir in 1119; Cluny must then be notably
earlier than 1119.

According to the documents, a consecration was celebrated at
Vézelay in 1104. It is probable that this referred only to the choir
which no longer exists. The nave which has been preserved to us
was apparently attacked immediately afterwards. There is not the
slightest evidence that the fire which in 1120 injured the monastery [1] occasioned damage to the structure of the stone and vaulted
church. In fact, an inscription on one of the key-stones explicitly
states that the church was only damaged by smoke.[2] The Pilgrims'
Guide, written probably in 1129, speaks of the church as if it were
finished.[3] The porch and the narthex were completed without doubt

[1] See de Lasteyrie, 425.
[2] SVM MODO FVMOSA SED ERO POST HEC SPECIOSA. Illustration by Porée, 17.
[3] In quo etiam loco ingens ac pulcherrima basilica monachorumque abbatia constituitur.
(Miracula S. Jacobi, IV, 8, ed. Fita, 29).

when "the church of the pilgrims" (*i.e.*, the narthex) was consecrated in 1132;[1] and the entire basilica was finished before 1138.[2]

Orthodox archaeology has as usual set aside the documents, and declared that the church must be later.

The proof is supposed to be the transept capital representing Adam and Eve (Ill. 28) which is said to be much more primitive in style than any other capital in the church.[3] Since this capital is also broken, it is identified as an authentic remnant of the church of 1104–1120; its presence, it is believed, suffices to show that the existing nave was erected after the fire of 1120.

Even were the capital in question earlier than the others, that would not prove that the existing church might not be of 1104–1120. An earlier fragment might as easily have been incorporated in a building begun in 1104 as in one begun in 1120.

As a matter of fact, however, the capital in question is certainly contemporary with the others in the church. The fact that it is broken means nothing; before the restoration many of the capitals were broken, as any one may see by a glance at the fragments in the narthex. This particular capital is, indeed, by the hand of one of the easily distinguishable sculptors at Vézelay, by whom are also other capitals (see for example, Ill. 29),[4] which no one has ever thought of calling primitive. Neither is the statement that the Adam and Eve capital was not made for its present position, true ; the necking fits the shaft (Ill. 28) perfectly. If the abacus appears too large for the capital (Ill. 28), it is because the broken volutes of the bell have not been restored, whereas the abacus, which was doubtless also broken, has been remade. The volutes once filled the now vacant angles, precisely as in the capital of the Death of Cain (Ill. 35). The Adam and Eve capital is therefore not an earlier fragment, but certainly sculptured for the existing church.

---

[1] Chérest, 197. Note, however, that there was a church of St. James at Vézelay, so that the application of this text to the narthex is not absolutely certain. For a discussion of the dates, see *Cong. Arch.*, LXXIV, 27; de Lasteyrie, 425.

[2] Porée, 15.

[3] Michel, I, 2, 638.

[4] Compare the head of the female figure second from the right (Ill. 29), with the head of Eve (Ill. 28).

Moreover, if we suppose that the new church of Vézelay was destroyed in 1120, we are forced to suppose that the ruins were cleared away and the great nave and narthex built in the twelve years that elapsed between the fire and the consecration of the narthex in 1132. The existing church is entirely homogeneous ; there are no breaks nor reconstructions visible in the masonry. From the work of 1104–1120, according to the orthodox theory, only one broken capital was saved. Now although Romanesque churches were undoubtedly often built more rapidly than is usually believed, it is hardly credible that the nave and narthex of Vézelay could have been erected in only twelve years.

The sculptured key-stone [1] is a dated monument of 1120, for the reference to the fire in the inscription makes it certain that the carving was executed immediately after that event. Now the style of this sculpture is evidently more advanced than the style of the capitals of the nave. The garments have ornamented borders, and folds indicated by parallel incised lines, features lacking in the earlier capitals of the nave, but present in the later capitals of the narthex. The nave capitals are therefore earlier than this dated sculpture of 1120 ; the narthex capitals contemporary with it.

There are, indeed, many proofs that the nave of Vézelay dates from exactly the time which the documents would lead us to suppose. If we compare its sculptures (Ill. 28–51) with those of Moreaux (Ill. 1067, 1068) dated about 1140 or with those of St.-Denis, dated 1137–1140 (Ill. 1437–1457,) we shall be convinced that they are earlier, and notably earlier. We must therefore place them in the first quarter of the XII century. That they are earlier, not later than 1120, may be proved by comparing them with the capitals of Saulieu, begun, as we have seen, in 1119. Those of Vézelay, and especially of the more eastern bays at Vézelay (Ill. 28, 31, 33, 42), are distinctly more primitive than those of Saulieu (Ill. 52–61). The chronological order is clearly : Cluny, Vézelay, Saulieu.

When we compare the capitals of Vézelay with those of Autun

[1] Illustrated by Porée, 17.

(Ill. 67–79), we see again that those of Vézelay are simpler, less developed, more archaic. Now Autun was begun about 1120.[1] Again we can without difficulty establish the chronological sequence: Cluny, Vézelay, Autun.

If we compare the capitals of Vézelay with those from Moûtier-St.-Jean (Ill. 62–66) now in the Fogg Museum,[2] remnants of the church built by the abbot Bernard II (1109–1133),[3] we perceive again that the nave of Vézelay is earlier, and that the chronological sequence runs: Cluny, Vézelay, Moûtier-St.-Jean.

If we compare the capital of Vézelay (Ill. 43) representing the Sacrifice of Bread in the Old Law, with Guglielmo's relief of Enoch and Elijah at Modena, dated 1099–1106,[4] and note the similarity of the figures and especially of the faces, we shall not doubt that the existing nave of Vézelay is the one begun in 1104.

If we compare the capital of Vézelay (Ill. 33) representing Daniel with the capital of the crypt of St.-Parize-le-Châtel (Ill. 25) representing the sciapodes, we can not doubt that the two are closely related and contemporary. Now the capital of St.-Parize-le-Châtel is dated 1113.

A point of support for dating the capitals of Vézelay is afforded by the sculptured key-stone representing the Church, a monument surely dated 1120 by the inscription. Characteristic of this sculpture are the ornamented border and the parallel drapery lines. These features are found only in the later capitals of Vézelay in the western part of the nave and in the narthex. The capitals of the eastern part of the nave are unmistakably earlier in style, therefore anterior to 1120.

A comparison of the capitals of Vézelay (Ill. 28–46) with those of Cluny (Ill. 5–9) shows that Cluny is the earlier of the two, and that the capitals of Vézelay are in fact thence in part copied.

Take for example the famous Adam and Eve capital at Vézelay

---

[1] De Fontenay et de Charmasse, 408.
[2] I have published these capitals in the Fogg Museum *Notes*, 1922, I, 2, 23.
[3] Plancher, I, 516.
[4] Illustrated in the *Gazette des Beaux Arts*, LXI, 1919, 50.

(Ill. 28) and place it beside the capital of Cluny representing the same
subject.[1] It is evident at a glance that the Cluny rendering is much
finer and more subtle. That of Vézelay is in comparison coarse and
commonplace. But it is no less evident that the Cluny capital is
earlier. The figures at Vézelay are more articulated, more plastic.
The anatomy is far more realistically rendered. The muscles of the
calves and thighs of Adam at Vézelay are carefully and thoroughly,
if incorrectly, expressed; at Cluny they are simply ignored. Eve's
breasts at Vézelay are portrayed with realism, but are passed by in
silence at Cluny. The faces, the eyes and the hair are all far more
naturalistic at Vézelay.

Or compare the Cluny capital representing the Rivers of Paradise
(Ill. 5) with the one of the same subject at Vézelay.[2] The relationship of the two is evident. There are the same volutes ending in each
case in a flourish of foliage. In both capitals one of the rivers is represented in each corner as a naked beardless figure crowned, holding
a stream in his hands. The convention for representing the flowing
water by means of parallel incised lines is the same. Obviously one
of these capitals must be a copy of the other. As to the relative quality we can not for a moment be in doubt. The delicacy, refinement
and charm which make of the Cluny fragment one of the masterpieces of mediaeval art have disappeared at Vézelay. It is clear that
Cluny is the inspired original, Vézelay, the commonplace copy. It
is equally clear that Vézelay shows a style later in date. The work
there is bolder, coarser, more plastic, more deeply undercut. The
faces are more naturalistic, more modelled and show greater feeling
for the third dimension. The crown which is simple at Cluny, is
given at Vézelay a gratuitous ornament.

The foliage of the Cluny Rivers of Paradise capital (Ill. 5) should
be compared with that of the hunting capital at Vézelay (Ill. 32).
The sculptor of Vézelay seems here to have taken over directly the
Cluny vine; but his design is coarser, less decorative. And note

---

[1] Illustrated by Terret, Pl. XLV.
[2] Illustrated by Pouzet, 105.

again that the Vézelay figures are more modelled, more naturalistic, but less beautiful.[1]

Let us continue the comparison to the two capitals representing the Four Winds (Ill. 31).[2] The similarity is again striking. There are the same volutes, the same foliage, the same four figures crouching over the same bellowses, and these bellowses are indicated by the same convention of wattling. Since the Winds are thus represented, to the extent of my knowledge, nowhere else in mediaeval art, there can be no question of the direct connection between Cluny and Vézelay. Again, however, we notice that Cluny is both simpler and of higher quality. How much broader and more beautiful is the treatment of the draperies, how much more delicate the feet! The grace and daintiness of Cluny are coarsened at Vézelay; the greater elaboration of the draperies, the stronger plastic feeling are powerless to compensate for the verve that is lost. In this case, moreover, we have absolute proof that Cluny is the original. The iconographic program is, as we have remarked, unusual. There is no especial reason why it should have been introduced at Vézelay among capitals representing unrelated subjects. At Cluny, on the other hand, it was logically included in the parallel between the eight Tones, the four virtues, the four seasons, the four Rivers of Paradise.

Now let us put the Vézelay Luxury (Ill. 34 a) beside the Cluny Rivers of Paradise (Ill. 5). The general similarity of the figures is again striking. The position is very similar; the right arms are held in the same attitude, the legs are very like. The serpent of the Vézelay figure has lines which resemble those of the river at Cluny. Again, however, we notice the same differences. Vézelay is larger in scale and coarser; the fine crispness of Cluny has disappeared; the foliage so dainty and fresh at Cluny has at Vézelay become rank; the hair so broad and simple at Cluny at Vézelay is more elaborate, but hardly as effective.

---

[1] This capital was imitated at Notre-Dame-du-Port of Clermont-Ferrand (Ill. 1174). *Facilis decensus Averno!*

[2] The Cluny capital is illustrated by Terret, Plate LVI.

Or take the Vézelay capital representing Daniel (Ill. 33). This is a strange iconographic conception — the placing of Daniel in an aureole would be singular, but the putting of the lions also in one is astounding. There can be no question that the sculptor was here solely occupied with reproducing the decorative effect produced by the aureoles of the Cluny capital of the Tones (Ill. 7). How clumsy and uninspired this Vézelay capital is, however, compared with the glorious original! How heavy and badly proportioned the body, how commonplace the face, how inexpressive the draperies! The figure of Daniel, indeed, is imitated not from the Cluny capital of the Tones, but from that of the Sacrifice of Isaac (Ill. 10). The hair and face of Daniel recall, in fact, the angel to the right of the Cluny capital. In other words, two distinct models by different hands are copied and combined in a single capital of Vézelay. One could hardly ask for more eloquent proof that Vézelay is a derivative of Cluny.

It is interesting to follow the further fortunes of this motive. It reappears at St.-Benoît-sur-Loire (Ill. 1415) and Rieux Minervois (Ill. 1404). Something very like it was found in a capital of Savigny, which I know only from the drawing published by Dalmace.[1] Judging on this insecure basis I should suppose that the capital in question was derived from Cluny rather than from Vézelay, for another capital of the same series seems to show unmistakably the direct influence of Cluny. Since the church of Savigny was in construction in the last years of the XI century, this analogy is another indication of the early date of Cluny.

It was undoubtedly the capital of Vézelay, however, that is copied in a capital of St.-Nectaire representing the martyrdom of St. Sebastian.[2] The aureole, the position of the figure, the draperies, the hair are all taken from the Vézelay capital of Daniel; but since the subject required an archer, the St.-Nectaire sculptor hunted about the Burgundian abbey until he came upon the figure of an archer in the capital representing the Death of Cain (Ill. 35). This he then

[1] 407.　　　　　　　[2] Published by Bréhier.

reproduced nearly without changes. We have here, therefore, clear proof of the genealogy Cluny, Vézelay, St.-Nectaire.

One of the striking facts which become evident from the comparison of the capitals of Cluny and Vézelay is that the easternmost, and therefore presumably earlier capitals at Vézelay, are the ones which are most nearly like Cluny. Among the numerous hands which may be distinguished at Vézelay it is that which I have ventured in the atlas to distinguish by the name of "Cluny master" who shows the closest affinities, and, indeed, in general contents himself with reproducing the models of Cluny (Ill. 30, 31, 32, 33). Now the work of this master is found only in the nave, and often rather far east in the nave. On the other hand, the "Bathsheba master" (Ill. 44), who worked on the western bays of the nave and on the narthex still copies Cluny, but in a different way. Compare, for example, his work at Vezelay with the Grammar of Cluny (Ill. 6). He seeks to reproduce the spirit rather than the letter of his great original. Certain details of the folds of the draperies, or of the shoes we find, indeed, taken over; but what impresses us is how this, the greatest of the Vézelay sculptors, has caught the line, the grace, the delicacy of his master. It is a calamity that the deplorable restoration of Viollet-le-Duc has left us only copies and scrapings of the work of this artist. In what remains, however, it is abundantly evident that his style in its more developed articulation, in the freedom of the drawing, in the realism of the faces, in the greater elaboration of the draperies belongs to a later age than that of Cluny.

From all this it seems certain that Cluny is anterior to Vézelay, and consequently to 1104.

Let us now examine whether the style of Cluny is really inconsistent with a date in the XI century.

Certainly among the striking characteristics of the Cluny capitals are their feeling for line, and their daintiness of execution. We have found that in these qualities the capitals are hardly equalled in the XII century, even in works directly inspired by Cluny. But it is easy to find parallels of the last quarter of the XI century. Put the capi-

tals of Cluny (Ill. 5–9) beside the sculptures of Santo Domingo de
Silos (Ill. 666–673). The spiritual relationship of the two works is
at once evident; there is the same sense of line, the same refinement,
the same delicacy, the same crispness. The folds of the draperies
although different, fall in similar broad curves; the zig-zag edges are
alike. The faces in both are archaic and unindividualized. The
letters of the inscriptions are generally similar. The raised hand of
God in the Adam and Eve capital of Cluny is the same dainty, un-
articulated XI century hand which we have learned to know at Silos.
Moreover, we notice that the subtle rhythm so characteristic of Silos
is also a conspicuous merit of Cluny. The hair convention of the
Third Tone at Cluny (Ill. 7) is the same as the hair convention used
at Silos, as is also the beard convention of the same figure. We notice
that the curious boots of the Cluny capitals (Ill. 6) reappear in the
Silos Deposition (Ill. 669) and in the Madrid Virgin of Sahagún
—1089–1099— (Ill. 770).

Delicacy like that of Cluny is also to be found in the miniatures of
the Greek Physiologus of Smyrna, edited by Strzygowski, a manuscript dating from about 1100.

Such delicacy is, moreover, characteristic of the Benedictine art
of Monte Cassino of the second half of the XI century, and it is,
indeed, probably from here that it came to Cluny. We find it, for
example, in the frescos of the lower church of S. Clemente at Rome
(1073–1084), with which Cluny presents so many other analogies as
well; and also in the Last Judgment of S. Angelo in Formis, painted
in the last quarter of the XI century.

The peculiar convention for representing the undersleeve in the
Cluny capital of Summer with a series of rings like bracelets, is char-
acteristic of the XI century. It is found, for example, in the Arca of
San Millán (Ill. 638) and in the Oviedo Arca Santa of 1075 (Ill. 657).

The elongation of the figures characteristic of the capitals of Cluny
(Ill. 5, 6) also accords with a date in the XI century. M. Diehl has
supposed that the mannerism originated in the mosaics of the dome
of Sta. Sophia of Salonica, of the first half of the XI century, and

that it was here instituted to off-set the effects of fore-shortening. I should question the explanation, for there is an example of marked attenuation in the miniature representing Christ in the house of Mary and Martha in the Perikopenbuch Kaiser Heinrichs II, which was executed before 1014.[1] It is probable, however, that the motive originated in the Orient, for it is found in a statue of Kwannon, believed to be Korean, in the Museum at Nara, and dating from the VII century.

In the second half of the XI century, and especially in the last quarter of that century, the motive was taken up by the school of Monte Cassino. It occurs in the miniatures of an unpublished manuscript which I have seen in the library of the abbey.[2] It also is found in the Last Judgment of S. Angelo in Formis, painted in the last quarter of the XI century, although it is absent in the earlier frescos of the same church. It is similarly very prominent in the frescos of the lower church of S. Clemente at Rome, executed before 1084.[3] It is found in a miniature of the Bible of S. Paolo at Rome, now in the Vatican.[4] By the beginning of the XII century the idea had spread throughout Europe; we find it in English miniatures of Bury St. Edmund's,[5] in Austrian miniatures of Salzburg[6] and in the Greek Physiologus of Smyrna.[7]

The wattling convention used to represent the folds of the socks on the capitals of Cluny (Ill. 7) is one of the peculiarities of the style, which was hence widely copied in XII-century sculpture. The motive may have been originally suggested by the thonging of the feet and ankles common in miniatures.[8] I know of no earlier instance of

---

[1] Illustrated by Leidinger, V, 34.

[2] *Homilae*, No. 98, H.

[3] Cf. Bertaux, *Ital. Mér.*, 276; Dans les oeuvres de technique aisée, comme la miniature et la peinture murale, les proportions des figures commencèrent à prendre, sous le gouvernement de l'abbé Oderisius (*i.e.*, in the late XI century) un allongement qui s'exagéra bientôt de façon ridicule (*sic*).

[4] Moscioni photograph, 8014.

[5] Illustrated in the *Burlington Catalogue*, Pl. 23, 28.

[6] Perikopenbuch von St.-Erentrud, Munich, Kgl. Hof- und Statsbibliothek, No. Clm. 15903.

[7] Ed. Strzygowski.

[8] See for example the Bible of Charles le Chauve in the Bibliothèque Nationale at Paris; a

the use of this mannerism in the West; it is, however, found in the colossal bronze statue of Barletta, believed to represent the emperor Heraclius and to have been executed in the VII century. The use of the motive at Cluny was consequently not entirely without precedent.

It may be objected that the arches which appear in the main arcades of the surviving transept of Cluny are pointed, and therefore inconsistent with the early date indicated by the documents. In point of fact, the arches of the ambulatory, which is the portion of the church with which we are here concerned, are shown as round in Sagot's lithograph;[1] but were they pointed, I should not be disquieted. Pointed arches were in fact known in the XI century. Indeed, they are used as early as the IX century in the Orient, as in the mosque of Ibn Tulun at Old Cairo,[2] and are frequent in the architecture of Armenia of the X century.[3] Apparently about the middle of the XI century the motive found its way into France at St.-Front of Périgueux. A few years later, between 1063 and 1095 we find it in the narthex of St. Mark's at Venice. Contemporaneously it appears in the cathedral of Pisa (begun in 1063).[4] Still another example is extant in the porch of S. Angelo in Formis, dating from the seventh decade of the XI century. That the pointed arch should therefore have found its way to Cluny by 1088 is neither impossible nor even surprising.

It should be observed that the legs of the Adam on the capital of Cluny are modelled very similarly to those of the Christ of the Madrid crucifix, a dated work of 1063 (Ill. 654).

The capitals of Cluny and Vézelay are, beyond any possible doubt, inspired chiefly by manuscripts, or a manuscript of the school of Winchester. This delightful type of English illumination came out of the Psalter of Utrecht, which is now thought to have been produced at or near Reims in the first third of the IX

Monte Cassino MS. of the late XI century illustrated by Bertaux, *Ital. Mér.*, 203; the Bari *Exultet*, etc.

[1] *Millénaire*, II, Pl. III.　　　　　　　[2] Rivoira, *Arch. Mus.*, 144.
[3] *Ibid.*, 232.　　　　　　　　　　　　　[4] Rizzo e Toesca, 550.

century.[1] The school of Winchester did not attain its zenith, however, until the second half of the X century. It came to an end with the Norman conquest in 1066.

Now the capitals of Cluny and Vézelay show all the characteristics of drawing of the miniatures of this school. The facial types are the same, and this is the more striking that they are highly distinctive. Compare, for example, the beardless faces of Vézelay (Ill. 28–46) with the miniature of 1016–1020 illustrated by Herbert,[2] or those of Cluny (Ill. 5–10) with the gospels of Besançon[3] or the Rouen missal.[4] The close relationship is obvious. The bearded as well as the beardless faces of the capitals approach very closely the Benedictional of St. Aethelwold, a dated manuscript of c. 980.[5] Compare especially such faces as that of the St. Anthony of the Vézelay narthex (Ill. 42). The St. Paul on folio 8 of the manuscript is like the St. Paul of the "mill" capital of Vézelay (Ill. 40) even to the peculiar shape of his head.

The draperies fluttering behind, so characteristic of the Burgundian school, are found in the Benedictional of St. Aethelwold, which dates from 980, in a miniature representing Christ in glory.[6] The spiral folds of the drapery, typical of Burgundian sculpture, are taken over from the same source, and perhaps originated in Carlovingian manuscripts. This convention in a miniature has a certain meaning, for it seeks to indicate the spherical form of certain portions of the anatomy; in sculpture it becomes purely decorative, for the form is already indicated by the relief. Nothing could prove more clearly the dependence of the sculptures upon the miniatures than the taking over of this singular convention. The clinging draperies introduced into Burgundian sculpture are similarly derived

[1] Erst die von Fleury vermittelte und von Männern wie Dunstan, Aethelwold und Oswald in den sechziger Jahren in Süd-England eingeführte Cluniacensische Reformbewegung hat, wie es scheint, den gewaltigen künstlerischen Aufschwung herbeigeführt, dem wir eine solche Fülle von Meisterwerken verdanken. (Homburger, 7).

[2] Pl. XIII.

[3] Homburger, Taf. VI.

[4] Ibid., Taf. X.

[5] Illustrated by Warner and Wilson.

[6] Homburger, I.

from the same source, in which they are constantly used. The slender long feet and hands, characteristic of the sculptures of Autun (Ill. 67–81) are found in the Benedictional of St. Aethelwold. In the Benedictional of Rouen [1] is represented, as in the tympanum of Vézelay (Ill. 47–49), Pentecost. The apostles are seated about a curved table as at Charlieu (Ill. 110). The edicular canopies so typical of Burgundian sculpture appear in this miniature as in one of the Benedictional of Paris. The calligraphic quality of Burgundian drawing is evidently derived from the delicate outlines in pen of the miniaturist. There are the same lyric curves, the same caressing outlines. The motive of crossed legs appears in the Besançon gospels. The Bodleian gospels [2] have flirted garments and attenuation. Flying angels, agitated draperies, aureoles, movement, contorted postures, revealing draperies, fluttering scarfs quite of the Burgundian manner, are found in the charter of King Edgar to New Minster, Winchester, a manuscript dated 966.[3] The strange lower borders of the garments in the Benedictional of St. Aethelwold reappear in the capitals of Cluny; there are the same loops, and the lower folds are over-turned similarly. The peculiar oval folds about the knees of certain figures of Cluny, like the Grammar (Ill. 6) are precisely like those of the XI-century miniature of St. John in the manuscript of Lord Leicester.[4] The flat folds of Burgundian draperies are anticipated in a south Anglo-Saxon manuscript of the XI century, the Bede of St. Petersburg [5] and in the gospel of St. Gallen.[6]

There was, therefore, nothing new in the artistic formula used by the sculptor of Cluny. He merely translated into stone the types of singular beauty perfected long before by the miniature artists of Winchester. When we look at the capitals of Cluny from this point of view, we are not at all surprised that they should have been executed in the XI century. We have seen abundant evidence that the

[1] Homburger, VI.   [2] *Ibid.*, XI.
[3] Brit. Mus. Cotton MS. Vespasian A. VIII, f. 2 b, illustrated in *British Museum Reproductions from Illuminated Manuscripts*, Series I, Pl. IV.
[4] Dorez, *Catalogue*, Pl. III.
[5] Lat. Q. v. I, n. 18, fol. 26 b, illustrated by Zimmermann, 332.
[6] No. 51, p. 267, illustrated by Zimmermann, 188.

artists of the XI century were fully masters of their chisels. There is no reason why they could not express in stone what they had long been accustomed to express with their pen. We perceive, too, why it is that Romanesque sculpture was never, in any true sense of the word, archaic.[1] It was not forced to pass through that struggle with material form which fell to the lot of other periods.

The style of the capitals of Cluny is, therefore, in entire agreement with the documentary evidence that they were executed between 1088 and 1095.

Before leaving the subject of the capitals of Cluny, the air should be cleared of a myth which has been widely circulated in regard to them. Orthodox archaeologists unwilling to admit that they date from the XI century, yet having too much conscience to disregard entirely the documentary evidence that the church was constructed from 1088–1113, have often suggested the hypothesis, nay, asserted as an obvious fact, that the capitals were carved long after having been placed in the building. This theory has been applied to other monuments as well; and as it has been made a basis for the late dating of much Romanesque sculpture, it will be well to remind the reader that mediaeval sculptures were carved before they were placed.

The question has already been investigated by Prof. Vöge in one of the most fundamental passages of his fundamental work.[2] His researches have made it perfectly clear that in the Romanesque period sculpture was executed before the blocks were set up in the building.

The evidence accumulated by Prof. Vöge on the subject is quite conclusive. Since, however, certain scholars have continued to date monuments on the opposite theory, it may be well to add further proofs.

There are extant a number of representations of mediaeval masters at work. At Maastricht[3] and in the cloisters of the cathedral of Gerona[4] we see masons sculpturing blocks before they are placed in the building. Whether in these cases we have to do with the carv-

[1] I owe this observation to Mr. Berenson.
[2] *Anfänge*, 267 f.
[3] Ligtenberg, Taf. XXIII.
[4] Michel, II 1, 256.

ing of capitals or reliefs, or only with the squaring of dressed blocks is not altogether clear. There is no doubt, however, that in two representations at S. Zeno of Verona, and in others at S. Maria Maggiore of Bergamo, at Modena,[1] in the museum of Toulouse [2] and at San Cugat del Vallès [3] we have represented the making of capitals. All these show that the capitals were sculptured in the atelier, and when held reversed between the knees of the sculptor, or, as at San Cugat and Toulouse, placed horizontally before him. The reliefs at Bergamo are late — 1405 — but they are of particular interest because they show a sculptor touching up a finished capital after it had been placed. This, as Prof. Vöge has recognized, was doubtless also the custom at an earlier period. A Byzantine miniature [4] representing the construction of a building, shows that capitals were carved before being placed, but touched up afterwards. A fresco of Benozzo Gozzoli in the Pisa Campo Santo shows that the practice of executing sculpture before placing the blocks in the building continued until the XV century; the builders at work upon the tower of Babel are hoisting into position the already carved architectural decorations. The evidence is conclusive; mediaeval sculptures were executed in the atelier, and merely touched up after being placed in position.

Indeed, the excellent craftsmanship displayed by mediaeval capitals could hardly have been attained if the sculptor had been obliged to work upon the stone in the disadvantageous position in which it was fixed after being placed in the building. We have only to examine the care and skill with which Romanesque sculpture is executed, to be convinced that the artists must have taken advantage of every means of securing technical excellence. In this connection the experience of the builders at Bryn Athyn is instructive. At first the capitals were carved after being placed in the modern manner; but it was soon found that the technical perfection of mediaeval work could be imitated only if the sculptor were enabled to work the capital at his

[1] For all these, see my *Lombard Architecture*, I, 14.
[2] Illustrated by Revoil, III, 26.
[3] Puig y Cadafalch, II, 61.
[4] Illustrated by Diehl, 369.

ease, turning it as he pleased. The system was therefore changed, and now capitals are carved before they are placed.

An examination of almost any capital of the XII century will show that the sculptor was able, during the execution, to place the capital so as to give a blow with his chisel from any angle or direction desired. It is clear that much of the work was done with the capital upside down, and held below the level of the eye of the artist. Capitals were in general intended to be looked up at; but obviously it would be exceedingly difficult for the artist to work them above his head. By holding them upside down below his eye, he was able to see them in the same relative position in which they would be seen when finished, and still work at them with ease.

The evidence of the buildings themselves re-enforces that which we have drawn from representations of masters at work. In the monastic buildings of Marcilhac are twin capitals (Ill. 1145) set side by side. The faces of these capitals which nearly touch are carved with the same finesse as the other faces. Now these interior faces not only can hardly be seen, but it would have been physically impossible to insert a chisel to sculpture them in the narrow space between the two capitals. They were then sculptured before they were set in position. Similar instances abound in mediaeval work.

In the portal of Romans (Ill. 1335) are inserted in either jamb a pair of sculptured figures. These piers, one suspects, were originally carved for a cloister, and later diverted to their present position; but however that may be, one of the figures on each side faces diagonally in against the wall. Now these figures are completely finished, even in the surfaces which nearly or actually touch the face of the wall. It is consequently certain that they were sculptured before they were set up.

In the northern upper lunette at Corme Royal (Ill. 1013) is a sculptured voussure. It is evident that owing to a miscalculation there was not space enough to fit in the two upper figures. Accordingly a slice has been sawed off the head of each to accommodate the sculpture to the space available. Clearly then these reliefs must have been made before being placed.

At S. Ambrogio of Milan, in the portal, is a capital with inscription inserted upside down. It is clear that by error two capitals were made for the right-hand side of the door. In order to make one fit the left-hand side, it had to be put in up-side down. The existence of such a mistake shows that capitals were carved before being placed in position, since otherwise it could not have occurred.

Often capitals forming an iconographic sequence are inserted out of order, as for example, in the cloister of the cathedral of Gerona.[1]

Had it been the custom to carve capitals after they were placed, we should certainly find, in view of the slow and frequently much delayed progress habitual in mediaeval building, numerous edifices with capitals of a much later period than the architecture, or in which the capitals had remained unfinished to our own days. Now there is nothing of the sort. I know of no instance of a mediaeval church with capitals carved at a much later period than the date of the structure itself. I have never seen a church of the XII century with capitals of the XIII or XIV century. We have a great number of churches begun in the XII century, left unfinished, and completed only in the Gothic period or perhaps not at all. In every one of these, the capitals of the Romanesque portions are Romanesque; we look in vain for an example of a capital in the Romanesque portion of the building finished in the Gothic style. What we do find rarely, are capitals left either partially or entirely unfinished. One of these for example exists at Aulnay,[2] another in the gallery of Notre-Dame of Paris. I have observed several examples in Auvergne, at St.-Menoux, St.-Genou, etc. A superficial criticism has concluded that the existence of such unfinished capitals proves that carving was executed after capitals were placed. But what justifies such a conclusion? Aside from the fact that many of these so-called unfinished capitals are really not unfinished at all, but have merely lost their original painted decoration, it is as easy to suppose that a capital which was left unfinished was intended to be carved in the chantier as in position. When the masons had to place a capital in the church,

---

[1] Puig y Cadafalch, III, 241–242.   [2] *Cong. Arch.*, 1913, I, p. 100.

before they could proceed to the construction of the arch above, it must inevitably have happened at times that a slow workman had not completed the carving of the capital. Suppose that it would take him two weeks more to finish it. Either the entire construction would have to be delayed two weeks, and the masons kept idle, or the capital would have to be inserted partially finished. The latter expedient was occasionally adopted. The very fact that these capitals remained unfinished may be interpreted as an indication that capitals were carved before being placed; otherwise they could easily have been completed afterwards.

It was probably precisely with a view to avoid blocking the construction by obliging the masons to wait for the completion of carved members, that such were generally executed at the very beginning of the construction. An instructive example has recently come to light in the church of the Annunciation at Nazareth.[1] A XII-century church was here in building, when the construction was brusquely and forever interrupted, presumably by the advance of the Saracens. Excavations have brought to light the mediaeval chantier, which was in the hands of European, and doubtless French, builders. We see a Romanesque church in the actual building. The foundations have barely been laid; only the base moulding of the portal is in position. Yet the elaborately and beautifully sculptured capitals of this portal are almost completed; most of them are entirely finished, on one alone there lack a few touches. It is certain that here the capitals were executed not only before being placed, but even before the building had been begun. It was only in this way that danger of blocking the masons by obliging them to wait for the work of the sculptors could be avoided.

In the abbey of S. Trinità at Venosa, in Apulia, we have another admirable opportunity to study the building methods of the XII century. This great building (Ill. 167–171) has remained half constructed. We see that it was built not in vertical sections, but in irregular horizontal sections. The piers of the nave have some of

[1] Egidi.

them been built and crowned with entirely finished capitals; but the archivolts were never placed upon them. As far as the construction has gone, not a bit of the decoration is unfinished. It is clear that here again the sculpture was executed before it was placed. In fact, capitals and lions, carved for this building, but never used, still exist in the neighbourhood in considerable abundance (Ill. 170, 171). The side portal (Ill. 169) is completely finished in the most minute detail, although not a stone of the clerestory has been laid.

Indeed, not only capitals, but all architectural sculptures, tympana, friezes, voussures or incidental reliefs were executed before being placed. In voussures, a single subject was commonly sculptured on each stone, for convenience in setting up, but often also a single subject runs over more than one block. In such cases the reliefs were carved just the same way in the atelier, were then taken apart, and put together again when they were set up in the building. Reliefs of considerable size almost always occupy more than one block. A careful inspection of any Romanesque tympanum will bring to light evidence that the stones were sculptured in the chantier, and assembled in the construction already carved. There is a particularly clear example at Donzy (Ill. 114). Here the block to the right of the three of which the tympanum is composed has been badly placed, so that the level of the background projects beyond that of the other two blocks. This fault is concealed by bevelling the edge of the projecting block. Such an error could only have occurred in sculptures carved before being placed.

It is sure that random bits of sculpture inserted in the façades of churches like S. Michele of Pavia or of the church at Champagne (Ardèche) must have been executed before being placed. Along the pilgrimage route and in Spain, it seems to have been the custom to accumulate great quantities of sculpture before the construction was begun. Either there was no very definite plan as to how this was to be used, or else the scheme was changed before the building was erected. At any event, the sculptures were commonly inserted quite at hap-hazard, and not in the positions they were intended to occupy.

Obviously, these reliefs were carved long before being placed. San-güesa (Ill. 749–754) and the Puerta de las Platerias at Santiago (Ill. 676) offer good examples of this manner of building in Spain, Civray (Ill. 1122–1131) and Loches (Ill. 1111–1119) in France. At Reims, statues executed for the west portal could not be placed as originally intended, because plans were radically changed between the time the sculptures were made, and the building of the portal. These statues were made a half century before the portal was actually erected. In the façade of Notre-Dame-la-Grande of Poitiers (Ill. 956) a column cuts across the figure of Adam. The string-course over the figure of *Nabacchodnosor* (Ill. 958) has a different profile from that over the prophets, and is discontinued altogether at their right (Ill. 958). Such irregularities could only have arisen in sculptures carved before being placed.[1]

In the light of all this evidence we may conclude that the capitals of the ambulatory of Cluny were not carved after being placed, and that they really were executed between 1088 and 1095.

It must not be forgotten that the abbey of Cluny possessed other Romanesque sculptures besides the ambulatory capitals. In the Musée Ochier there is preserved a capital, quite different in style from those of the ambulatory, and coming from the church (Ill. 10). I conjecture that it belonged to the nave. The style is puzzling. The heavy stocky figures are at the opposite pole from the delicate graceful work of the ambulatory; they seem to be related, though in general character rather in detail, to the work at Charlieu (Ill. 4). At first they give the impression of being earlier than the ambulatory capitals; but on closer study, especially of the faces, it becomes clear that the reverse is the case. This capital was, however, in all probability, executed before 1108.

---

[1] Certain reliefs of Poitou have uncarved blocks inserted in the middle. Such are found, for example, in the Constantine (Ill. 1126) and voussures of Civray, in the voussures of St.-Pompain (Ill. 1058), and before the restoration existed in the voussures of Ste.-Croix of Bordeaux. These uncarved blocks must have been inserted to replace weathered portions of the sculptures in some restoration, perhaps of the XVIII century. It was doubtless the intention to carve them, but this was never carried out. The same explanation applies to the uncarved blocks replacing statues on the façade of Pérignac (Ill. 1020, 1021).

The great portal at Cluny was part of the church of 1088–1113.[1]
Since it was situated at the western end of the church, it would presumably have been erected rather towards the end of this time. It
has been totally destroyed, and Sagot's lithograph appears to be phe-
nomenally inaccurate, so that it is impossible to judge of the style.
The composition is known from descriptions and the lithograph.[2]
In the immense tympanum, sixteen feet broad, appeared the figure
of Christ in an aureole sustained by four angels; about were the
symbols of the four evangelists. Below, on the lintel were the four
and twenty elders; and above, in the spandrels, four apostles. In the
inner row of voussures about the tympanum were sculptured reliefs
of angels; and on the third voussure were twenty-five medallions,
each containing a head in profile.

[1] I was wrong in my surmise that it was one of the portions of the church rebuilt in 1125–
1131. The proofs that it must have belonged to the earlier construction will appear in a later
chapter.

[2] *Millénaire*, II, Plate II.

VII

THE DIFFUSION OF CLUNIAC ART
IN BURGUNDY

THE glorious tympanum of Vézelay (Ill. 47–49), like so much else in that abbey, is evidently derived from Cluny. The subject, it is true, has been changed; we no longer have the *Majestas Domini* of the Cluny tympanum, but Pentecost.[1] The great figure of the Deity in an aureole still, however, continues to be the central point of the composition; there is still a lintel forming a base to the tympanum; and the great size of this superb lunette could only have been inspired by Cluny.

The nave of Vézelay was finished in 1120, the narthex was consecrated in 1132. The portal would seem to belong to the nave rather than to the narthex, and consequently to belong with the earlier rather than with the later date. However, it should be observed that the hand of the master of the tympanum can be recognized in none of the capitals of the nave, but only in those of the narthex. This seems to indicate that the master of the tympanum was not at work at Vézelay when the nave was being built, but that he was there when the narthex was being constructed. The conclusion is therefore justified that the tympanum dates from shortly before 1132.

Another derivative of the tympanum of Cluny is that of Autun (Ill. 80, 81). Although not a Cluniac priory, like Vézelay, the cathedral of Autun was nevertheless closely connected with the great

---

[1] The iconography of Vézelay should be compared with the mosaic in one of the domes of St. Mark's at Venice representing the same subject. Here below the apostles are shown the nations called to the faith — Romani, Judaei, Cretes, Arabes, Parthi, Medi, Aelamitae, Mesopotamia, Judaea, Cappadocia, Pontum, Asiatici, Phrygia, Pamphylia, Aegyptus, Lybia. According to Marco Polo there were dog-headed men in the island of Agaman (Andaman) in the Gulf of Bengal. These are illustrated with a miniature in the manuscript Fr. 2810 of the Bibliothèque Nationale. The same conception re-appears in Oderico da Pordenone's description of Nicobar, also illustrated in the same manuscript. The conception of dog-headed men is familiar in Japanese and Chinese art.

abbey. The bishop Etienne de Bâge (1112–1139) by whom the cathedral was built, went to Cluny to die; documents speak of the cathedral as associated (*conjuncta*) with Cluny.[1] The subject of the tympanum is changed again; in this case it is the Last Judgment. The theme once established at Autun was sculptured in the western tympana of countless churches of the Occident. Perhaps it came to Autun from the painted Last Judgment, which St. Hugh had caused to be executed in the refectory which he had built at Cluny.[2] The subject is ultimately of Oriental origin.[3]

The composition of the tympanum retains the essential lines of that of Cluny. Again there is the figure of Christ in the aureole in the centre; again the narrow lintel crowded with little figures. Again the tympanum is of enormous size.

We are fortunate in knowing the name of the sculptor who executed the tympanum of Autun; he has signed his name, *Gislebertus* — Gilbert.[4]

It is evident that Gilbert's manner, like that of the sculptor of the Cluny capitals, was largely formed on miniatures. The angels plunging downwards head-foremost, recall, for example, the Sacramentary of Henry II [5] and the IX-century Apocalypse of Trèves.[6] The spiral belly folds must certainly have come from a manuscript— we find precisely such in a miniature representing Christ between evangelists and prophets in the Louvre Bible of Charles-le-Chauve, in a miniature of St. Matthew in the Perikopenbuch Kaiser Heinrichs II, a work of the Reichenau school of before 1014;[7] in another

---

[1] *Bullarium*, 215.   [2] Lorain, 91.

[3] Last Judgments had been painted in fresco in the West at St. George, on the island of Reichenau, about the middle of the XI century, and at S. Angelo in Formis at the end of the XI century. The subject appears to have been represented as early as the end of the IX century in the lower church of S. Clemente at Rome. That the iconographical conception came from the Orient is the opinion of Bertaux (*Ital. Mér.*, 259). M. Diehl (228) has remarked that it appears in the *Cosmas Indicopleustes*, which is a IX-century copy of a VI-century original.

[4] GISLEBERTVS HOC FECIT

[5] Illustrated in Michel, I, 2, 733.

[6] Bibl. de la Ville, No. 31, illustrated by Boinet, Pl. CLV. The motive also occurs in an ivory of the Kaiser Friederich Museum at Berlin. This work, which dates from the middle of the XI century, has been illustrated by Goldschmidt, II, No. 34.

[7] Illustrated by Leidinger, V, 2.

miniature, representing the dormition of the Virgin in the same manuscript,[1] in an Armenian manuscript of the X–XII centuries,[2] and in the Benedictional of St. Aethelwold of the school of Winchester.[3] The motive may be traced back as far as an ivory diptych of the VI century in the British Museum.[4]

Gilbert's manner of covering his draperies with a net-work of fine lines is also probably derived from a manuscript. We find something very similar in the IX-century gospels of Lothaire. The motive may very probably have originated in Byzantium. It is found on the Christ of the gold and enamel paliotto of St. Mark's at Venice;[5] this appears to be a Byzantine work of the X century. In sculpture we find similar technique in the late XI century in a capital of Otranto,[6] and at the end of the XII and beginning of the XIII centuries in sculptures of Catalonia, at Perpignan (Ill. 618–620), Elne (Ill. 623–626), Arles-sur-Tech (Ill. 627).

The curious leg-bands which appear on the thighs of several of Gilbert's figures, perhaps originated in a bracelet, which was misunderstood and transferred from the arm or ankle to the thigh and treated as a part of the drapery. Such leg-bands are probably of Byzantine origin, since they are found in Japanese art also. In occidental art we find them in a miniature of the Evangelium Kaiser Otto III,[7] and in a IX-century German pyxis in ivory of the British Museum.[8] The motive became characteristic of English miniatures of the School of Winchester.[9] It is also found in the XI-century Arca of San Felices at S. Millán de la Cogolla (Ill. 662), and had appeared

---

[1] Illustrated by Leidinger, V, 33.
[2] Paris, Bib. Nat. Syriaque 344, fol. 5 verso.
[3] Illustrated by Homburger, I.
[4] Illustrated by Pelka, 69.
[5] Illustrated by Venturi, II, 649.
[6] Illustrated by Wackernagel, Taf. IX e.
[7] Illustrated by Leidinger, I, 13.
[8] Illustrated by Dalton, Pl. XXIII, 43.
[9] It is found, for example, in the Descent to Limbo of the Benedictional of St. Aethelwold of c. 980, illustrated by Homburger, I; in the Register of New Minster, Winchester of c. 1030, British Museum, Stowe MS. 960, illustrated by Bond, Thompson and Warner, II, 17; and in a miniature of the end of the X century representing St. Michael, in Cottonian Psalter, Tiberius C VI, British Museum, illustrated by Westwood, Pl. 46.

in sculpture in the *St. James* of the Puerta de las Platerias at Santiago (Ill. 676) before it found its way to Autun.

A figure with its head turned directly back, like the soul on the left-hand side of the tympanum of Autun (Ill. 80) is found in the Register of New Minster, of the Winchester School.[1] The capital of the nave of Autun, by Gilbert, representing the angel appearing to St. Peter in prison (Ill. 79) has the subject enclosed in an arch, as do the miniatures of the Benedictional of St. Aethelwold. The devil represented on one of the capitals of the nave[2] is precisely like the devil of a miniature of the *Liber Vitae* of the school of Winchester.[3]

From these analogies, we may draw the conclusion that Gilbert founded his art upon Cluniac tradition, but that he was deeply influenced, like all Burgundian sculptors, by miniatures of the school of Winchester. He also probably knew German miniatures.

The cathedral of Autun was begun in 1119 or 1120; it was consecrated in 1132 and a second time in 1146.[4] The capitals of the nave and the tympanum belong to the campaign of 1119–1132.

That the nave is substantially contemporary with the tympanum is proved by the fact that the hand of Gilbert may be recognized in several of the capitals — those representing the Fall of Simon Magus (Ill. 75), St. Peter in Prison (Ill. 79), Music, *Noli me tangere* (Ill. 78), the Ravishing of the Magdalen,[5] the Temptation.[6]

If we compare the tympanum of Autun (Ill. 80, 81) with that of Vézelay (Ill. 47–49), we shall easily convince ourselves that the two are contemporary. The style is very different — each is the work of a highly individual hand. They are none the less clearly products of the same art and of the same time. Now we have found reason to believe that the tympanum of Vézelay was sculptured before 1132. We are therefore justified in believing that the tympanum and nave

[1] British Museum, Stowe MS. 960, illustrated by Bond, Thompson and Warner, II, 17.
[2] Illustrated by Terrey, Pl. I.
[3] British Museum, Stowe MS. 944, illustrated by Herbert, Pl. XIII.
[4] For a study of the documents, see De Fontenay and De Charmasse, p. cxlj f.
[5] The authorship of this capital was first recognized by M. Mâle.
[6] Illustrated by Déchelette, 20 ter.

capitals of Autun belong to the period of building activity at Autun extending from 1119 to 1132.

When we compare the capitals of the nave of Autun (Ill. 67–79) with those of the nave of Vézelay (Ill. 28–46), executed between 1104 and 1120, we perceive that the Vézelay work is rougher, more vigorous, less refined. The Autun capitals have a decadent quality that is lacking at Vézelay. We easily perceive that the nave of Vézelay is earlier than the nave of Autun.

It is only in the western bays of the nave at Vézelay, and especially in the narthex, built from 1120 to 1132, that we find capitals really analogous to those of Autun. The work of the "Bathsheba Master" (Ill. 44) has the same languor, the same sweet sweeping lines, the same refinement, the same seduction of decadence that is characteristic of the work at Autun (Ill. 68–81). The "Tympanum Master" of Vézelay in his capital representing Samson and the Lion (Ill. 46) approaches so closely the capital representing Duke Hugh II presenting the cathedral to St.-Lazare at Autun (Ill. 74)[1] that one is tempted to call them the work of the same hand. It seems to me that it is more probable, however, that we have merely a strong influence exerted by the master of the Vézelay tympanum upon a sculptor of Autun.[2]

Our impression of the date of the capitals and tympanum of Autun is confirmed by a study of the capitals of Saulieu. This collegiate church was associated with Cluny;[3] the existing nave was erected after the translation of relics in 1119.[4]

When we compare the capitals (Ill. 52–61) with those of the nave of Vézelay (Ill. 28–35, 39–42, 44), we perceive that those of Saulieu are later. At Saulieu there is more attenuation, more manner, more movement, more disparity of scale in the figures. If, for example, we put the Vézelay capital of the Death of Cain (Ill. 35) beside the

[1] I am mortified to be obliged to illustrate this capital from the modern copy. A photograph of the original has been published by Déchelette, 20.

[2] I presume it must have been these capitals that M. Mâle had in mind when he stated that the same sculptors worked at Vézelay and at Autun.

[3] *Bullarium*, 216; Bruel, IV, 410.

[4] De Fontenay et De Charmasse, p. cxlj.

Saulieu capital of the *Noli me tangere* (Ill. 55, we shall be convinced that the Saulieu master is softer, more graceful, more decadent. Or if we compare the facial types in the Vézelay capital of the Stolen Blessing (Ill. 37) with that of the Balaam at Saulieu (Ill. 56), we shall quickly convince ourselves that Saulieu is more realistic, more plastic, less archaic. Compare also the draperies in the same two capitals — it is evident how much more naturalistic are those of Saulieu. When we put the Saulieu capital of the Temptation (Ill. 53) beside that of the Vézelay Temptation of St. Anthony (Ill. 42) we see at once that the Saulieu demon is more accomplished, more exaggerated, more naturalistically rendered. Or if we compare the lions on the Vézelay capital of the burial of St. Paul[1] with those of the capital at Saulieu (Ill. 61), it becomes evident how much more naturalistic is the work at Saulieu.

From all this we may conclude that the nave of Saulieu was built not before, but after, the translation of relics in 1119.

That on the other hand Saulieu is not later than the third decade of the XII century, is proved by comparing the capitals with those of Moûtier-St.-Jean, now in the Fogg Museum. These capitals are certainly earlier than 1133, since the church from which they come was built by the abbot Bernard II who died in that year.[2]

Now if we compare the lion of the Moûtier-St.-Jean capital representing Samson[3] with that of the capital of Saulieu, we shall at once perceive how closely the two resemble each other. If we put the Moûtier-St.-Jean Journey to Emmaus (Ill. 65) beside the Saulieu *Noli me tangere* (Ill. 55), we see that the facial types in the two works are very similar, the eyes indicated by the same convention, the hands similarly rendered, the hair and beard represented in the same way, the draperies adorned with the same bead border. Moûtier-St.-Jean seems contemporary with, or if any thing a little later than, Saulieu. Similarly, if we place the Moûtier-St.-Jean capital of Cain and Abel (Ill. 66) beside the Saulieu capital of the Temptation

---

[1] F. M. S. phot. 7789.   [2] Plancher, I, 516.
[3] Illustrated in the Fogg Museum *Notes*, I, 2, Fig. 6.

(Ill. 53), and compare the face of Christ at Saulieu with that of Cain at Moûtier-St.-Jean and the draperies of the two capitals, we shall be convinced that the two works are contemporary. The capitals of Saulieu must consequently have been sculptured in the years immediately following 1119.[1]

When we compare the capitals of Saulieu (Ill. 52–61) with those of Autun (Ill. 67–79), we perceive that the latter are less vigorous, but more lyric. Yet the two are so much alike that we can not doubt that the two are contemporary. Take, for example, the two Flights into Egypt (Ill. 54 and Ill. 71). The close resemblance of the two representations, extending even to the strange rosettes under the feet of the donkey,[2] is evident. If Saulieu is more naturalistic, Autun is more polished and refined. The donkey in the Autun capital reproduces, almost line for line, the donkey of Balaam at Saulieu (Ill. 56). The Devil in the Judas capital of Saulieu (Ill. 52) is very like the Devil in the Temptation at Autun. The Judas of Saulieu (Ill. 52) seems clearly contemporary with the disciple to the left in the Washing of the Feet at Autun (Ill. 70). We have, therefore, another indication that the capitals of the nave of Autun are of 1120–1132.

Still further confirmation is afforded by comparison with the capitals of Moûtier-St.-Jean, which, as we have seen, must be earlier than 1133. The general similarity in the types and in the draperies is evident at a glance. (Compare Ill. 62–66 with Ill. 67–79.) The wing of the angel in the Moûtier-St.-Jean capital of the Journey to Emmaus[3] is precisely like the wing in the Autun Fall of Simon Magus (Ill. 75). If we put the Fogg Annunciation to Zacharias (Ill. 63) beside the Autun Washing of the Feet (Ill. 70), we shall perceive that there are the same draperies, the same working of the eye, the

---

[1] Capitals strikingly analogous to the unfigured capitals of Saulieu are found in the cathedral of Troia in Apulia (illustrated by Bertaux, *Ital. Mér.*, 459). One of the bronze doors of this nave was made in 1119, the other in 1127, so the structure must be about contemporary with Saulieu.

[2] Similar rosettes are found on a capital of the crypt of Otranto in Apulia which was consecrated in 1088 (illustrated by Wackernagel, IX b). Are they connected with the lotus-blossoms of Oriental art?

[3] Illustrated in the Fogg Museum *Notes*, I, 2, Fig. 4.

same conventions for the hair and beard, the same facial types. It is impossible to doubt that works so similar are contemporary. We therefore again conclude that the nave of Autun is of 1120–1132.

As closely as Autun resembles these works of the third decade of the XII century, does it differ from those of the fifth. In the Archaeological Museum of Dijon is preserved a tympanum representing the *Majestas Domini* (Ill. 134, 135), found in 1833 embedded in the substructions of a buttress on the east side of the north transept of the church of St.-Bénigne. This relief bears an inscription stating that it was restored under the abbot Peter.[1]

As there were two abbots of St.-Bénigne by the name of Peter, one of whom held office from 1129–1142 and the other from 1142–1145, it is not clear to which the inscription refers — we can only be certain that the relief is anterior to 1145.

However, it is known that in 1137 the city and suburbs of Dijon were devastated by a great fire. "L'église de Saint-Bénigne en fut presqu'entièrement ruinée; il fallut dix ans entiers pour la rétablir."[2] Now there can be no doubt that our tympanum was part of the restorations carried out by either one or the other Peter after this fire; it therefore dates from between 1137 and 1145.

The composition of this tympanum (Ill. 134, 135) shows that it is another derivative of the destroyed portal of Cluny. We have only to put it beside the tympanum of Autun (Ill. 80, 81) to be convinced that it is much later than Autun in style. This difference is so marked that since the Dijon tympanum can not be later than 1145, we must place the Autun tympanum at least as early as 1132.

Nor does the *Majestas* at Dijon stand alone. In the same Archaeological Museum is preserved another tympanum (Ill. 136) representing the Last Supper. This also comes from St.-Bénigne, and more precisely from the portal of the refectory, where it was seen and engraved by Dom Plancher[3] in the early part of the XVIII century.

[1] REDDEDIT AMISSVM MICHI PETRI CVRA DECOREM
✠ ET DEDIT ANTIQVA FORMAM MVLTO MELIOREM
[2] Plancher, I, 494.
[3] I, 520.

His drawing shows it surmounted by a row of sculptured voussures, purely Gothic in character. Now this tympanum also bears an inscription, similarly stating that it was restored by the abbot Peter.[1] It therefore is contemporary with the first relief, and dated between 1137 and 1145.

When we compare this second tympanum with Autun (Ill. 80, 81), we again perceive that Autun must be at least as early as 1132.

A comparison of the two tympana of Dijon (Ill. 134, 135 and Ill. 136) with each other shows that marked difference of style which we have already found is so often characteristic of contemporary sculptors in Burgundy, even when working in the same atelier. The tympanum of the Last Supper is obviously an imitation of the work of the head master at Chartres — the latter must in consequence be earlier than 1145. Although drinking from fountain-heads of such purity, the sculptor of the tympanum of the Last Supper shows the same defects of weakness and decadence that are characteristic of the *Majestas Domini*. In any other period these productions would pass as masterpieces; but when we come fresh from Autun and Cluny, they seem faded.

There remains one other monument of Burgundian sculpture of certain date. It is the tomb of St. Lazare of the cathedral of Autun, carved by a monk of the name of Martin in the time of the bishop Stephen (1170–1189), as is known from a destroyed inscription.[2] The monument has been broken up, but fragments are preserved in the Musée Lapidaire installed in the church of St.-Pierre. In quality these sculptures (Ill. 147–149) are among the finest productions of the second half of the XII century. The style evidently takes us into a different era from the one which we have been studying.

There are therefore not a few monuments of Burgundian sculpture, the date of which can be determined by documentary evidence. These all seem entirely consistent with each other, and show a logical

[1] ✝ CV RUDIS ANTE FORM DEDIT HANC MICHI PETRVS HONOREM
✝ MVTANS HORROREM FORMA MELIORE PRIO[REM].
[2] De Mély, 36.

and convincing evolution of the style. There is consequently no necessity for setting aside this mass of documentary evidence. The monuments and the documents correspond in an entirely satisfactory and convincing manner.

The dated monuments are distributed over the century from 1080 to 1180 with sufficient evenness to form an outline into which it is not difficult to fit the monuments for which there is no documentary evidence of date.

The new art created at Cluny spread quickly through Burgundy. The earliest extant imitation appears to be the altar at Avenas (Ill. 11–15). Surely no other sculptor came as close to the manner of the great original (Ill. 5–10). Yet his inferiority is, of course, patent. Compare the Third Tone at Cluny (Ill. 7) with the Christ at Avenas (Ill. 12). The coarseness, rigidity, jerkiness of the Avenas figure contrast with the exquisite grace and rhythm of Cluny; the great clumsy hands of Avenas are doubly disquieting when placed in juxtaposition to those of Cluny; the dainty grace of the Cluniac draperies makes those of Avenas seem rigid and not well understood. But the Avenas altar still remains a work of great merit. The sculptor has certainly sought his inspiration at Cluny, but he has not merely copied. He has developed a style of his own, which is of decided originality and charm; his work haunts the memory with singular persistence. We can not but respect the crispness of his carving, the sureness of his touch.

As for date, his work must evidently be later than Cluny, therefore later than 1095. On the other hand, his style seems entirely free from the influence of the other great ateliers which soon succeeded Cluny. I can detect no signs of the influence of Vézelay (Ill. 28–51). Compared with Vézelay indeed, Avenas seems distinctly earlier. If we put, for example, the Christ of Avenas (Ill. 12) beside the Daniel of Vézelay (Ill. 33), we see 'that at Vézelay the eye is drawn more naturalistically, and the draperies are more advanced. It is probable, therefore, that Avenas is earlier than 1104. We shall not go far astray if we ascribe its production to c. 1100.

The relief of the refectory at Charlieu (Ill. 16), on the other hand, is obviously later. The relationship to Cluny is still patent; but the draperies are more complicated than at Avenas, and a border ornament of perforated holes is introduced. This is evidently a very archaic example of a motive developed at Saulieu (Ill. 55) and destined to attain great popularity about the middle of the XII century. The eyes in the Charlieu relief are rendered by the same peculiar convention which is characteristic of the "Vézelay Master No. 1" (Ill. 34). We may consequently conclude that the Charlieu relief is contemporary with the atelier of Vézelay (1104-1120). It is a singular fact that the wings of the angel seem to be executed in the Toulousan, not in the Burgundian manner; they resemble those of the reliefs of the ambulatory of St.-Sernin (Ill. 297-300) — *c*. 1105 — rather than those of the tympanum of that church (Ill. 309) — *c*. 1115. This would lead us to place the Charlieu relief about 1110. That such a dating is approximately correct we may convince ourselves by comparing the relief with the earlier tympanum of 1094 (Ill. 4) on the one hand, and the later porch of *c*. 1140 (Ill. 108-110) on the other. The refectory relief is obviously closer to the former than to the latter.

An entirely new note is struck by the superb *Christ* of St.-Amour (Ill. 106). This is one of the unforgettable creations of mediaeval art, in its way as inspired and as imaginative as the capitals of Cluny. The style falls quite outside the development of the Burgundian manner; the forms of beauty which crowded to the mind of this artist were as impatient of conventional expression as of realism and the possibilities of space. He makes us think on the one hand of the wild fantasies of the Irish miniaturists; on the other of the sculptures at Nara.[1] His is, in its way, an equally supreme achievement. The date of this masterpiece is not easy to determine, because of its very originality. Surely such draperies could not have been conceived

---

[1] His draperies are indeed much closer to those of Japanese art than any I know in the Occident. See especially the gilt bronze figure earlier than 781, owned by the Imperial Household, and exhibited in the Kyoto Exposition. It is illustrated in the catalogue. I am indebted to Mr. Clapp for making me acquainted with this, and so many other superlative examples of Far-Eastern art.

before Cluny. On the other hand, they are in some respects rather similar to, though apparently earlier than, those of the tympanum of Fleury-la-Montagne (Ill. 107) which seems to be an inferior production of *c.* 1120. The chair at St.-Amour is like the chair of the Christ at Avenas (Ill. 12). If we place St.-Amour about 1110, we shall probably not be very wide of the mark.

Perrecey-les-Forges was a priory dependent upon St.-Benoît-sur-Loire.[1] The tympanum (Ill. 84) certainly belongs to the first half of the XII century. This Christ in majesty, mysterious and silent as a sphinx, charms as does a madonna of Bellini, but never cloys. The cherubim flanking the aureole are superbly mannered. Chronologically, the sculpture must be placed between the archaic simplicity of the older portal at Charlieu (Ill. 4) — 1094 — and the refined mannerism of Gilbert's tympanum at Autun (Ill. 80) — 1132. It seems more advanced than the capitals of the nave of Vézelay (1104–1120) (Ill. 28–44). It may therefore be assigned to about 1125.

Anzy-le-Duc was a priory dependent upon St.-Martin of Autun.[2] The architecture of the church seems imitated from Charlieu; it is consequently later than 1094. The sculptured capitals (Ill. 17–23) are exuberant, even rough; but finely spirited and full of imagination. Chronologically they seem about abreast of the tympanum of Fleury-la-Montagne (Ill. 107), a monument of *c.* 1120.

The capitals of the nave of Anzy-le-Duc (Ill. 17–23) should be compared with those of the crypt of St.-Parize-le-Châtel (Ill. 25, 26). If we put that of Anzy representing an acrobat (Ill. 21) beside that of St.-Parize representing the Sciapodes (Ill. 25), we shall be convinced that the two are very closely related. Now it is known that in 1113 the bishop Hugh IV of Nevers gave the church of St.-Parize to the canons of his cathedral.[3] There seems every reason to suppose that the crypt of St.-Parize belonged to a reconstruction undertaken in consequence of this donation. The capitals may in consequence be

---

[1] Mortet, 507.
[2] Thiollier, 73; Rhein in *Cong. Arch.*, LXXX, 269.
[3] *Le Nivernois*, 237.

considered dated monuments of 1113. The nave of Anzy-le-Duc must also date from about the same time.

The western portal of Anzy-le-Duc is of a different and much more developed art. The style (Ill. 96, 97) seems clearly more archaic than that of the tympana of Vézelay (Ill. 47–51) and Autun (Ill. 80, 81), both dating from about 1132. It may therefore be assigned to about 1125. The elders floating upon the voussures suggest the influence of the school of the West.

A second portal is preserved at Anzy-le-Duc (Ill. 95), not in the church, but in the priory buildings. The style is totally different from that of either the capitals or the western portal of the church; and when we come to the portal that has been transferred to Paray-le-Monial (Ill. 98, 99), we shall find still a fourth manner of sculpture. All these must have flourished at Anzy-le-Duc within a few years of each other. It is usually supposed that the portal of the priory is much earlier than that of the church, but I do not believe that this point of view can be justified. The style in fact shows many points of contact with the tympana of Vézelay (Ill. 47–51) and Autun (Ill. 80, 81), both monuments of about 1132. It is, therefore, probable that the two portals of Anzy-le-Duc are about contemporary with each other.

The same serpentine, El Greco-like style is found in the portal at Neuilly-en-Donjon (Ill. 93, 94). We have here the work of a hand very closely related to, if not identical with, the one that sculptured the priory portal at Anzy-le-Duc (Ill. 95).

From the priory portal at Anzy-le-Duc and the tympanum of Neuilly-en-Donjon seem to be descended the celebrated outer portal of Charlieu (Ill. 108–110).[1] This imaginative work possesses a Hindu-like exuberance of ornamentation. As for its date, a glance is sufficient to reveal that we are here dealing with the late autumn of Burgundian art. The Charlieu sculptures (Ill. 108–110) are ranker, more mannered, less fresh than the tympana of Vézelay (Ill. 47–51)

---

[1] The circular table in the Last Supper suggests Byzantine influence; compare the Armenian manuscript of the Bibliothèque Nationale, Etchmiadzin, 362 G. fol. 8 vo.; Codex Purpureus of Rosano of the VI century, illustrated by Haseloff, Taf. V.

and Autun (Ill. 80, 81), hence later than 1132. On the other hand, the puristic tendencies of Chartres are notably absent. We have already seen that these began to make themselves felt in Burgundy before 1145. Charlieu can consequently not be later than 1140. The tympanum of St.-Julien-de-Jonzy (Ill. 111), smaller, but better preserved, is a work of the same hand. Its composition is the same as that of the older portal at Charlieu (Ill. 4).

The delicate tympanum of Montceaux-l'Etoile (Ill. 104, 105) and the sculptures of St.-Paul-de-Varax (Ill. 86–91), with their striking effects of space, both are close to the tympana of the side portals of Vézelay (Ill. 50, 51). The enigmatic tympanum which is the most conspicuous remains of the ancient cathedral of St.-Vincent at Mâcon (Ill. 92) seems to be a conglomeration of fragments which were perhaps disposed like the sculptures of St.-Paul-de-Varax. The original tympanum of much smaller size, representing the *Majestas Domini*, the apostles and the two witnesses of the Apocalypse was at a later period combined with parts of a frieze like that of St.-Paul-de-Varax (Ill. 86, 87, 89, 90) to form a much larger tympanum representing the Last Judgment. The wings of the upper angels recall Perrecey-les-Forges (Ill. 84). The original sculptures may have dated from about 1130. Montceaux-l'Etoile (Ill. 104, 105) is perhaps a little earlier, St.-Paul-de-Varax (Ill. 86–91) a little later, than the Vézelay work. A third portal of Anzy-le-Duc, now in the Musée Eucharistique at Paray-le-Monial (Ill. 98, 99) is marked by a style which is more advanced than that of St.-Paul-de-Varax. The draperies of Christ seem already to show something very like the Chartres-esque formula. On the other hand this tympanum seems distinctly earlier than the Dijon tympana (Ill. 134, 136) and also earlier than the outer portal at Charlieu (Ill. 108–110). It may therefore be as early as 1135.

The fragments of the church of St.-Sauveur of Nevers (Ill. 126–133), gathered together in the Musée de la Porte du Croux, are of more than common interest. The capital representing St. Peter and St. John (Ill. 132) shows points of marked similarity with the capital of Tobias (Ill. 45) in the narthex of Vézelay. Since the latter dates from before 1132, the Nevers capital may very probably be of *c.* 1135. The tympanum representing the Giving of the Keys (Ill. 133) is by the same hand as the capital. Since the tympanum is signed, we have the name of this interesting, if somewhat mediocre sculptor — Mavo.

The style of the work at St.-Sauveur of Nevers does not seem entirely Burgundian. It has a certain dryness which recalls much more the school of the West. The gracious movement, the swirling lines, the fluttering draperies of Burgundy are strangely absent. We are therefore not entirely surprised to find the hand of this same artist in a capital of Fontevrault (Ill. 923). The abbey of Fontevrault was consecrated in 1119; his work there must then be considerably earlier than that at Nevers. It is strange that at Fontevrault in the heart of the West, Mavo seems as Burgundian as he seems Western at Nevers. He was possibly born and formed in the region between Burgundy and the West.

When we compare the tympanum of St.-Sauveur (Ill. 133) with that of St.-Bénigne of Dijon representing the Last Supper (Ill. 136), we are in no doubt that St.-Sauveur is earlier. It is clear that the St.-Bénigne tympanum was executed under the strong influence of the head-master of Chartres. This is evident not only in the facial types, the draperies, the borders of the garments, the folds of the table-cloth, but even, as Mr. Priest observes, in the composition. This is, in fact, a reversal of the composition of the Last Supper on one of the capitals of Chartres.[1] Now these Chartres-esque mannerisms which abound at St.-Bénigne, are lacking at Nevers. We may consequently conclude that Nevers is earlier. Since the St.-Bénigne Last Supper is anterior to 1145, the Giving of the Keys of St.-Sauveur must be still earlier, or of about 1135.

Indeed, the comparison of the tympana of these two Cluniac priories suggests a more daring conclusion. If we divest the Dijon

---

[1] The composition was made popular at Chartres (it was copied thence also on a capital of La Daurade of Toulouse — Ill. 471 —), but was not originated there. Mr. Cook has called my attention to the fact that it is found in the Arca of S. Felices at S. Millán (Ill. 661).

Last Supper of its Chartres-esque mannerisms, so evidently a super-ficial affectation, we should have left a style strangely like that of the Nevers Giving of the Keys. The head of the right-hand apostle at Nevers is very like that of the third from the right at Dijon. There is the same trick of shortening the figures to make them fit under the curve of the lunette. There are the same faults of proportion — com-pare for example the figure second from the left in both tympana. At Dijon have we Mavo trying to imitate Chartres?

It is clear that the sculptor of the tympanum of Donzy (Ill. 112–114) also knew Chartres. If we compare his composition with the tympanum of the southern portal at Chartres, we shall have no doubt of the fact. His Virgin sits in the same position, holding the Child straight in front of her; in each case she is under a canopy sup-ported on columns (that at Chartres has been broken away); the posture of the angel to the left, the sweep of his wings, even the posi-tion of his left hand and arm is the same. The bottom folds of the drapery of the Virgin's dress are in the two cases very similar. The crowns are alike. The right hands of the Virgins are precisely the same. The tympanum of Donzy is certainly inspired by Chartres.

Yet at Donzy there is much more than mere copying of Chartres. It is impossible to remain in the presence of this noble work, without the conviction that it was produced by an artist of strong individual-ity, with a vision of beauty that was characteristically his own. Now this personality which persists underneath the superficial influence of the Master of the Angels, is singularly like that of the sculptor of the outer porch of Charlieu (Ill. 108–110) and of St.-Julien-de-Jonzy (Ill. 111). If we compare the face of the angel at Donzy (Ill. 112) with the face of the angel in the corresponding position at St.-Julien (Ill. 111); the flutter of drapery in front of the angel at Donzy (Ill. 112) with that behind the left-hand angel at St.-Julien; the folds and lower edge of the garment about the left knee of the left-hand angel at Charlieu (Ill. 108) with the fold about the right knee of the Virgin at Donzy (Ill. 113); the execution of the feathers of the wing of the angel at St.-Julien (Ill. 111) with that of the wing of the angel at

Donzy (Ill. 112); the draperies to the right of the feet of the Deity at Charlieu (Ill. 108) with those about the feet of the Child at Donzy (Ill. 113), we shall, I think, be tempted to conjecture that all three tympana are by the same sculptor.

A problem no less interesting is afforded by the two portals of La Charité-sur-Loire (Ill. 115–122). Here, again, the composition of the lintel repeats with extraordinary exactitude that of the lintels of the south portal of Chartres. In this instance the question is complicated by the existence of a third rendering of the same theme in the frieze of Montmorillon (Ill. 1072 a, 1073). If we place the three versions beside each other,[1] we shall be in no doubt that they are closely related. The similarities are extraordinary. The scene of the Nativity, for example, is represented in all in the same peculiar way; the Virgin lies in bed; above her is a sort of shelf, on which the Christ Child, the ox and the ass are, or were, placed. St. Joseph stands in all cases at the head of this arrangement; his garment falls over his left arm in precisely the same way. The angel of the Annunciation at Chartres and La Charité is represented in the same manner; his wings are similarly placed,[2] even the feathers are executed with the same convention. At Montmorillon this angel has been transferred from the scene of the Annunciation to that of the Shepherds.[3] The

[1] Excellent reproductions of the sculptures of Chartres are available in the monograph of M. Houvet.

[2] This arrangement of the wings is an old Byzantine motive, the history of which I have sketched in *Lombard Architecture*, I, 285. In addition to the instances there cited it should be remarked that it also occurs in a manuscript of Monte Cassino, dated 1072, No. 99 H, *Homiliae diversae;* in an ivory-carving representing the Dream of Joseph in the South Kensington Museum, called an Italian work of the XI–XII centuries, and illustrated by Graeven, II, 57; in another in the same museum, a work of the Ada group dating from the IX century illustrated by Goldschmidt, I, No. 14. This motive had been naturalized in the sculpture of western France from at least the time when the sculptures of Villogen (Ill. 1083) were executed. We have here another indication that the composition which we are studying originated where this motive was at home, *i.e.*, at Montmorillon, and not in Burgundy nor the Ile-de-France, where it had been previously unknown.

The angel of the Montmorillon Annunciation is very like the second angel from the bottom in the inner voussure on the right-hand side at Le Mans. It is evident, however, that the Montmorillon angel is the original, the Le Mans version a derivative.

[3] This detail is puzzling, and to some extent contradicts the conclusions at which we shall arrive. I can only suppose that the St.-Gilles Master of Chartres, a veritable vagabond, knew the rendering of the theme at La Charité as well as that at Montmorillon. Mr. Priest has observed that certain heads at La Charité — notably the Virgin (Ill. 118) and the second king

altar on which the Christ Child is presented is of the same peculiar form;[1] in all it resembles a pagan pedestal. But enough has been said of the similarities, which no one will doubt. The differences are more significant for our purpose.

We notice, therefore, that the Montmorillon sculptor is fond of movement, which the sculptor of Chartres avoids. Compare, for example, the two angels of the Annunciation. That at Montmorillon rushes, while that at Chartres hardly moves. The shepherds at Chartres are more rigid than those at Montmorillon; the virgin in bed raises her knees and lifts her elbows; at Chartres she lies corpse-like. The work at Chartres is more monumental and architectural; that at Montmorillon more lively and naturalistic. The figures at Montmorillon have not the attenuated proportions of those of Chartres. The draperies, moreover, have a different character. At Montmorillon the folds are broader and more theatrical.

All these facts seem to indicate that Chartres is later than Montmorillon. The great changes of style introduced by the atelier of Chartres were the abandonment of the movement which had been before in vogue, and the elaboration of a new type of drapery.

However, the instances we have already found of minor sculptors in the provinces who reproduced pages of the gospel of Chartres, and numerous others of similar character which we shall come upon in the future, raise the *a priori* suspicion that we may have here merely another instance of the diffusion of a Chartrain motive. It is hence desirable to find definite proof that Chartres can not be the original from which the other two are derived.

Fortunately, such is at hand. At Chartres the scene of the Adoration of the Magi is omitted, but this is included at both Montmorillon

of the Adoration (Ill. 118) have a somewhat Chartres-esque quality, while others recall the Betrayal of the St.-Gilles frieze (Ill. 1319, 1320). Did the St.-Gilles Master, who worked at St.-Gilles and Chartres, and who also knew La Charité, bring thither these ideas?

[1] A similar altar is found in the lintel of Bitonto (Ill. 232). In the Benedictional of St. Aethelwold, a manuscript of the School of Winchester of *c.* 980 preserved at Chatsworth, is a miniature representing the Presentation, with a square altar seen diagonally. The Virgin holds the Child somewhat as at Montmorillon. Illustrated by Wilson and Warner, folio 35.

(Ill. 1073) and La Charité (Ill. 118).[1] The composition, it is true, is reversed; but details like the peculiar caned chair with a footstool in which the Virgin is seated (such a chair is found nowhere at Chartres); the halo of the Christ Child; the drawing of the first magus, prove that the two compositions are related. Another detail is also conclusive. At Montmorillon (Ill. 1073) and La Charité (Ill. 119) in the scene of the Presentation the Christ Child is held above the altar; at Chartres he stands upon it. That Montmorillon and La Charité have common characteristics different from Chartres proves that Chartres is not the common ancestor.

We notice, furthermore, that La Charité shows little trace of the style of Chartres in the details of the execution. On the other hand, the influence of Montmorillon is patent. The folds of the drapery falling from the left arm of the Christ in the tympanum of La Charité (Ill. 116) are evidently inspired by those of the Joseph in the Presentation of Montmorillon (Ill. 1073). The halo of Mary in the Presentation at La Charité (Ill. 119) is bent back over the stringcourse, precisely as are the halos at Montmorillon (Ill. 1072 a, 1073); there is nothing analogous to this at Chartres. The little square altar which appears in all these reliefs in the scene of the Presentation has no prototype in Burgundy nor in the Ile-de-France. It is, however, at home in the West, being found in a capital of L'Ile-Bouchard (Ill. 1102), in which the Presentation is represented with this same peculiar iconographic formula. The style of the sculptor of La Charité shows numerous signs of having been influenced by the West. One suspects, indeed, that he is not Burgundian at all. The prophets flanking the aureole (Ill. 115, 117) are not very close to the nearest Burgundian prototypes, like the figures of the "Mill" capital of Vézelay (Ill. 40); their scrolls, their beards, their sinuous contours show that they must be rather descendants of the Isaiah of Souillac (Ill. 344). The crouching figure in the right-hand corner of the

[1] The scene of the Visitation, which occurs at Chartres and at La Charité, does not appear at Montmorillon. It certainly, however, once existed. These reliefs are not in their original position. When they were moved this panel must have been destroyed. Part of it is still visible to the right of the Annunciation (Ill. 1072 a).

tympanum at La Charité (Ill. 117) looks as if it might be a derivative
of the figures in the same position at Angoulême (Ill. 937). All this
gives reason to believe that Montmorillon is the common ancestor,
La Charité and Chartres derivatives.

We may even go so far as to conclude that Chartres is later than
La Charité. If we compare the latter with the Dijon *Majestas
Domini*, we shall be convinced that the two are closely related. The
right hand of the Christ at Dijon (Ill. 135), for example, is precisely
like the right hand of the Christ at La Charité (Ill. 116); the similarity of feeling in the draperies and various details is unmistakable.
It is, however, equally clear that La Charité is more archaic. Dijon
is notably more sugary, more relaxed, more naturalistic. Since the
Dijon relief can not be later than 1145, it can not be much later than
Chartres; La Charité, which seems so much more primitive, must be
earlier.

It seems surprising that the great atelier of Chartres should have
condescended to copying works so little known as Montmorillon and
La Charité. Should we, therefore, suppose the existence of a common
prototype, now lost, for all these works? I do not think the hypothesis is necessary. The lintel at Chartres in which this passage
occurs is not by any of the four great masters who worked upon that
façade, but by a fifth and much inferior hand, that of the St.-Gilles
master. We shall later see that one of the chief characteristics of this
sculptor was the literalness with which he reproduced other people's
compositions.

Moreover, the atelier of Montmorillon which seems obscure to us
to-day may not have been so in the XII century. The provenance of
these sculptures is unknown. That they exerted great influence upon
Romanesque art is proved not only by the copies at Chartres and La
Charité, but also by the sculptures of the west wall at Souvigny
(Ill. 124, 125). This Cluniac priory is situated a little to the west of
Burgundy; it is still, however, geographically far removed from
Poitou. The débris of sculptures which have been set up in their
present position in modern times, perhaps originally belonged to a

jubé;[1] they were already in their present position when drawn by Chenevard in 1838. The style is evidently closely related to Montmorillon. The wings of the angel are broken, but were probably held as in the Montmorillon *Shepherds*; the draperies are precisely those of Montmorillon; and the curious caning of the chair is like that of the chair and the bed at Montmorillon.

The new style introduced at Souvigny seems to have spread to St.-Menoux in Auvergne. In the narthex of this church (Ill. 1257, 1258), and in the museum at Moulins (Ill. 1259) are preserved fragments of a screen similar to that of Souvigny. When we compare the Christ of St.-Menoux (Ill. 1257) with that of Souvigny (Ill. 125), we perceive how painstakingly the Auvergnat sculptor has copied his original. The folds of the drapery are precisely the same. It is evident, however, that all the freshness and vigour of the work at Souvigny are lost in this uninspired imitation. In the bishop at St.-Menoux (Ill. 1257) is reproduced line for line, the bishop of Souvigny (Ill. 124).

The sculptures from Ebreuil (Ill. 1254–1256), now in the museum of Moulins, are a hardly less patent imitation of Souvigny. Compare, for example, the undergarment of Christ in the two works (Ill. 125 and Ill. 1254). Ebreuil is, however, even clumsier and more uncouth than St.-Menoux. Another echo of Souvigny may be found in the Christ at Vizille (Ill. 1185).

To return from this digression in uncreative Auvergne to the fertile soil of Burgundy, we find one more monument which shows relationship to La Charité. It is the tomb of Ste. Magnance (Ill. 146). While the facial types and the general treatment are clearly close to La Charité (compare, for example, with the Mary in the Presentation — Ill. 119), the workmanship is distinctly inferior. The execution of the folds of the draperies is very similar to that of the Christ at St.-Menoux (Ill. 1257); I should not be surprised if it proved to be another production of the same plodding hand.[2]

---

[1] Crosnier's drawing seems to show at La Charité fragments of a screen like the one at Souvigny. Compare also the fragments of an altar reredos at Maastricht, illustrated by Ligtenberg, Taf. IV.

[2] I am indebted to Mr. Royall Tyler for having called my attention to the existence of sculptures at Ste.-Magnance.

It is a delight to turn from such troubled waters to the limpid beauty of the little relief at Bois-Ste.-Marie. I can detect no traces of Chartrain influence in this masterpiece (Ill. 142); the style seems wholly Burgundian, a development of the lyric mood already initiated in the lintel of Anzy-le-Duc (Ill. 98) now at Paray-le-Monial. The naturalism of the drawing argues a date about 1160; so satisfying a composition was hardly again achieved until Benedetto created his lunette in the Parma baptistry.

Delightful, too, is the portal at Avallon (Ill. 137–141). Of all the Chartres-esque portals of France, this is the most archaic and the most crisp. At Ivry-la-Bataille the jamb figure is more elongated (Ill. 1478), but the voussures (Ill. 1474–1477) show an art which is already Gothic in feeling, while those of Avallon are still thoroughly Romanesque. They are, indeed, closely imitated from the portal at Vézelay; and the style of the tympanum sculptures, with figures of extreme elongation, recalls works like those of the Tobias master at Vézelay (Ill. 45). Obviously this good Burgundian sculptor let himself be dazzled only to a very limited extent by the glitter of Chartres. An innovation of capital importance was the division of the portal into two halves by a central column with arches.[1] At Santiago twin portals had been used, and at Vézelay there had been introduced a trumeau (Ill. 47). At Avallon, however, there were twin arches under a single great tympanum,[2] now unfortunately destroyed.

The type of Burgundian portal initiated at Avallon was developed in the west portal of St.-Bénigne of Dijon, now entirely destroyed. From the engraving of Dom Plancher[3] (Ill. 144) we are able to reconstruct the composition. Like the destroyed tympanum of Avallon this was another derivative of the portal at Cluny, but into the *Majestas Domini* was unexpectedly projected (at least if the drawing

[1] According to Revoil, III, 22, there was an earlier example of this motive at St.-Pons; but the upper tympanum was not sculptured, whereas the two minor portals had sculptured tympana.

[2] This tympanum represented the *Majestas Domini*. St. Lazare was on the trumeau; on the jambs to the left was the Annunciation, on those to the right two prophets (Fleury, 132, citing a document of 1482). Drawings of the portals, showing three jamb figures in the central portal, and four in the side portal were published by Plancher (I, 514) in 1739.

[3] I, 503.

may be trusted) the Church and the Synagogue. The voussures were all sculptured in the Gothic manner, so the portal is presumably later than Avallon. The extreme elongation of the jamb figures has also been discarded; it is striking that they have been moved up to the top of the columns. On the trumeau was a great statue of St.-Bénigne. The head of this statue, after having been long exposed in the wall of the Hotel Gossin, has found its way into the archaeological museum at Dijon. The style (Ill. 145) shows evident kinship with the St. Andrew from the tomb of St. Lazare at Autun (Ill. 149); the Dijon portal may, therefore, be assigned to *c.* 1170.

The arches at St.-Bénigne are still all semicircular; among the sculptured Romanesque portals of Burgundy, it is only at Semur-en-Brionnais (Ill. 143) that the pointed arch appears. The composition of the Semur tympanum, like that of the tympanum at Charlieu (Ill. 108), repeats once more the formula enunciated at Cluny.

VIII

THE DIFFUSION OF CLUNIAC ART OUTSIDE
OF BURGUNDY

WE have seen that in Burgundy, and possibly at Charlieu (Ill. 4), was originated a new formula of composition for tympana. This consisted of the representation of the Deity in an aureole supported by angels. Variously embellished and amplified, the motive was constantly repeated in monuments of Burgundy.

It was, indeed, destined to spread far beyond the limits of that province, and its frequent presence in distant lands is proof of the far-reaching influence exerted by the Cluniac school of sculpture. Thus we find it in Auvergne (in more or less modified form), at Thuret (Ill. 1139), Meillers (Ill. 1251), Mars (Ill. 1140), Autry-Issard (Ill. 1141) and Mauriac (Ill. 1246); in Languedoc at St.-Chamant (Ill. 1276); in Germany in the Marktportal at Mainz,[1] and in the tympanum from Petershausen near Constance, now in the Vereinigte Sammlungen at Karlsruhe;[2] in Austria, at St. Stephen of Vienna;[3] in England at Ely,[4] Water Stratford[5] and in the south portal of Malmesbury abbey;[6] in Lombardy at Torre dei Piccenardi;[7] in Tuscany at the cathedral of Lucca (Ill. 247); in the Capitanata at S. Leonardo (Ill. 214);[8] in Catalonia at Corneilla (Ill. 528), and in a

---

[1] Illustrated by Dehio und von Bezold, XII, 12.
[2] Illustrated *ibid.*, XII, 9.
[3] Illustrated *ibid.*, XII, 12.
[4] Illustrated by Prior and Gardner, 206.
[5] Illustrated *ibid.*, 195.
[6] Illustrated in Bell's handbook, 72.
[7] Illustrated in Porter, *Lombard Architecture*, IV, Plate 115, Fig. 3.
[8] These sculptures are not as late as has been supposed. They should be classed not so much with the tympanum of S. Maria at Monte S. Angelo (Ill. 231) as with the sculptures by Acuto at Pianella in the Abruzzi (Ill. 217, 218). Indeed, I almost question whether they be not by the very hand of Acuto. Now Pianella was rebuilt after a destruction in 1158. The lintel (Ill. 218) is closely related to that of S. Clemente di Casauria (Ill. 220) which is a dated monument of 1176. The style of the sculptures at S. Leonardo is also similar to that of the master who worked upon the cathedral (Ill. 204–206, 208–211) and Ognisanti (Ill. 201–203) of Trani. The

somewhat modified form (the Labarum being substituted for the Deity in an aureole), at St.-Féliu-d'Amont (Ill. 548); in Aragon at San Juan de la Peña (Ill. 545) and with the same modification at Huesca (Ill. 529, 531, 532); and in the Basque provinces, in an even more modified form, at Armentía (Ill. 766).

The Burgundian lintel, as well as the Burgundian tympanum, was copied throughout the length and breadth of Europe. At Charlieu (Ill. 4) the motive is enunciated in its essence; here the cycle of the apostles is represented, each under the arch of an arcade. Lintels so composed had been known in Burgundy before Charlieu, since one is already found at Châteauneuf (Ill. 2); and something very like the motive occurs at St.-Genis-des-Fontaines (Ill. 513) and St.-André-de-Sorrède (Ill. 514) in the Pyrenees. Charlieu, however, appears to be the earliest instance extant in which such a lintel is placed below a tympanum.

The motive in whole or in part was repeated in various regions. At Rutigliano in Apulia (Ill. 163) it was reproduced quite exactly as early as 1108. In Germany, the portal of Petershausen, near Constance, now in the Vereinigte Sammlungen at Karlsruhe,[1] echoes all the essential parts of the Charlieu composition, except that the arcades of the lintel are omitted. In the Galluspforte at Basel, on the other hand, the composition has been entirely changed; only the fact of the lintel witnesses the survival of the Burgundian tradition.[2] In Lombardy the lintel with the arcade was taken over by Nicolò and used by him at Piacenza,[3] Ferrara [4] and S. Zeno of Verona.[5] But for the single figures of apostles which at Charlieu had been placed beneath the arches of the arcade, Nicolò substituted reliefs representing scenes usually from the life of Christ. This version of the motive was then carried back again to France at Bourg-Argental

---

bronze doors of the cathedral of Trani were made about 1175; it is absurd to suppose that the jambs can be later. All this brings us to about 1175 for the date of the S. Leonardo sculptures.

[1] Illustrated by Dehio und von Bezold, XII, 9.

[2] *Ibid.*, XII, 9.

[3] Illustrated in my *Lombard Architecture*, IV, Plate 181, Fig. 1; Plate 182, Fig. 4.

[4] Illustrated *ibid.*, Plate 89, Fig. 5.

[5] Illustrated *ibid.*, Plate 225, Fig. 2.

(Ill. 1150), Valence (Ill. 1188) and — in a frieze — at St.-Trophîme of Arles (Ill. 1374).[1]

At St.-Trophîme of Arles (Ill. 1366) and St.-Chamant (Ill. 1276) the Burgundian apostles were again reinstated in the lintel below the *Majestas Domini* of the tympanum. Thence the motive made its way, without the tympanum, to several monuments of Tuscany of the second half of the XII or the XIII century — it is found at S. Bartolommeo in Pantano (Ill. 190) and S. Pietro Maggiore (Ill. 228) of Pistoia and S. Giovanni of Lucca (Ill. 227). Only at the cathedral of Lucca (Ill. 247) is it found in connection with a tympanum.

In France, the motive made its way to Ganagobie (Ill. 1236), to Mauriac (Ill. 1247), to St.-Bertrand-de-Comminges (Ill. 323), to St.-Sernin of Toulouse (Ill. 310) and to Cahors (Ill. 422). At St.-Sernin (Ill. 310) and Mauriac (Ill. 1247) the arches are omitted, so the lintels show, perhaps, the influence of Cluny rather than of Charlieu. There is, at any rate, no doubt that the row of elders below the tympanum of Moissac (Ill. 339) is derived from Cluny, since here as there elders are substituted for apostles. At Moissac (Ill. 339) the lintel tends to be absorbed in the tympanum; at Beaulieu (Ill. 409) the reduction of the lintel was carried still further, and at St.-Denis it disappeared altogether (Ill. 1439). The lintel was, however, reinstated by the head-master at Chartres. Here we have an archaistic revival of the motive in its original Burgundian form; every essential feature of Charlieu (Ill. 4) is present, including the arches and the apostles. The only innovation was the addition of two extra figures, possibly intended to represent the witnesses of the Apocalypse.[2] These seem to be derived from the lintel of Etampes (Ill. 1462) which, together with the tympanum, forms a composition representing the Ascension, a subject in which the witnesses are regularly represented with the apostles, in accordance with the Biblical text. From Chartres the motive spread in all directions — we find it repeated in

---

[1] It was probably from Provence that the sculptor of the tomb of S. Vicente at Avila came by the motive, which he combines with Etampes canopies (Ill. 850, 851).

[2] This idea was first suggested to me by Mr. C. S. Niver.

France at Le Mans, at Bourges, at St.-Loup-de-Naud (Ill. 1492);
it formerly existed at Angers, St.-Ayoul of Provins and Ivry-la-
Bataille. It travelled as far as Sangüesa in Spain (Ill. 742), and in a
modified form to the cathedral of Genoa in Italy (Ill. 254).

In the portal of Cluny, as we have seen, a notable advance was
made over Charlieu. The tympanum was made of immense size —
sixteen feet in width. The arches in the lintel were suppressed, and
for the twelve apostles were substituted the four and twenty elders.
In the tympanum were introduced, in addition to the *Majestas
Domini* and angels, the symbols of the four evangelists.

The composition of the tympanum of Cluny was reproduced at
Moissac (Ill. 339); the only essential difference is that at Moissac,
for lack of space, some of the elders are crowded over into the tympanum. This tympanum, like that of Cluny, is of great size, whereas
the earlier tympana of Aquitaine and Spain, like St.-Sernin (Ill. 308)
and Santiago (Ill. 678–680) had been of small dimensions.

The style of the tympanum of Moissac is entirely different from
that previously practised by the sculptors of Languedoc. It is only
necessary to compare the photographs of it (Ill. 339–342) with those
of the earlier work at Moissac (Ill. 262–287) and Toulouse (Ill. 288–
322) on the one hand, and with the capitals of Cluny (Ill. 5–10) and
the tympanum of Vézelay (Ill. 47–49) on the other, to be convinced
that the sculptor, while undoubtedly influenced by local tradition,
was still essentially Cluniac. It was only in Burgundy that he could
have learned his elongated proportions, his calligraphic lines, all without precedent at Toulouse. Compare, for example, the angel to the
left in the Moissac tympanum (Ill. 340) with the Grammar of Cluny
(Ill. 6). We are at once struck by the similarity in the bend of the
figures, the tip of the heads, the movement of line, the attenuation.
The resemblance extends even to details. The folds of the drapery of
the left knees fall in the same characteristic oval lines. Now put
beside these two figures the angel in the corresponding position of the
St.-Sernin tympanum (Ill. 308). It is clear what a gulf separates
Moissac from the heavy massive art of Toulouse, and what close

bonds connect it with Cluny. The face of the Deity at Moissac (Ill. 341) is totally different from that of the Deity at St.-Sernin (Ill. 309), whereas it closely resembles the Deity in the tympanum of Vézelay (Ill. 48 a) — there are the same eyes, the same long narrow head, the same extraordinary beard with little strands ending in spirals and with moustache carried over the beard, the same convention for indicating the hair, the same nose. The broad flat folds of the Moissac draperies (Ill. 340–342) are essentially Cluniac, and entirely different from the round folds of St.-Sernin (Ill. 309, 310). The drapery edges at Moissac as, for example, on the cloak falling in the lap of the Deity (Ill. 341), are without analogy at Toulouse (Ill. 308–321), but are very similar to the draperies of Cluny — see, for example, the veil of the figure called Iron Work (Ill. 9). The striking beards of the Moissac elders (Ill. 340) are without resemblance to the beards of the St.-Sernin sculptures (Ill. 310), but are an obvious elaboration of such beards as that of the Third Tone at Cluny (Ill. 7). Even where Moissac seems to resemble St.-Sernin, it is probable that both may be derived from Cluny, for, as we shall presently see, there is no doubt that the St.-Sernin portal was influenced also by the Burgundian monastery. Thus the tipped heads of the apostles at St.-Sernin (Ill. 310) might easily seem to be the prototype of the same motive found in the elders of Moissac (Ill. 339). But Sagot's lithograph,[1] inaccurate as it is, suggests that the heads of the elders at Cluny were also tipped. Similarly, the face of the left-hand angel at Moissac (Ill. 340) seems to be a development of that of the angel in the corresponding position of the tympanum of St.-Sernin (Ill. 308). But here again the type of face seems to be Burgundian rather than Toulousan; it goes back rather to the Grammar of Cluny (Ill. 6) than to such figures as the angels of the St.-Sernin ambulatory (Ill. 297–302). Nor is the movement, which begins in the St.-Sernin tympanum (Ill. 308) and is carried much farther in the tympanum of Moissac (Ill. 339), a native growth. It had been, we have seen, one of the chief characteristics of the art of Cluny, and before that of the

---

[1] Reproduced in *Millénaire*, II, Pl. II.

miniatures of the school of Winchester. The tympanum of Moissac may therefore be considered essentially Burgundian in style.

The date of the tympanum of Moissac has been much discussed. A late chronicle calls it the work of the abbot Ansquitil (1085–1115). This statement would seem entirely credible, did not the chronicler Aymery proceed to give his reasons. These are couched in a Latin that is unintelligible;[1] the attempts to explain the passage made by modern scholars do not carry conviction, so that we are left in doubt as to what the chronicler's authority for his statement may have been, and the suspicion that it was not very good.

Above the porch is the statue of the abbot Roger (1115–1131). In the inscription the abbot is called "*beatus*"; the statue was consequently set up after his death, or after 1131. Now the style of this statue (Ill. 379) seems to differ materially from that of the porch below (Ill. 360–377); but that of the companion statue (Ill. 380) is less unlike the work on the porch. The conclusion seems justified that the statue of Roger was here placed because the porch was the work of the abbot in question, and that hence the porch was erected between 1115 and 1131.

In this connection attention should be called to the fact that in 1122 relics were translated into the abbey.[2] It may well be that the works of embellishment of which the porch was part, were undertaken in consequence of this translation.

The style of the sculptures of the porch differs notably from that of the tympanum. Although the technical details are closely copied, so as to give the work the appearance of a sort of unity, the trumeau and porch are surely by a weaker and far inferior hand. We have only to place the St. Peter of the jambs (Ill. 360) beside the angel to the left in the tympanum (Ill. 340) to perceive the superiority of the latter; the carving is crisper and more vigorous, the draperies far better understood and more competently rendered. The face of St. Peter is more advanced and naturalistic than the faces of the elders of the tympanum (Ill. 339–342); but how much more commonplace,

[1] See Mortet.   [2] Rupin, 66 f.

less characterful, less original. Compare the left arm of the St. Peter (Ill. 360) with the right arm of the Deity in the tympanum (Ill. 341); how the defects of the latter have been caricatured, its beauty lost in the poor copy. The fussy and weak border ornaments of the draperies of the St. Peter and Isaiah of the jambs (Ill. 360, 361) contrast with the strong vigorous ornaments in the tympanum (Ill. 340–342). Or compare the weak characterless faces of the Virgin and Child in the Adoration (Ill. 375) with the strong archaic beauty of the face of the angel to the left in the tympanum (Ill. 340). There can be no question that the sculptures of the porch are inferior in quality.

There are good archaeological reasons for believing that the tympanum is not now in its original position, but that it was moved from over the western portal when the existing porch was erected.[1] We must, therefore, conclude that the tympanum is earlier than the porch.

Are we justified in placing it as early as the time of Ansquitil, or before 1115? We can only arrive at a satisfactory answer to the problem by comparing it with other works of the Cluniac school to which it belongs.

When we compare the tympanum of Moissac (Ill. 339) with that of Vézelay (Ill. 47) dated 1132, we see at once that Moissac is earlier. The composition is much closer to that of Cluny; the draperies are far simpler and more Cluny-like; the manner is less extreme; the facial types less varied and less naturalistic. In the light of the much more advanced manner of Vézelay we are forced to conclude that the tympanum of Moissac can hardly be later than 1120.

Similarly, when we compare the tympanum of Moissac (Ill. 340–342) with the capitals by the "Bathsheba Master" at Vézelay (Ill. 44), a sculptor who worked on the western bays of the nave and the narthex, and who was consequently active about 1115–1132, we feel that Moissac is more archaic. There is a perfection, a refinement, a decadent quality in the work of the exquisite artist of Vézelay, which makes Moissac seem very vigorous, very primitive. It is

[1] Fleury, 91.

only when we compare the Moissac tympanum (Ill. 340–342) with the masters of the nave of Vézelay who were active before 1120, that we find real points of contact. Thus the beards of the "Vézelay Master No. 3" as, for example, in the capital representing the Mill of St. Paul (Ill. 40), are not without analogy with the beards of the Moissac elders; the facial types of this capital distinctly recall those of the Moissac elders; the faces of the Moissac angels are evidently analogous to the beardless faces of the "Cluny Master" as seen, for example, in the capitals of the Winds (Ill. 31) and of Daniel (Ill. 33).

From all this we may, I think, safely infer that the Moissac tympanum can not be very much later than 1120. Whether it be as early as 1115, and hence the work of Ansquitil, seems to me too delicate a question to be safely decided on the basis of the evidence available. Until the corrupt text of Aymery has been satisfactorily elucidated, I should not be ready to conclude that his statement is untrustworthy.

Archaeologists have probably been influenced in assigning a late date to the tympanum of Moissac by the circumstance that it is evidently contemporary with the rib vault of the porch, since the latter rests on capitals by the same hand (Ill. 337–338). It was formerly believed that the rib vault found its way into the Midi only at an advanced period of the XII century. However, the rib vault was known in Lombardy from shortly after 1040; it is found in Apulia in the church of S. Benedetto of Brindisi, begun in 1090, where it is already profiled; in 1093 the profiled form was already known at Durham in England; it is found in Brittany in the church of Ste.-Croix of Quimperlé consecrated in 1073; in Poitou, in the clocher of St.-Hilaire of Poitiers, consecrated in 1096; in Provence in the porch of St.-Victor of Marseille, which must date from the last years of the XI century, in an ornamented form in the choir of St.-Gilles, a church begun in 1116 and the façade of which was in construction c. 1140, and in the profiled form at St.-Jean of Valence, which appears to be of the first quarter of the XII century. In the Ile-de-France, the profiled form had certainly been in regular use since before 1100. The use of the unprofiled rib vault at Moissac is, therefore, no reason for believing that the tympanum could not have been sculptured about 1120, or in 1115, for that matter.

The influence of the tympanum of Cluny by no means ended with Moissac. The tympanum of Rochester in England reproduces the composition exactly.[1] There are other derivatives at Champniers,[2] Ganagobie (Ill. 1236), Sauveterre (Ill. 488) and Bourg-Argental (Ill. 1150). In the fourth decade of the XII century, an abbreviated version came into popularity. In this the angels supporting the aureole are omitted; the composition is reduced to the figure of the Deity in an aureole surrounded by the symbols of the four evangelists. An early rendering of the theme so modified seems to have existed in the Puerta Francigena at Santiago. It was this form of the motive which undoubtedly existed at St.-Gilles (Ill. 1318), although the original sculptures have been replaced by Renaissance imitations; it was repeated in several monuments derived from St.-Gilles — Arles (Ill. 1372), Vizille (Ill. 1185), Maguelonne (Ill. 1384), and the destroyed portal of Nantua. The head master of Chartres influenced doubtless by some frescoed arts of the Bawit type took the motive over and from here it ran through Europe. Thus we find it at Angers (Ill. 1501), at Issy (Ill. 1489), at St.-Loup-de-Naud (Ill. 1492), in both churches at Provins (Ill. 1490 and Ill. 1496), at Le Mans, at Bourges, at St.-Benoît-sur-Loire (Ill. 1519, 1520), at St.-Pierre-le-Moûtier (Ill. 1275), at Valcabrère (Ill. 501, 502), at St.-Aventin (Ill. 508); it formerly existed at Châlons-sur-Marne and Ivry-la-Bataille (Ill. 1474). Outside of France we find it in Spain at Tarragona (Ill. 603), at Besalú (Ill. 602), at Tudela, at Sepúlveda (Ill. 799), at Agüero (Ill. 547) and at Soria (Ill. 795); at the cathedral of Genoa (Ill. 254) in Italy, in Germany at Soest;[3] in Austria and Hungary at Lavanthal[4] and at Tischnowitz.[5]

[1] Illustrated by Prior and Gardner, 198.
[2] There is a wretched reproduction of this relief in the *Catalogue du Musée de la Société Archéologique et Historique de la Charente*, 157.
[3] Illustrated by Dehio und von Bezold, XII, 8.
[4] Hamann, 125.   [5] *Ibid.*, 126.

Another composition for the tympanum possibly invented in Burgundy was also destined to have illustrious descendants. At Anzy-le-Duc (Ill. 96) the Ascension was represented. It was a variation of the *Majestas Domini* motive, and is repeated in a very similar form at Montceaux-l'Etoile (Ill. 104), and St.-Paul-de-Varax (Ill. 88). The earliest example of this subject in a tympanum which I know is not in Burgundy, but at St.-Sernin of Toulouse (Ill. 308). The motive also found its way to Etampes (Ill. 1462). It was taken over in the northern tympanum of Chartres, a work of the Master of the Angels. The composition at Chartres approaches very closely that at Etampes; but it is certain that the Master of the Angels knew, and knew well, the tympanum of Anzy-le-Duc (Ill. 97). It is thence that his angels of the southern tympanum are derived. The angels of the northern tympanum must also be of Burgundian origin.

It must then be admitted that Burgundian tympana in general, and the tympanum of Cluny in particular, exerted an enormous influence upon the art of Europe. Shall we go still farther and say that all tympana, that the motive of the tympanum itself, is thence derived? It has recently been claimed that the sculptured tympanum is a French invention, and that all sculptured tympana are to be classed as French, all portals without tympana as Italian.

Such assertions are not comforted by the facts. The motive of the sculptured tympanum originated neither in France nor in Italy; it is found in the East from a very early period, as, for example, in the portal of Daschlut [1] now in the Cairo Museum. It was from the Orient that it came to Italy and France and Spain as well. The sculptured tympanum of the north portal of the cathedral at Borgo S. Donnino [2] is as little French as the tympanum-less portals of the cathedral of Reims are Italian.

The portal of Cluny must be credited with an important part in spreading through Europe the motive of the elders. There is an earlier rendering of the subject in sculpture on a capital of the clois-

[1] Illustrated by Strzygowski, *Hell. und Kopt. Kunst,* 22.
[2] Illustrated in my *Lombard Architecture,* IV, Plate 29, Fig. 5.

ter of Santo Domingo de Silos (Ill. 668), so that the popularity of
the theme is evidently not entirely due to Cluny; there can, however,
be little question that its use on the portal of Cluny was observed
and copied by sculptors in widely separated regions.

This motive of the elders seems to have originated in Roman
mosaics. It appeared in the arch of triumph of S. Paolo f. l. m. in
440; it was repeated in the apse arch of S. Prassede, 817–824, and
in the frescos of Castel S. Elia in the first half of the XI century.
The composition of the Cluny portal, with a lunette above, and
a base band beneath, recalls Roman mosaics, like the apse of S.
Prassede. A certain influence of Roman mosaics upon French
sculpture must be admitted. The tympanum of Senlis appears to
have been inspired by the apse of S. Maria in Trastevere. The four
figures in the spandrels at Cluny recall the six in the spandrels at S.
Clemente, which is the earliest example I know of this persistent
motive.

At S. Paolo and S. Prassede, the elders had been represented bare-
headed and bare-footed, carrying their crowns in their hands. At
Castel S. Elia they still stand erect, or rather move slowly in stately
procession, and they are bare-footed; but their crowns are on their
heads, and in their right hands they carry a chalice on a veil. In the
capital of Santo Domingo de Silos of the last third of the XI century
(Ill. 668) they are still erect, but they carry not chalices, but musical
instruments and phials. At Cluny they were erect and carried musical instruments.[1] They were represented on the destroyed Arca of
St.-Gilles, and must here have carried musical instruments, for the
inscription preserved in the *Pilgrim's Guide* contained the line:
Dulcia qui citharis decantant cantica claris. On the tomb of St.-
Junien (Ill. 450) the elders are seated and carry musical instruments
and phials. This iconography perhaps originated in Beatus manuscripts like that of St.-Sever, in which elders of this type are associated with the Apocalyptic Vision. Such miniatures may have
influenced the iconography and even the composition of the tym-

[1] Terret, in *Millénaire*, II, 3.

pana of Cluny and Moissac, although I can detect no stylistic
affinities. At Moissac (Ill. 339) the elders are seated, crowned,
bare-footed, and they hold chalices and musical instruments. In
the upper gallery at Parthenay (Ill. 1055, 1056) they were erect,
and held phials and musical instruments. The veiled hands recall
Castel S. Elia, and foreshadow Chartres. At Airvault and Anzy-
le-Duc (Ill. 96) the elders were represented upon the voussures of
the portal. The motive is developed in the portal of Parthenay
(Ill. 1048, 1051); from this model it found its way to the Ile-de-
France, to St.-Denis (Ill. 1439), to Etampes (Ill. 1461) and to
Chartres. Like everything at Chartres, the voussures with the
elders were imitated. They were repeated almost literally at Angers
(Ill. 1502), at Avallon (Ill. 137, 138). Meanwhile in the West, a
new form of the motive had been developed. At Ste.-Croix of
Bordeaux (Ill. 920), at Aulnay (Ill. 979) and at Varaize (Ill. 1001),
the elders are placed in the voussures, but turned at right angles,
so as to radiate. This version became especially popular in Spain.
We find it at Soria (Ill. 797), at Sepúlveda (Ill. 800), at Toro (Ill.
735), at Carrión de los Condes and in the Pórtico de la Gloria of
Santiago (Ill. 824–828). At Morlaas, Oloron-Ste.-Marie (Ill. 461),
and St.-Guilhem-le-Désert (Ill. 1400–1402), the Santiago version of
the theme was repeated. The processions of the elders at Ripoll (Ill.
585) and S. Isidoro of Léon (Ill. 696) are not derived from Chartres,
but more probably from Cluny directly.

The motive of spandrel figures, which we have seen, came to the
portal of Cluny from Roman mosaics,[1] spread from Cluny to the
School of the Pilgrimage. It seems probable that the portals of
Santiago were influenced by the Burgundian monastery. In the
destroyed Puerta Francigena, the composition of the tympanum
which represented Christ in an aureole surrounded by the evangelists
was perhaps derived from Cluny. The spandrel figures which still
exist in the Puerta de las Platerias (Ill. 675–677) I suppose to have
come from the same source. At Cluny we know that the spandrel

---

[1] See above, p. 142.

figures represented the four apostles James, Peter, Paul and John. The *Pilgrim's Guide* tells us that at Santiago three of these — James, Peter, John — reappeared. There can, therefore, be no question of the relationship. This same motive found its way subsequently to St.-Sernin of Toulouse (Ill. 311, 312), S. Isidoro of Léon (Ill. 696, 697, 700, 701), S. Salvador of Leire (Ill. 712–714) and La Madeleine of Châteaudun (Ill. 1425). It was later taken over by Nicolò in Lombardy, and repeated at Piacenza,[1] Ferrara,[2] the cathedral[3] and S. Zeno[4] of Verona. Angels were substituted for prophets in the destroyed metal altar-piece of the abbey of Stavelot, in Belgium, dating from soon after 1130, and known from a drawing reproduced by Helbig.[5] Angels in the spandrels of arches also appear at Bourg-Argental (Ill. 1149), Notre-Dame of Etampes (Ill. 1460) and S. Niccola of Bari (Ill. 200).

At Cluny, in the inner row of voussures were sculptured under little arches the figures of fourteen angels in adoration, and in the centre, Christ, also under a little arch.[6] In the third voussures were sculptured a series of heads in medallions.[7] It seems probable that we have here the prototype of the motive of voussure sculptures developed in the West into forms of such loveliness.

The angels' heads, without the little arches, were reproduced in Apulia, in the archivolt of the cathedral of Monopoli (Ill. 158–162) begun in 1107. At Conversano in Apulia (Ill. 179) the motive of heads in medallions is also introduced in the archivolt. This portal is a dated monument of 1159–1174.[8]

---

[1] Ilustrated in Porter, *Lombard Architecture*, IV, Plate 181, Fig. 1.
[2] Illustrated *ibid.*, Plate 88, Fig. 3.
[3] Illustrated *ibid.*, Plate 217, Fig. 5.
[4] Illustrated *ibid.*, Plate 225, Fig. 2.   [5] 56.
[6] La première archivolte qui couronnait le bas-relief se composait d'une suite de petits cintres, sous chacun desquels étaient des anges en adoration, hors dans celui du milieu qu'occupait le Père éternel. (Lorain.)
[7] Deux autres archivoltes concentriques à la précédente présentaient la première des feuillages, et la seconde, des médaillons d'où sortaient des têtes toutes variées d'expression. '(*Ibid.*)
[8] The dates were misread 1369 and 1373 by Schulz, I, 94. The inscription is:
† A. D. M. C. LIX. PSES ECCLIA. CU. EI'. ALIS. ICEPTA FUIT.
PSIDETE. DÑO. P. DE ITO. EPO CVP(ER)SAÑ. PTER. T. T. IPI' ECC.
ET FINITA. TEPOR. EIUSDE. A. M. C. LXXIIII. Q. FIERI FE
CIT. P(RO)RIS. SUPTIB. HOSPICIU. NOUU. SIC. P(RO)TEDIT. A. CAPPE

The archivolt of Calvenzano in Lombardy [1] has radiating compartments like those of the tympanum of Vézelay (Ill. 47–49) also suggesting proto-voussures. The style of Calvenzano is, however, far more primitive than that of Vézelay, being, indeed, allied to that of the sculptures in another Cluniac priory of Lombardy, Pontida.[2] The latter are dated 1095. Pontida, in turn, seems to be stylistically related to the capital of the nave of Cluny (Ill. 10).

The heads in medallions of the third archivolt of the portal at Cluny reappear in the archivolt at Bourg-Argental (Ill. 1149). Evidently then the sculptor of this remarkable portal knew Cluny. The zodiac of his outer archivolt is placed under little arches, precisely as had been the angels of the Cluny archivolt. Clearest proof of all, the composition of the tympanum with the *Majestas Domini* and angels is clearly derived from the tympanum of Cluny.

But Cluny was far from being all that the sculptor of Bourg-Argental knew. The figures in relief at the summits of his archivolts have a curiously Catalan air, and bring to mind the much later work at Agramunt (Ill. 633).

It is, however, with the work of the Lombard sculptor Nicolò that the Bourg-Argental portal shows the most striking analogies. The very idea of a porch in relief, supported on columns rising above the archivolts, is without analogy in France, but is an evident modification of the Lombard porch used by Nicolò at Piacenza,[3] at Ferrara[4] and at the cathedral[5] and S. Zeno[6] of Verona.[7] The rinceau and

LLA. IPI'. HOSPICII. USQ. AD. ECCLIA. ET MLTA. ALIA. BNFIA.
FECIT. ITUS. ET. EX. CIUITATE. CUIUS. ANIMA. REQUIE
SCAT. I. PAC. AMEN.

[1] Illustrated in Porter, *Lombard Architecture*, IV. Plate 42, Fig. 7.

[2] Illustrated in Porter, *Lombard Architecture*, Plate 189, Fig. 1, 2.

[3] The work of Nicolò at Piacenza is illustrated in my *Lombard Architecture*, Plate 181, Fig. 1; Plate 182, Fig. 4.

[4] Illustrated *ibid.*, Plate 88, Fig. 1, 2, 3; Plate 89, Fig. 3, 4, 5.

[5] Illustrated *ibid.*, Plate 217, Fig. 1, 2, 3, 5.

[6] Illustrated *ibid.*, Plate 225, Fig. 2; Plate 227, Fig. 4; Plate 229, Fig. 2, 3, 4; Plate 234, Fig. 3.

[7] The porch at Bourg really resembles the Apulian porch of S. Niccola at Bari (Ill. 200) more closely than any of the Lombard examples, not only because of the angels in the spandrels (see above, p. 144), but also because the columns are carried to the level of the top of the archivolts, whereas in Lombardy the capitals are at the level of the imposts of the archivolts. The columns are however restored.

guilloche beneath the lintel are very similar in feeling to those of the Ferrara and Verona portals. The lintel is divided into a series of arcades by little arches supported on colonnettes, and in these arcades are sculptured reliefs. Now this motive, we have already seen, is characteristic of the work of Nicolò, being found at Piacenza, at Ferrara and at S. Zeno of Verona,[1] but is exceedingly rare in France.[2] Moreover, the analogies in the execution of this series of reliefs in arcades at Bourg and in the works of Nicolò are close. Thus in the spandrels of the arches at Bourg are little circular turrets; these reappear at both Ferrara and Piacenza. In both cases the colonnettes of the arcade are decorated with diaper patterns; now the spiral which occurs on the two extreme colonnettes at Bourg is the same as that on the colonnette between the Baptism and the Flight at Piacenza. The second, fourth and fifth colonnettes at Bourg have a pattern of interlacing strings; so has the colonnette in the midst of the Piacenza Temptation. The Adoration of the Magi at Bourg is the only subject which is given more space than a single arcade; it runs over into three. Similarly at Ferrara the same subject is the only one accorded more than a single arcade. The iconography of Bourg follows incident for incident that of the north portal at Piacenza, with, however, the peculiarity, common in mediaeval copies, that the composition is reversed. The Visitation at Bourg reproduces line for line the Visitations at Piacenza and especially at Ferrara;[3] the posture of the arms, the placing of the figures, even the facial types are the same. The Virgin in the Adoration at Bourg is a reversal of the Virgin in the same subject at Piacenza. In the scene of the Nativity, the Christ Child appears in the same cradle, wrapped in the same swaddling clothes, and below the same ox and ass at Ferrara and at Bourg. Inscriptions are placed on the horizontal bands dividing or limiting the composition at both Bourg and Pia-

---

[1] See above, p. 133.

[2] The only analogy I know north of the Alps is the font at Hulla, illustrated by Roosval, Taf. XII.

[3] The same composition is found on a capital of Gargilesse (Ill. 83) and on the voussures of St.-Loup-de-Naud (Ill. 1492).

cenza. The horse of the magi at Bourg repeats line for line the horse of the Flight in the Piacenza archivolt, except in the head, where the inferior sculptor found himself unable to copy his model. Finally, the important motive of jamb sculptures, which is one of the most striking characteristics of the Bourg portal, is also found in Nicolò's jambs at Ferrara and the cathedral of Verona.

A hand as crabbed and constipated as that which we have learned to know in the portal at Bourg-Argental — if indeed it be not the same — reappears in the lintel now in the wall adjoining the façade of the church of St.-Martin-d'Ainay at Lyon. There is the same jerky dividing up of the lintel into separate compositions; the same use of arcades; the same square undercutting; the same puggy faces; the same scratched draperies. The Lyon relief shows, however, less evidently the influence of Cluny and Nicolò.

Are we to conclude from this that the sculptor of Bourg was a native of Lyon or of the Rhône valley? The fact that this relief is the only work in the region related to his style would seem to indicate that such is not the case. The capitals of the choir of St.-Martin-d'Ainay belong to the church consecrated in 1107; they are rough works [1] obviously influenced by Guglielmo da Modena, and not without points of contact with the capitals of Gofridus at Chauvigny (Ill. 904, 905) and the sculptures of Ste.-Radegonde of Poitiers (Ill. 907–911). Except, however, for the common fact of crudity and Lombard influence, they show no points of contact with the portal at Bourg, which must be besides some thirty years later. The capitals of the nave at St.-Martin-d'Ainay are polished works of the school of Burgundy, at the opposite pole from Bourg. Nor do the sculptures of the Manécanterie at Lyon (Ill. 1243, 1244) offer analogies with those of our sculptor. The Bourg artist has, therefore, little connection with the school of Lyon.

To understand the real character of this sculptor, we must imagine him divested of the superficial elements which he evidently absorbed from the study of highly polished works like the portal of Cluny and

[1] Good illustrations in the *Cong. Arch.*, LXXIV, 530, 532.

the sculptures of Nicolò. It is reasonable to suppose that from such masterpieces he must have borrowed not only the formulae of certain compositions, but also details of style, the handling of draperies, a certain restraint. Now if we imagine the sculptor of the Bourg portal stripped of the Cluniac and Nicolò-esque influences, we should have left a personality strangely like that of the master of the cloisters of S. Orso at Aosta.[1] The all-over decoration applied to the colonnettes at Bourg (Ill. 1149) recalls the decorated columns characteristic of the Aosta school, and found, for example, in the pulpit at Isola S. Giulio.[2] The strong classic feeling in the cornice of the Bourg portal is analogous to the classic feeling in the pulpit. Many technical details are common both to the Aosta cloisters and the Bourg portal. Thus the curious little trick of finishing the lower end of the sleeve with a series of concentric rings like bracelets occurs on the right arm of Rebecca at Aosta, and on the right arm of the Deity at Bourg-Argental; the same strange hair convention appears in the Jacob at Aosta and in the Deity at Bourg; the beards of the same two figures are exactly alike; so, too, the moustache and the mouth; the same widely spreading broad noses are found in both; Jacob's skirts at Aosta resemble those of the Deity and first magus at Bourg; the convention for the eyes is precisely the same in both works, and different from any other, to the extent of my knowledge, in mediaeval art; the cowl of Rebecca at Aosta is not without points of contact with the cowl of Elizabeth at Bourg. The figure of Nebuchadnezzar eating grass on one of the capitals of Bourg is particularly close to the figures at Aosta. The most convincing similarity of all, however, is a certain feeling of the personality of the artist, a comic uncouthness, a jerkiness, which is toned down at Bourg by the influence of more refined sculptors, but which still shows through, while it is unrestrained at Aosta.[3]

[1] Illustrated in my *Lombard Architecture*, IV, Plate 13, Fig. 1, 3; Plate 14, Fig. 1, 2, 3; Plate 15, Fig. 3.

[2] I have illustrated this pulpit in the *American Journal of Archaeology*, 1920, XXIV, 126. It was, I suppose, from Lombardy that the motive found its way to St.-Denis (Ill. 1443, 1444).

[3] Before leaving Bourg-Argental and the subject of Italian influences in France, I take advantage of the opportunity to add two notes to the study of the style of Nicolò which I have already published in my *Lombard Architecture* (I, 277 f.). The first is that the draperies of

Let us now return to the study of the influence exerted by the sculpture of Cluny.

It should be remarked that the folds falling in broad ovals over the legs in the Grammar (Ill. 6) of Cluny reappear in the tomb of Widukind at Herford in Germany.[1] This tomb Creutz has shown dates from the very beginning of the XII century. It gives then another proof of the early date of Cluny. The shoes and sloping shelf beneath the feet of the Herford figure, as well as the arch in which he is placed, recall not Cluny but Santo Domingo de Silos (Ill. 669–673). The horizontal lines on the shelf are analogous to the Moissac cloister reliefs (Ill. 262–273).

The broad folds of the drapery to the right of the Externstein[2] seem to show the influence of Cluny. The figure of God above to the left is distinctly Burgundian, and already suggests the manner of Montceaux-l'Etoile (Ill. 104). The Externstein is a dated monument of 1115.

The influence of Burgundy soon spread to Auvergne. The sculptured capitals of the ambulatories of Clermont-Ferrand, Issoire, St.-Nectaire, Volvic, merely repeat the motive initiated at Cluny. The horizontal band running about the capital at Issoire representing the Last Supper (Ill. 1214), formed by the table, and cutting the capital in two parts, is a reminiscence of the capital of the Tones at Cluny (Ill. 8). The virtues of the Psychomachia capital at Clermont-Ferrand (Ill. 1182) are copies of the Prudence of Cluny. We have already seen[3] that the St. Sebastian capital at St.-Nectaire is a copy of the capital of the Tones at Cluny (Ill. 7). At Gargilesse (Ill. 82, 83) and St.-Révérien (Ill. 100–103) are sculptures completely Bur-

---

Nicolò at S. Zeno of Verona, executed in 1138, already show the influence of those of St.-Denis, begun in 1137 — a remarkable example of the celerity with which artistic ideas were transmitted across Europe in the XII century. The second is that the composition of Nicolò's reliefs at S. Zeno, especially the Creation of Eve and the Creation of the Animals, is analogous to the Salerno altar-frontal.

[1] Illustrated by Creutz, Taf. III, b.

[2] Illustrated *ibid.*, Taf. V.

[3] See above, p. 94.

gundian in style. They are both among the inspired productions of mediaeval art.

In the museum at Toulouse are preserved fragments coming from the destroyed cloister of St.-Etienne (Ill. 434–449). These consist of five capitals and twelve reliefs representing the apostles. The reliefs originally belonged to the jambs of the portal of the chapter-house. There are four pairs coupled together, and four single figures. An old drawing[1] seems to show that there was a pair and two single figures on either jamb; the position of the remaining two pairs of figures is not indicated, and it is far from being certain how far the drawing is to be trusted. St. Andrew and St. Thomas (Ill. 434) are distinguished among the apostles by inscriptions with their names; St. Peter (Ill. 440) may be recognized by his keys; the apostle coupled with him carrying a book (Ill. 440) may be St. Paul; and St. Philip carries a cross with a double bar (Ill. 443). The others can not be identified.

The two labelled statues of St. Andrew and St. Thomas were also signed. Each bore at the base an inscription with the name of *Gilabertus* — Gilbert. These inscriptions have been broken away with the exception of the initial letter "G," but are known from copies in old catalogues of the museum.[2]

The hand of Gilbert may be found not only in the two signed statues of the Toulouse museum. The Virgin of the Cloister at Solsona in Catalonia (Ill. 552) is in my opinion also his work.[3]

If we compare this Virgin (Ill. 552) with the Toulouse *St. Thomas* (Ill. 436), we perceive that the facial type is similar — both heads are imprinted with the same grave beauty. The drawing of the eye in the two is identical. The right hand of the Solsona Virgin is the same as the right hand of the Toulouse *St. Thomas*. In both the gar-

---

[1] Nodier, Taylor et de Cailleux, *Languedoc*, Pl. 29–30.

[2] In the catalogue of 1818 the inscriptions are given: (under the St. Thomas) Gilabertus me fecit (87); (under the St. Andrew) Vir non incertus me celavit Gilabertus (88). The inscriptions are given in the same form in the two catalogues of du Mège of 1828 (107, 310) and 1835 (200) and in that of Roschach of 1865.

[3] This statue has been published by Riu, who believed it to be a work of the VIII century.

ments are trimmed with an elaborate border; [1] now the pattern of this border consisting of circles in squares with a border of dots is the same in the border running diagonally over the *Virgin's* breast, and the neck band of the *St. Thomas*. The draperies are extraordinarily alike; in both the surface is covered with a net-work of fine lines; the peculiar and characteristic folds of the right shin of the *St. Thomas* and the left shin of the *St. Andrew* are but slightly varied on the left shin of the *Virgin;* the folds of the draperies on the *Virgin's* right knee are like those below *St. Andrew's* left hand; the draperies of *St. Andrew's* right sleeve are repeated on the thigh of the Child at Solsona; all three figures have the same narrow, sloping shoulders.

When we turn to the remaining apostles of the St.-Etienne series with the knowledge of the personality of Gilbert gained from these three statues, it is at once clear that they are not by his hand. We have only to put the *St. Philip* (Ill. 443) beside the real works of Gilbert to perceive how utterly different and how much inferior it is. The refinement and delicacy of Gilbert are at the opposite pole from the rough vigour of this Toulousan master. This same inferior hand appears in the apostle now beside the *St. Philip* (Ill. 443). The head of this figure (Ill. 442) is an attempted imitation of the head of Gilbert (Ill. 436); but how weak in comparison! It is clear, therefore, that in the apostles of St.-Etienne we have two sculptors at work — Gilbert who did with his own hand the *St. Andrew* and the *St. Thomas;* and a Toulousan assistant who did the *St. Philip* and the companion apostle.

The remaining apostles at Toulouse are the work of the inferior master, who, however, consciously imitated Gilbert. It is probable that Gilbert even personally touched up in places the work of his companion, just as the head master at Chartres touched up the work of the St.-Gilles master, and the draperies of the Etampes master (for example, the lower part of the inner figure of the north jamb of

---

[1] Such borders to garments hardly appear in French sculpture before the time of Gilbert. They are, however, of much more ancient origin, since they are found in the art of the Far East from a very early period.

the northern portal). Thus at Toulouse in the *St. Peter* (Ill. 440) and the *St. Paul* (Ill. 440) border ornaments such as we have learned to recognize as characteristic of Gilbert are introduced; on the left-hand edge of *St. Peter's* drapery is the same ornament of little dots as in the corresponding positions of the *St. Andrew* (Ill. 434) and the *St. Thomas* (Ill. 436); the drapery of *St. Peter's* right thigh repeats that of the right thigh of *St. Thomas*; the zig-zags in which it ends are identical; the draperies of *St. Peter's* right shin are like those of *St. Thomas'* right shin; the curious little zig-zag ornament on the folds is the same. The folds of *St. Peter's* under-garment are the same as those in the corresponding position of *St. Thomas*. Yet we have only to compare the hands, or the faces, or the proportions or the composition of the *St. Peter* and *St. Paul* with the *St. Andrew* and the *St. Thomas*, to perceive that the former can not be by Gilbert, but must on the contrary be by his assistant, working, however, under his direction, and perhaps with his help.

A similar problem is offered by the capitals of St.-Etienne (Ill. 444–449). These, like the apostles, show a sliding scale of style. That representing the Passion of the Baptist (Ill. 446) is most like Gilbert; then that representing the Wise Virgins (Ill. 445); the others somewhat less so. The evidences of relationship between these capitals and the style of Gilbert are numerous and striking. The facial types are similar; the draperies in both cases are indicated by a net-work of fine lines; the garments have the same borders as those of Gilbert; the crown of Herod is not unlike that of the Virgin of Solsona (Ill. 552); the sceptre of the Virgin at Solsona is identical with that of the Virgin of the Toulouse Adoration (Ill. 447); the beaded slipper of the Solsona Virgin reappears in the Toulouse Salome (Ill. 446); the star-inscribed halos of the capitals are like those of Gilbert's assistant (Ill. 436–443).[1]

[1] This motive was probably of Byzantine origin, and found its way into the art of China and Japan as well as into that of the Occident. It was very widely diffused in Europe. We find it, for example, in the Ada gospels of Trèves, Bib. de la Ville, No. 22, illustrated by Boinet, Pl. VIII; in the IX century Gospel of Lorsch, Rome, Vat. Pal. Lat., 50, illustrated *ibid.*, Pl. XVII; in the IX century Gospel of St.-Médard of Soissons, Bib. Nat. lat. 8850, illustrated by Boinet,

Nevertheless, these capitals are all of inferior quality to the authentic work of Gilbert, and must, I think, be the work of another
assistant working under his direction. The Wise Virgins (Ill. 444),
for example, display a heavy stocky character, which is certainly not
that of Gilbert's figures. The heads are too big, the legs are too short.
The square hunchy shoulders of the second virgin from the left
contrast strongly with Gilbert's slim slinking shoulders. The legs of
the virgins, especially those which are crossed, seem to lack knees;
they are round and heavy, very different from Gilbert's slender,
well-articulated legs. The handling of the drapery is heavy and
stupid; the folds are meaningless copies of Gilbert's formulae, not
understood; the attack entirely lacks Gilbert's crispness. The
clumsy hands are not Gilbert's hands, and are too large for the
bodies.

The hand of this assistant of Gilbert's may, I think, be recognized
in the tomb of St.-Junien (Ill. 450–452). The Virgin here (Ill. 451)
recalls the Virgin of Solsona (Ill. 552) and that of the Adoration of
the St.-Etienne capital (Ill. 447). Her bordered garment falls diagonally across her breast, like that of Herod in the St.-Etienne capital
of the Passion of the Baptist (Ill. 446). She holds a sceptre of the
same peculiar form as the sceptres of the Virgins of the St.-Etienne
Adoration (Ill. 447) and of Solsona (Ill. 552). The posture of the
figure is identical, except that the legs are a little more widely spread
apart. All three Virgins are alike in that the Child is not held directly in front, as was usual in the XII century, but naturalistically,
to one side, as in an Italian Quattrocento Madonna. The folds of
the drapery are very similar; the borders of the garments of the St.-
Junien *Christ* (Ill. 452) have ornamented bands. The Virgin at St.-
Junien (Ill. 451) has a star-inscribed halo, like the saints at Toulouse.
The faces are of the same type. The colonnettes of the St.-Junien

Pl. XXI; in a Carlovingian ivory of the IX century in the British Museum, illustrated by
Dalton, Pl. XXII, 42; in the frescos of the ceiling of Bjeresjö, illustrated by Roosval, Taf. LX;
in the tympanum of the Cäcilienkirche at Cologne (illustrated by Clemen, 788); in the Grab-
stein der hl. Plektrudus (illustrated *ibid.*, 789); in the archivolts of S. Marco at Venice, at
Bamberg, in Nicolò's sculptures at Ferrara, at Bourg-Argental, in the vault sculptures of
Crouzilles, etc.

tomb are ornamented with the same patterns as the colonnettes of Nicolò's architraves; and we shall see that there is obvious connection between the art of Nicolò and that of Gilbert's assistant at Toulouse. The beards of the elders at St.-Junien are some of them of the same type as Gilbert's *St. Thomas*. The drapery of the left knee of the elder in the top row to the left at St.-Junien is precisely like the drapery of the left knee of the *Virgin* at Solsona. The folds between the legs of the elder to the right in the upper row at St.-Junien are identical with those between the legs of the Solsona *Virgin*.

There can therefore be no doubt of the close relationship of the tomb of St.-Junien to the atelier of Gilbert. On the other hand, it can not be by the master himself. We have only to put the photographs of the tomb (Ill. 450–452) beside those of the authentic works of Gilbert (Ill. 434–436, 479, 552) to perceive what a great difference in quality separates the two. The dry plodding execution at St.-Junien is far inferior to that of either the Solsona *Virgin* or the Toulouse *St. Andrew* and *St. Thomas*. The character of the carving is different; the draperies are clumsier, the facial types less clarified.

Now in all these points in which the tomb of St.-Junien differs from the manner of Gilbert, it resembles that of his assistant on the capitals of St.-Etienne.

In fact, if we make mental abstraction of the touches by Gilbert on the St.-Etienne capitals (Ill. 444–447) and compare what is left with the St.-Junien tomb (Ill. 450–452), we shall perceive how very much alike the two are. The rounded jointless knees of the St.-Etienne Wise Virgins (Ill. 444) which impressed us as being so un-Gilbertian, are entirely matched by the upper angels about the aureole of the Virgin at St.-Junien (Ill. 451). The crown of the Virgin at St.-Junien (Ill. 451) is exactly the crown of the Herod on the front face of the St.-Etienne capital of the Passion of the Baptist (Ill. 446). The convention of representing the lower sleeve by a series of rings, unthinkable in Gilbert, occurs constantly both at St.-Junien (*e.g.*, on the sleeves of the Virgin — Ill. 451 —) and on the Toulouse capitals (*e.g.*, on the right sleeve of the Wise Virgin to the right of Ill. 444). The stupid wattling of the sleeve of the Christ at St.-Junien (Ill. 452) or of the figure with the "pudding cap" in the St.-Etienne capital of the Passion of the Baptist (Ill. 446) is equally discordant with the manner of Gilbert. The facial types are precisely the same at St.-Junien and in the St.-Etienne capitals, flabbier and less characterful than those of Gilbert. The draperies, the hair and beard conventions, the petalled halos, the drawing of the hands are all the same at St.-Junien and in the St.-Etienne capitals. It seems, therefore, clear that the capitals of St.-Etienne are by the St.-Junien Master, with a few retouches by Gilbert.

Comte de Lasteyrie, in studying the tomb of St.-Junien, which he assigned to the school of the West,[1] wrote of it: "C'est une oeuvre d'un style remarquable, s'il est vrai qu'elle a été exécutée par ordre du prévôt Ramnulfe au commencement du XIIe siècle."[1] In view of the sad results which have come about from following theory rather than documents I am sorry to have to confess that in this case I entirely share the eminent archaeologist's mistrust of the evidence of a late chronicle. It is difficult for me to believe that the tomb of St.-Junien can be earlier than about the middle of the XII century.

When we compare the Virgin of St.-Junien (Ill. 451) with the Virgin of Marseille (Ill. 1284) dated 1122, we note a marked resemblance, especially in the facial types. The Marseille Virgin however seems stiffer, more mannered, more archaic. It seems as if the St.-Junien Virgin must be notably more advanced, hence later than 1122.

The St.-Junien tomb must be later than the St.-Etienne capitals. The Chartrain and Burgundian character, which is its most striking characteristic, can only be due to the influence of Gilbert. There is nothing in Languedoc from which it could have sprung. Neither Moissac (Ill. 360–380) nor Beaulieu (Ill. 409–420) nor St.-Antonin (Ill. 358, 359) nor the tympanum of Conques (Ill. 392–401) has anything similar to show.[2] The facial types are obviously of Gilbertian

[1] 666.

[2] It is only in the Annunciation of the transept at Conques (Ill. 386) that we find draperies which tend towards something of the same character. But even here the difference is so great as to be unbridgeable. The draperies of the Conques Annunciation (Ill. 386) are derived from

inspiration, as are also many details of the [style at St.-Junien, such as the petalled halos, the borders of the garments, the sceptre of the Virgin, the drawing of the feet of the Christ, the position of the Child. Since the St.-Etienne capitals are not anterior to the fifth decade of the XII century, we are forced to conclude that the St.-Junien tomb can not be earlier than 1150.

If, indeed, we compare the tomb of St.-Junien (Ill. 450–452) with the fragments of what must have been a tomb very similar in composition at St.-Sernin (Ill. 296–305), we shall perceive at once what a wide gap stylistically separates the two. Now the St.-Sernin tomb we have seen really does date from the early years of the XII century. It is clear that St.-Junien must be at least half a century later.

The canopies over the elders on the St.-Junien tomb (Ill. 450) are totally different from the canopies of the early XII century, as, for example, those of the cloisters of Moissac (Ill. 262–273), a dated monument of 1100. They are more elaborate than those of the façade of St.-Denis, a monument of 1137–1140 (Ill. 1441, 1442), or of the Arca of Santo Domingo de Silos which dates from about 1150. They are, on the other hand, very similar to those of Cahors (Ill. 427), which date from the sixth decade of the XII century. This is another indication that the St.-Junien tomb dates from shortly after 1150.

Still another train of reasoning leads us to the same result. The draperies of the St.-Junien tomb are very like the work in the side portals at St.-Gilles. The curious folds about the breast of the Virgin at St.-Junien (Ill. 451) are singularly like those about the breasts of the Synagogue (Ill. 1385) in the St.-Gilles tympanum of the Crucifixion. The girdle of the Virgin at St.-Junien is very like the girdle of the St. John in the St.-Gilles tympanum (Ill. 1385). The movement of the St.-Junien angels is like that of the St.-Gilles Synagogue. The folds about the knee of the St. John in the St.-Gilles tympanum (Ill. 1385) recall those about the knee of the St.-Junien Christ (Ill. 452). The feeling of the draperies throughout the later work at St.-Gilles

the Puerta de las Platerias at Santiago (Ill. 675–693), which is also the ultimate source for the Gilbertian draperies in part at least.

is very like that of St.-Junien. It is certain that there must be a close connection between the two. There are, it seems to me, good reasons for believing that the side portals at St.-Gilles are later than the central part of the façade and may in fact date from as late as about 1180. St.-Junien can, therefore, hardly be earlier than 1150.

The tomb of St.-Junien belongs indeed to an art which is widely diffused, the roots of which perhaps spring from Burgundy and which was elaborated in southern France about the middle of the XII century. In addition to the monuments already mentioned, Nantua in Dauphiné (Ill. 1214 a), the southern portal of S. Salvatore in Lucca (Ill. 225), the lintel of S. Giovanni Fuorcivitas in Pistoia (Ill. 199) dated 1162, and the work of Benedetto in Lombardy (last quarter of the XII century) are closely related.

Another assistant of Gilbert seems to have accompanied him into Catalonia. A column of the cloister of Solsona, which has given its name to Gilbert's Virgin, is sculptured with four engaged figures (Ill. 551). These are obviously related to the apostles of St.-Etienne, but are by the hand neither of Gilbert nor of any of the assistants who worked with him on the Toulouse jamb figures. Yet it is obviously a production of the atelier of Gilbert. The draperies over the heads of the female figures of the Solsona column are exactly like the draperies on the heads of the Toulouse virgins (Ill. 444). The faces are the same, with the same small eyes, the same round cheeks; the leaf of the capital overhanging the figures recalls the niche in which stand the Toulouse apostles; there are the same folds of the draperies, executed in the same heavy way as in the St.-Junien tomb (Ill. 450–452).

The question remains whether the Gilbert of Toulouse can be identified with the Gilbert whom we have already learned to know at Autun.

It must be granted, to begin with, that the manner of the Gilbert of Toulouse shows little connection with the style of Languedoc. His delicacy, his refinement are totally unlike any works produced by that school. We have only to compare his apostles at St.-Etienne

(Ill. 434) or his Virgin at Solsona (Ill. 552) with the tympanum of St.-Sernin (Ill. 309) or with that already largely Burgundian one of Moissac (Ill. 340–342) to be convinced of the fact. He was a foreigner at Toulouse, who introduced a strange and new style, unrelated to what had gone before.

Now as completely as Gilbert's style differs from that of Languedoc, does it resemble that of Autun.

Let us place Gilbert of Autun's capital representing the angel appearing to Peter (Ill. 79), beside Gilbert of Toulouse's *St. Thomas* (Ill. 436). We perceive that the facial types are identical. The beard and hair conventions are very similar. The drapery on the right leg of the Toulouse figure, and which we have seen is one of the most persistent mannerisms in the work of Gilbert of Toulouse, is identical with that on the left leg of the Autun St. Peter — in each case there are three little parallel oval welts. The border of St. Peter's sleeve has a pattern of dots like the falling edge of *St. Thomas'* mantle. The ear of the Autun angel is the same peculiar ear as the ear of the Toulouse *St. Andrew* (Ill. 435); the ear of the Autun St. Peter is like that of Herod in the Toulouse Dance of Salome (Ill. 446). The capitals of the niche at Autun have foliage of the same character as the capitals of the niches at Toulouse. At Toulouse and at Autun there is the same fondness for border ornaments; the same pre-occupation with covering the entire surface with decorative lines. The feet are not very dissimilar — compare the St. Peter of the Autun tympanum (Ill. 80) with the Toulouse Christ (Ill. 445). The horizontal bandings, so characteristic of Autun, reappear on the leg of the Virgin at Solsona (Ill. 552) and on the capitals of Toulouse (Ill. 446). The slim sloping shoulders characteristic of Autun reappear at Toulouse. The legs of the beardless apostle holding a scroll at Toulouse (Ill. 438) have draperies very like those of the right leg of the tall standing figure to the left of the Autun aureole (Ill. 80). The drapery over the left knee of the angel supporting the aureole below to the right in the Autun tympanum (Ill. 81) is the same as that which falls from the left hand of the *St. Andrew* at Toulouse (Ill. 434).

These resemblances make it clear that the art of Gilbert of Toulouse is the art of Autun. Since the name Gilbert is not of the commonest, the simple explanation seems to be to suppose that at Toulouse we have a later phase of the artist we have learned to know and admire at Autun.

It must be admitted that there are notable differences between his work at Autun and at Toulouse. The attenuation and movement which are so striking at Autun have disappeared at Toulouse; the manner is much less exaggerated.

We are, perhaps, apt to underestimate the variations in manner which mediaeval artists might undergo. The cloister of Moissac and the portal of Chartres might have been executed within the life-time of a single sculptor. Obviously a man who in 1100 was working in the manner of Moissac must in 1140 have been working in a very different manner. We are all aware how versatile are living artists of to-day. Paradoxical as the statement may seem, it is probably true that mediaeval sculptors were more individualized, freer, less trammelled by convention than artists of the present time. We have already found several instances in which a sculptor's manner was notably altered by the sight of a new masterpiece.

Now differences of style between the sculptures of Autun and those of Toulouse are precisely such as we would imagine might have been produced upon a sensitive artist by an acquaintance with the work which was produced shortly after the completion of Autun at St.-Denis and Chartres. The obvious and close relationship between Gilbert's apostles at Toulouse (Ill. 434–443) and the destroyed jambs of St.-Denis (Ill. 1445–1457) is well known; since it is not disputed, it is unnecessary to weary the reader by insistence upon the fact. It seems to me certain that Gilbert of Toulouse knew the new art of the North. The problem consequently appears to be very simply solved. Gilbert of Autun, plus St.-Denis, equals Gilbert of Toulouse.[1]

---

[1] That a Burgundian sculptor should have been called to Toulouse is to be explained not only by the fact that Toulouse was a focal point of the pilgrimage road, but also by the fact

There can be no question that Gilbert did much to spread Burgundian art through southern France and Spain. His Virgin and the column of his assistant at Solsona exerted great influence upon the sculpture of Catalonia and the Pyrenees in the second half of the XII century. They were, indeed, imitated even beyond the boundaries of Catalonia. The column in the cloister of St.-Bertrand-de-Comminges (Ill. 492–495, 497) must have been inspired by that of Solsona. The draperies of the Annunciation (Ill. 553–554) [1] from the old cathedral of Lérida show the covering of the surface with fine lines, characteristic of the manner of Gilbert. The introduction of jamb sculptures at Ripoll (Ill. 572, 573) must be credited to his account. So, too, a group of monuments of the very end of the XII or beginning of the XIII century, in which the draperies are indicated by a net-work of lines covering the entire surface of the stone — the sculptures at Perpignan (Ill. 618–620), the tombs at Elne (Ill. 623–626), Arles-sur-Tech (Ill. 627) and St.-Genis-des-Fontaines (Ill. 621-622). [2]

that the canons regular of St.-Etienne had been put under the jurisdiction of Cluny by Isarnus in 1077 (Bruel, IV, 630).

[1] I am indebted to Miss King for having called my attention to these sculptures, and to Miss E. H. Lorober for her photographs of them, which she has kindly allowed me to reproduce.

[2] These Catalan draperies without question also show the influence of Tuscan sculpture.

The Tuscan school may be considered to have been formed by Guglielmo da Innspruch with the production of his Pisa pulpit (Ill. 186–188) now at Cagliari. In this he applied the draperies of Provence to native Tuscan figures and to the type of pulpit which had before his time been consecrated at Pisa (Ill. 181–185) and which continued to be popular with the Tuscan school until the time of Giovanni Pisano. It is a curious fact that the supporting lions which formed so characteristic a feature of Tuscan pulpits seem to have been derived by Guglielmo da Innspruch, not from neighbouring Lombardy, as might be supposed, but from Arles. At least, the face of the surviving lion of the Cagliari pulpit (Ill. 188) seems to have been inspired by the face of the lion beneath St. Peter on the façade of St.-Trophîme (Ill. 1371).

The work of Guglielmo da Innspruch had enormous influence. He was himself called to execute the lintel of S. Bartolommeo in Pantano at Pistoia (Ill. 190) in 1167. This introduced his manner at Pistoia. The artists who worked upon the lintel of S. Andrea in the same city (Ill. 191) were influenced by him, as he was himself in turn influenced by Gruamonte; and Guido da Como, when many years later he executed the pulpit at S. Bartolommeo in Pantano (Ill. 234) could do nothing better than copy Guglielmo's Pisa pulpit (Ill. 186–188). Guglielmo's "organ-pipe" draperies run through much of the subsequent work in Tuscany — we recognize them in the pulpit at Volterra (Ill. 196), in the lintel of S. Giovanni Fuorcivitas of Pistoia (Ill. 199), in Biduino's western portal of S. Casciano of 1180 (Ill. 223), in the lintel of the southern portal of S. Salvatore of Lucca (Ill. 225) and in the pulpit (Ill. 229) and St. Michael (Ill. 230) of Groppoli, of 1194.

The capitals of St.-Etienne were closely, though feebly, imitated by one of the sculptors who worked, perhaps much later, upon the second campaign in the cloister of La Daurade at Toulouse (Ill. 464–471). The jamb sculptures of the chapter-house of the same priory (Ill. 474–479) obviously owe much to the cycle of Gilbert and his assistant.

Gilbert's art at Autun shows points of contact with Germany. His extreme elongation is matched in certain miniatures of the XII century.[1] A book-cover in the University Library of Würzburg[2] is strangely like the Autun capitals. The divided beard of the *St. Andrew* possibly echoes the tradition witnessed by the St. Paul of an ivory-carving in the Cluny Museum at Paris, by the Echternach master, dating from the end of the X century.[3]

In the Autun capital of the angel appearing to St. Peter (Ill. 79) the latter crosses his arms with a gesture which recalls in spirit rather than in detail Sienese Virgins of the Annunciation like the Andrea Vanni Annunciation of Death in the Fogg Museum. A marked, though not always definable, kinship of feeling unites the arts of Romanesque France, Trecento Siena and Tang China.

The sculptures at Malmesbury in England show strong Burgundian influence. We have already remarked that the southern tympanum repeats the composition of Charlieu. The style is exceedingly close to St.-Sauveur of Nevers — compare, for example, the detail illustrated by Messrs. Prior and Gardner[4] with the St. Peter and St. John capital in the Musée de la Porte du Croux (Ill. 132). The voussures of the southern portal[5] are very like those of Avallon (Ill. 137–138). All this offers an interesting confirmation of Prof. Moore's dating of Malmesbury to 1140, arrived at by an entirely different chain of reasoning.

The type of twin portal initiated at Avallon was repeated at

[1] See, for example, the Traité de Musique, at the Imperial Library of Vienna, MS. 51, fol. 35 vo., illustrated by Soc. Fr. Rep. Min. Peint., 1913, Pl. XIX.
[2] Illustrated by Pelka, 156.
[3] The Toulouse *St. Andrew* and *St. Thomas* should also be compared with the Harbaville triptych of the Louvre.
[4] 188.　　　　　　　　　　[5] Illustrated by Prior and Gardner, 54.

Oloron-Ste.-Marie (Ill. 461), Sauveterre (Ill. 488) and Morlaas (Ill. 458) [1] in France and S. Vicente of Avila (Ill. 844) in Spain.

The composition of the Presentation of the architrave of La Charité-sur-Loire (Ill. 119) reappears in the wooden doors of St. Marien im Kapitol at Cologne.[2]

The western portal of St.-Bénigne of Dijon (Ill. 144) inspired the composition of the Pórtico de la Gloria at Santiago (Ill. 820–840).

Burgundian influence was also diffused through Chartres. We have already seen that the head master picked up ancient Burgundian motives to re-use in his central tympanum and lintel. There can be no doubt that he owed much else besides to Burgundy, directly or indirectly. It is only from Burgundy ultimately that he could have derived his ideals of delicacy and refinement. The tympana of Autun (Ill. 80, 81) and Vézelay (Ill. 47–49) offer prototypes of his draperies. Compare, for example, the folds and edge of the upper drapery falling over the right knee of the seated apostle to the right of the aureole in the Vézelay tympanum (Ill. 48 a) with the draperies in the corresponding position of the Christ at Chartres.[3] Or put the same draperies at Chartres beside those of the right leg of the angel to the right of the aureole at Autun (Ill. 81). Or compare the bottom folds over the feet of the Christs at Chartres and Autun (Ill. 81). The Master of the Angels at Chartres manifestly found the inspiration for the lovely angels of the tympana of the side portals in the no less lovely and more vigorous angels of the tympanum of Anzy-le-Duc (Ill. 96, 97).[4] It is certain that the school of the West,

---

[1] It is possible that Morlaas may be derived from St.-Pons.

[2] Illustrated by Dehio und von Bezold, XII, 13.

[3] Illustrations by Houvet.

[4] See the forthcoming article by Mr. Priest in *Art Studies*.

The Master of the Angels at Chartres seems also to have known ivory-carvings. His draperies recall an Ada group panel now in the Victoria and Albert Museum at London (illustrated by Goldschmidt, I, No. 14). The nervous line formed by the upper garment cutting across the knees of his angel to the left in the southern tympanum at Chartres (Houvet, Pl. 59) should be compared with the corresponding drapery edge of the St. John in the ivory. The drapery folds to the right of the left knee of the St. John in the ivory are like those to the right of the right knee of the angel to the right of the southern tympanum at Chartres (illustrated by Houvet, Pl. 51). The folds at the bottom of the draperies of the angel to the left of the southern tympanum at Chartres (illustrated by Houvet, Pl. 59) are like those of the corresponding position

which also shows so many connections with Chartres, came under the strong influence of Burgundy; but such close resemblances as exist between Burgundy and Chartres can not be explained on the supposition of an indirect influence of Burgundy upon Chartres by way of the West; the head master, and the Master of the Angels must have drunk at the fountain-head.

Of the five sculptors who collaborated upon the western portal of Chartres, the most Burgundian is assuredly the master of Etampes. By his hand are the three northern jamb sculptures of the northern portal, less the heads which do not belong to the statues, and less much work upon the innermost figure which was certainly touched up by the head master. To him should also be credited considerable work upon the capitals — we easily recognize his touch in the Anne and Joachim story; but it is difficult to be sure that he may not here have been collaborating with another sculptor. Certain capitals, like the Adoration of the Magi, must surely be the work of the St.-Denis master, and others look as though they were the joint work of the Etampes and St.-Denis masters and possibly other hands as well.

The master of Etampes seems to have worked unaided upon the portal at Etampes (Ill. 1460–1464).

His style is strongly Burgundian, and is close especially to the work of Gilbert both at Autun and at Toulouse. He has the border-ornaments, the characteristic shin draperies, the leg bands we have learned to recognize as characteristic of this sculptor. The braided hair of the left-hand figure of the west jamb at Etampes (Ill. 1463) is like that of the Virgin at Solsona (Ill. 552). The same curious zig-zagging occurs upon the fold of the right thigh of the central figure at Chartres and in the folds at the bottom between the legs of the apostles at Toulouse. The draperies which fall from the left hand of the central figure of the left jamb at Etampes (Ill. 1463) are the same

in the Virgin of the ivory. The flutters of drapery falling from the arms of the two angels in the upper compartment of the ivory, recall those falling from the right-hand arm of the elder to the left in Houvet's Plate 50.

as those which fall from the left hand of the *St. Andrew* at Toulouse
(Ill. 434). The hand of the *St. Andrew* is very like the hand of the
innermost figure of the left-hand jamb at Etampes. The pattern of
dots we have noticed as characteristic of Gilbert is found on the
border of the book of the central figure of the jamb at Chartres. The
draperies which flutter at the sides of the angels in the Etampes
spandrels (Ill. 1460, 1461) and certain figures in the Anne and Joachim capital are very like the draperies fluttering behind Christ in
the Autun capital of the Temptation.

These similarities made me at one time suppose that the master of
Etampes was only another phase of the versatile personality of Gilbert. In this, however, I was wrong. Gilbert at Autun and Toulouse
is refined; the Etampes master has a streak of coarseness which can
not be reconciled with the blithe character of the Autun sculptor.
The rank folds of his drapery fairly out-Charlieu the Charlieu master (Ill. 108–111); we are surely here at the very end of a decadent
tradition. But the analogies between Gilbert and the Etampes master abundantly prove the closest connection between the two; each
must have exerted a strong direct influence upon the other.

Prof. Vöge is inclined to identify with the master of Etampes some
of the work upon La Madeleine at Châteaudun. The rough drawings
of the destroyed sculptures certainly suggest in their vagaries the
work of the master of Etampes (Ill. 1426, 1427); however, the fragments of sculpture which still remain in the other portal seem to
show that the Châteaudun sculptor was another, although equally
bizarre, artist (Ill. 1428–1430), who derives his art, quite naturally,
from such work as the Wheel of Fortune at Beauvais (Ill. 1423,
1424).

An interesting problem is that of the relative age of the portals at
Chartres and Etampes. It is the orthodox view that Chartres is
earlier; but Dr. Buschbeck, one of the most intelligent students of
Romanesque sculpture, has lately advanced the opposite view, unfortunately without stating his reasons. Mr. Priest is inclined to
agree with Dr. Buschbeck. He observes that the canopies at Char-

tres are more elaborate;[1] that the Etampes sculptures show no trace
of the influence of Chartres, and it is almost inconceivable that a
man who had worked at Chartres should not have been affected by
the style of the head master; that the work of the Etampes master
at Chartres is unmistakably finer and more advanced than at
Etampes; that the work at Etampes struggles unsuccessfully with
several problems which had been solved at Chartres. It is obvious
that Etampes is more Burgundian than the work by the Etampes
Master at Chartres; the figures have more movement, and occasionally, as in the angels of the spandrels, burst into Autunian agita-
tion and swirls.

These arguments seem to me convincing, and to out-weigh those
which may be urged on the other side. It must be admitted, however, that the voussures at Etampes look more advanced than those
of Chartres.

A school of sculpture not unrelated to the master of Etampes
flourished in Vienne about the middle of the XII century. The point
of departure for the study of this important and little known group
of monuments is the church of St.-André-le-Bas (Ill. 1218, 1219).
An inscription on the base of one of the piers gives the date, 1152,
and the name of the sculptor, Guillaume, son of Martin.[2] The style
of the capitals shows affinity with the school of Provence; the Job
(Ill. 1218) repeats almost line for line the right-hand patriarch of the

---

[1] The Etampes canopies are probably a development of those which had been characteristic
of Spanish monuments of the XI century, like the San Isidoro casket (Ill. 651–653) or the
cloisters of Santo Domingo de Silos (Ill. 671). They are found in the Ile-de-France in the altar-
frontal of St.-Benoît-sur-Loire (Ill. 1421, 1422), a monument which adjoins the school of the
West, and in the retable of Carrière-St.-Denis, now in the Louvre (Ill. 1485), a monument
which is by the hand of a Western artist. In the West itself the motive is found in the sculptures of Giraud Audebert at Foussais (Ill. 1063). Did the Etampes master derive this feature
as well as his voussures from the West? At all events, the motive spread to Spain; it was
adopted in the tympanum of Cahors (Ill. 422) and in the frieze of Carrión (Ill. 722). It is also
found at Estabaliz (Ill. 772), in a capital of the Museo Arqueológico of Madrid (Ill. 792). In
Dauphiné we find the Etampes canopies copied in capitals of the cathedral of Vienne: it was
from this region, doubtless, that the motive was exported to the Church of the Annunciation
at Nazareth.

[2] ADORATE DNM IN AVLA SCA EIV
✚ ET CV STATIS ADORANDV RE[MI]TTITE SI QVID HABETIS ADVERSVS
ALIQVE VSQ LXXES VIIES ✚ VVILLELMVS M[ART]INI ME FECIT ANO MILL.
C. LII. AB INC D

Arles façade (Ill. 1370) — the two faces are, in fact, identical to the drawing of the cheek-bone and the wrinkles of the nose. The Samson (Ill. 1219), on the other hand, seems derived from the youth to the right in the scene of the money-changers of the St.-Gilles frieze (Ill. 1316). The facial type is the same; there is the same wattling of the sleeves; the drawing of the eye is like that of the master of the St.-Gilles frieze (Ill. 1316), the draperies are those of Brunus (Ill. 1302, 1303, 1306–1311). Moreover the Samson capital presents evident affinities with the capital depicting the same subject, coming from the cloister of Notre-Dame-des-Doms [1] at Avignon, and now in the Fogg Museum (Ill. 1342). There are besides at Vienne indications of that Apulian-Lombard influence so characteristic of the art of Provence. At St.-André-le-Bas is a Lombard supporting figure; in the museum which has been gathered together at the church of St.-Pierre are two lions, of completely Lombard character, and which once evidently supported the columns of a Lombard porch; a similar one is in a neighbouring garden. [2]

Guillaume has left traces of his activity not only at St.-André-le-Bas. Closely related to him, if not by his hand, is a relief from the tympanum of St.-Pierre (Ill. 1219 a); engaged sculptures representing St. Paul (Ill. 1217), St. Peter (Ill. 1216) and St. John (Ill. 1215), now in the north porch of the cathedral, and perhaps jambs from a destroyed portal; a capital of the cathedral of Lyon; [3] and several of the cathedral St.-Maurice of Vienne. [4] Now the jamb sculptures of St.-Maurice show manifest affinity with the jamb sculptures of the Etampes master (Ill. 1463, 1464); the garments have the same borders, there are similar leg bands, the posture of the figures is evidently analogous. Moreover, several capitals of the cathedral have canopies of the peculiar type characteristic of Chartres and Etampes (Ill. 1463, 1464). Evidently then, the school of Guillaume was in-

[1] Labande: De Lasteyrie, 631. A capital of unknown provenance representing the story of Job and now in the Musée Calvet of Avignon (Ill. 1341) is by the same hand.
[2] I am indebted for these indications and a photograph to Major Royall Tyler.
[3] Illustrated by Bégule, 106.
[4] Illustrated ibid., 116, 121, 122, 131.

fluenced by the North as well as by the South. The spirit of his art is closely allied to that of the master of Etampes. His spiral folds and violent movement could only have come out of Burgundy. As so often in Romanesque art, we have influences converging from many directions.

It is with this group of sculptors, partly Chartrain, partly Burgundian, partly Provençal that should be classed the hand which executed in far-away Palestine and in the year 1187 the capitals of the church of the Annunciation in Nazareth, destined to remain unfinished.[1] This artist is a little finer, a little more Burgundian than Guillaume; his draperies have, however, the same spiral folds, the same heaviness, the same admixture of Provençal elements. The leg bands and borders of the garments are like the Etampes master, and so is the spirit of the execution. The canopies recall equally Chartres and Vienne.

Thus we see the influence of the art of Cluny extending as far as England, Galicia, Germany, Apulia, and even to Palestine.

[1] Illustrated by Egidi.

PART II
PILGRIMAGE SCULPTURE

PILGRIMAGE SCULPTURE

I

THE PILGRIMAGE TO COMPOSTELA

It seems, singularly enough, that the modern age of creeping scholarship is moved by the tomb of St. James, less universally surely, but perhaps hardly less potently, than the Middle Age of flying faith. The cult of the students began when Fita published, a half century ago, the itinerary of the pilgrims, contained in the last part of the pseudo-Callistine codex. His was, certainly, a beautiful discovery; and a paper-bound pamphlet of a few badly printed pages has guided scholars toward the solution of their difficulties, much as the stars of the milky way reminded the mediaeval sinner of the road to Compostela. And the modern pilgrimages have also been illuminated with miracles. On the road to St. James, M. Bédier has found the key which unlocks mediaeval literature. Sceptics may doubt whether the body at Compostela be that of St. James; but it is certain that there lies buried the mystery of the XII century.

The modern pilgrim to Santiago journeys those long, but delicious kilometres, not entirely, nor even chiefly, to admire the miracles of scholarship already performed, nor even in the hope (inevitably present, however fatuous) of himself assisting at others. There is in the place, and in the road, a singular poetry. One feels, as nowhere else, wrapped about by the beauty of the Middle Age. One is, as perhaps never before, emotionally and intellectually stimulated. Chords of the memory, long unused, are set vibrating. The actuality of the pilgrimage, like a cosmic phenomenon, overwhelms with the sense of its force, its inevitability. It seduces one, irresistibly, farther and farther from his way, to linger over every turning; not, as the student is possibly simple enough to believe, because the pilgrimage peppered the art of Europe with stars and cockle-shells; nor even because of its deeper and more spiritual impress upon culture, so that to it we owe much that is fine in XII-century music, the *chansons de geste* and the Gothic cathedrals; nor yet because of a sentimental sympathy with the myriad human beings who trudged unending leagues to lay their gratitude and their remorse, their wealth and their sins at the feet of the apostle; nor because of all these and many other like things together; but because of an inner vitality, whether poetic or spiritual I know not, but still forcefully living at Santiago, and unquenchably beautiful there; beautiful none the less because seen across swarms of well-fed priests and a pestilence of syphilitic beggars, just as the living Romanesque core of the basilica shines out through an external coating of barocco, fine, too, in its way, yet writhing in the agony of dissolution.

Hardly less poignant, emotionally, than the road itself, is the twin-sister of the road, the Callistine codex. It is regrettable that no complete edition of this manuscript has yet appeared; and although the different parts have been separately printed, they are dispersed among books all of which are seldom to be found in the same library.[1] The dividing up of the manuscript began in the XVI century, when some zealous cleric, loving Saint James more fervently than the truth, sought to save the credit of the *Miracles* for a sceptical age by tearing from them the *Chronicle of Turpin*. Fita, in recent years, detected the trick, and restored the codex to its integrity. But the parts had been edited separately. The absence of a critical edition of the entire codex is the more unfortunate, because appreciation of the quality of the book as a whole depends upon grasping its unity.

The codex opens with a liturgical introduction, which is, indeed, extended to disproportionate lengths. The ritual is interspersed with sonorous prophecies, authentic and apocryphal, and punctuated by lyrics and a miracle play.

The ultramundane prologue is followed by the intensely human

---

[1] López Ferreiro, *Hist. Sant.*, I, 412 f.; Bollandists, *Acta Sanctorum*, t. VI de Julio, 47 f.; Castets, *Turpini Historia Karoli Magni*, Montpellier, Société pour l'Etude des Langues Romanes, 1880; Fita y Vinson, *Le codex de Saint Jacques de Compostelle. Liber de Miraculis sancti Jacobi, Liber IV*. Paris, 1882.

book of the *Miracles*. Tender as the *Fioretti*, romantic as a play of Calderon, this is one of the great imaginative productions of the Middle Ages. The legends deal with pilgrims, and the scene is the road.

The next part of the codex deals with the end of the pilgrimage, the tomb of the apostle. His life and passion are told; how he preached in Spain; how he became bishop of Jerusalem; and how he was beheaded by Herod. But the strangest part of the tale follows — how his disciples carried his body into a boat; how they brought it without sails or rudder to Galicia; how it lay for long centuries unknown; and how it was miraculously revealed.

Suddenly the codex becomes epic. It is the famous chronicle of the pseudo-Turpin. Saint James appears to the emperor Charlemagne. "You who have freed all other lands, why have you not freed my land and my road!" Charlemagne becomes the first pilgrim to Compostela; the archbishop Turpin dedicates the basilica. The emperor conquers all Spain; at his approach the walls of Pamplona sink; at his curse Luçerna is turned into a salt lake, inhabited only by large, black fish. Before the reader passes the glamour of chivalry, the superdeeds of heroes, the Christian conquering the infidel, the dream of a Spain liberated from the Saracens by the help of France. Against this background is woven the story of Roland — his duel with the giant Ferragudo, the battle of Roncevaux, and the wail of the oliphant, echoing through the ports of the Pyrenees.

But it is the last book, the *Pilgrim's Guide*, which for the modern reader is the most precious. Under the guidance of the writer, we suddenly become XII-century pilgrims, setting out on the journey to Compostela. Through his eyes we see all. We learn the details of the roads — the alternate routes, how they forked and intersected. We journey across the plains of France, through the mountains and plateaux of Spain. We stop to worship at the tombs of saints along the way. Here and there we catch glimpses of great Romanesque basilicas just finished or in building. We learn the characteristics of various nations — which peoples were kindly, which treacherous, which dirty; where wine was good, and where food was bad; at what places rivers could be forded, and where inns or hospices afforded shelter for the night. Finally, our author leads us into the cathedral of Santiago; he shows us every detail of the architecture and arrangement. Through his XII-century eyes we see the XII-century basilica. We examine the sculptures in detail; he patiently explains to us the iconography. We compare, stone by stone, the existing church with the basilica of the XII century. Our eyes are no longer blinded by the deceptions of eight centuries. Mystery after mystery of XII-century art is suddenly revealed. What had been most obscure, now is evident.

That the codex might carry greater authority, the propagandist who compiled it thought it well to ascribe the various portions to different well-known people. It is a question immaterial to our purpose how far he himself may have believed in these attributions, and to what extent he consciously fabricated them. It is certain that those to the archbishop Turpin and the pope Callixtus are false.

There has been much discussion as to the date at which the propagandist did his work. It was surely in the first half of the XII century, that is to say, at a time when the pilgrimage had already been in full progress for upwards of a hundred years. The pseudo-Callistine codex was, therefore, less a cause than a product of the pilgrimage. It is undoubtedly this fact that gives the book its peculiar vitality. In the last analysis it is folk-lore, of which the fundamental character is not altered by forged signatures. The pilgrimage grew up spontaneously in the heart of the mediaeval world; but from an early period it was exploited by scheming clerks.

Surely no capitalist of the XIX century ever promoted more shrewdly, nor any diplomat of the XVI played politics more cleverly, than the Cluniac monks, who to, if not for, their own advantage, set all Europe a-journeying, quite literally, to the ends of the world. The rulers of the great abbey were quick to realize the success of the pilgrimage, and far-sighted in driving, at an early date, their finger-nails firmly into the carrot of Saint James.

The pilgrimage road may be compared to a great river, emptying into the sea at Santiago, and formed by many tributaries which have their sources in the far regions of Europe. All these streams, gathering force as they descend, flowed together at Puente la Reyna, whence the river runs in its full strength to Compostela.

Now Cluny possessed priories or affiliations along the pilgrimage route at St.-Martin-des-Champs and St.-Julien-le-Pauvre of Paris; at Longpont, Montlhéry, Vézelay, Blazimont, Moissac, St.-Gilles, St.-Jean-d'Angély, Montierneuf of Poitiers, St.-Eutrope of Saintes, St.-Martial of Limoges, St.-Etienne of Nevers, Morlaas, La Sauve Majeure, St.-Macaire, La Daurade and St.-Etienne of Toulouse, Lézat, San Juan de la Peña, Leyre, Estella, Irache, Nájera, Santa Colomba of Burgos, San Pedro de la Cardeña, Frómista, Carrión de los Condes, Benevívere, Sahagún, San Pedro de las Dueñas, San Salvador of Astorga, Villafranca, Ferreiros.[1] On referring to the list of establishments affiliated with Cluny published in the *Bullarium,* one is surprised to find included in the number not only direct dependencies, but cathedral churches, colleges of canons and even monasteries of other orders. Among the churches along the road given in this list as Cluniac are: St.-Vincent of Mâcon, St.-Philibert of Tournus, the cathedrals of Autun and Narbonne, St.-Benoît-sur-Loire, St.-Denis, St.-Martin of Tours, the abbey of Bernay, St.-Pons, Montmajour, St.-Androche of Saulieu, the cathedral of Santiago, St.-Hilaire of Poitiers, the cathedral of Pamplona, Sagra S. Michele, S. Isidoro of Léon, the cathedral of Nîmes, the cathedral of Burgos, Montierneuf of Poitiers, Beaulieu, Donzy, La Charité-sur-Loire, St.-Etienne of Nevers, St.-Martial of Limoges. It is therefore evident that Cluny

---

[1] Bruel, V, 256 mentions the following Cluniac dependencies which may have been on the road: S. Martini de Juvia quod in diocesi Minduniensis ecclesie situm esse cognoscitur juxta flumen Juvie in territorio Trasanguis; Sancta Crux, in Castanneda, juxta ripam fluminis quod vocatur Pisuenna; San Salvador de Comeliana quod situm est apud Asturias, in territorii de Salas inter duo flumina, Nouaia et Narceia; Botinio in Gallicia in terra Tuorii, in ripa fluminis Munei, territorio Rudensi, prope ipsam urbem Tudam, ad radicem rupis magne, que vocatur Vulturaria; Sancte Marie, quod cognomento Vimiverium vocatur in territorio Bracarensi. Cf. also Marrier, 1746: Prioratus S. Saluatoris de Villaviridi in Gallicia, Austericensis diocesis; Prioratus de Valla-viridi, in Gallicia, Lucensis diocesis; Prioratus S. Vincentij de Palumberiis in Gallicia, Lucensis diocesis.

held in her grip the entire lower, and consequently richer, course of the gold-scattering stream, as well as the strategic points of the head-waters.

The pilgrimage to Saint James thus became for Cluny an important source of material prosperity. A quaint document of 1188 [1] shows that the clergy were quite conscious of these benefits. The prior of Villafranca brought suit against the prior of a neighbouring hospital, because the latter *in peregrinis sua jura injuste usurpabat !* It is therefore not surprising that Cluny should have stood ready to help Santiago to crush, or compromise with, rivals in relics, and in every way to foster the pilgrimage.

We may gather from a few instances the means by which Cluny was enabled to control even those important churches along the road which were not directly subjected to her discipline. The bishop of Santiago, Dalmatius, under whom the choir was constructed, and who gave the golden altar, was an ex-Cluniac monk, who returned to Cluny to die in 1095. Isarne, who became bishop of Toulouse in 1071, was a strong supporter of Cluny. In 1074, he donated the *locum de S. Genio* to the Burgundian monastery. Three years later, he made a much more important donation of the great Cluniac monastery of La Daurade. He reformed his own canons, doubtless according to Cluniac ideas. We shall study later his attempt to transfer St.-Sernin to Cluny. In 1088 and 1096 the same bishop again appears as the strong supporter of Cluny. His successor, Amelius, gave a church to Cluny in 1110; and in this same year one to Moissac and another to Cluny. Durande, the predecessor of Isarne, was a Cluniac monk and abbot of Moissac. It is therefore clear that the two crucial bishoprics of Santiago and Toulouse were completely under the control of Cluny. Her alliance with the secular powers was not less firm. Among all the benefactors of the monastery, none was so circumstantially honoured as the Aragonese king, Alfonso. He, doubtless, was the most generous of all to the abbey, and it seems to have been chiefly at his expense that the new church of Cluny was

---

[1] Buel, V, 680.

built. It is unnecessary to question the sincerity of his piety. But one more than suspects that he saw in Cluny a material as well as an immaterial comfort. Cluny aided in bringing French pilgrims to Santiago; these pilgrims were potential crusaders capable of playing an important rôle in driving the Moors from Spain.

Thus by the skilful playing of many cards, bit by bit, the fame of Saint James and his road was increased. The journey to Galicia became incredibly popular. The only remaining rivals were Jerusalem and Rome. The wisest policy, and the one doubtless at first adopted, was to pool the interests of all three, and encourage a circular pilgrimage which should include the Holy Land and Italy as well as Galicia. It was folly for Santiago to enter into rivalry with Jerusalem and Rome. The bishop of Santiago, Diego Gelmirez, nevertheless embarked on this ill-advised course. The outstripping of Rome may have been the work the pseudo-Callistine codex was intended to accomplish. We begin to suspect why it was put in the mouth of a Roman pontiff. At any rate the doubt soon began to be whispered abroad, whether, after all, Saint James was not greater than Saint Peter. In the portals of many pilgrimage churches, the son of Zebedee elbows from the position of honour the prince of the apostles.

About the pilgrimage was thrown every lure that could fascinate the mediaeval mind. Relics were the passion of the age, and these in profusion were dangled before the eyes of the intending pilgrim to Compostela. The tomb of the apostle was of course the goal of his journey; at Santiago were also the relics of the lesser St. James; on the way there and back many spiritual treasures could be visited with little extra effort. The itinerary of the pilgrims was arranged with especial care from this point of view. The tomb of Ste. Foy at Conques; that of St. Trophîme at Arles; that of St. Gilles in the monastery of the same name; that of St. Guilhem in his desert; that of St. Sernin at Toulouse; that of S. Isidoro at Léon; that of St. Léonard near Limoges; that of St. Front at Périgueux; those of Ste. Radegonde and St. Hilaire at Poitiers; that of the Magdalen at Vézelay; that of St. Eutrope at Saintes; that of St. Seurin at Bor-

deaux; that of St. Veronica at Soulac; that of St. Facundus and
St. Primitivus at Sahagún; that of St. Martin at Tours are only a
few among the more important of an unending number of relics
which lined the road to Santiago. Hardly less seductive to the mediaeval pilgrims were the associations of the *chansons de geste.* The
Church cleverly extended to these secular heroes the cloak of sanctity. On the road were seen and visited the very field of Roncevaux;
Blaye where St. Roland was buried; Bordeaux where the oliphant
was preserved (St.-Sernin of Toulouse also claimed to have the oliphant, but the Guide passes this pretention by with scornful silence);
Belin, where were buried Oliver and other piers of Charlemagne;
Sahagún, near which the Christians' spears burst into foliage.

Into the psychology of the pilgrimage there must also have entered love of wandering for its own sweet sake. Ever since the days
of Odysseus, and doubtless long before, men have passionately desired to see strange countries. The same restlessness that creates the
modern tourist spurred on the men of the Middle Ages to rove.
Chaucer's pilgrims to Canterbury told their tales to while away the
time on their journey; it is easy to see that the pilgrimage on the
whole was a thoroughly delightful experience. The pilgrims of Saint
James similarly sought solace from monotony in the *Chanson de
Roland* and the *Chanson de Guillaume;* they, too, doubtless found
travelling, for all its discomforts and even perils, pleasurable. The
efforts of Cluny and of pious individuals had resulted in making the
road relatively safe and comfortable. Hospices were provided at
needed points,[1] bridges built, the roads repaired.[2] The Callistine codex lays great stress upon the terrible vengeance that Saint James
might be expected to visit upon whoever molested, or even failed to
aid, his pilgrims. His wrath, it was known, was especially liable to
fall upon unscrupulous inn-keepers. No sin could be more heinous
than to defraud pilgrims of money which otherwise would be given

---

[1] As early as 969 a donation was made in *pago Matisconensi* (Mâcon), *in Villa Rufiacensi* to
Cluny *ut peregrini et non habentes inde sustententur et recreentur* (Bruel, II, 345).

[2] A merit of Santo Domingo de la Calzada was, as his name implies, that he built and kept in
repair a portion of the road of St. James.

to the Church. Fraternities were formed everywhere to aid pilgrims. He who went to Saint James was wrapped about by a sort of sanctity that was a powerful protection and a help in case of need.

So the journey was not over-full of hardships. Neither was it very expensive. M. Thorel has estimated that the return trip from Amiens cost about $200 in modern money. This certainly seems reasonable for a journey that must have lasted several months, since we are told that the return trip from Toulouse required thirty-six days. Travelling was assuredly slower than to-day, but perhaps not dearer nor less agreeable. This explains the fact that the pilgrims were not satisfied with their long trip to Santiago. They pushed on two long days further to see where St. James landed at Padrón, and to gather cockle-shells on the shores of the western ocean. Indeed, the going to Notre-Dame of Finisterre, the westernmost land, was an integral part of the regular pilgrimage route.

By no means the least glamour of the pilgrimage was and is that of art. The four roads to Santiago lead, even to-day, past an incomparable series of mediaeval monuments.

Leaving St.-Jacques of Paris, of which only the tower remains to-day, passing under the shadow of the cathedral, near St.-Julien-le-Pauvre and St.-Germain-des-Prés out the rue St.-Jacques and through the Porte St.-Jacques the pilgrims went to Longpont, St.-Sulpice-de-Favières, Etampes, Orléans, Blois, Amboise, Tours, Cormery, Beaulieu-les-Loches, Loches, Parthenay, Thouars, St.-Jouin-de-Marne, Champdeniers, Poitiers, Montmorillon, Moreaux, Civray, Melle, Aulnay, Saintes, Bordeaux, Dax, Mimizan, Bayonne, Sauveterre, Roncevaux, Pamplona, Puente la Reina, Estella, Hirache, Logroño, Nájera, Santo Domingo de la Calzada, Burgos, Frómista, Villacázar, Carrión de los Condes, Sahagún, San Miguel de Escalada, Léon, Astorga and so to Santiago ; returning they might pass Oviedo, Santa Maria de Lena, Arbas, Armentía, Vitoria, Estibaliz, Leyre, San Juan de la Peña, Santa Cruz de la Serós, Jaca, Oloron-Ste.-Marie, Morlaas, St.-Bertrand-de-Comminges, Valcabrère, Lézat, Toulouse, Carcassonne, Rieux-Minervois, Narbonne, Béziers, St.-Guilhem-le-

Désert, Aniane, Montpellier, Maguelonne, St.-Gilles, Arles, Nîmes, Le Puy, Brioude, Lavaudieu, Issoire, St.-Saturnin, Clermont-Ferrand; or if the alternate routes were chosen, Hagetmau, Bazas, Blazimont, Périgueux, Limoges, St.-Léonard, Nevers, Vézelay, Castelvieil, La Sauve Majeure; Moissac, Cordes, Conques; and possibly Cahors, Rocamadour, Figeac, Souillac, Martel, Carennac, Beaulieu. Kilometre for kilometre it would be, I think, impossible to trace another itinerary in Europe passing as many important monuments of the early part of the XII century. It is clear that there was a distinct tendency for Cluniac priories, for relics, and for monumental sculpture to gather along the road.

That the road should have been adorned with art, as it was with legends and epics, is in no way surprising. The mere material prosperity brought by the streams of pilgrims would explain much. Moreover, large towns and arteries of communication naturally gravitate together. Behind all this there was however, I suspect, the directing hand of the monks of Cluny. At this period Cluny was the champion of all the arts, but especially of sculpture. It was through Cluny that stone sculpture was first really popularized in the West; and Cluny remained the chief foyer of the art until the rising power of Cîteaux broke the prestige of the older order, and soured its sweetness with the gloom of Puritanism. After Saint Bernard, art could hardly flourish in any monastery, more than it could, after Luther, in any church. But in the first third of the XII century Cluny, the lover of art and beauty, was still at the zenith of her power; and those precious moments never to return she used to line the road, from Paris to Santiago, with a series of masterworks. The influence exerted upon sculpture by these pilgrimage churches was exceedingly great.

Many of the sculptures of northern Spain not upon the road seem to be derivatives of monuments which are. Santa Marta de Terra comes out of Santiago (Ill. 675–691). Moarves (Ill. 729) is evidently copied from Carrión de los Condes (Ill. 722–726). The jamb sculptures of San Martín at Segóvia (Ill. 755–756) may have been inspired

by Sangüesa (Ill. 743–746). The large figures in the cloister of Santillana del Mar (Ill. 867–868) come out of Oviedo (Ill. 869, 870). The
caryatid figures under the cupola at Santiago (Ill. 694, 695) [1] are
analogous to those at Hirache, Armentía (Ill. 767), Ciudad Rodrigo,
Toro, Salamanca (Ill. 736–739), Conques (Ill. 388, 389), Aix, Venasque and Carpentras.

The history of Spanish Romanesque sculpture might be graphi-
cally represented by taking a pen, full of ink, and tracing with it upon
wet blotting paper, the road of St. James.

Nor, does it appear, was the case in France essentially otherwise.
Certainly the school of the West had important centres at Blazimont,
Parthenay, Melle, Aulnay, Saintes and Poitiers, all on the road. The
school of Provence similarly centres in Arles, St.-Gilles, Nîmes, St.-
Guilhem-le-Désert, all on the road. That of Velay radiates from Le
Puy, which is on the road. That of Auvergne is grouped about
Issoire and Clermont-Ferrand, both on the road. By far the most
important centres of south-western France were Moissac and Toulouse, both on the road. The Burgundian-Languedocian manner was
originated at Cluniac Moissac (Ill. 339–342), on the road; thence it
spread to Beaulieu (Ill. 409–420). Other centres were formed at
Cahors (Ill. 422–429) and Conques (Ill. 386–401), both on the road.
From Conques, the art spread to Espalion (Ill. 402). The last phase
of Languedocian Romanesque sculpture, characterized by the appearance of the influence of Chartres, found centres in the Cluniac
priory of La Daurade at Toulouse (Ill. 462–479), on the road, and at
St.-Etienne (Ill. 434–449) of the same city, hence also on the road,
and also under strong Cluniac influence.

Lombardy was connected with the rest of Europe by the pilgrimage routes. Many Lombards made the journey to Compostela, as we
learn from the book of the miracles and other sources. Nicolò, who

[1] The motive is doubtless of Byzantine origin, since found in Armenia at Kumurdo, a church
which according to Strzygowski, 782, dates from the second half of the X century. In Byzantine mosaics the evangelists were regularly represented in this position.

The existing sculptures in the pendentives of Santiago seem related in style to the work of
Mateo and are perhaps not earlier than the second half of the XII century, but they must
replace earlier sculptures of the same subject.

had certainly been in Spain, carved the figures of Roland and Oliver on the jambs of the cathedral of Verona. Moreover, two important pilgrimage routes, those to Rome and Jerusalem, crossed Lombardy, passing through Susa, Sagra S. Michele, Vercelli, Sannazaro Sesia, Pavia, Piacenza, Borgo S. Donnino, Parma, Modena, Bologna.

Indeed, the roads to Rome and to the Holy Land were connected with that to Compostela, and were no less important in transmitting artistic influences. A long series of accounts written by pilgrims at various periods of the Middle Ages has been published by the Palestine Pilgrims' Text Society. Less condensed and vivid than the Guide to Compostela, this valuable series of documents nevertheless informs us in detail of the journey to the Holy Land in mediaeval times. The great number of alternative routes is sharply brought to our attention. We are apt to forget that in the XII century, as now, there were many different ways of going from one place to another. Pilgrims who had gone to Santiago by the regular route, might return by way of Catalonia, visiting the great shrines at Zaragoza and Montserrat, and passing, perhaps, by Solsona or Ripoll, thence via Puigcerda to Villefranche with its church of St.-Jacques and the pilgrimage of Mont Romeu. So pilgrims to the Holy Land went occasionally, especially in early times, over-land the entire distance — this was the route taken by the Bordeaux pilgrim in 333, by St. Antoninus *c.* 570 and by Mandeville. In the XII century, however, the usual route was by sea. The pilgrim might embark at Venice or at Rome, but he was more likely to sail from an Apulian port. The one selected seems to have depended upon circumstances. Seawulf (1102–1103) writes: "Some embark at Bari, some at Barletta, some at Siponto or Trani, and some even at Otranto. We, however, went on board ship at Monopoli." After having been shipwrecked, he re-embarked at Brindisi. Other pilgrims mention that they took ship at Taranto. The great shrines at Monte Gargano and Bari were, however, regularly included in the itinerary.

The pilgrimages to Rome and the Holy Land undoubtedly played a large part in uniting the art of Apulia and Lombardy with that of the rest of Europe. We find the influence of Lombard architecture appearing in Normandy, at Jumièges, at precisely the moment when the Normans began to pass through Lombardy frequently on their way to Apulia. The connection between the Bayeux tapestry, the relief at Angoulême (Ill. 939), the Porta della Pescheria at Modena, and the Porta dei Leoni at S. Niccola of Bari (Ill. 156) has doubtless the same explanation. The occupation of Apulia by the Normans must have caused much travelling back and forth from Normandy through Lombardy to Apulia even by those who were not pilgrims. Journeys undertaken for many different reasons led travellers along the same routes. Suger, for example, made three trips to Italy, and went as far south as S. Niccola of Bari. We are not therefore surprised to find him introducing at St.-Denis numerous features of Italian art — mosaics, Lombard anthemia, bronze doors, jamb sculptures. Artists themselves often travelled. We have already found many instances, and shall find even more striking ones in subsequent chapters. The pilgrim who signed his initials and added the word *peregrini* to the marble epitaph of Ponce de Brou at Narbonne [1] was only one of many who combined the business of art with the spiritual benefits of a pilgrimage. It was another, I suspect, who (*pelegrinus*, not *Pellegrinus*) executed in 1273 the windows for Charles d'Anjou in the castle of Pontano at Foggia.[2]

The roads crossing Lombardy without question aided in the transmission of artistic ideas to and from that province. Lombard sculpture was formed at Modena, which lies on the road.

From Modena it spread to Nonantola, to Cremona, to the Cluniac S. Benedetto Po. The second phase of Lombard sculpture was formed by Nicolò at Sagra S. Michele and Piacenza, both on the road. From there it spread to Ferrara and Verona. From Ferrara the style was carried to France, to Chamalières (Ill. 1154–1156) in the Cévennes. At Parma, on the road, was formed the art of Benedetto, which spread to Milan, to Venice, throughout Lombardy.

Corneto, on the road to Rome, and the Apulian cities on the road

[1] de Mély, 61.   [2] Lenormant, I, 40.

to the Holy Land, both developed during the XII century an art of the pilgrimage type. In both the architectural forms in the early part of the century are Lombard; in both these are later supplanted by the early Gothic forms of northern France. The same succession of Lombard and French influences is notable in the sculpture of Apulia. In other provinces of Italy the influences of the pilgrimages can be traced. The sculptures of the cathedral of Genoa (Ill. 254–258) are derived from Chartres; those of the cathedral of Lucca (Ill. 247) from Burgundy. I suspect that Giovanni Pisano may have absorbed the French influences which form so important an element in his style from pilgrims and travellers passing through Pisa on their way to Rome.

The discoveries of Strzygowski leave no doubt as to the reality of Byzantine influence over the art of the Occident. A venerable tradition had, indeed, always asserted the fact, and Syrian monuments had already given good reason to suspect that the Orient counted for more in Western productions than the wildest dreamer could have imagined. Now that Armenian architecture has been opened up to us, we are face to face with the fact that Western art was largely inspired by the East. Thence were derived many motives we have considered characteristic of Western Romanesque — cubic capitals, triangular arches, arched corbel-tables (?), blind arches, plans of the Germigny-lès-Prés type, arched squinches, apses polygonal externally semicircular internally, barrel-vaulted naves with transverse arches, compound piers, Le Puy vaults, pointed arches, horse-shoe arches, alternation of supports, griffes, sculptured tympana, columns supported on lions (?), figure sculpture, zig-zag dentil string-courses, transverse arches, squinch sculptures. From the East came the Auvergnat vaulted basilicas, with central cupola buttressed by vaults raised over the side aisles. Thence also were derived the mosaic pavements characteristic of Romanesque churches in Italy and France — such pavements were common in Byzantine churches of the IV–VI centuries in the East.[1] To the

[1] Diehl, 211.

same source was due sculpture in stone which is found in Armenia in the church of Mzchet, dating apparently from the VIII century,[1] at Kars (928–951)[2] and at Achthamar (921.)

Not only separate motives, but entire buildings appear to have been transported, as it were bodily, either from Armenia or from the source of Armenian architecture. Among these is the cathedral of Pisa, a city on the road to Rome. The cathedral of Pisa seems to have inspired in turn an entire school of Romanesque architecture in Tuscany; and it was also copied in the cathedral of Troia in Apulia, which in turn was reproduced at Foggia and Siponto.

An undoubted result of the pilgrimages was to diffuse through the West copies of the church of the Holy Sepulchre at Jerusalem. The characteristic features of this structure were: first, that it was of central or circular type; and second, that it consisted of a building within a building, since the rotunda had been constructed about the tomb itself. Avowed or evident reproductions are numerous in the West, and exist, or existed at St.-Léonard, Montmorillon, Parthenay, Ste.-Croix of Quimperlé, St.-Bonnet-la-Rivière, Laon, Neuvy-St.-Sépulcre, Eunate, El Sepulcro of Torres, Santa Cruz of Segóvia, Cambridge, the Temple Church at London, S. Sepolcro of Barletta, S. Stefano of Bologna. M. Bréhier has suggested that the old rotunda of St.-Bénigne of Dijon should be added to the list, and the strange church of Charroux should almost certainly be grouped under this head.

Western iconography, until 1140 almost exclusively, and always in great part, was under the influence of Byzantine models. The pilgrimages may have played no small part in carrying such conceptions from the East, and in renewing constantly contact with the fountain-heads.

S. Marco of Venice, and the domed churches of the west of France, are certainly derived from Eastern models. This type of architecture may well have been brought to the West by means of the pilgrimages. The church of Canosa in Apulia was vaulted with domes on penden-

[1] Strzygowski, 81.   [2] *Ibid.*, 84.

tives of the same diameter in 1101; this church and S. Marco and St.-Front of Périgueux were all important pilgrimage centres.

Other types of vault may well have come from the East. The barrel-vaulted basilicas of the Asturias recall strangely those of Asia Minor. The singular ribbed cupola of Casale Monferrato is precisely like the similar vaults at Cordoba and San Baudelio in Spain and Aklepat in Armenia.

Along the road of St. James followed by the Lombard pilgrims, the forms of Lombard art begin to appear, and spread thence to the neighbouring districts. The apse of St.-Guilhem-le-Désert, on the road, is completely Lombard. The alternate system, introduced at St.-Nazaire of Carcassonne, on the road, spread thence to Bozouls. The rib vault is introduced at Fréjus, on the road (for pilgrims doubt-less came by the shore as well as by the Mt.-Cenis), at St.-Victor of Marseille, on the road, at Maguelonne, on the road, at St.-Etienne of Toulouse, on the road, at Moissac, on the road, at St.-Hilaire of Poitiers, on the road.[1] The Cistercian rib vaults of Lombardy[2] pene-trated into the porches of St.-Guilhem-le-Désert on the road and St.-Martin-de-Londres. These Lombard influences were doubtless brought not only by pilgrims. The architecture of Catalonia, French as well as Spanish, was under strong Lombard influence. Lombard masters were probably often employed — at least it is certain that this was the case at Seu d'Urgell. These masters journeyed over the same road taken by the pilgrims.

Lombard rib vaults were introduced into Central Italy at Corneto and at Montefiascone on the road. Thence the idea spread to S. Robano, to Sovana, perhaps even to Aversa, Teramo and S. Maria di Ronzano. In Apulia Lombard rib vaults were introduced at S. Bene-detto of Brindisi, on the road.

The type of Romanesque cloister, consisting of twin columns sup-porting round arches with piers at the angles, is closely associated

[1] The rib vault of Ste.-Croix of Quimperlé, however, appears to be earlier than any of the examples on the road. The construction early spread to the Ile-de-France and to England.

[2] Or did these profiled ribs come from the North? St.-Jean of Valence gives some reason to think such may have been the case.

with the pilgrimage road. We find it at Santo Domingo de Silos in
the eighth decade of the XI century (Ill. 666). Such cloisters be-
came characteristic of the Romanesque architecture of Spain and
Catalonia; they are found at the cathedral and Sant Pere de Galli-
gans of Gerona, Estany, Perelada, Bages, Sant Pere de Roda, Sant
Pere de les Puelles (destroyed), Ripoll, Elne, San Cugat del Vallès,
San Pedro of Huesca, San Pedro of Estella, Santillana del Mar. In
France the type was introduced from Spain, at Moissac, on the road.
Later it appears at St.-Trophîme of Arles, on the road, at Mont-
majour, at St.-Bertrand-de-Comminges, on the road, at Notre-
Dames-des-Doms of Avignon (now destroyed), and at Aix-en-Pro-
vence. It found its way, too, into Lombardy; to S. Orso of Aosta,
S. Stefano of Bologna, the cathedral and S. Zeno of Verona; thence
to Ss. Quattro Coronati (c. 1113) and other cloisters of Rome and
Sicily. It was doubtless one of the many artistic ideas which the
Lombard pilgrims brought back from their journey to Compostela.

The motive of crossed legs in sculpture, wherever it originated,
found itself established at an early period in the Spanish-Aquitanian
school. At Compostela and Toulouse it was known from at least the
second decade of the XII century. Thence it spread through the pilgrimages over Europe — to Ferrara in Lombardy, to Bamberg in
Germany, to St.-Gilles in Provence, to St.-Denis and Senlis in northern France.

Architectural motives travelled as easily along the pilgrimage
routes. Miss King has shown that the west front of Le Puy, on the
road, is derived from Santiago, and Lampérez that the cusping of
St.-Michel-de-l'Aiguille is inspired by the same source.

It has long been known that the horsemen sculptured on the façades of several churches in the west of France represent Constantine. It has been conjectured that pilgrims to Rome had been impressed by the statue of Marcus Aurelius, now on the Capitoline,
but then near the Lateran, and which had mistakenly been believed
to represent Constantine. Upon returning home, it is supposed, they
caused the statue to be copied.

The fact, however, I confess, seems to me far from certain. Constantine is a subject well known to Byzantine iconography. Strzygowski [1] has suggested that the motive of the victorious rider, transfixing with his spear his fallen enemy is of ancient Egyptian origin, since it is found in a relief representing Horus, now in the Louvre. In any event, the motive was very frequent in the Christian art of the Copts; almost any saint [2] might be represented in this form, among others, Constantine. [3] Now there are several clear indications that the Constantines of western France are derived from Eastern tradition, not from the Marcus Aurelius of Rome.

Constantine was represented in a mosaic of the church of the Holy Sepulchre at Jerusalem. [4] This monument has unhappily perished, and we know it only through over-brief descriptions. One detail is, however, significant. Opposite the emperor was represented the female figure of the empress Helena. This suggests an explanation of the female figure which appears beside the Constantines at Châ-

[1] *Hell. und Kopt. Kunst*, 26.

[2] Clermont-Ganneau, 398, mentions an instance in which Christ is represented as a horseman; he also speaks of "deux intailles d'hématite à la Bibliothèque Nationale, où l'on voit un cavalier perçant de sa lance un ennemi à terre, avec le nom de Salomon." Every one is familiar with representations of St. George and St. Martin as horsemen. According to Strzygowski, *Kopt. Reit.*, 51, there are at the monastery of St. Paul at Mar frescos of 1713 representing six cavaliers, all different saints and labelled. In the south monastery of St. Anthony at Gallale are ten or twelve riders (52), and many single representations occur elsewhere (53).

[3] Grueneissen, 63. A partir de l'époque impériale, les images des vainqueurs terrassant l'ennemi sont multiples : on les voit sur les bas-reliefs, sur les médailles et ailleurs. . . . Le type de cavalier vainqueur foulant aux pieds l'ennemi désarmé était très repandu dans l'art alexandrin populaire. De petites figurines en argile, créées pour le grand marché, prouvent avec évidence, que la formule simplificatrice n'est point une invention copte. L'image de Constantin est la première dans la longue série des saints guerriers intrépides, et celle de saint George ne sera pas, certainement, en Egypte, la plus fréquente. Dans le nombre des cavaliers qui ornent les murs de Baouit, on trouve les noms de St. Victor, de Orion, Bonakh et Askla, de Sisinnios. Dans la chapelle XXVI sont représentés quatre cavaliers affrontés dont un seul conserve la légende fragmentaire; peut-être Jean le martyre. Sur une ampoule en plomb, on trouve un cavalier avec le nom de S. Théodore. Enfin, il existe beaucoup d'autres cavaliers, surtout dans l'art textile, mais ils ne sont pas encore identifiés. Strzygowski (*Aachen*, 48) has identified the Barberini ivory of the Louvre as a Constantine, and believes that it was executed at Alexandria in the IV century. For the origin of the iconographical tradition of representing Constantine as a horseman, see Clermont-Ganneau, 398 : "L'empereur (Constantin) s'était fait représenter en personne dans le rôle d'adversaire du dragon. Ce fait enregistré par Eusèbe, confirmé par la numismatique, est également attesté par les historiens orientaux qui mentionnent, parmi les statues d'airain de Constantinople, un cavalier armé d'une lance et perçant un serpent."

[4] Jeffery, 36.

teauneuf-sur-Charente (Ill. 1008), Angoulême and St.-Jouin-de-Marne (Ill. 947). These, I suspect, represent not the Church, as M. Mâle has supposed, but Helena. The presence of these female figures in several of the French monuments, inexplicable on the theory that the theme is derived from the Roman Marcus Aurelius, is easily comprehensible in the light of Byzantine tradition.[1]

The prostrate figure at the feet of the horse, characteristic of the French sculptures, might well be derived from the East. Such a figure occurs under the feet of one of the four horsemen represented on a Byzantine ivory box of the X century in the museum at Arezzo. One, too, is found in the Barberini ivory of the Louvre, which is an Alexandrine work of the IV century. The same motive recurs in a Coptic manuscript of the X or XI century and in a miniature of the Chludoff psalter, a palimpset erased in the XII century, but of which the illustrations belong to an earlier period.[2] The fifty-ninth psalm appears, in fact, to have been interpreted as symbolical of Constantine. We find the prostrate figure at the feet of the horseman also in the XIII century wooden doors of Kasr-es-Scham'a at Old Cairo.[3] There is nothing in this motive therefore which might not have found its way into French sculpture from Oriental sources.[4]

In western France, Constantine on horseback is regularly balanced by Samson wrestling with the lion. The Hebrew hero is astride the back of the monster, and breaks his jaws with his hands. Now this peculiar iconography seems to be taken over from reliefs representing Mithra and the bull[5] which were common in Egypt as well as elsewhere. In these Mithra is seen on the back of the ani-

---

[1] Helena is often represented with Constantine in Byzantine iconography, as *e.g.*, in an ivory triptych of the X century in the Bibliothèque Nationale, illustrated by Schlumberger, *Ep. Byz.*, I, 17; in an ivory triptych of the XI century in the Berlin museum, illustrated *ibid.*, II, 76; in a reliquary of the XI–XII centuries at Nonantola, illustrated *ibid.*, II, 81; in a reliquary of Cologne, illustrated *ibid.*, II, 177; in a steatite carving of the XI–XII centuries in the cathedral of Lentini, illustrated *ibid.*, III, 804.

[2] Illustrated by Tikkanen, Taf. I, Fig. 1. Compare also Lefebvre des Noëttes, Fig. 6.

[3] Strzygowski, *Kopt. Reit.*, 55.

[4] The horseman at S. Maria Antiqua, Rome, seems to have had two prostrate figures beneath his horse's hoofs (Grüneisen, Pl. IC. XVI).

[5] Two of these are illustrated by Strzygowski, *Cairo Cat.*, 8–10. Many others illustrated by Frothingham, *passim*.

mal, grasping its head in precisely the same manner. Both Constantine and Samson appear therefore to be motives of Egyptian origin.

Several of the earlier Constantines in the West — those of St.-Jouin-de-Marne (Ill. 947) and Angoulême — are low reliefs, and in the former case of very small dimensions. The early cavalier of Parthenay-le-Vieux (Ill. 924), it is true, is of the established type; but in general there seems to be a distinct evolution towards larger and higher reliefs, a fact which makes it seem probable that the western cavaliers are derived from miniatures rather than from the Roman statue in the round.

It is certain that the silver Constantine presented by Charles, Duke of Berry, in 1414, had a Greek inscription.[1] Therefore at least one image of Constantine had been imported into France from the East. Nor is there reason to suppose that it was the only one.

A marked peculiarity of the Constantines in the West is the coat fluttering behind. This is excellently preserved, for example, at Surgères (Ill. 1092, 1093) and Parthenay-le-Vieux (Ill. 924). Now this motive is characteristic of Byzantine art,[2] but is not found in the Marcus Aurelius. This fact is conclusive.

Indeed, a well-known anecdote suggests that the Marcus Aurelius,

[1] Strzygowski, *Hell. und Kopt. Kunst*, 27–28.

[2] The coat flutters behind Constantine on horse-back in a Byzantine miniature of the X century in the Bibliothèque Nationale, illustrated by Schlumberger, I, 605. It also flutters behind the equestrian St. Sisinnios of Bawit illustrated by Grüneisen, Pl. XXXV. St. Minas is depicted as a horseman with coat fluttering behind, and a naked bather at the feet of his horse in a Nubian miniature of the IX century, illustrated by Kaufmann, 33. Horsemen in Byzantine art are, in fact, regularly represented with the coat fluttering behind — *e.g.*, on an ivory box of the XI century at Troyes, illustrated by Diehl, 615; in an ivory casket of the X century at Liverpool, illustrated by Graeven, I, 13; in a miniature illustrated by Schlumberger, *Ep. Byz.*, I, 740; in an ivory of the XI or XII century in the museum of Angers, illustrated *ibid.*, II, 132; in a miniature of the X–XI centuries in the library of St. Mark's at Venice; illustrated *ibid.*, II, 473; in an ivory box of the X or XI century in the Bargello at Florence, illustrated *ibid.*, III, 17; in miniatures of the XI century at Jerusalem, illustrated *ibid.*, III, 32, 37; in a casket of the XI century at Bologna, illustrated by Graeven, II, 4; in a miniature of the Utrecht Psalter (f. 7 b); in one of the four horsemen of the Apocalypse of St.-Sever (1028–1072), illustrated by Haseloff in Michel, II, 1, 752; in the rider of the pulpit at Aachen, an ivory plaque of ancient Alexandrian origin inserted in the Romanesque work of 1002–1024; in the rider of the tympanum at Daschlut, illustrated by Strzygowski, *Hell. und Kopt. Kunst*, 21; in a miniature of the Greek manuscript, Vatican 1156, illustrated by Millet, Fig. 95; in a Tétrevangile of the Bibliothèque Nationale, Paris, 74, illustrated *ibid.*, Fig. 100; in a fresco of Kalinîc, illustrated *ibid.*, Fig. 154; in a Macedonian relief of the Louvre, illustrated by Lefebvre des Noëttes, Fig. 21.

far from inspiring the French statues, was dubbed a Constantine from its resemblance to the traditional representations of that saint. It is said that a French noble when visiting Rome was so shocked to find the statue deprived of the cloak usual in his country, that he presented one. It is certain that in the XII century the significance of the Marcus Aurelius was disputed. In the *Descriptio Plenaria* [1] we read: *Laterani est quidam caballus aereus qui dicitur Constantini, sed non ita est.* Another pagan statue near by was called Samson, probably because Samson commonly balanced Constantine on the façades of Pictave churches. [2]

Not all the cavaliers of western France are Constantines. Very few of them are actually named; because it is known that equestrian statues of Constantine existed, it has been assumed that all equestrian statues represent Constantine. Such, however, is not the case. At Surgères (Ill. 1092, 1093) there are two horsemen, only one of whom can be Constantine. The second figure is inexplicable on the theory that these cavaliers are derived from the Roman Marcus Aurelius. In the East, however, we have seen that many different saints, of whom Constantine was only one, were represented as horsemen. [3] In the frescos of St.-Jean of Poitiers, in addition to the Constantine, three other horsemen appear. This iconographical scheme has no analogy with the Marcus Aurelius; on the other hand, it is entirely parallel to the chapel at Bawit, also adorned with four cavaliers in fresco [4] and to the southern monastery of St. Anthony at Gallale, where the same peculiar iconographic composition is repeated. [5] It therefore seems certain that the French cavaliers are derived not from Rome, but from the East.

At Bamberg, where the influence of the East as well as of France is strong, is a rider whom there is no especial reason for believing a representation of Constantine.

---

[1] Ed. Urlichs, 98.   [2] *Ibid.,* 136.

[3] At S. Zeno of Verona, Theodoric appears as a horseman, as he did also in the pediment of his palace at Ravenna.

[4] Grüneisen.

[5] These frescos are of 1508–1540. See Strzygowski, *Kopt. Reit.,* 55.

Two reliefs in Spain, at Santa Maria of Carrión de los Condes (Ill. 774) and at Armentía (Ill. 763) show every characteristic of the French Constantines. But here again the significance is not certain. At a later period St. James in Spain often appears in the form of a victorious horseman,[1] and the conquered province at his feet becomes a Moor. The researches of Miss King have proved that the conception of St. James as a horseman is indeed at least as old as the end of the XI century; it is he who appears in the psychostasy at Pontida.[2]

What part, if any, the pilgrimages played in diffusing the motive of the rider through western Europe remains then problematical.

In other features of iconography, however, the influence of the pilgrimages is unmistakable. It is evident that the popularity of St. James reflected glory on his colleagues. Through the pilgrimage of Santiago, the entire group of the apostles came to the foreground with a conspicuousness that they had never before enjoyed. Their images commenced first to be represented in the pilgrimage churches. An early sculptured cycle of the apostles is found in the cloister of Moissac (Ill. 262–273). Soon after, the subject was taken up at Santiago, and many times repeated; then it occurs in the cloister of St.-Etienne of Toulouse, which adjoined the pilgrims' hospital; then at Oviedo, then in the Cluniac Daurade of Toulouse, then in Mateo's Pórtico de la Gloria. From the pilgrimage churches it spread to northern France, to Chartres, to Amiens and to Reims. Even as late as 1324 the cycle of the apostles was repeated in the pilgrimage chapel at Paris. Five of these statues, the work of Robert de Launoy, have been excavated and are in the Museum of Cluny. Germany also brought back from Spain the cycle of the apostles, and adopted it with enthusiasm. Certain of the apostles of the Liebfrauenkirche of Halberstadt have their legs crossed, probably an indication that

---

[1] He is already so represented at Betanzos (Ill. 895). The female figure here is, I suppose, a donor.

[2] I illustrated this relief, of which I missed the iconographic significance, in my *Lombard Architecture*, IV, Plate 189, Fig. 2. Santiago is conceived of as a cavalier in the XIX miracle of the Callistine codex, ed. Lopez-Aydillo, 45. He also appears as such in the codex known as Tumbo A of the cathedral archives at Santiago, Mas phot., C 29435.

they are derived from the South-west. The apostles of Bamberg evidently owe much to Toulouse and Santiago.

The basilica at Compostela was begun in 1078; the choir was consecrated in 1102; and in 1124 the building was finished. This edifice marks a notable advance in architectural art. It has been much discussed whether the church should be classed as French or Spanish.

In point of fact, at Santiago, as in other important mediaeval buildings, the best workmen were summoned from wherever they could be found, and artistic ideas were collected wherever suitable ones could be met with. From these mixed elements was formed an indigenous atelier. Precisely the same process took place when the basilica of St.-Denis and the cathedral of Canterbury were constructed, and was the natural proceeding when there must be built a church so great as to be beyond the ordinary resources of the country.

It may well be that the master-builders of Santiago, Bernard and Robert, were Frenchmen. It is certain that closer precedents for the style of the building are to be found in France than in Spain. The ambulatory, the most conspicuous feature of the plan, is surely not of Spanish origin. The motive appeared in Lombardy toward the end of the X century — at S. Stefano of Verona, c. 990 and in the cathedral of Ivrea c. 1000 — and also, it seems, about the same time in France. The earliest extant example north of the Alps is at Tournus.[1] It was certainly from France and more precisely from northern

---

[1] M. Bréhier believes that the motive of the ambulatory was originated in the cathedral of Clermont consecrated in 946, and was copied thence at St.-Martin of Tours, Ste.-Croix of Orléans (989), Notre-Dame-de-la-Couture of Le Mans (c. 997) and the cathedral of Le Mans (951–970). I confess, however, to distrust of deductive reasoning based solely upon excavated foundations. Nothing is easier to misunderstand. The dates can not be controlled by study of the style. Especially hazardous in my opinion are the conclusions which have been risked upon St.-Martin of Tours. If we believe Comte de Lasteyrie and M. Mâle the basilica erected there in 994 was the prototype of the entire Santiagoan family of churches. This theory is based upon the admittedly inaccurate reports of excavations conducted in an entirely unscientific manner. Such evidence hardly justifies the assumption that a church of this type existed at Tours a century earlier than elsewhere; especially since we have the explicit statement of the contemporary *Pilgrim's Guide* that the church of St.-Martin was built in imitation of that of Compostela: *super quem* (the tomb of St. Martin) *ingens basilica veneranda sub eius honore, ad similitudinem scilicet beati Jacobi, miro opere fabricatur*. The Santiagoan church was doubtless erected after the fire of 1123. It is less improbable that the church of St.-Martial of Limoges, begun in 1063 and consecrated in 1095, was of the Santiagoan type shown in drawings of the edifice destroyed in the XVIII century that have come down to us. The débris

Auvergne that the ambulatory, and other features of design also, were brought to Compostela. The significant fact, however, is that out of these ancient elements was produced a new whole; that the atelier of Santiago became, for a century, one of the most advanced and productive centres of artistic creation in Europe; and that it exerted a dominating influence upon the development of architecture and sculpture in the XII century.

The type of architecture originated at Santiago became the standard for a great number of churches along the pilgrimage road, and in whole districts of France. St.-Sernin of Toulouse is an evident copy of the basilica at Compostela; so is Ste.-Foy of Conques and so were probably St.-Martin of Tours and St.-Martial of Limoges. The great abbey of Cluny itself was influenced by Santiago. From these centres, all, except Cluny, on the road, the type spread through whole districts of France, through Limousin, through Languedoc, through Auvergne, through Burgundy. Compostela was the model from which, directly or indirectly, was derived a majority of the great Romanesque churches of the XII century in France. The type, modified it is true, but still unmistakable, was carried into Italy, to Acerenza, to Venosa, to Aversa, to S. Antimo. The church at Cavagnolo Po, dedicated to the pilgrimage saint, Ste. Foy, clearly shows the influence of this type of construction. In Languedoc and Provence a modification of the Santiagoan type was introduced. The ambulatory was replaced by apses, and the barrel vaults were pointed. St.-Trophîme of Arles, on the road, may have been one of the centres from which the type spread.

The Ile-de-France owes much to Compostela. We have already remarked that the broad-leaved and crocketed capitals characteristic of the transitional style of the middle of the XII century are inspired, not by nature, as has been supposed, but by the XI-century work at Santiago. The half-barrel vaults thrown across the galleries

of the abbey, now gathered together in the Musée Adrien Dubouché (No. 35, 36, 37, 38, 39, 41, 45, 46, 47, 48, 49, 50, 51, 52, 53, 54, 72 — see Texier, Pl. I, Fig. 3), show such nondescript workmanship that it is difficult to judge of their date. It is however more natural to suppose that the church of St.-Martial was reconstructed after the fire of 1122 (C. de Lasteyrie, 295).

of St.-Etienne of Caen, and long erroneously (as M. Lefèvre-Pontalis has shown) believed to be the germ from which the flying buttress developed, may have come to Caen from the pilgrimage churches as well as from Auvergne.[1]

With the XII century passed the glory of Cluny. The power of the art-loving monastery was supplanted by that of the art-hating Cistercians. The popularity of the pilgrimage continued, but the first fine fire of enthusiasm had passed. And Spanish sculpture began to decline. Like the pilgrimage, Spanish plastic art reached its highest point of development in the XII century. Nevertheless, even in decadence, the pilgrimage road continued to be the centre from which artistic influences spread. It was, however, as in France itself, no longer the Cluniac monasteries, but the secular churches, which fostered the ateliers. On the pilgrimage route there sprang up in Santo Sepolcro of Estella and in the cathedrals of Léon, Burgos, Vitoria and Pamplona schools of sculpture completely French in character. From these centres the art spread throughout Spain. At Villacázar on the road was another centre, cruder, less purely French in character. From the centre at Santo Domingo de la Calzada on the road, still another manner of sculpture spread to San Millán.

The developed Gothic architecture of northern France was introduced into Spain in the cathedrals of Léon and Burgos, on the road; thence it spread. In southern France a local Gothic style appeared at St.-Nazaire of Carcassonne, St.-Etienne of Toulouse and the Cathedral of Narbonne, all on the road. It was a style of merit which, as in the cathedral of Narbonne with its flying battlements, rises at times to an unexpected height.

The stained glass of the North was introduced at Béziers and St.-Nazaire of Carcassonne on the road. The latter atelier seems to show affiliations with that of Ste.-Radegonde of Poitiers. The art spread to St.-Michel at Carcassonne, to Albi, to Santes Creuz in Catalonia and to Narbonne. St.-Nazaire of Carcassonne became, indeed, the centre of an important school of glass-making, which preserved the

[1] Half-barrel vaults over the galleries buttressed the dome of St.-Bénigne of Dijon.

traditions of the XIII century almost unmodified long after they had been abandoned in the North. The church at Caylus contains a window with small medallions and Gothic colouring executed in the XV century. At Léon, on the road, arose another school of glass-painting.

As late as the XV century the Romanesque architecture of Compostela still haunted the memory of artists in northern Europe. The background of Van Eyck's Annunciation at St. Petersburg represents the interior of the transept of the cathedral at Santiago.[1]

It is therefore evident that the pilgrimages are an important fact in the history of mediaeval art. The pilgrimage roads were a route along which ideas travelled in both directions with extraordinary facility. The pilgrimages united the art of all Europe and even of Asia. But the most important contribution of the pilgrimages to mediaeval art was the group of sculptures produced in the XII century along the lower part of the road of St. James. It is to these remarkable monuments and their influence that will be devoted the remaining chapters of this book.

[1] *Bulletin Monumental*, 1909, 150–151.

II

MOISSAC AND SOUILLAC

"*Pour la sculpture romane*," M. Bertaux has written, "*il n'y a pas de Pyrénées.*" It is a commonplace of history that the existing frontier between France and Spain was first established by St. Louis. Before the XIII century the mountains formed no barrier. The same peoples, Basques or Catalans, lived, as they still live, on both slopes.

This fundamental fact has nevertheless been ignored by archaeologists and historians of art. All students of Romanesque sculpture have followed one another in establishing a rigid division following the modern frontier. They have seen in Toulouse one school, in Spain another school. And especially if the author was French, he has found at Toulouse originality, power, inventiveness; in Spain thoughtless copying of French motives. The fact that at this period Toulouse was not French had no power to dampen the enthusiasm of patriotism. National vanity found the liveliest satisfaction in depreciating the monuments on the Spanish side of the frontier, and in praising those on the French side.

Interest in this sport appears to have blinded all eyes to the still surely obvious truth, that the art of the two sides of the frontier is precisely the same. One style stretched from Santiago along the pilgrimage road to Toulouse and Moissac and Conques. This art is neither French nor Spanish. It is the art of the pilgrimage. It is as idle to discuss whether its creative centre was at Toulouse or at Santiago, as it is to discuss whether that of northern French sculpture was at Chartres or Reims. Both Toulouse and Santiago were centres. The same sculptors were active at both. Religiously and consequently financially, Santiago was certainly the more important. The cathedral possessed six sculptured portals against the single one of St.-Sernin. The atelier at Santiago hence naturally employed more artists than that of Toulouse; among the extant fragments we can

trace seven times as many hands at Santiago (Ill. 674–695) as at St.-
Sernin (Ill. 296–322). The average quality of the work at Toulouse
may be slightly above the average at Santiago, although the best
work at Compostela equals if it does not surpass anything at St.-
Sernin. Nothing in Spain is more degraded than the portal at Espalion (Ill. 402–408), or some of the work at St.-Aventin (Ill. 508–
510) and St.-Bertrand-de-Comminges (Ill. 323–326). Sculptors from
Santiago — not from Toulouse — were called to work upon the church
of San Isidoro of Léon (Ill. 696–702) and upon Ste.-Foy of Conques
(Ill. 386, 392–401).

A peculiarity of the school of the pilgrimages is the creation of
oases of art in the midst of deserts. Sculpture flourished, as a rule,
only in pilgrimage churches throughout the entire South-west. Toulouse and Moissac are as isolated in sterile Languedoc as Santiago in
the wilds of Galicia. Exceptionally the art spread from the pilgrimage churches to the abbeys or cathedrals or parish churches not on
the road — to Segóvia (Ill. 755–760), Sepúlveda (Ill. 799–805) or
Soria (Ill. 795–798) in Spain, to Albi (Ill. 453–455) or St.-Antonin
(Ill. 358–359) in France. Several of the off-shoots north of the
Garonne showed great vitality; but in southern Languedoc, as in
Spain, they withered and died. It was from the pilgrimages that the
art was born; it was by the pilgrimages that it lived; and it was only
in the pilgrimage churches that it really flowered.

The earliest extant monument of pilgrimage art is really the cloister of Santo Domingo de Silos that we have already studied. The
monastery lies to the south of Burgos, and a day's journey from the
regular route of the Pilgrims. It may be conjectured, however, that
not a few would detour to visit so holy a place; the pilgrim's wallet
and cockle-shell of the Christ in the Journey to Emmaus (Ill. 667)
argue that pilgrims were often seen in the abbey. This is, I believe,
the first time in art that Christ at Emmaus is represented as a pilgrim to St. James.[1]

---

[1] M. Omont has published from a manuscript of Beauvais a mystery of the XII century
dealing with the Journey to Emmaus.

The school of sculpture, so brilliantly inaugurated at Santo Domingo de Silos, did not remain without descendants. At Souillac, in
the valley of the Dordogne, are incorporated in the west wall of the
church fragments of an ancient portal (Ill. 343–352). These sculptures, it is evident enough, are closely related to those of Santo Domingo (Ill. 666–673), but one feels, especially in certain of the faces,
the freshness of the fountain-head of Cluny. The aesthetic value of
the work is uneven. Something of the sense for composition of the
Santo Domingo sculptor is carried over into the relief with the story
of Theophilus (Ill. 347–348). The two seated saints flank the central
group, as Memmi's Santa Giulitta and Sant' Ansano flank Simone's
Annunciation. The figure of the prostrate Theophilus, to whom the
Virgin returns his bond, combines with the shrine to form a sort of
arch over the four figures enacting the central portion of the drama.
It is, indeed, probable that this composition is taken over directly
from Silos. In the wall of that church, near the door of the Cámara
Santa, is a relief of the XIII century representing Santo Domingo
like a good pilgrimage saint delivering prisoners.[1] Now the composition of this late relief, with a large figure at either side, while the
prisoners are grouped in the centre under an arch, is strikingly like
that of the Souillac Theophilus. It is probable that there was in the
cloister at Silos, or at least by the sculptor of the cloister, a relief with
this composition which was reproduced at Souillac and by the later
sculptor at Silos.

The same sense for composition which is remarkable in the Souillac
Theophilus, presides also in the altogether remarkable trumeau
(Ill. 349–352). Here in the midst of apparent confusion all is order.
The thrice repeated figure of a bird-headed monster divides the front
face into carefully balanced and rhythmic patterns. The entwined
figures of the farther side (Ill. 350) are among the inspired creations
of mediaeval art. Satisfying, too, even in ruin, is the Joseph (Ill.
343, 346) that once doubtless flanked the portal; while the opposite
Isaiah (Ill. 344–345) haunts every memory. There is, it is true, in this

[1] Illustrated by Roulin, 9.

figure a certain something which leads one to understand why solemn archaeologists, notwithstanding his clearly engraved name and ample beard, have set him down as a "foolish virgin"; but the movement of the figure is so stimulating, the swirl of the draperies so intoxicating, the lines of the scroll so decorative, that the severest critic must capitulate.

The sculptor of Souillac worked also upon the portal of St.-Martin of Brive (Ill. 353–354). Fragments of this which have been recovered by excavations are now assembled in the Musée Massenat.[1] It is curious, in view of the Spanish origin of this master, to observe that Viollet-le-Duc remarked Arab character in the capitals.[2]

The capitals of St.-Martin of Brive are not by the hand of the master of Souillac. We have only to compare the clumsy and formless draperies (Ill. 355–357) with the exquisitely modelled ones of the trumeau at Souillac (Ill. 349–352); the heavy proportions and overlarge heads of the capitals of St.-Martin (Ill. 355–357) with the slender proportions and dainty heads of the master of Souillac (Ill. 343–354); or most of all the general inferiority of execution in the capitals (Ill. 355–357) with the superlative technique of the Souillac artist (Ill. 343–354) to be convinced of the fact. However, it is none the less certain that the sculptor of the capitals imitated carefully the style of the master of Souillac. The head of his Christ (Ill. 355) is an obvious copy of the Souillac master's Adam (Ill. 353). The face of his executioner (Ill. 355) recalls that of the St. Stephen at Souillac (Ill. 347). The draperies of his angel (Ill. 356) are evidently an imitation of draperies of the type of those of the Souillac *Isaiah* (Ill. 344). We have, therefore, in the St.-Martin capitals an inferior sculptor who imitates very exactly certain details of the style of the Souillac master.

A problem of unusual interest is the question of the relationship of the St.-Martin capitals to the pulpit at Volterra, in distant Tuscany (Ill. 194–196). The style of the pulpit is clearly compounded of many different elements. The Visitation (Ill. 196) reproduces line for line

[1] Bonnay, 237.   [2] Forot, 68.

the same subject on the impost of S. Andrea of Pistoia, by Enrico
(Ill. 192). A much stronger influence, however, is that of St.-Gilles.
The ram in the bushes of the Volterra Sacrifice of Isaac (Ill. 195) reproduces precisely the last sheep to the right in the St.-Gilles scene
of the Money Changers (Ill. 1317). The curious draperies, the folds
of which are indicated by a slash ending in an "eye," for example in
the Abraham (Ill. 195), could only have been derived from the work
of Brunus at St.-Gilles (Ill. 1303). The facial types are many of them
directly taken over from St.-Gilles — the Zacharias (Ill. 196) reproduces the last figure to the right in the lintel of the central portal at
St.-Gilles (Ill. 1318); the face of the angel at Volterra (Ill. 196) is like
that of the executioner to the left in the St.-Gilles Betrayal (Ill.
1319); the facial types in the Volterra Last Supper (Ill. 194) are
analogous to those of the St.-Gilles Betrayal (Ill. 1319, 1320).

It is certain, therefore, that the sculptor of the Volterra pulpit had
been at St.-Gilles, and had taken thence many details of his style.
Now if we subtract from his work at Volterra what he had learned at
St.-Gilles and at Pistoia, we have left a personality strangely like
that of the master of the Brive capitals. The head of the Abraham
at Volterra (Ill. 195) is a head of the Souillac master, precisely like
that which the sculptor of the capitals had reproduced in his Christ
at Brive (Ill. 355). The head at the feet of the Volterra Abraham
(Ill. 195) recalls the seated executioner in the Brive capital (Ill. 355).
The head of the angel at Volterra (Ill. 195) is like that of the executioner at Brive (Ill. 355). The face of St. Peter in the Brive Giving
of the Keys is reproduced in that of Christ in the Volterra Last Supper (Ill. 194). There are at Brive and Volterra the same heavy figures, the same disproportionate heads. There is the same copying of
the manner of more gifted sculptors. I have little hesitation in concluding that the Volterra pulpit, although the style seems superfi-
cially so different, is really by the same artist as the Brive capitals,
but executed at a later phase of his career, and after he had studied
St.-Gilles and the sculptures of Tuscany.

We have remarked that the Volterra pulpit shows draperies copied from those of Enrico at S. Andrea of Pistoia. Now these draperies of Enrico are themselves in turn derived from the Pisa pulpit of Guglielmo Tedesco now at Cagliari (Ill. 186–188). Since this pulpit was executed in 1158–1162, we may infer that the work of Enrico at S. Andrea of Pistoia (Ill. 191–193) is later than 1162, and the Volterra pulpit later still.

Romanesque sculpture offers no more baffling problem than the relationship of Souillac to the porch at Moissac. It seems clear that the tympanum of Moissac (Ill. 339–342) is earlier than any of the work at Souillac (Ill. 343–352). On the other hand, the reliefs of the porch at Moissac (Ill. 360–377) appear to be the work of an inferior artist who imitated alternately the earlier tympanum (Ill. 339–342) and Souillac (Ill. 343–352). His trumeau (Ill. 362) is inspired by that of Souillac (Ill. 349–352); but the admirably subordinated detail of the original has been suppressed, and the crisscrossed monsters are copied from the earlier capitals (Ill. 337) of the Moissac porch. The trumeau (Ill. 362) has gained a certain brutal power, but has lost the finer and more imaginative qualities of the Souillac original (Ill. 349–352). The prophet (Ill. 363, 365) in relief on the east side of the trumeau is obviously imitated from the Souillac Isaiah (Ill. 344, 345); but the life, the movement and the vigour of the original figure are lacking. Santo Domingo draperies have been supplanted by the Cluniac draperies of the tympanum; the figure, notwithstanding its mannerisms, is dull. Even more commonplace is the prophet of the west jamb (Ill. 364), and how inferior to the *Joseph* of Souillac (Ill. 343)! But it is in the *Peter* (Ill. 360) and the *Isaiah* (Ill. 361) flanking the doorway that the inferiority of the Moissac artist is most apparent. The *Peter* (Ill. 360) is an unhappy adaptation of the angel to the left in the tympanum (Ill. 340); the *Isaiah* (Ill. 361) repeats the outlines of the Souillac *Joseph* (Ill. 343). The reliefs with scenes from the story of Lazarus (Ill. 366–369), like those opposite dealing with the early life of Christ (Ill. 372–375), are plodding imitations of the manner of the tympanum. In the representation of the vice of Luxury (Ill. 371), however, the sculptor shows quite unexpectedly wealth of imagination and tragic power. This is a great grotesque. Opposite, the Visitation (Ill. 377) also rises to extraordinary heights. I should hardly know where to find more sensitive line, more expressive drawing, more delicate finish. One is tempted to conjecture that these masterpieces are by another and much finer hand.

The influence of Santo Domingo de Silos continued to be exerted until a late period of the XII century. The series of reliefs, part of which is preserved at St.-Guilhem-le-Désert (Ill. 1399) and part at the University of Montpellier (Ill. 1397, 1398), is derived from this original.[1]

The cloister of Moissac (Ill. 262–287) was, as an inscription proves, in construction in 1100, and the pier sculptures appear to have been executed in this year. Moissac was a Cluniac abbey on the road; but inspiration was sought not in Burgundy, but in Santo Domingo de Silos (Ill. 666–673). Thence is derived the architecture of the cloister with its coupled columns (the pointed arches are, of course, the result of a later reconstruction); thence the pier sculptures, thence the plastic style.

The Cluniac grace and movement which bubble at Santo Domingo have dried up at Moissac. These reliefs seem made of cast iron. The scale has been coarsened; the figures appear frozen. This immobility produces at first sight an impression of archaism; but on closer study it becomes evident that the Moissac sculptures must be later than Santo Domingo. The facial types, while closely related to those of the Spanish cloister, are more varied and far better characterized. The conventions for the hair and beard, while very similar, are at Moissac more naturalistic. The gestures are more varied and freer than at Santo Domingo. Finally, to resort to a mechanical proof, the form of the letters of the inscriptions at Santo Domingo is more primitive than at Moissac.

The internal evidence of style entirely reinforces, therefore, the documentary evidence that the Moissac cloister is later than Santo Domingo. It is hardly necessary to point out how closely the Moissac

[1] They are executed by the hand of the Third Master of St.-Gilles.

sculptor has followed his predecessor. The convention of two parallel lines used to indicate the folds of the draperies, the drawing of the eyes, the gestures, the position of the feet placed on a sloping shelf, many other details betray a close relationship. Indeed the Spanish influence at Moissac was always strong. "*On remarque sur un chapiteau des caractères arabes maladroitement copiés par un lapidaire ignorant leur signification.*" [1] The crossed animals of the porch capital are similar to those of a Mozarabic codex of the X century published by Gómez-Moreno.

Like the sculptor of Santo Domingo, the master of the Moissac cloister made much use of ivory-carvings. It seems to have been directly from this source, rather than from Santo Domingo, that he derived the arches under which his figures are placed. The horizontal bottom line of the draperies and the modelling of the faces is strikingly analogous to the ivories of the Fitzwilliam Museum at Cambridge [2] and the Stiftsbibliothek of Frankfurt. [3] The motive of two angels carrying a medallion, which is found on one of the capitals of the Moissac cloister, also occurs in an ivory of the Ada group, now in the Victoria and Albert Museum of London. [4] The face of the St. James of the cloister pier (Ill. 265) and which later reappears in the Christ of the Flagellation in the tympanum of Santiago (Ill. 680) is closely analogous to that of St. Peter in an ivory of the Museo Civico of Bologna assigned to *c*. 500. There is the nose, the same eye, the same mouth. [5] I suspect, indeed, that the sculptor of the Moissac cloister held in his hand an ivory, probably of the Ada group. The peculiar stiffness and coarseness of his figures can only be due to this inspiration. So, too, their strength. After all, this the earliest [6] extant cycle of the apostles in French sculpture is also the most unforgettable.

---

[1] Michel, I, 2, 617.

[2] Goldschmidt, I, No. 120.　　　　　　[3] *Ibid.*, No. 121.

[4] *Ibid.*, No. 14. This motive occurs frequently on ancient sarcophagi. But I can see little evidence that the master of the Moissac cloister made any use of Roman models. The motives of ancient sculpture which are found in his work may well have come to him through the ivories.

[5] Illustrated by Graeven, II, 1.　　　　　　[6] Except Azay-le-Rideau (Ill. 896).

It may be common derivation from Ada group ivories (or, as Mr. Morey would have it, miniatures) which explains the analogies between the cloister of Moissac and the works of Guglielmo da Modena. At all events it is certain that the latter also fell under this influence. His style is distinctly foreshadowed in an ivory of the X century in the John Rylands collection at Manchester;[1] while his curls, which also appear at Moissac, may be traced as far back as Irish manuscripts.[2]

The capitals of the Moissac cloister (Ill. 274–287) are the work of the same atelier that executed the pier sculptures, if not of the same master. They are less under the influence of Santo Domingo de Silos. There was here originated an iconographic program to which the XII century repeatedly turned for inspiration.

In the ambulatory of St.-Sernin of Toulouse are enwalled sculptures (Ill. 296–305) which are clearly related to the pier reliefs of Moissac. Since the original position of these reliefs in the church is unknown, it is impossible to determine their date with accuracy by documentary evidence, although the building dates of the church have come down to us. A new basilica was begun, presumably soon after the foundation of the chapter regular in 1077; this was consecrated a first time in 1096 and a second time in 1119. When St. Raymond died in 1118, the nave was finished up to the level of the clerestory windows.[3]

St.-Sernin stood in the same relation to Compostela as S. Niccola of Trani to S. Niccola of Bari — it was an imitation which threatened to develop into a serious rival. Among the fabulous relics claimed by the chapter were the oliphant and the bodies of six apostles, including "the greater part" of that of St. James himself! The new basilica,

---

[1] Illustrated by Goldschmidt, I, No. 27.

[2] See the Landisfarne Gospels, Book of St. Chad, Litchfield, fol. 142, illustrated by Zimmermann, 246. From Irish manuscripts, too, seems to have come the wavy line of the lower edges of the draperies, characteristic both of Lombardy and of Aquitaine — see the Kells Gospel, Trinity College, Dublin, No. A. 1. 6., fol. 32 b, illustrated by Zimmermann, 171.

[3] Quid tandem de egregio ecclesie Sancti Saturnini opere, cui per multa annorum tempora prefuit, et preter capitis membrum, quod jam completum fuerat, corpus a fundamentis incipiens, ante obitus sui (diem), divina opitulante misericordia, parietes in circuitu ad fenestrarum completionem usque perduxit (cit. Mortet, 262).

begun in the latter part of the XI century, was almost the exact duplicate of the great church at Compostela. All this was too much for
the patience of Cluny which had the interests of the pilgrimage so
vitally at heart. The Cluniacizing bishop of Toulouse found a pre-
text for expelling the canons (1082), and installed monks of Cluny in
their place.[1] But a year later the pope, who doubtless began to be
already somewhat alarmed at the growing power of Santiago, inter-
vened through his legate to restore the canons. These had now, however, learned their lesson; they perceived that their best interests,
like those of Cluny, lay in fostering the pilgrimage. The guide of the
XII century makes of St.-Sernin one of the principal pilgrimage
churches, but the author feels called upon to warn the reader against
the spurious relics of St. James.

The provenance of the sculptures now enwalled in the ambulatory
of St.-Sernin (Ill. 296–305) has remained a mystery. The suggestion
that they are fragments of a destroyed tympanum is so obviously
wide of the mark that it may be at once dismissed. The close resemblance of the Toulouse reliefs to those of the piers of Moissac (Ill.
262–273) has given some ground for supposing that the St.-Sernin
sculptures are fragments from a similar cloister, which were enwalled
in the ambulatory at a comparatively recent date. It is, however,
evident that the St.-Sernin sculptures could never have been placed
on the piers of a cloister. The *Majestas Domini* (Ill. 296) must have
once formed the centre of a composition; to the right of Christ stood
the cherub (Ill. 297) and to the left the seraph (Ill. 298) as indicated
by the inscriptions. The other two angels (Ill. 300, 302) similarly
form a pair, which presumably also flanked a now lost central composition, perhaps a Virgin. Finally the two saints (Ill. 303, 304) also
must have been symmetrically disposed. Now these balanced reliefs
would be inexplicable in a cloister; they might, however, very easily

---

[1] (Isarnus episcopus) querelam habuit cum canonicis sancti Saturnini, qui pontificiam sub-
jectionem detrectabant; quapropter Hunaldo Moissiacensi et Hugoni Cluniacensi abbatibus
eorum ecclesiam tradidit an. 1082, instante Guillelmo comite pro monachis canonicorum loco
substituendis; sed donatio contradicente Richardo pontificio legato, suum sortita non est
effectum, nam anno sequente canonici regulares revocati sunt in eamdem ecclesiam (*Gallia
Christiana*, XIII, 13).

have been arranged about an altar; on the chief face the *Majestas Domini*, the cherub and the seraph (Ill. 296, 297, 298); on the reverse the lost Virgin flanked two angels (Ill. 300, 302); on either end a saint (Ill. 303, 304).

The St.-Sernin relief of the *Majestas Domini* follows precisely the formula consecrated for altar-frontals. Christ is seated in an oval aureole, pointed at the top and bottom (Ill. 296); at the four corners are the symbols of the four Evangelists, bringing the panel to a rectangular shape, higher than broad. This peculiar composition was probably first invented for a book-cover,[1] but in the XII century had become the stock theme for the decoration of the front face of antependia. In the Palio d'Oro of S. Ambrogio,[2] which dates from the IX century, the *Majestas Domini* already occupies the centre of the principal face, but the symbols of the Evangelists, instead of being in the corners, are in the arms of the cross radiating from the central medallion. In the even earlier altar of Cividale [3] Christ in an aureole similarly occupies the centre of the front face. In later times the *Majestas Domini* was regularly represented in the frontals of altars in precisely the peculiar oblong composition we find in the St.-Sernin relief. We learn from the Pilgrims' Guide that the destroyed Arca of St.-Gilles had on the front a *Majestas Domini* placed between a cherub and a seraph; the analógy with St.-Sernin is therefore complete. At St.-Junien (Ill. 450–452) the *Majestas Domini* is in the panel at the end, instead of in the front; the composition is, however precisely that of the St.-Sernin relief. At Airvault (Ill. 964) there is extant an altar-frontal which presents the closest points of contact with the St.-Sernin fragments. The *Majestas Domini* shows the usual composition; and this central group is flanked by figures standing in arches, exactly like the cherub and seraph of St.-Sernin. The *Majestas Domini* from Briare (Ill. 1434) now in the museum at Orléans is a fragment of an altar-frontal also very similar in composition

[1] See, for example, the silver one at Spalato, illustrated by Folnesics, *Dalmatien*, 104.
[2] Illustrated in Porter, *Lombard Architecture*, IV, Plate 122, Fig. 3; Plate 123, Fig. 1, 2; Plate 124, Fig. 1, 2.
[3] Illustrated *ibid.*, Plate 3, Fig. 2.

to the Toulouse relief of the same subject. The fragments of the other
altar at St.-Benoît-sur-Loire (Ill. 1421, 1422) show that here, too,
there was a series of figures under arches. The usual composition of
the *Majestas Domini* is found on the front face of the altar at Avenas
(Ill. 11). Similar, too, is the *Majestas Domini* of the Arca Santa of
Oviedo (Ill. 656) and here, also, is found the motive of flanking figures in arches. The same composition is repeated in a wooden altar-
frontal from Sigena, now in the museum of Lérida (Ill. 555) and in
another of the museum of Vich. The formula more or less varied is
repeated many times in the superb collections of painted antependia
assembled in the museums of Barcelona and Vich. A composition
precisely analogous to that of St.-Sernin, with a *Majestas Domini*
flanked by figures of equal height under arches, is found in the enamel
altar-frontal of Santo Domingo de Silos now in the museum of Burgos. The altar-frontal of S. Marco at Venice was made originally in
1105, but in 1205 enamels from Constantinople executed between
1118 and 1143 were added, and the whole was re-made in 1345. On
this is represented the *Majestas Domini*, and St. Michael bearing the
scroll ΑΓΙΟΣ, ΑΓΙΟΣ, ΑΓΙΟΣ which is the Greek version of the
words *Sanctus, Sanctus, Sanctus* inscribed on the scrolls of the St.-
Sernin cherub and seraph. The altar-frontal of Città di Castello has
the *Majestas Domini* like that of St.-Sernin, and the frontal from
Bâle now in the Musée de Cluny has full-length flanking figures under
arches like St.-Sernin. In view of these analogies there can be little
doubt that notwithstanding their somewhat extraordinary height
the St.-Sernin fragments are from a sculptured altar or Arca.

It remains uncertain whether this was the high altar of the church.
It is tempting to connect the sculptures with the consecration of
1096; but the style gives reason to believe that they are a decade
later. In fact, the sculptures of the St.-Sernin ambulatory (Ill. 296–
305) seem to be derived from the reliefs of the piers of Moissac (Ill.
262–273), which are dated 1100. The close relationship of the two is
obvious. Figures of the same adamantine hardness are placed under
similar arches; the proportions and the general effect are strikingly

analogous. The curious wings of the Toulouse angels recur in certain capitals of the Moissac cloisters (Ill. 281, 282, 284). The Toulouse sculptures appear, however, later and inferior. The drapery folds, although very similar, are more complicated and less well understood; the eyebrows are rendered by a convention more naturalistic, but less effective; the drawing of the feet is much poorer; the faces are less well done; the hair conventions are weaker. On the other hand, it is certain that the sculptor of St.-Sernin was also influenced by Spanish art. His style shows close analogies with the Arca of San Felices (Ill. 661–664). The facial types, the folds of the drapery indicated by two parallel lines, the fondness for beardless faces, the hands raised, palm outwards, the hair conventions to a certain extent, but much more the conventions of the beard, and the peculiar diamond ornament introduced on the edges of the tunic of Christ in the Arca (Ill. 661) and in the aureole at Toulouse (Ill. 296) all bear witness to a close relationship. The drapery folds indicated by two parallel lines is an old motive, which can be found almost anywhere; Spain, however, possesses, I believe, the earliest example in the celebrated "Lady of Elche." [1] The convention persisted in later times, being found, for example, in the Bible of Avila. [2] It may have come to both Moissac and Toulouse from Spain. The peculiar shin line, characteristic of the Toulouse sculptures (Ill. 304), is found as early as 1075 on the Arca Santa of Oviedo (Ill. 658). The composition of the *Majestas Domini* of the St.-Sernin ambulatory was precisely that destined to become so popular in the Catalan antependia.

The sculptor of the St.-Sernin ambulatory reliefs was also influenced by Santo Domingo de Silos. If we compare the face of his seraph (Ill. 299) with the harpies of the dated capital of 1073–1076 at Santo Domingo (Ill. 666), we find the same long nose, the same badly placed eye, the same low head, the same omission of the forehead. The Toulouse ambulatory sculptures are, in fact, extraordinarily unpleasant productions. They may be assigned to about the

---

[1] See the illustration in the *American Journal of Archaeology*, 1921, 368.
[2] Illustrated by Schultz.

year 1105, and it may be conjectured that the canons of St.-Sernin having learned of the new sculptures of Moissac, lost no time in causing them to be imitated.

Thus the sculpture of Languedoc, like nearly all mediaeval art, was compounded of many elements derived from various sources. German ivories, Spanish manuscripts, Spanish sculpture and Burgundian sculpture each contributed a quota. It has been believed that the sculpture of Languedoc gave all and received nothing. Such a facile formula will hardly satisfy longer thoughtful students. Moissac and Toulouse in the XII century not only radiated influences to the other schools of sculpture in Europe, but received influences.

III

LA PUERTA DE LAS PLATERIAS

THE Mephistophelian south portal of St.-Sernin (Ill. 308–315) must have been executed before, and probably considerably before, the consecration of 1119. It has evidently undergone a very radical restoration in modern times, presumably under Viollet-le-Duc in 1855. The first impression, indeed, is that of being in the presence of a modern work. The restoration may account, at least in part, for the ugliness. We are fortunately able to judge of what must have been the quality of the original from other productions of the same artist — a fragment of a seated figure in the museum of Toulouse (Ill. 306), and certain sculptures at Santiago (Ill. 679, 681, 684). This master appears, as has often been pointed out, to have derived his art from the ambulatory sculptures. Undoubtedly, however, he also sought inspiration in Burgundy; thence must have come the movement, the composition of the lintel, the throwing back of the heads of the apostles.

In the spandrels, on either side of the archivolt, were placed the figures of St. James (Ill. 311) and St. Peter (Ill. 312). M. Mâle believes that these are by the same hand as the similar figures at Santiago (Ill. 676). There is, beyond question, a resemblance; but the much finer quality of the Santiago figures (Ill. 676) and numerous other differences seem to indicate that these are not the works of the same master. It is, however, evident that one must have influenced the other. Which is the original?

The documents do not determine the question. The St.-Sernin portal was doubtless finished before the consecration of 1119; but it is hardly conceivable that it could have been executed before 1110. The choir of Santiago appears to have been completed in 1102; the nave was at once attacked, and finished in 1124. The transept portals would presumably have been sculptured in the earlier rather than in the later part of this building campaign, say between 1102 and 1112. No definite conclusion as to priority between the sculptures of Santiago and those of St.-Sernin can be drawn from these data.

The internal evidence of the Santiago portal is in the highest degree confusing and complicated. M. Bertaux was the first to observe that the sculptures (Ill. 674–691) are not all of the same style; he believed that he could distinguish the work of two different hands. It seems to me that the sculptures are the work of many distinct artists, perhaps as many as fourteen.

A glance at the present Puerta de las Platerias suffices to reveal the fact that we have to do with a conglomeration of fragments not in their original position. No order is traceable in the composition as a whole. Little statues, big statues, pieces of statues are walled in helter-skelter. The little figures of apostles above the eastern portal (Ill. 676) look as if they were fragments of a stone altar-frontal like that of Tahull. The man riding on a monster of the west tympanum (Ill. 679) is inserted horizontally. The woman holding a skull just below (Ill. 679) has had her shoulder and part of her head cut off to adapt her to her present position. The flying angel in the spandrel to the right, above this same tympanum, cuts across the archivolt (Ill. 676). Romanesque sculptures, we have seen, were carved before being placed; and Spanish Romanesque builders were notoriously careless in their assembling of these previously prepared decorations. It is, however, incredible that misfitting should have been carried to this degree. Moreover, details like the beginning of an archivolt under the feet of the third apostle, upper row, left-hand side (Ill. 675), show that certain sculptures have been wrested from a very definite place in which they belonged.

The description in the Pilgrims' Guide proves, indeed, that certain ones — the Expulsion [1] (Ill. 675) and the sign of the zodiac, Sagittarius (Ill. 675) — which are now in the south portal were originally

---

[1] The companion relief of the Expulsion, mentioned in the Guide as in the north portal and representing God reproving Adam and Eve is now in the museum (Ill. 693).

in the north portal. It has been supposed that when the latter was reconstructed in the XVII century, the discarded reliefs were added to the previously intact sculpture of the south portal. That sculptures of the north portal were introduced into the south portal is certainly true. But recognition of that fact does not solve the mystery of the south portal.

The truth is, I think, that the Puerta de las Platerias has been twice rebuilt. The mouldings of the two arches have advanced Gothic profiles (Ill. 676). They are far more developed than, for example, those of the portal of St.-Sernin (Ill. 308). The bracketed lintel (Ill. 681) is similar to Mateo's in the Pórtico de la Gloria (Ill. 829). The least difficult hypothesis seems to be that Mateo reconstructed the Puerta de las Platerias in the second half of the XII century. It may be conjectured that at this time he incorporated fragments from the west façade. In fact, the God the Father in white marble (Ill. 676), now in the spandrel between the two portals, may be, I suspect, the same as that described in the Guide as forming part of the Transfiguration of the west façade.

The incoherencies of the composition, it is true, can only be partially explained on this hypothesis. The same extraordinary mixture of subjects that exists to-day in the tympana (Ill. 678–680) is very exactly described in the XII-century Guide. The four angels in the spandrels (Ill. 675–677), the lions over the central columns are all as they were. On the other hand, there are notable points of divergence between the description and the existing monument. One of the *"feroces leones"* has disappeared.[1] The jamb sculptures are not those described in the Guide. Instead of the existing Sign of the Lion, St. Andrew, Moses and a bishop, there were four apostles. *"In liminaribus eiusdem introitus, sunt duo apostoli quasi valvarum custodes, unus ad dexteram, et alius ad sinistram, similiter in alio introitu sinistrali, in liminaribus scilicet, alii duo apostoli habentur."*

---

[1] These lions (Ill. 674) were copied nearly half a century later by the sculptor who executed the fragments now incorporated in the so-called "throne of the popes" in the cathedral of Avignon (Ill. 1339, 1340). Here the lion of St. Mark (Ill. 1339) has the same peculiar paws, the same sardonic expression and the same tail curled around behind his leg.

Such discrepancies indicate that the portal has undergone a radical reconstruction. The jamb sculptures could hardly have been changed without tearing the portal down and rebuilding it.

The Puerta de las Platerias, therefore, consists of fragments of at least three different portals, heaped together at two reconstructions, one of the second half of the XII century and the other of the XVII century. Fortunately, however, the description mentions specifically certain reliefs which can still be identified. These must without any question have belonged to the original portal.

Among the sculptures thus described in the Guide is the St. James (Ill. 676),[1] which resembles the statue at Toulouse (Ill. 311)[2] and the Christ (Ill. 676) in the spandrel between the two arches. These figures the Guide tells us belonged to a cycle of Christ and the apostles, several other figures (Ill. 676) of which, more or less mutilated, are still in their original position, while others have disappeared. Happily for our investigations, the description mentions in detail the woman holding a skull in her lap of the west tympanum (Ill. 679). It gives, indeed, an explanation of the subject which otherwise would entirely escape us. The figure represents the vice of Luxury, typified by the legend of the adulterous wife, whose husband forced her to fondle twice a day the head of her lover while it corrupted in her hands. This same subject is represented in a capital of Santa Marta de Tera,[3] a church in which the Toulousan master seems also to have worked.

The interesting part of this relief is that it really is by the hand of the sculptor of the portal of St.-Sernin. Doubt is not possible. Not

---

[1] Some light upon the singular form given to the cypress trees in the Santiago and Toulouse reliefs is furnished by a Byzantine ivory triptych of the X century at the Louvre. On the reverse of this (illustrated by Schlumberger, I, 128), are represented unmistakable cypress trees with a vine wound around them. The peculiar trees at Santiago must be a further conventionalization of a form like this.

[2] Miss King, *op. cit.* III, 252, deduces, from the iconography that the Toulouse St. James must be derived from the similar figure at Santiago. This conclusion is confirmed by the study of the style of the two sculptures. There must have been a continual interchange of masters between the two ateliers of Toulouse and Santiago.

[3] See the illuminating publication by Gómez-Moreno who appears to have been the first to perceive the relationship of Santiago to the rest of Europe in its true light.

only are the types, facial modelling, draperies, hands, feet and hair conventions identical, but there are the same mannerisms like the horizontal line following down the shin line and the incision in the bulge of the drapery folds.

The work of our sculptor at Santiago did not end with the Luxury. The man riding a monster inserted horizontally above (Ill. 679) is by his hand; as are also two of the jamb sculptures, the St. Andrew of the east jamb of the west portal (Ill. 681) and the woman with crossed legs holding a lion of the east jamb of the east portal (Ill. 684) and the boy holding a cock just below her.

These unrestored sculptures give an opportunity to judge of the artistic stature of our artist. He is surely of higher rank than one would suspect from St.-Sernin. He possesses vigour and power, and attains a certain effect at the expense of the finer qualities.

The woman holding the lion (Ill. 684) is a strange subject. We should be entirely embarrassed for an explanation, were it not that the theme recurs in a relief now in the museum of Toulouse and coming from St.-Sernin (Ill. 322). Here are seen two women, similarly seated with crossed legs, one holding in her lap a lion, the other a lamb. It is the illustration, as Lahondès recognized, of a legend attributed to St. Augustine, but manifestly of much later date, according to which, in the time of Julius Caesar, strange prodigies took place at Toulouse, at Rome and at Jerusalem. At Toulouse, notably, two women bore one a lion, the other a lamb, symbolic of the two natures of the coming Messiah.[1] It is evident that we have here another attempt of the canons of St.-Sernin to rival Santiago. For the usual triad Compostela, Rome, Jerusalem, is substituted the triad Toulouse, Rome, Jerusalem. It was entirely natural that the miracle should have been commemorated in the sculpture of St.-Sernin. The meaning was underscored by the inscriptions, which have, however, been so strangely misunderstood — *Signum leonis. Signum arietis. Hoc fuit factum T(olosae) tempore Julii Cesaris.*

Now there can be little doubt that this subject was originally

[1] Lahondès, 460.

created at Toulouse, where it was at home, and copied at Santiago, where there was no reason for it to be represented. Hence several important conclusions. The Toulouse sculptures of the lion and the ram, although of much finer quality than those of the south portal, must be about contemporary with them; and our sculptor of the south porch of Santiago and of the south portal of St.-Sernin must have been at Toulouse, and, presumably, have worked there, before he copied at Santiago the productions of his more gifted contemporary.

But we are by no means at the end of the complications! Did the sculptor of the Toulouse "Signs" also work at Santiago? Close to his manner are the David (Ill. 687), the Creation of Adam (Ill. 686) and the Sacrifice of Abraham (Ill. 690). These works are much finer than the sculptures of the master of the south portal of St.-Sernin, or for that matter than anything in the lower portion of the Puerta de las Platerias. On the other hand, they seem a little off from the Signs of St.-Sernin, as if an inferior artist had collaborated. But the fragments of the cycle of the apostles in the spandrels is of the very highest quality, and obviously related to the "Signs" on the one hand, and the group of lower sculptures we have indicated at Santiago on the other. The close relationship of all these sculptures is undeniable, and so is their superior excellence. An easy explanation seems to be to suppose that they are the work of one gifted and highly versatile artist. Whether this sculptor was a native of Santiago or of Toulouse there is nothing to indicate. His David (Ill. 687) sits under an arch like those of the Moissac cloister (Ill. 262–273); but this same motive had long been characteristic of the art of Spain, being found, for example, in the Arca Santa of Oviedo (Ill. 656). The motive, moreover, we have seen was characteristic of ivories, and our sculptor betrays knowledge of this medium. The *David* (Ill. 687) recalls an ivory of the same subject at the Bargello at Florence.[1] In the two works, the mantle slung from shoulder to shoulder falls in the same "U" curves. The type of face is similar, in both the eyes are curi--

[1] Illustrated by Graeven, II, 23.

ously round, and similarly drawn.[1] Folds of the drapery like those of the Santiago *David* (Ill. 687) are found in two ivories of the X century of the British Museum.[2] The long straight legs of the Adam in the Santiago Creation (Ill. 686) recall those of the scenes of Genesis in a Byzantine ivory casket of the X–XI centuries at Darmstadt.[3] This Adam also shows analogies with the Adam and Eve capital of Cluny; our sculptor was perhaps influenced by Burgundian models here and in the fluttering draperies of the "Signs." He is certainly an important figure in the history of art. Nothing at Toulouse equals or foreshadows the superb Christ of the spandrel (Ill. 676), a figure which was a century ahead of its time, and inspired whole cycles of later art. Among other things which must be set down to the credit of this artist is the idea of representing the Sacrifice of Abraham with upright figures on the jambs of the portal (Ill. 690) — a motive later taken over and developed by the Gothic sculptors of Senlis (Ill. 1508) and Chartres.

It is important to observe that the master of the south porch of St.-Sernin may have executed jamb sculptures at Santiago. Two of his works — the St. Andrew (Ill. 681) and the Sign of the Lion (Ill. 684) — are now used as jamb figures, and jamb figures of the most primitive type; that is, reliefs of the inner jamb, at right angles to the door. The description makes it certain that in the early XII century both the northern and southern portals had jamb sculptures. Those of the north portal represented the four apostles, St. Peter, St. Paul, St. James and St. John; all held books in their left hands, and their right hands were raised in benediction. The relief embedded in the west buttress (Ill. 685), next to the lion, may be one of these apostles. In the jambs of the south portal were four other apostles whom the Guide does not name more specifically; it is probable that St. Andrew may have been among them, and that the *St. Andrew* (Ill. 681) which still exists is in the original position.

---

[1] This ivory is called a *French* work of the X century — but is it?
[2] Illustrated by Dalton, Pl. XXIV, 46.
[3] Illustrated by Schlumberger, I, 59.

The fact that jamb sculptures, set at right angles to the door, were found at Santiago, is significant. Guglielmo used this same motive at precisely this moment at Cremona (1107–1117); his prophets, like the Santiago apostles, are on the inner face of the jambs, at right angles to the door. Did Guglielmo copy from Santiago or the Santiagoan sculptor from Guglielmo? Or both from a common original?

The idea of flanking a portal with full-length figures in relief is at least as old as the Heroön at Tyrsa. In this, which is probably the most primitive form of the motive, the statues are placed not in the jambs of the portal, but in the wall beside it. In such a form the motive is found at Elindsche, near Garni in Armenia.[1] This simple version also found its way into the Occident. At La Couture of Le Mans (Ill. 1412) in northern France there exists an example very crude in style, and presumably of early date. We find the motive in southern France and in Italy, at Souillac (Ill. 343, 344), Moissac (Ill. 360, 361), Beaulieu (Ill. 417, 418), Notre-Dame-du-Port of Clermont-Ferrand (Ill. 1162, 1163), S. Maria Maggiore of Toscanella, S. Antonino of Piacenza, S. Quirico d'Orcia. It probably also existed at St.-Michel-de-Cuxa in Catalonia (Ill. 558, 559), although the fragments of the portal are no longer in their original position. The only instance of the motive that I know in Spain is in the comparatively late work at Leire (Ill. 715). In Dalmatia the motive appears in the portal at Traù. It is also found at Zara; here we have older fragments of the XII century, incorporated in the portal of 1320. The reliefs are at present in two rows; very possibly the original arrangement in this particular may be preserved, for jamb sculptures in two rows, first initiated by Guglielmo at Cremona were frequently repeated in later monuments.[2] Of the simple flanking type, like those of Zara, examples are extant in the Abruzzi at S. Clemente de Casauria (Ill. 219) and in the Basilicata at Marsico Nuovo.

[1] Illustrated by Strzygowski, *Arm.*, 812 f.
[2] At Bamberg in Germany, at Las Caldas de Oviedo and San Julián de Moraime in Spain.

The second step in the evolution of jamb sculptures would be to transfer the relief which had been placed in the wall flanking the portal, to the face of the jamb, at right angles to the door. This form of the motive we find at Santiago and Cremona. It appears to have been more at home in Italy than in Spain, for it survives in several late monuments all in Italy — the cathedral of Foligno, the cathedral of Lodi, S. Andrea of Barletta (Ill. 252).

What seems to be a development of the motive is found at St.-Antonin (Ill. 358, 359) in Aquitaine. The gallery of the Hôtel-de-Ville has piers upon which are engaged sculptures that produce the effect of adossed reliefs. These may conceivably be inspired by the jambs of Santiago. The Adam of St.-Antonin (Ill. 358) faintly recalls the Adam of the Creation at Santiago (Ill. 686). Stylistically, however, the work at St.-Antonin shows the influence of Burgundy in the draperies, and especially in the spirals of the knees. Its closest relative is the tympanum at Moissac (Ill. 339–342).

The third step in the evolution of the Gothic portal was to replace the sculptures of the inner jambs by a series of sculptures on the various orders of the portal. At first these sculptures were placed in niches upon rectangular members. In this form the motive is found on the portal of the cathedral of Ferrara, sculptured by Nicolò in 1135. It was repeated soon after in the portal of the chapter-house of St.-Etienne of Toulouse (Ill. 434–443).[1] The sculptures in niches are re-echoed in Nicolò's holy-water font at Chamalières (Ill. 1154–1156).

The fourth step was to transfer these little figures in niches on the rectangular members of the portal to the engaged colonnettes of the portal, without altering the size of the sculptures. This phase we find in Nicolò's portal of the cathedral of Verona of 1139. It is echoed in late monuments in widely separated regions — in the strongly Lombard façade of the Schottenkirche at Regensburg, and in two destroyed churches of Holland — the Johanniskirche of Utrecht

---

[1] There was probably a lost original from which both these works are derived.

(rebuilt after a fire in 1148) and St. Odilienberg.[1] In Spain the motive in this form is found only in late monuments — at Monterey,[2] Las Caldas de Oviedo (Ill. 881–882), Villaviciosa (Ill. 884, 885) and San Julián de Moraime.[3]

We must at this point turn aside to consider an alternative possibility in the development of jamb sculptures.[4]

In the portal of Santiago are incorporated three marble columns (Ill. 688, 690, 691) entirely covered with sculptures of figures standing in arched niches. Since the description of the XII century refers to these remarkable productions, there is no doubt that they belonged to the original construction. To cover a column with arched niches filled with reliefs is a Byzantine idea; it occurs in the columns of the ciborio of S. Marco at Venice.[5] The actual workmanship at Compostela is undoubtedly local; the figures are of the pilgrimage style, and similar to the other reliefs executed before 1124.

The suspicion arises that these columns may have inspired the much later colonnettes of the convent of the Benedictine nuns (Ill. 705–708). On each are adossed the figures of three apostles.[6] I was unable to obtain access to the originals of these sculptures, which I know only from the casts in the chapter-house of the cathedral. Hence I have no helps but the style to establish the date. It is evident that they must be much later than the work anterior to 1124 in the Puerta de las Platerias. The close analogy between the heads (Ill. 708) and that of Nicolò's Oliver at the cathedral of Verona suggests that the Santiago colonnettes are not earlier than the fourth or fifth decade of the XII century. On the other hand they certainly

---

[1] The fragments of the former are in the Städischen Museum at Utrecht, those of the latter in the Niederländischen Museum at the Hague. Illustrated by Litgenberg, Taf. V.

[2] Illustrated by Fatigati, 18.

[3] Illustrated by García de Pruneda, 159.

[4] Something like jamb sculptures are found at Grossenlinden in Germany and Millstadt am See in Austria. (Illustrated by Hamann 1, 130).

[5] The motive was taken over in the west portal of Chartres, probably from Santiago. Illustration by Houvet, 11.

[6] The handle of a flabellum of the XII century, called southern French, in the British Museum, has apostles coupled in niches in the manner of the Santiago columns. This has been illustrated by Dalton, Pl. XXXVI, 76.

appear much more primitive than the jamb sculptures of St.-Etienne of Toulouse (Ill. 434-443).

There exist several other examples of the motive of three or more figures adossed to a column. The earliest is at Solsona in Catalonia (Ill. 551). From there the motive was carried to St.-Bertrand-de-Comminges in the French Pyrenees (Ill. 492). It is also found in a fragment from Notre-Dame of Châlons-sur-Marne of unknown date (Ill. 1487) which has found its way to the Louvre.[1]

Now it is easy to imagine that the three or four figures engaged upon a column of a cloister might easily have been reduced to one. And in fact we find numerous examples of such in nearly all parts of Europe. One of the most significant are the three colonnettes from St.-Quentin-lès-Beauvais, now in the Museum of Beauvais (Ill. 1431-1433). The style of these figures is primitive — they have every appearance of being earlier than St.-Denis (Ill. 1437-1457).

Similar sculptured colonnettes are found in the museum which has been installed in the archevêché at Albi (Ill. 453-455). These are said to be fragments of a secular building, such as the sculptures of St.-Antonin (Ill. 358, 359) still adorn. Inscriptions — REX SAUL, REX SALAMON — leave no doubt as to the iconographical meaning of two of the figures. Of the other two, representing women, one (Ill. 454) is probably the Queen of Sheba. The style seems to show derivation from many different sources. Draperies of Chartres and Beauvais, postures from the Moissac porch, limbs of Santiago, hands of Rieux-Minervois (Ill. 1404) are combined with the manner of the third quarter of the XII century.

Elsewhere in France we find the motive in the cloisters of Aix (Ill. 1407, 1408), and Ganogobie (Ill. 1237, 1238). An old drawing shows that it formerly existed in the cloisters of St.-Georges-de-Bocherville in Normandy [2] — this is significant, as the monument appears to have dated from about 1140. The theme also formerly existed in the

---

[1] In the museum of Calcutta, India, is a square pillar, coming from Bharhut, on which are adossed three figures in relief. (Illustrated by L. A. Waddell, in the *Asiatic Quarterly Review*, 3d series, 1912, XXXIII, 104.)

[2] Nodier, Tayler et de Cailleux, II, Pl. 116, Fig. 2, 9.

cloisters of Lavaudieu [1] and Avignon,[2] the latter dating from about 1155.

Outside of France we find sculptures adossed to colonnettes at Chur in Switzerland, and in the façades of the cathedral at Genoa and the Pieve at Arezzo.

Now it is easy to imagine the motive of a sculptured column like those of the museum at Beauvais transferred from a cloister to the portal of a church. The portal of St.-Denis might have been produced in this way as well as by copying of the Italian portals.

Between the two genealogies, — Cremona, Ferrara, destroyed monument like the cathedral of Verona, St.-Denis; and Santiago sculptured column, colonnette of the convent of Benedictine nuns, Beauvais colonnettes, St.-Denis — it is not altogether easy to choose. The former, on the whole, seems perhaps somewhat smoother and more convincing, but gives no explanation of the fact that sculptured colonnettes seem to have existed before St.-Denis. The truth probably is that both evolutions took place, not independently, but with constant cross-influences.

When in 1137 the abbot Suger undertook the reconstruction of St.-Denis, he faced a peculiar situation, which it is well to bear in mind in studying his work.

First of all, Cluny was already discredited. The art-loving order was on the wane, and the art-hating Cistercians were waxing in power and prosperity. St. Bernard's strictures had killed the tender art of the early XII century. A wave of puritanical austerity swept across Europe. An order which condemned sculpture, which banished stained-glass and frescos, which reduced architecture to dreary and barn-like monotony, became the fashion of the hour. It was a tide too strong to be opposed. The downfall of Cluny and of Cluniac ideals of art became certain.

Suger, a clever politician, was assuredly not unaware of the Cistercian tide, nor could he have failed to be influenced by the current

[1] The sculptured column of Lavaudieu has been sold.
[2] Illustrated by Labande, Pl. LXXVI.

running so strongly in his time. And in fact the element of Cistercian austerity was an important one in his achievement, and perhaps its chief defect. It must be said in Suger's praise, however, that by nature he was little inclined to puritanical ideals. His personal relations with St. Bernard show him as a temporizing, but never enthusiastic, follower of the great reformer. The Cistercian movement, we feel, was a force so powerful that he dared not but conform to it, although his heart was cold. When St. Bernard praises Suger's behaviour, we seem to read between the lines that the actions commended had been motived by fear rather than by love.

We may conjecture that Suger felt notably that the hostility towards art preached by the Cistercians was a mistake. His own tastes, doubtless, corresponded much more nearly with the Cluniac ideal. He perhaps viewed with something like dismay a movement which threatened to stamp out Romanesque art. His politician's mind conceived the idea of producing a new style, which should preserve the loveliness of Cluniac production, while at the same time satisfying the Cistercian austerity. Cluniac art should, in fact, by a process of reform, be made endurable for Cistercian Puritans.

Suger was regent of France, and St.-Denis was the royal abbey. The abbot had the interests of the crown at heart. He was, moreover, a man who had travelled wide, and seen many countries, notably Italy. He was aware of what had been produced by the architecture of other lands, and surely perceived how far that of his own country lagged behind. It is perhaps not too much to credit him with an understanding of the advantages a superior art could bring to the French crown. In any event, whether by conscious reasoning or by intuition, what he did was to create a national style. The political importance of this move can hardly be over-estimated. It was an important step in that centralizing policy, which became for so many centuries the aim of the French kings, and which is still a living factor in French economy. The value of a national and centralized art, first perceived by Suger, was understood by his followers in the French government throughout the centuries. It is still part of the French government policy of to-day.

The problem of Suger was, therefore, to create an art which should be national, that should be recognized as superior even by foreign nations, thus gathering glory for the name of France, that should perpetuate what was great in the art of Cluny, and that should satisfy the puritanical exactions of the Cistercians.

He found native in the Ile-de-France a finely archaic architecture well suited for his purpose. His task was to combine this architecture with the figure arts of the south, so as to produce a whole which might be impregnated with theological and scholastic dogma to an extent which would disarm the strictures of the Cistercians, and at the same time produce a compelling work of art.

Thus St.-Denis was compounded of elements brought from many sources. It combines the building forms of the Ile-de-France with sexpartite vaults of Normandy, sculptures of Aquitaine and voussures of Saintonge. Enamel workers were summoned from Germany. M. Mâle believes that even the hollow work at Beaulieu contributed its quota. Whence the glass came, no one knows, but it is hardly likely that Suger invented the art. The windows of St.-Denis are obviously not the first attempt of a novice, but the production of artists who were working in a medium with which they were well acquainted. Suger, moreover, expressly states that his glass-workers were imported. It is also sure that Suger was in touch with the building operations at Cluny. He writes of bringing marble columns by water from Rome in evident imitation of what had actually been accomplished in the Burgundian monastery.

It is not less certain that the art of St.-Denis was influenced by Lombardy, especially in its ornamental and decorative details. The mosaics were assuredly purely Italian.[1] The sculpture is as little indigenous. The style shows no relationship to the crude earlier work

---

[1] Mosaic pavements are found in Germany and in several French churches, such as Cruas and Thiers, as well as in Italy. Cruas is dated 1098. Thiers must be of the XII century, although it has been called Carolingian. The mosaics of St.-Denis differ from these because partially made of glass.

in the Ile-de-France at St.-Etienne of Beauvais (Ill. 1423, 1424), St.-Quentin-lès-Beauvais (Ill. 1431–1433), Bury. The supporting figures of the western portal are a characteristically Guglielmo-esque motive (Ill. 1438, 1441–1443), though derived perhaps via Beaulieu (Ill. 416).[1] Nothing could be more completely Lombard than the lion with his tail between his legs supporting the colonnette (Ill. 1443). This colonnette is decorated with spirals and ornaments in the manner peculiar to the masters of the Isola S. Giulio pulpit and S. Orso cloister. The reliefs of the zodiac show analogies with the sculptures of the same subject at Modena. A capital of the crypt has on its abacus a completely Lombardic anthemion (Ill. 1436). The angels in the voussures (Ill. 1440), heavy and expressionless, are of Lombardic rather than of Aquitanian type. The figures of the virgins in arches surmounted by tabernacles (Ill. 1441, 1442) recall Guglielmo's prophets at Modena. The peasant quality of the broad, squat figures is also reminiscent of Guglielmo.

It is therefore entirely within the bounds of possibility that the jamb sculptures of St.-Denis came from Lombardy. On the other hand, it is certain that St.-Denis was much influenced by pilgrimage art. It was itself a pilgrimage church, part of the chain which stretched from Santiago to the remote ends of Europe. It is certain that the sculptor whom we call the St.-Denis Master owes important peculiarities of his style to the West and South.

Before leaving the subject of jamb sculptures, a word should be said of the holy-water basin at Chamalières (Ill. 1153–1156). This has four adossed figures in niches, like the jamb sculptures of the cathedral of Ferrara and of the chapter-house of St.-Etienne of Toulouse (Ill. 434–443). It is evident, however, that the Chamalières basin is related to Nicolò's work at Ferrara much more closely than to the Toulouse apostles. In fact, the Chamalières basin appears to be a work by Nicolò's own hand, and dating from his Ferrarese period. The style is far more suave and developed than in his earlier productions at Piacenza. On the other hand it seems less mannered

---

[1] The Bury figures beneath the vault show the same influence.

than the jamb sculptures of the cathedral of Verona. The peculiar braided ornament on the border of the drapery of one of the figures of the Chamalières basin recurs on the St. John the Baptist in the spandrels of S. Zeno at Verona. It is, however, with Nicolò's work at Ferrara that the Chamalières basin shows the closest analogies. There are the same draperies, the same hands, the same eyes, the same beards, the same noses, the same lips, the same scrolls, the same niches, the same hair. Indeed, the basin at Chamalières resembles the jambs of Ferrara much more closely than do Nicolò's signed works at Sagra S. Michele and Verona. It seems, therefore, impossible to doubt that it is by his hand.

The question arises how this work found its way into the heart of the Cévennes. Did Nicolò undertake a journey into the Velay? There is plenty of evidence to show that he did travel in France, although rather in the South-west, in Languedoc and Aquitaine. It seems to me, however, more probable that the basin was exported from Italy, and carried to Chamalières. It will doubtless be objected that the basin is an exceedingly heavy object to have been transported in this manner. Yet we know that far more complicated shipments were made in the XII century. The great ambulatory columns of Cluny, for example, the transportation of which would be something of a problem at the present day, and in comparison with which the Chamalières basin seems a trifle, were brought all the way from Rome to Burgundy. The transportation of the Chamalières basin would have been comparatively easy, because it could have been sent most of the way by water, across the sea, and up the Rhône.

But the fortunes of the motive of jamb sculptures have led us far away from Santiago. Returning thither we notice that the sculptured columns of the Puerta de las Platerias are by no means the only traces of Byzàntine influence. One suspects it, indeed, of underlying much of the work, and if we knew more of Byzantine sculpture, it is likely that we could detect definite traces. One fragment is, indeed, certainly Byzantine. It is that strange bust (Ill. 676) inserted in the spandrel between the two doorways, and which the Guide shows to have originally belonged to the Transfiguration of the west façade. The Byzantine foliage in the boss betrays the origin of the sculptor. But this is not all. A head of similar character is found in a relief of S. Marco at Venice representing the sacrifice of Isaac.[1]

There is a head resembling the one at Santiago (Ill. 676) in the portal of Santillana del Mar (Ill. 860). The other sculptures of this façade are of far inferior quality.

In the relief of the Temptation in the western tympanum of the Puerta de las Platerias is introduced the trilobed arch, destined to become important in northern art. The motive is found in a Carlovingian miniature of the Gospels of Soissons, in what would seem the more advanced polylobed form; [2] it also occurs in the trilobed form in an Anglo-Saxon manuscript of the IX century,[3] and there is something very like it in the scene of the Adoration of the Magi [4] of the Hildesheim doors. The popularity of the motive, however, especially in architecture seems to have been established by Spain. It is found in Mohammedan architecture from the IX century,[5] coming according to Rivoira from India,[6] and in the X century it is already acclimated in the mosque of Cordoba. It occurs in the Arca de San Felices (Ill. 661) in a form very similar to that of the Puerta de las Platerias. At Santiago it is used not only in the relief, but architecturally as well. Its diffusion thence in architecture we have already noticed.[7] In the plastic arts we find it reproduced in a miniature representing the Feast at Emmaus in a Limoges manuscript of the XII

---

[1] This relief has been variously assigned from the III to the XIII century. It is, however, certainly of the early XII century. This may be proved by comparing it with the relief of Hercules and the Ceryneian deer of the same basilica. The latter is a Venetian copy of a Byzantine work, not earlier than the XII century. It is evident that the heads in the two works have the same character. Probably much Byzantine sculpture dates from the XI–XII centuries. The relief at Xeropotamon (Mt. Athos) reproduced by Brockhaus Taf. 9 reproduces line for line an ivory of the XI century in the museum of Berlin (illustrated by Schlumberger, II, 89).
That the S. Marco Sacrifice of Isaac is Byzantine, seems to me certain. It has nothing to do with contemporary work in Italy. Was it imported from Constantinople in 1204, like so many other marbles of S. Marco, or was it executed *in situ* by a wandering Byzantine sculptor?
[2] Paris, Bibl. Nat. lat. 8850, illustrated by Boinet, Pl. XXI.
[3] Lord of Leicester's Library, illustrated by Dorez, *Catalogue*, Pl. III. Cf. a miniature in the Gebhards-Bibel at Admont, illustrated by Buberl, 25.
[4] Illustrated by Dibelius, Taf. 8.   [5] Puig, III, 385.
[6] *Arch. Mus.*, 374.   [7] See above, p. 187.

century in the Morgan Library [1] and in the altar-piece of the abbey
of Stavelot in Belgium, known from a drawing reproduced by Helbig,[2] and dating from soon after 1130.

One of the most interesting of the artists who worked at Santiago
is the master who executed the three figures, probably of apostles, at
the left-hand edge of the upper row (Ill. 675), the Expulsion just below (Ill. 675), the relief representing God reproving Adam and Eve
now in the museum at Santiago (Ill. 693), the angels blowing trumpets (Ill. 675–677), the lions (Ill. 674), four figures at the right-hand
edge of the lower row (Ill. 677), the figure just above the Sacrifice of
Abraham in the east buttress (Ill. 688), the Healing of the Blind
(Ill. 680),[3] the Adoration of the Magi (Ill. 680) [3] and the Betrayal of
the eastern tympanum (Ill. 680). Since the Expulsion is mentioned
in the description of the XII century, our master worked upon the
original construction.

This artist shows close relationship to some of the work at Conques.
If we compare the draperies of Christ and Judas in the Santiagoan
Betrayal (Ill. 680) with those of the prophets in the niche to the left
of the Abraham at Conques (Ill. 397); the head of Christ in the Santiagoan Betrayal (Ill. 680) with the head of the second prophet in the
niche to the left of Abraham at Conques (Ill. 397); the rosettes in the
cornice at Santiago (Ill. 677) with the stars inside the aureole of
Conques (Ill. 393); the angels blowing trumpets at Santiago (Ill.
675–677) with the angels of Conques (Ill. 394), we shall be convinced
that the two groups are related. Conques seems distinctly more
naturalistic and advanced in style than Santiago.

Another sculptor at Santiago shows even closer analogies with a
second sculptor at Conques. This is the artist who executed at Compostela the Flagellation (Ill. 680) and the Crowning with Thorns
(Ill. 680) in the centre of the lower register of the east tympanum;
the Adoration of the Magi (Ill. 680) just above;[4] the neighbouring
grotesque (Ill. 680);[4] an angel carrying a crown near by (Ill. 680);[4]

[1] No. 101.   [2] 56.
[3] In these works, I suspect, another sculptor collaborated.
[4] In these works his companion seems to me to have collaborated.

the Temptation of the western tympanum (Ill. 678, 679); and the west jamb figure of either portal representing Moses with the tablets of the law (Ill. 682) and a bishop (Ill. 683). A curious convention for representing the lower edge of the draperies with redoubled folds is like the signature of this artist. Now precisely this same convention recurs at Conques in the group of figures to the left of Christ (Ill. 395, 396). The similarities do not end here. The figures in the two monuments are of the same stocky types. The head of the Christ in the Flagellation at Santiago (Ill. 680) is like the head of the king at Conques (Ill. 395). The short skirts of the executioner at Santiago are like those of the same figure at Conques (compare Ill. 680 with Ill. 395). The square hair line is characteristic of both works. The draperies of the Moses at Santiago (Ill. 682) are entirely similar to those of the abbot leading the king (Ill. 395) at Conques.

The figures in both works wear the same block shoes. The face of the abbot at Conques (Ill. 396) is the same as the face of the executioner to the left at Santiago (Ill. 680). The attitude of the angel Gabriel in the Annunciation of the transept at Conques (Ill. 386) is taken, line for line, partly from the Christ, partly from the angel in the Temptation of the Santiago tympanum (Ill. 678). The face of the Virgin in the same relief at Conques (Ill. 386) is the face of the angel swinging a censor in the same relief of Santiago (Ill. 678). The lower fringe of the drapery of the handmaiden in the Conques Annunciation is the same as that of the Christ at Santiago (Ill. 678). That the two groups are by the same hand seems certain. Again, however, we note that the sculptures of Conques are more advanced.

The Betrayal by the first master of Santiago must have formed part of the same series of reliefs with the Crowning with Thorns and Flagellation by the second. Therefore the two worked together at Santiago. We are justified in concluding that the same pair worked together also at Conques.

The question of the origin of these sculptors is an interesting problem. I can see no reason to doubt that the one who executed the Flagellation at Santiago is Spanish. The work at Conques is evidently more advanced than that at Compostela. It is, moreover, as evidently of Spanish character. The brilliant polychromy suggests a Spanish origin; it is, perhaps, by way of Conques that the tradition reached Auvergne. The facial types are thoroughly Spanish; they already foreshadow those of Mateo. The devils, too, are of Spanish type, and not unlike those of the western tympanum of Santiago. Moreover, the manner of this sculptor is very close to the Bible of Avila, a XII century manuscript of Spanish origin in the Madrid Library.[1] The only analogies with his work outside of Spain that I know are not more than might easily have come to him second-hand. Thus his characteristic folds are somewhat like those of the bronze tomb-stone of Rudolf von Schwaben, a monument of the Dom at Mersburg, dating from soon after 1080.[2] They also resemble those of an ivory-carving of the South Kensington Museum, called Italian of the XI–XII centuries.[3] But his personality at bottom is, so far as I know, unlike anything outside of Spain.

The case is different with the other sculptor whom we may call the Master of the Santiago Betrayal. There is a close prototype to his style at Conques itself. The tomb of the abbot Bégon III in the exterior of the south wall of the nave does not seem to have attracted the attention of archaeologists to the extent it deserves. This tomb is adorned with a relief (Ill. 387) which represents Christ, two angels and Ste. Foy (she is the figure to the right — her crown is the same peculiar one that appears in the golden image —) receiving into paradise the dead abbot. Since this tomb was presumably erected soon after the death of the abbot, it may be considered a dated monument of 1107.

Now the style of this relief shows singular points of contact with that of the Betrayal Master. Compare, for example, the face of the Christ (Ill. 387) with that of the Christ in the Santiago Betrayal (Ill. 680). There are the same eyes, the same type of face. The face

---

[1] Illustrated in the Boletín de la Sociedad Española de Excursiones, Año V, 1897, 100.
[2] Illustrated by Dehio, abb. 420.
[3] Illustrated by Graeven, 57.

of Ste. Foy is like that of the figure to the right in the Betrayal. The hair of the angels in the Conques relief (Ill. 387) is like the hair of Christ at Santiago (Ill. 680). The draperies of the right shoulder of Christ at Conques (Ill. 387) are the same as those of the right shoulder of Judas at Santiago (Ill. 680). The bottom folds of the draperies at Conques have something of the character with which we are already familiar in the draperies of the Betrayal Master at Santiago. On the other hand the tomb of Bégon is distinctly cruder, distinctly earlier. The work at Santiago shows the strong influence of the sculptor of the south portal of St.-Sernin, which is lacking at Conques.

Let us now extend our study to the angels in the pendentives of Conques (Ill. 388, 389). Compared with the tomb of Bégon III (Ill. 387), the Conques angels appear much superior (Ill. 388, 389). The draperies are more coherent and better rendered; they tend already to approach the Santiagoan type; the proportions are better and more slender. The facial types, however, are the same and the draperies fundamentally alike. It is evident that the angels represent the tomb of Bégon plus an immense improvement brought about by the influence of Santiago. The angels are, however, still far from equalling the work of the Betrayal Master at Santiago (Ill. 680). Were we placing these reliefs in order, we should certainly arrange them: tomb of Bégon, angels of Conques pendentives, Betrayal Master at Santiago, Betrayal Master at Conques.

The sculptures of the transepts (Ill. 390, 391) are assuredly more advanced than the angels of the pendentives (Ill. 388, 389). The influence of Santiago is stronger. The folds of the mantle of Isaiah (Ill. 391) are a debased copy of the much finer ones of the mantle of David at Compostela (Ill. 687). The facial types are, however, those of the tomb of Bégon (Ill. 387) and of the angels of the pendentives (Ill. 388, 389). We are still less advanced than the work of the Betrayal Master at Santiago. Our series must be extended: tomb of Bégon, angels of Conques pendentives, transept sculptures, Betrayal Master at Santiago, Betrayal Master in the western tympanum of Conques.

I confess that between the tomb of Bégon and the western tympanum of Conques there seems to be a difference not only of style, but of quality, that makes it difficult to believe that all these works can be by the same hand. They would, however, have fallen within a single lifetime; and if we suppose two hands, it is very difficult to say where one stops and the other begins. What seems certain is this. There existed at Conques from the beginning of the XII century an atelier of sculpture, which from crudity rapidly rose to great excellence under the influence of Santiago; and this atelier culminated in the production of the western tympanum of Conques (Ill. 392–401), the work of two masters, both of whom had worked at Santiago, one of whom was perhaps Spanish by birth, but the other of whom came out of the native atelier of Conques.

It is evident that orthodox archaeology has made a serious error in ascribing the tympanum of Conques to the end of the XII or to the XIII century. The style is entirely that of the second quarter of the XII century. The faces (Ill. 393–401) are analogous to those of Vézelay (Ill. 28–46) — 1104–1120. Certain figures, like the one with the cane, the third to the left of Christ (Ill. 396), show points of contact with the pulpit of Isola S. Giulio, which dates from c. 1120.[1] The star-bedecked aureole, and other peculiarities as well, recall the Salerno altar-frontal which dates from the last quarter of the XI century. The conspicuous position given to the cross in the composition of the tympanum at Conques (Ill. 392) shows that the work is not later than the middle of the XII century. It was in the XI century that the cross became a prominent feature of Last Judgments. It is inconspicuous in the early XI century at Oberzell in Reichenau, but it is central in the late XI century at Burgfelden.[2] In the Perikopenbuch of Kaiser Heinrich II, the cross already holds a prominent place in the composition of the Last Judgment.[3] In sculpture of the first half of the XII century, the cross is prominent; it dominates the com-

---

[1] Noak, in the *Dritten Bericht über die Denkmäler Deutscher Kunst*, 43, notes analogies between the pulpit at Isola and the east choir at Mainz. The latter he dates 1125 on independent grounds. It is reassuring that his chronology, arrived at by entirely other ways, should agree to within a year with mine.

[2] Dehio, abb. 360, 361.   [3] Ed. Leidinger, V, 38.

position at Beaulieu (Ill. 409) and at St.-Denis (Ill. 1439). It was
first dropped at Autun (Ill. 80). After St.-Denis (1140) it no longer
is conspicuous. In this particular, therefore, Conques shows the
manner of the third or fourth decade of the XII century. The
iconography of the tympanum is, moreover, in other respects archaic.
Christ does not show his wounds as at St.-Denis (Ill. 1439) and in
later works. The Gothic formula has not yet been found—the composition is arranged in a fashion that foreshadows the final solution,
but which is evidently earlier and tentative.[1]

The evidence of the iconography is confirmed by that of the style.
Since sculptors who worked at Santiago before 1124, and presumably considerably before, executed the tympanum of Conques, it is
evident that the latter must certainly fall within the first half of the
XII century. Is it possible to determine the date more exactly?

The tomb of Bégon furnishes a sort of speedometre by which we
can measure the rate of progress in the atelier of Conques. We can
compare the state of sculpture in 1107 as witnessed in this monument
(Ill. 387) with that attained by the Betrayal Master at Santiago (Ill.
680) before 1124. If so much water had flowed under the bridges in
seventeen years or less, we can hardly assume that more than ten
years separated the Puerta de las Platerias (Ill. 674–691) from the
western tympanum at Conques (Ill. 392–401). That would bring us
to 1134 at latest for the date of the latter.

This agrees well with what we can deduce of the history of the
building of the basilica at Conques. We know from the epitaph of
Bégon III, who as we have seen died in 1107, that he constructed the
cloister, in the north gallery of which he was buried. His epitaph
says nothing of his having reconstructed the church; evidently then
the church had not been begun at the time of his death.

It must, however, have been commenced very soon afterwards.
There are many proofs that the existing church is later than the
cloister. The masonry of the south transept reveals that the church

---

[1] There are striking similarities between the inscriptions at Conques and those at St.-Denis.
It is a question, however, how far either are to be trusted.

was built around the previously existing cloister. The earliest capitals of the church — those of the east end — are evidently later in style (but only slightly later) than those which still survive of the cloister.[1] The angels of the pendentives (Ill. 388, 389), falling midway in style between the tomb of Bégon of 1107 (Ill. 387) and the Puerta de las Platerias (Ill. 674–691), can hardly be later than 1115. The choir must already have been in construction at this time. Fifteen years later the western façade might well have been building. Everything, therefore, indicates that the tympanum was executed between 1130 and 1135, contemporaneously with the other great tympana of Autun (Ill. 80), Vézelay (Ill. 47) and Beaulieu (Ill. 409).

Ste.-Foy of Conques, inspired by Santiago, seems on the other hand to have been the point of departure for the Romanesque school of Auvergne. The latter appears to have been formed at Notre-Dame-du-Port of Clermont-Ferrand, an edifice later than c. 1140.[2] The crudity of many works in this remote and mountainous region

[1] The *enfeu* of Bégon III seems to have been established in its present form after the reconstruction of the church, but of the fragments of the original tomb.

[2] There is indeed a text which proves that work was still in progress upon the church as late as 1185 (Michel, I, 2, 605). The sculptured capital of the southern side aisle representing the Temptation (Ill. 1184) shows a style notably later than that of either the ambulatory capitals (Ill. 1167–1183) or the sculptures of the portal (Ill. 1158–1163). If the church was begun about 1145 with the east end (as usual the sculptures for the ambulatory capitals and the portal would have been the first things executed), it is easily conceivable that the nave might not have been entirely finished forty years later. It has been supposed that the finer sculptures of the lintel are of a later period than the capitals of the ambulatory, and the former have been associated with the document of 1185. It is true that two very different hands may be distinguished in the portal at Notre-Dame-du-Port. Robert, who comes out of the atelier of Conques, executed all the capitals of the ambulatory (Ill. 1167–1183), that of the exterior of the south transept representing the Sacrifice of Abraham (Ill. 1165), the *St. John* (Ill. 1163) and the *Isaiah* (Ill. 1162) of the portal, and the reliefs of the Annunciation (Ill. 1164) and Nativity (Ill. 1166) above. The second hand, which as we shall see comes out of Souvigny, executed the lintel (Ill. 1158, 1159) and tympanum (Ill. 1160, 1161). Now it is impossible to put thirty-five years between the work of these two masters. They certainly were active at Notre-Dame-du-Port at the same time. The analogies of the second master to Souvigny show that he worked in the fifth or sixth decade of the XII century, which is precisely the time to which the work of the first master must also be ascribed. More than this the two masters evidently co-operated upon the south portal, since the hands of both can there be found. Finally the *Isaiah* of Robert (Ill. 1162) shows copying of the style of the second master. The folds of the draperies over his left knee (Ill. 1162) obviously reproduce those over the left knee of the Christ in the tympanum (Ill. 1158). Both sculptors are therefore contemporary, and were active upon the church about 1145–1150.

handicapped by rough and unworkable building materials has led to their being generally considered older than they probably are in fact.

At any event there can be no question of the great debt which Notre-Dame-du-Port owes to Conques. We have only to compare the *St. John* of Conques (Ill. 390) with the *St. John* of Notre-Dame-du-Port (Ill. 1163), or the *Isaiah* of Notre-Dame (Ill. 1162) with the angel in the pendentives at Conques (Ill. 388, 389), or the long scroll of the *Isaiah* of Conques (Ill. 391) with those of the capitals at Clermont (Ill. 1179) to be convinced of the fact. But Notre-Dame is clearly a later and inferior copy. Compare the face of the Conques *St. John* (Ill. 1163) with the Clermont rendering of the same subject (Ill. 390). How the fine spirituality of the Conques face has vanished in the Clermont version, and there remains an unmeaning expression of tricky slyness. The Clermont sculptor has been able to imitate very exactly the strands of the hair, the folds of the drapery; but he has been powerless to give his figure the dignity of pose, the expressive significance of the Conques prototype. It is in vain that he has covered every inch of the surface with fussy ornament. The effect of austerity and dignity which the Conques master attained by this means entirely slips through his fingers. Similarly when we compare the *Isaiah* of Clermont (Ill. 1162) with the angel of Conques (Ill. 388) we are at once conscious, for all the similarities of posture and of detail, how much more significant the figure at Conques is. The raised right hand of the Conques angel (Ill. 388) convinces us, whereas that of the Clermont *Isaiah* seems futile (Ill. 1162). The resemblance of the draperies is patent, although the Clermont sculptor has evidently attempted to introduce certain new improvements; but how much better contained is the Conques figure, how much firmer the outlines.

It was not only to Conques that the sculptors of Notre-Dame went to seek models. The lintel (Ill. 1160, 1161) is a close imitation of the screen at Souvigny (Ill. 124, 125). The draperies of the Virgin in the Clermont Adoration (Ill. 1160), for example, are clearly thence derived. The folds of the upper part of her garment (Ill. 1160) reproduce line for line those in the corresponding position of the Christ at Souvigny (Ill. 125); those of her skirts recall the figure to the left of the Souvigny Christ (the extreme figure to the left in Ill. 125). The draperies about the knees of Christ in the Clermont tympanum (Ill. 1160) are imitated from those about the knees of the Christ at Souvigny (Ill. 125). Since Souvigny is not earlier than *c.* 1140, the sculpture at Notre-Dame-du-Port must be later than that date.

The hand of the master of the Clermont-Ferrand lintel reappears in the tympanum of Valence (Ill. 1189). The style of the two works is so similar that it is difficult to determine which is older; Valence, however, seems somewhat more purely Burgundian than Notre-Dame-du-Port.

One of the features introduced at Conques and taken over at Notre-Dame-du-Port is the pedimented lintel. The origin of the motive is obscure. The earliest example with which I am acquainted is that of the church of S. Lorenzo of Zara, now in the museum assembled at S. Donato.[1] It is, perhaps, not earlier than the XI century, although it has been called Carlovingian. The motive also found its way to Belgium. It seems to have been known in Spain, since it is found at Barbedelo, Santa Maria del Sar and perhaps at S. Isidoro of Léon.[2] It was probably from Spain that it came to Conques. At all events there can be no doubt that from Conques it was taken over at Notre-Dame-du-Port (Ill. 1160, 1161) and copied thence throughout Auvergne — at Mozat (Ill. 1223), in the lintel now enwalled in the Place des Gras at Clermont-Ferrand (Ill. 1205), at Chambon (Ill. 1250), at Thuret (Ill. 1139), at Meillers (Ill. 1251), at Champagne and at Autry-Issard (Ill. 1141).

Reliefs inserted in the exterior of the church of St.-Austremoine at Issoire representing the Sacrifice of Abraham (Ill. 1210), Abraham and the Three Angels (Ill. 1209) and the Miracle of the Loaves and Fishes (Ill. 1211) are obviously derived from the atelier of Conques. The style approaches closely that of the angels of the Conques pendentives (Ill. 388, 389). One is almost tempted to suppose that they

---

[1] Illustrated by Gurlitt, 70.   [2] King, II, 192.

are earlier fragments re-employed in the existing church. However, certain details, like the folds about the left leg of the angel in the centre of the Three Angels appearing to Abraham (Ill. 1209), or the perforated borders of the garments show that we have here late imitations of earlier models. The style is entirely different from that of other reliefs enwalled in the choir representing the zodiac (Ill. 1208) and also from that of the capitals of the ambulatory (Ill. 1212–1214). These all, like the capitals of the ambulatory at Notre-Dame-du-Port of Clermont-Ferrand (Ill. 1167–1183) show a strong classic character, and the influence of southern models — especially of the frieze at Beaucaire (Ill. 1292–1298) and the works of Guglielmo and Nicolò in Lombardy. At Issoire, as at Notre-Dame-du-Port we doubtless have two ateliers, with widely divergent manners, working upon the church contemporaneously, or nearly so. Notre-Dame-du-Port seems to stand in relation to Auvergne in much the same relation that Cluny stands to Burgundy. It is the centre from which radiate the influences which bore fruit at Champagne (Ill. 1186), St.-Nectaire (Ill. 1190–1204), Volvic (Ill. 1206, 1207), Issoire (Ill. 1208–1214), Mozat (Ill. 1223–1227) and many minor edifices.[1]

The Virgin of the Annunciation at Conques (Ill. 386) appears to have been known to the sculptor who executed the Virgin of the Annunciation under the vaulting ribs of La Trinité at Vendôme (Ill. 1517).[2]

The influence of Conques was therefore exceedingly great. Nor is the impression which it produced upon contemporary artists to be wondered at. It moves as profoundly the spectator of to-day. Notwithstanding the somewhat restless and confused effect of the division into zones by bands with inscriptions, the freshness of the polychromy, the quaintness of the faces, and the vigour of the modelling

---

[1] St.-Nectaire and Champagne resemble Notre-Dame-du-Port most closely. Issoire is more advanced, while Mozat shows the style in its ultimate phase. Indeed, the style of the capitals at Mozat (Ill. 1224–1227) seems about abreast of that of the tomb in the church of La Magdalena at Zamora (Ill. 890, 891), a monument which is probably not anterior to the XIII century.

[2] An unexpected relationship of the Vendôme sculptures is with the work of Nicolò. The head of the youthful bishop at Vendôme (Ill. 1518) reproduces almost line for line the head of the St. Zeno in the tympanum of S. Zeno at Verona.

combine to make of this one of the grand achievements of Romanesque art.

Before leaving this pair of sculptors who worked together at Santiago and at Conques, it is interesting to note that the relief of the
Flagellation (Ill. 680) at Santiago appears to have been the starting-
point for a whole group of interesting sculptures. If we compare this
Flagellation with the one at Beaucaire (Ill. 1297), we shall be in no
doubt as to whence the Beaucaire sculptor derived his inspiration.
Now from Beaucaire in turn are derived the series of reliefs dealing with the Passion which belonged to the pulpit and screens
of the cathedral at Modena, and the celebrated frieze of St.-
Gilles.

Still another sculptor of Santiago has left us the relief of the Creation of Adam embedded in the east buttress (Ill. 689). He is an inferior creature who plods along at a respectful distance behind the
master of the south portal of St.-Sernin. He follows him so faithfully
that he must have worked about the same time.

The hand of the same master may be recognized in the portals of
San Isidoro of Léon (Ill. 696–702).[1] This church seems to have been
the object of a number of reconstructions which succeeded each other
from the middle of the XI century until the final consecration of
1149. The style of the sculptures of S. Isidoro is not sensibly different from that of the works of the same master in the Puerta de las
Platerias. His *Santa Sabina* (Ill. 697) shows him still assiduously
copying the work of his more gifted contemporary and co-worker
upon the Puerta de las Platerias; his *S. Isidoro* (Ill. 698) is a faithful
reproduction of the *St. Peter* by the same master at Toulouse (Ill.
312). The tympana of S. Isidoro have a certain impressionistic effect
which is finer than anything our master accomplished at Santiago;
I can not detect, however, any real sign of progress or of development
in his style. It is therefore probable that the work at S. Isidoro is

[1] The eastern portal (Ill. 696–699) is perhaps later than the western (Ill. 700–702). The heads
of the spandrel figures (Ill. 700, 701) have been remade. The draperies of the tympanum
(Ill. 702) show the influence of Aragon (Ill. 535–543), those of the spandrel figures (Ill. 700,
701) of Moissac (Ill. 262–273).

approximately contemporary with that at Compostela. We may consequently assign it to about 1120.

It was apparently from the already troubled waters of Léon that somewhat later the sculptor of St.-Bertrand-de-Comminges drew the inspiration — if that word can be applied to so sorry a performance — for his tympanum (Ill. 323–326).

IV

LATER PILGRIMAGE SCULPTURE

WITH the completion of the cathedral of Santiago in 1124 ends the great creative cycle of the pilgrimage school. From this time the sculpture of Spain and Aquitaine reflects various foreign influences. It veers about like a weathercock, pointing now to Burgundy, now to Lombardy, now to the West, now to Provence, now to the Ile-de-France. The strangers, constantly passing back and forth on the road, brought with them motives from the four quarters of the world. The most distant and unexpected models were copied. The pilgrimage churches became an international mixing-pot of styles.

In the third decade of the XII century, the influence of Burgundy was assuredly the most prominent. The great tympanum of Moissac (Ill. 339–342), we have seen, was executed under this inspiration. At Leire (Ill. 711–716) Burgundian influences are at work too; but combined with other elements. The St. James (Ill. 713) is another replica of the over-copied *St. Peter* (Ill. 312) of Toulouse; the Annunciation (Ill. 714) is reminiscent of that of the Moissac porch (Ill. 376); the skirts of the figures in the tympanum fall in folds precisely like those of the figure to the right in the tomb of Bégon at Conques (Ill. 387), the flaring lower garment and the trailing sleeves recall Notre-Dame-la-Grande of Poitiers (Ill. 960, 961); the caryatid lions, Lombardy.

The same polyglot and cosmopolitan character permeates the well-known jamb sculptures from the chapter-house of St.-Etienne in Toulouse (Ill. 434–443). The assistant of Gilbert marks at once the extreme development and the extreme degradation of the Toulousan style. Cynicism could go no further. These strange creations in their mocking, demoniac attitudes, their stocky proportions, their coarse quality make us understand the character of the Albigensian heresy; after studying them, one almost finds St. Louis sympathetic. Like

all the sculpture of the South-west of this period they reflect a multitude of foreign influences. The sculptor seems to have been formed
in that atelier of ivory-carving which produced the New York Journey to Emmaus and *Noli me tangere* (Ill. 709). His facial types seem
to be derived from a master of Santiago — the one who did the *St.
James* (Ill. 676) and the *St. Peter* (Ill. 675). They are, however, obviously much later and more advanced. Some of the draperies come
from the same source. The master also knew the "Signs" (Ill. 322)
of St.-Sernin. Other draperies are inspired by the tympanum of
Moissac (Ill. 339–442). Nicolò's earlier, crisper and more archaic
work at Ferrara is perhaps derived from the same lost original as the
figures of Gilbert's assistant.[1] The capitals of the niches show the
influence of the Moissac cloister (Ill. 262–273). The movement of the
draperies of certain figures is Burgundian, the draperies, the hair and
beard conventions, and the ornamented borders of others are derived
from St.-Denis (1137–1140) — Ill. 1437–1457 — or Chartres. There
is a XIII century feeling in the faces and hair conventions which
suggests a date in the second half of the XII century. If we compare these heads with those of Beaulieu (*c.* 1135) — Ill. 409–420 — ,
we shall be convinced that they are notably later. The tomb of
Dona Blanca (1156) — Ill. 719 — at Nájera [2] is from the point of
view of style closely related to the St.-Etienne sculptures. The
analogies in the draperies are striking. Two capitals of the cloister of
St.-Etienne show motives (lions' heads from which issues a stem (Ill.
448), little nude men climbing among vines) [3] that are familiar in
Apulian art of the second half of the XII century (see, for example,
the Duomo and later portions of S. Niccola at Bari). Other decoration is very analogous to that of the tomb of the bishop Jean at St.-
Etienne of Périgueux (†1169). Compared with the sculptures of St.-

---

[1] The Ferrara sculptures can not be derived from the Toulouse cycle, for they are earlier in
date. Moreover, the work at Ferrara shows points of contact only with Gilbert's assistant,
not with Gilbert himself. This would hardly be conceivable, had Nicolò seen the work at
Toulouse.

[2] The tomb at Nájera is in turn closely related to the portal of Santa Maria at Sepúlveda
(Ill. 799–804).

[3] This motive is also found on one of the columns of the west façade of Chartres.

Denis (Ill. 1437–1457) the faces of Gilbert's assistant appear more advanced and Gothic-like than any of the work in that portal. Moreover, the Toulouse apostles are all of the same height; now in the early cycles at Verona, at St.-Denis, at Etampes and at Chartres the statues had been of varying heights — it was only later that they were made uniform as in the Toulouse series. From all this we conclude that the activity of Gilbert's assistant can hardly fall before the fifth decade of the XII century.

The study of the style of Gilbert himself leads us to the same conclusion. He comes out of Autun (1132) — Ill. 67–81 — and shows the strong influence of St.-Denis (1137–1140) — Ill. 1437–1457 — if not also of Chartres. He has close points of contact with Chadennac (Ill. 1034–1040), which is a dated monument of 1140. Compared with St.-Denis (Ill. 1437–1457) his draperies are clearly finer, more elaborate, more complicated, more advanced. The draperies of his Virgin at Solsona (Ill. 552) are indeed strikingly analogous to those of the tympanum of St.-Trophîme of Arles (Ill. 1372) which dates from 1152. A date about 1145 for the cloister of St.-Etienne would, therefore, be in accordance with what we can deduce from the style of the two masters.

The capitals of the cloister of La Daurade at Toulouse, now gathered together in the museum, are of two distinct periods. The earlier group (Ill. 288–295) is closely analogous to the cloister at Moissac (Ill. 274–287), as we may easily convince ourselves by comparing the two Daniels (Ill. 278 and Ill. 288). It is, indeed, difficult to determine which is the older. On the whole, the Daurade seems to be slightly the more archaic; but in any case the two monuments must be nearly contemporaneous. It is evident that the cloister of Santo Domingo de Silos (Ill. 666–673) was well known to these artists. The second group of Daurade capitals (Ill. 462–473) is of much later date. Some of them are by the same hand as the jamb sculptures of the chapterhouse (Ill. 474–479); others show clumsy imitation of the capitals of Gilbert's assistant at St.-Etienne (Ill. 444–447). A peculiarity of several of these capitals is the hanging arches from the abacus dividing the bell of the capital into two fields (Ill. 464–466, 468, 469). This motive is also found on a capital of Notre-Dame-des-Doms at Avignon, now in the Musée Calvet,[1] a monument which dates certainly from the second half of the XII century. Buschbeck[2] has recognized that the later capitals of La Daurade (Ill. 462–473) are closely related stylistically with the cloister of St.-Bertrand-de-Comminges (Ill. 492, 494, 496).

The sculptures of the jambs of the chapter-house of La Daurade were seen by Du Mège while they were still in their original position, before the destruction of the cloister in 1813. He thus describes them: "La porte de la Chapelle du chapitre avait huit statues tenant lieu de colonnes; le montant de gauche contenait un bas-relief en marbre peint, représentant la Sainte-Vierge tenant l'Enfant-Divin sur ses genoux; en regard paraissait David assis, accordant sa harpe. . . . En avant du portail et faisant saillie, étaient, de chaque côté deux bas-reliefs représentant un Roi, une Reine et deux saints ou prophètes. Dans l'épaisseur de la saillie et dans le retour, il y avait, de chaque côté, et faisant de même avant-corps, un bas-relief."[3]

The fact that the reliefs of La Daurade were jamb sculptures inserted in the door of the chapter-house at once suggests that they are derived from the analogous sculptures of St.-Etienne. The style of the Daurade fragments (Ill. 474–479) is, however, notably different from that of the St.-Etienne apostles (Ill. 434–443). It is evident at a glance that they are much less vital. They are, as Vöge recognized nearly thirty years ago, flat imitations of Chartres. One perceives, however, that they are much later in date than their original. This is clear not only in the less vigorous modelling, in the monotony of the composition, and the general commonplaceness of the execution, but in certain of the heads which have already Gothic character.

There is, indeed, proof that this master worked about the end of the century.[4] The draperies of the jamb sculptures of the Daurade

---

[1] Illustrated by Labande, Pl. LXXVIII.   [2] 54.

[3] Du Mège, 246–247.

[4] Buschbeck, 40, has discovered documentary evidence that the cloister was finished before 1205.

(Ill. 474–479) are precisely like those of the celebrated Annunciation of the Toulouse Museum (Ill. 480, 481).[1] The head of the Gabriel (Ill. 482, 483) [2] is exceedingly like that of one of the Daurade prophets (Ill. 474, figure at right). The draperies of the Virgin of the Annunciation (Ill. 481) are like those of the next Daurade prophet (Ill. 474). The lower border of the garment of the Gabriel (Ill. 480) is similar to that of the Daurade *Virgin* (Ill. 479). But the quality of the Daurade sculptures is much poorer than that of the Annunciation. It is evident that the master of the Daurade jambs knew and copied the Annunciation. Therefore the Daurade must be later.

But can we determine the date of the Annunciation?

The head of the Gabriel (Ill. 482, 483) is very similar to the heads of the jamb sculptures (Ill. 498–500) that raise the portal of Valcabrère to more than antique heights. There is in both the same pointed chin, the same mouth with lips rising in the corners, the same long hooked nose, the same low forehead, the same naturalistic ear. Moreover, in both works the eye is placed in the horizontal (or nearly so) portion of the socket, not vertically in the cheek as in nature. It is this peculiarity which gives the sculptures their character.

On observing more attentively the sculptures of Valcabrère, we perceive that the radiance of this remarkable work proceeds from the heads, or to be more exact, from three of the heads, and from the outer figure on the right-hand side; the rest is not only inferior, but intolerably blundering. There can be no doubt that two very unequal hands worked together on this portal.

The finer of these hands, as we have said, is close to the master of

---

[1] The types of the Toulouse Annunciation could only have originated in Byzantium. Their spirit can hardly be equalled except in the technically dissimilar relief of Adalia, illustrated by Pace, 103. The closest prototype which I know is the ivory Annunciation in the Trivulzio collection at Milan, illustrated by Venturi, II, 616. This it is now believed to be a fragment of the Grado throne, an Alexandrine work of the VI century. During the XI and XII centuries the Grado throne seems to have been copied by artists of widely separated parts of Europe. It served as model to the ivory-carver of the altar-frontal at Salerno, and to Nicolò when he composed his reliefs on the façade of S. Zeno of Verona. The Toulouse Annunciation may be another derivative, direct or indirect. The close resemblance of the Toulouse angel to the Byzantine angels of S. Marco at Venice has been remarked by Buschbeck (39) — see especially the one illustrated by Ongania, Pl. 376.

[2] Unfortunately the nose of the Virgin (Ill. 484, 485) is modern.

the Toulouse Annunciation. His heads have the same stern quality as that of the Gabriel; like that, one could almost believe them inspired by an archaic Greek model. They are, indeed, extraordinarily fine. In looking at them, we seem to breathe the atmosphere of demigods and heroes. This XII-century artist of the Pyrenees attains all that Rome would have been, but never was.

His uncouth assistant (Ill. 501–502) is of little intrinsic merit, and probably a local light, since we find his hand again in the adossed figures of the neighbouring cloisters of St.-Bertrand-de-Comminges (Ill. 492–495, 496).[1] In the tympanum of Valcabrère (Ill. 501, 502) he seems to be trying feebly to imitate Burgundian models. His was clearly an unskilful chisel of the end of the XII century.

Indeed, the significance of the Valcabrère sculptures in this connection lies in the fact that their date can be determined. The church of Valcabrère was consecrated in 1200. The portal must, therefore, have been executed somewhat before this time.

All this brings the date of the Toulouse Annunciation and the Daurade fragments down to at least the last quarter of the XII century. It is exceedingly improbable that they are earlier than 1175.

Other trains of reasoning bring us to the same conclusion. If we compare the Virgin (Ill. 479) with the Virgin of Gilbert at Solsona (Ill. 552) or with those of his assistants at St.-Junien (Ill. 451) or on the capitals of St.-Etienne (Ill. 447), we shall perceive that the sculptor of the Daurade owed much to the art of Gilbert. The facial type of his Virgin (Ill. 479) is, indeed, that of the Virgin of Solsona (Ill. 552); but how weak and spineless it is in comparison, how lacking in character! We feel in one the strength and vigour of a living and progressing tradition, in the other the languid imitation of a decadent age.

It was, however, not only in Spain that the master of the Daurade cloisters sought inspiration. The canopy under which his Virgin sits connects his work with a series of Virgins similarly placed under canopies. The earliest example of this type I suppose to be the Virgin

[1] The same, or a very closely related hand, worked also at St.-Aventin (Ill. 508–510).

(Ill. 1299) which once formed part of the Adoration in the tympanum at Beaucaire, and which, wickedly restored, still exists in the house of the priest in that city. This probably inspired by some means the very different version of the theme in the southern tympanum of Chartres as it did the Virgin at York in England.[1] The Virgin at Donzy (Ill. 113) is obviously a derivative of the one at Chartres. The sculptor of La Daurade certainly knew Chartres; but it is rather in the Midi that he sought the inspiration for his Virgin. The statue of Beaucaire (Ill. 1299) had had descendants along the Mediterranean as well as in the North. The Virgin from Fontfroide, now at the University of Montpellier (Ill. 1301) is certainly a derivative. Here, too, the subject is the Adoration; the posture of the child is identical; the Virgin is in the same position, her right hand similarly raised, the knees spread apart in the same manner. The similarity of the long folds of the draperies over the knees is unmistakable. Indeed, the two sculptures were, perhaps, more closely alike than we should suspect, for the head of the Beaucaire statue is a modern restoration. The chief difference in the two works, and what shows the Fontfroide Virgin to be later, is not only its inferior quality, but the less attenuated proportions. In the second half of the XII century attenuation went out of fashion, and the figures tend to become ever heavier.

In the northern tympanum of St.-Gilles is another Adoration (Ill. 1386) which must be a third member of this series. The relationship to Beaucaire (Ill. 1299) is clear — in both we have the Virgin in the Adoration seated under a canopy in the middle of a tympanum. The position of Virgin and Child is still precisely the same. The Child is still seated on the left knee of His mother; He raises His right hand with exactly the same gesture; the Virgin has the same knees, widely spread apart; her right hand is in the same position. The folds of the left knee of the Virgin (Ill. 1386) resemble those of the Virgin of Fontfroide (Ill. 1301) rather than those of the Virgin of Beaucaire (Ill.

---

[1] Illustrated by Prior and Gardner, 135. I am indebted to Mr. Eric Maclagen for having suggested to me this comparison.

1299). The chair of St.-Gilles is also the chair of Fontfroide, not that of Beaucaire. But the composition, the placing of the subject in a tympanum, must have come from Beaucaire, not from Fontfroide. Therefore, the sculptor of St.-Gilles knew both Beaucaire and Font-froide. He is consequently the latest of the three. This conclusion is confirmed when we observe that his proportions are heavier than those even of the Fontfroide sculptor; attenuation has definitely dis-appeared. The series therefore runs: Beaucaire, Fontfroide, St.-Gilles.

Now we shall see that the tympanum of St.-Gilles is certainly later than the central portion of the façade, which was erected about 1140; and there is reason to believe that it may not have been executed until about 1180.[1]

When we place the Virgin of La Daurade (Ill. 479) in comparison with this series we easily perceive that she is the latest of the se-quence. The proportions are the heaviest of all. The draperies full of many fine folds at Beaucaire gradually become simpler and broader at Fontfroide and St.-Gilles, but at La Daurade they are the simplest and broadest of all. The canopies at Beaucaire and St.-Gilles are destroyed, but it is clear that that of La Daurade is far more elaborate and developed than that of Fontfroide. The engaged pediment over the arch with plate tracery indeed is strangely like Gothic architecture of c. 1200.

Another Virgin of this series is in the cloister of Santillana del Mar (Ill. 867). She is obviously the broadest, the squatest, and the latest of them all. In fact, there are independent reasons for believing that she can hardly be earlier than the end of the XII century. Yet it is evident that this very late Virgin is a close relative of the Virgin of La Daurade. The capitals and ornament of the canopy are very much the same; the folds of the drapery over the right knees, the right upper arms and the lower edge of the garments are similar.

A clumsy imitator of Gilbert's assistant, if I mistake not the very

---

[1] See below, p. 301. For a discussion of the fragmentary Adoration of the Magi at St.-Gilles, and other works which also belong to this series, see below, p. 277.

same who is responsible for many of the Daurade capitals of the second series (Ill. 462–473), executed the holy-water basin from Narbonne, now in the Toulouse Museum (Ill. 486, 487). This, too, must then date from about the eighth decade of the XII century.

A tympanum of peculiar interest is that of the Cluniac priory of Carennac (Ill. 381–385). This is by the hand of a sculptor whom we have little difficulty in recognizing in the tympanum of another Cluniac priory, that of Mauriac (Ill. 1246, 1247) in Auvergne. This artist certainly has little connection with the school of Toulouse. I should not be surprised if he came out of some such atelier as that which created the tomb of the daughters of Ramiro I at Jaca (Ill. 527). But if he was Aragonese by birth, it is clear that he wandered far, and absorbed a curious mixture of foreign influences. One of the most notable is that of Lombardy. The head of the apostle to Christ's left in the second row of the Carennac tympanum (Ill. 383) is a faithful reproduction of that of Guglielmo's *Jeremiah* at Cremona. The lion beneath the jambs at Mauriac (Ill. 1249) is certainly the echo of a Lombard motive. It may be debated whether our sculptor, if he be Aragonese, derived his knowledge of Lombard art directly or from the atelier in which he was educated. The school of Aragon shows the strong influence of Guglielmo, from whose art it is assuredly derived. The draperies of the skirts of the two figures supporting the aureole in the tomb of the daughters of Ramiro I (Ill. 527) are precisely like those of Enoch and Elijah in the Cremona relief.[1] The gesture and posture of the angels is exactly that of the Cremona prophets. In the tomb, draperies are indicated by two parallel incised lines, just as in the works of Guglielmo. There can then be no doubt of the very close dependence of the school of Aragon upon Lombardy. Our sculptor's Lombard draperies, lions and facial types may then have come to him without a trip to Lombardy.

The *Majestas Domini* which occupies the centre of the Carennac tympanum (Ill. 383) may be derived from the fragments of the St.-Sernin altar, now enwalled in the ambulatory (Ill. 296–307). The

---

[1] I have illustrated this relief in the *Gazette des Beaux-Arts*, 1919, LXI, 51.

peculiar division by vertical and horizontal bands in the Carennac tympanum seems, in fact, to be due to the attempt to adjust to a lunette a composition which was certainly created for a field of far different shape. We can feel the effort of the sculptor to accommodate a rectangular original to the space of a tympanum.

The horizontal and vertical bands which he introduces recall Conques (Ill. 392) on the one hand, and St.-Junien (Ill. 450) on the other.

An unexpected affinity of our sculptor is with Germany. The figure to the extreme right in the upper zone of the tympanum at Carennac (Ill. 384) reproduces line for line the figure in the right-hand corner of a miniature of the Perikopenbuch von St. Erentrud in Munich [1] representing the Crucifixion. There is an unmistakable similarity between the style of the Carennac artist and that of the master who executed the tympanum of the Galluspforte at Basel.[2]

The animals in the decorative frieze which runs below the tympanum at Carennac (Ill. 382, 383) are among the most spirited and naturalistic in mediaeval art. They are only rivalled by those of the St.-Gilles frieze (Ill. 1315–1317; 1321, 1322), and perhaps also come eventually from Apulia.

The tympanum at Mauriac (Ill. 1246, 1247) is certainly later than that at Carennac (Ill. 381–385). Burgundian influence is barely perceptible at Carennac (Ill. 381–385); [3] at Mauriac it is predominate (Ill. 1246, 1247). It is apparent in the composition, which is precisely that of Montceaux-l'Etoile (Ill. 104), in the angels in violent movement on either side of the aureole and in the leg bands of several of the apostles (Ill. 1247). We may safely conjecture that our master went to Burgundy after he executed Carennac, and before he worked at Mauriac.

This journey to Burgundy probably took place about 1130, since our artist brought back the composition of the tympanum of Mont-

---

[1] Illustrated by Swarzenski, No. 200.

[2] Illustrated by Dehio und von Bezold, XII, 9.

[3] Chiefly in the drapery edge of the upper garment falling diagonally across the knees of Christ (Ill. 383).

ceaux-l'Etoile and the motive of leg bands, both of which were con-
spicuously in the air about that time.

Another pilgrimage sculptor of interest is the one who executed the
tympanum of Cahors (Ill. 421–429) and whose hand it is easy to
recognize also in the sculptures of St.-Martin of Souillac (Ill. 430)
and in the tympanum of Martel (Ill. 431–433). The latter, indeed,
if abstraction be made of the modern heads, is one of the most·
heraldic and haunting compositions achieved by the school of
Languedoc. The artistic genealogy of our master is not altogether
easy to disentangle. The faces of the Cahors apostles are certainly
derived from the Carennac Master — compare, for example, the
apostle to the right in Ill. 427 with the one to the right in Ill. 382.
The angels on either side of the aureole (Ill. 422, 424) are literal copies
of those of the tympanum of Mauriac (Ill. 1246), which is a work of
the Carennac Master. In the folds of the draperies (Ill. 429, apostle
with crossed legs, lower half) our sculptor shows knowledge of the
porch of Moissac (Ill. 377). The composition of the tympanum is
obviously inspired by that of the tympanum of Moissac. (Compare
Ill. 339 with Ill. 422.) Other draperies (for example, the skirts of the
apostle with crossed legs, Ill. 429) seem derived from the work of the
Angoulême Master of St.-Gilles (Ill. 1304). The short tunics of the
figures in the scenes from the life of St. Stephen (Ill. 423, 426) recall
those of the frieze of St.-Gilles (Ill. 1315–1322).[1] Our artist uses constantly the whisk of drapery consisting of a groove separated by two
sharp edges from turned-over folds (e. g., apostle to extreme right, Ill.
429, drapery between feet) which we shall see was invented at Beaucaire (Ill. 1299) and copied at St.-Gilles.[2] His canopies seem a development of those of the capitals of Chartres, but the trilobed arch
is a Spanish motive. From all this we conclude that the Cahors
tympanum was hardly produced before about 1150. It is probably
the latest work of the series; the fine simplicity of Martel suggests
that it is earlier, while St.-Martin of Souillac is dull, and presumably
immature.

[1] This was suggested to me by Mr. Priest.
[2] See below, p. 277, 278.

It is obvious that the chief inspiration for the frieze of Carrión de los Condes (Ill. 722–726) was the lintel of Cahors (Ill. 427–429). In the broad lines of the composition, the *Majestas Domini* reproduces the type which we have found at St.-Sernin (Ill. 296), Carennac (Ill. 381–385) and St.-Junien (Ill. 450). Here again we have the impression that an arca has been reproduced — the apostles in arches recall the elders at St.-Junien (Ill. 450). But in this case I suspect that the inspiration came not so much from a sculptured tomb, as from a Limoges châsse. I even venture to suggest that the very model may have been the reliquary formerly at Santo Domingo de Silos, but now preserved in the museum of Burgos.

The Limoges origin of this arca, generally admitted, has recently been combatted by Leguina [1] who supposes it made in Orense. The purely Spanish type of the figures will be denied by no one familiar with Romanesque sculpture, but precisely such figures are characteristic of the entire group of enamels that pass as work of Limoges. Limoges was a station on the pilgrimage road; its great basilica was another replica of Santiago, and the enamels called Limoges are only a branch of the art of the pilgrimage.[2] Enamels may be credited with having played a large part in carrying to the Rhine, and indeed throughout the world, the forms of pilgrimage sculpture.

There is the same uncertainty regarding the date of the Silos arca as about its place of origin. Rupin, with evident error, assigns it to the XIII century. Roulin was doubtless closer to the mark in ascribing it to the last third of the XII century, and Dieulafoy closer still in placing it in the second half of the XII century.[3] Its figures, in fact, show the style of *c.* 1150.

Now the composition of this châsse is similar to that of the Carrión frieze; and there is furthermore good reason to believe that the

---

[1] 167 f.

[2] Cf. Molinier, in Michel, I, 2, 871 discussing this arca: Il semblerait même, à certains détails de dessin, que les ouvriers qui ont imaginé cette décoration ont pu avoir sous les yeux certains modèles orientaux importés d'Espagne. La chose ne serait pas autrement étonnante puisque, sur un assez grand nombre de monuments limousins, nous relevons des imitations de caractères arabes transformés en ornement et n'ayant plus aucune signification littérale.

[3] 7. Dieulafoy suspected the piece might be Spanish.

head master at Carrión (for he obviously did not work alone) had seen the châsse. His style shows close relationship to that of the well-known Annunciation of the Santo Domingo cloister (Ill. 721).[1] I almost question, in fact, whether that work be not by his very hand. In any event, the master of Carrión had certainly been at Silos. The châsse must then almost surely have come under his observation.

He also sought inspiration in many other quarters besides. He seems to have known the work of the Charlieu master (Ill. 108–111), and to have derived thence his hands and feet of such peculiar type, and the angel sculptured in relief on the column. The draperies of his Christ are very similar to those of the Virgin of the Charlieu master at Donzy (Ill. 112–114).[2] The canopies which surmount the apostles are no longer the simple round arches of the Silos arca, which are so strangely like those of St.-Denis (Ill. 1441, 1442), but elaborate polylobed canopies which must have come directly from the lintel of Cahors (Ill. 427), but ultimately from the capitals of Chartres or Etampes (Ill. 1463, 1464). It should be observed, however, that these canopies probably first originated in Spain, in ivories like the San Isidoro casket (Ill. 651–653).[3] Certain capitals of Carrión and the "organ-pipe" draperies are taken from the façade of St.-Trophîme of Arles (Ill. 1366–1377). From Provence came also, probably, the idea of a sculptured frieze, although the composition at Carrión resembles Ripoll (Ill. 584, 587) and Sangüesa (Ill. 748) more closely than anything beyond the Pyrenees. The bestarred aureole may have been inspired by Conques (Ill. 393). The drapery about the legs of the second apostle from the left at Carrión (Ill. 722) is like that about the legs of the Virgin in the cathedral of Zamora (Ill. 740). The voussures are derived from some monument of Saintonge, possibly Aulnay (Ill. 979). Numerous motives have been taken from Toulouse and the Puerta de las Platerias (Ill. 674–691).

---

[1] The flying angels about the head of the Virgin in this Annunciation seem to have been copied at St.-Jean-le-Vieux of Perpignan (Ill. 618).

[2] Such tortured draperies are already found in a Carlovingian ivory of the IX century in the British Museum, illustrated by Dalton, Pl. XXII, 42.

[3] See what has been said of this motive above, p. 45 f.

Since our sculptor knew the façade of St.-Trophîme (Ill. 1366–1377), he must have worked after 1152. On the other hand, he was earlier than Mateo. He shows no knowledge of the Pórtico de la Gloria (Ill. 820–840), although he was clearly acquainted with the earlier work at Santiago (Ill. 674–691). The activity of Mateo must have begun in the early 70's. We may, therefore, date the Carrión frieze to *c.* 1165.

Aesthetically, this is one of the grand achievements of the XII century. Ruined and battered as it is, we recognize in it immediately the expression of a great creative mind. The apostles, especially to the left, are of superb contour and delicious rhythm.

The much-restored Christ of the north portal of Lugo (Ill. 728) is inspired by the Christ of Carrión (Ill. 724).

The inferior and later work at Mimizan (Ill. 490, 491) also evidently owes much to Carrión. Not only is the motive of a frieze with the *Majestas Domini* in the centre and six apostles on either side taken over directly — for without doubt the fragments of Mimizan (Ill. 490, 491) must have formed precisely such a composition — but numerous details of the drawing of the draperies, the faces, the posture of several of the apostles as well. Mimizan (Ill. 490, 491) in turn seems to be related to the north transept portal of Chartres, built by the Spanish queen, Blanche of Castile. The sculptures of Mimizan were also certainly known to the sculptor of the north portal at St.-Benoît-sur-Loire (Ill. 1519–1527) who perhaps also saw Carrión (Ill. 722–726).[1]

A curious combination of influences is shown by a capital coming from Sahagún, now at San Marcos of Léon (Ill. 768). The artist had been to Santo Domingo de Silos and had been impressed by the sculptures in the cloister. He combines heads copied from the early work of the XI century (Ill. 671) with draperies taken from the Annunciation (Ill. 721). He must, therefore, have worked after 1160. His activity is doubtless to be connected with the consecration of 1183.

---

[1] The tympanum of St.-Pierre-le-Moûtier (Ill. 1275) is an evident copy of St.-Benoît-sur-Loire (Ill. 1519, 1520).

A different set of influences came to the front in the extraordinary sculptures of Sangüesa (Ill. 742–754). The close relationship to the jamb sculptures of Chartres is obvious. The master of the left-hand side (Ill. 746) — he has signed his name, Leodegarius (Léger) — seems, indeed, to have drawn his inspiration solely from Chartres; but the finer artist of the right-hand jamb (Ill. 743–745) knew St.-Loup-de-Naud and Autun as well. The head of the central figure of the right-hand jamb at Sangüesa (Ill. 744) is like that of the jamb figure left of the portal at St.-Loup (Ill. 1493).[1] The sensitively modelled heads and the draperies of the master of the right jamb of Sangüesa (Ill. 746) both recall the Autun tympanum (Ill. 80, 81). In the tympanum (Ill. 747) and upper part of the façade (Ill. 748–754) at Sangüesa other hands are at work. The Last Judgment (Ill. 747) of rudimentary type recalls the Moissac tympanum (Ill. 339), but it surmounts a Virgin and Apostles in arches after the manner of Chartres. The spandrels are filled with miscellaneous bits of sculpture, some of which show Lombard influence; the upper part of the portal with statues in niches is inspired by Pictave models. The style of certain of the statues in niches is like that of the sculptures flanking the shafts on the façade of Civray (Ill. 1122, 1123, 1125). The all-over sculpture of the spandrels, and in fact the entire architectural composition, recall Notre-Dame-la-Grande of Poitiers (Ill. 951–962). The rows of damned and blest in the tympanum (Ill. 747) seem analogous to those of the frieze of St.-Trophîme (Ill. 1366, 1375).

The date of Sangüesa is a delicate question. The church was given, it is known, to St. John of Jerusalem in 1132. It would be natural to suppose that the reconstruction was begun immediately afterwards. The sculptors of the portals, however, knew Chartres; and it is the orthodox belief that the portal of Chartres was not begun until 1145. Of all the derivatives of Chartres, Sangüesa is by far the most archaic; we may, therefore, assign the portal to c. 1155.

---

[1] It is just possible, however, that both may be derived from the work of the head master at Chartres — see the figure to the left, in Houvet's Plate 42.

The same combination of widely divergent influences is characteristic of the remarkable sculptures of Ripoll. Mediaeval art has
created little that is lovelier than certain passages of this rich façade
(Ill. 560–593). The jamb sculptures (Ill. 572, 573) must be due to the
influence of Gilbert — his peculiar draperies are reproduced in the
folds of the leg of *St. Paul*. We also notice rinceaux taken from
Nicolò's work at Sagra S. Michele, voussures from St.-Denis, a saw-
tooth moulding from Rome, monsters from Lombardy, drapery and
heads from the work of Guglielmo. The most significant analogy,
however, is with the bronze doors of Novgorod in Russia. The similarity in the treatment of the draperies is indeed striking. That there
is a direct connection does not seem open to doubt, and in this case
we are able to guess at an explanation. The bronze doors of Novgorod came originally from Plock in Poland.[1] Closely related doors
are those which still exist at Gnesen (Gniezno). Now these Polish
doors were perhaps actually manufactured in Germany; at any event
they belong to the Teutonic tradition of bronze-casting which
centred at Hildesheim. On the other hand, a local tradition, referred
to by Lampérez [2] claims the façade of Ripoll as the work of a German
monk. We can therefore easily understand how the basis of the art
of this master was the technique of the Saxon bronze-casters. We
can also understand how in his travels a multitude of foreign influences were grafted upon it.

Since our sculptor worked in Catalonia it is not surprising that he
absorbed elements of the local style. It was perhaps at Solsona that
he came to know the work of Gilbert. Certain of his draperies (Ill.
565) suggest that he had seen the *St. Peter* (Ill. 558) and the *St. Paul*
(Ill. 559) of St.-Michel-de-Cuxa. Others are like those of the Joseph
in the Huesca Adoration (Ill. 532). But we can trace even more exactly how the master of Ripoll absorbed Catalan influences. Señor
Pijoan has demonstrated that in sculpturing the façade of Ripoll the
artist held in his hand a Catalan miniatured Bible of the X century
like the Bible of Farfa — perhaps that very Bible itself — and trans-

---

[1] Furmankiewicz, 365.   [2] I, 399.

ferred from its pages to his walls scene after scene with only minor changes.

As for date, the façade of Ripoll gives the impression of being later than Sangüesa, but it must have been executed before 1160.

San Miguel of Estella (Ill. 777–785) is distinctly more advanced. The convention of hatching to represent the feathers of the wings, common in Spanish sculpture of this period, is, perhaps, derived from Byzantine originals through ivories of the Ada group. The heads of the adossed figures of Estella (Ill. 782, 784) are inspired by those of the right jamb at Sangüesa (Ill. 743–745), but are coarser and later. Certain draperies seem to have been influenced by the master of Carrión (Ill. 722–726). Others recall the façade of St.-Trophîme of Arles (Ill. 1366–1377). The prophets seem inspired by those of the Daurade at Toulouse (Ill. 474–478). We are evidently about 1185.

The master of San Miguel of Estella worked also at Tudela (Ill. 786–791) and in the cloister of Salamanca (Ill. 775, 776). Although the Tudela sculptures have been extravagantly praised, they do not seem, in point of fact, to be of extraordinary merit.

The work at Armentía (Ill. 761–767) is more interesting. This is in some ways the most typical of all the pilgrimage churches. Ideas are borrowed from everywhere, and the motives of other sculptors are reproduced with a fidelity that is extraordinary.

A most striking analogy exists between the relief of the Entombment at Armentía (Ill. 761) and that representing the same subject at Santo Domingo de Silos (Ill. 670). The composition of the two is the same. The field in each case is divided into two halves by the horizontal line formed by the tomb, on which lies the body of Christ. Below are the sleeping guards — an unusual addition to the scene of the Entombment, found only so far as I know in these two representations. Above to the right in both reliefs is the group of the three Maries; Joseph of Arimathea and Nicodemus bend over the body of Christ, the empty spaces are filled with angels. There can be no doubt, therefore, that the composition of the Armentía relief was directly taken over from Santo Domingo. Indeed, the sculptor of

Armentía copied more than the composition of his great predecessor. The faces of his three Maries are precisely those of the three Maries of Santo Domingo— the two middle ones are so similar that we might easily take them to be the work of the same hand, instead of separated by nearly a century. The wings of the angel to the right of the Armentía relief are clearly copied from the wings of the angel at Santo Domingo. The body of Christ at Armentía is a crude imitation of the splendid body of Christ at Santo Domingo. The draperies of the Maries at Armentía are obviously inspired by the much better draperies of the corresponding figures at Santo Domingo. The flame-shaped pebbles below the sarcophagus at Armentía recall those of the Deposition at Silos (Ill. 669).

How weak and emaciated is, however, the Armentía version compared with the vigour and noble simplicity of the Silos original! Nor has the Armentía sculptor been able to avoid the introduction of mannerisms of his later age. The round holes on his sarcophagus recall the friezes of Beaucaire (Ill. 1298) and St.-Gilles (Ill. 1391); the flying angels to the left above (Ill. 761) make us think of the later work at Santo Domingo (Ill. 721). The supporting figures (Ill. 761) recall Civray (Ill. 1128, 1129) and St. Jacob of Regensburg.

But it was not only at Santo Domingo de Silos that our sculptor sought inspiration. His adossed figures must come ultimately from Chartres — not directly, but through some intermediary which I can not determine;[1] the porch with side reliefs was probably copied from that of St.-Martin of Brive (Ill. 353, 354) which also was sculptured with reliefs representing the Harrowing of Hell; in the pendentives of the dome tetramorphs (Ill. 767) replace the angels of Compostela (Ill. 694, 695);[2] the tympanum (Ill. 764, 765) seems like the weakest and faintest echo of Autun (Ill. 80, 81); the Annuncia-

---

[1] Probably not Civray (Ill. 1122–1131).

[2] The style of the Santiago angels seems related to that of Mateo. To place the evangelists in pendentives was in accordance with a venerable Byzantine tradition. For the iconography of the tetramorphs see Bertaux, *Italie Méridionale*, 218. The motive which originated in the Orient at least as early as the VI century was soon diffused in the West. It is found, for example, in an early Irish manuscript — the Gospel of Kells, at Trinity College, Dublin (No. A. 1. 6 (58), fol. 28 ver. illustrated by Zimmermann, 173); in a Merovingian manuscript illustrated by

tion (Ill. 762) recalls the later work in the cloisters of Santo Domingo de Silos (Ill. 721); draperies are borrowed now from Arles (Ill. 1366–1377), now from the master of Carrión (Ill. 722–726), now from Chartres; a labarum and two angels (Ill. 766) are like the magnification of an abacus in the cloister of Moissac (Ill. 282). Yet for all the plagiarism and obviously second-rate quality the sculpture at Armentía is far from being despicable. These artists have known how to impart to their borrowings an atmosphere of wistful tenderness. We return to their works with a pleasure which is surprising in view of the technical mediocrity.

The sculptures of Armentía were donated by the bishop of Calahorra, D. Rodrigo Cascante (1146–1190). The style indicates that they were executed in the later rather than in the earlier part of his pontificate. The work at Armentía seems about abreast of that of San Miguel of Estella (Ill. 777–781). On the other hand the sculptors do not seem to have known Mateo's work at Santiago (Ill. 820–840). We may infer, therefore, that Armentía dates from about 1180.

A typical monument of pilgrimage art is, or alas was, the church of Ste.-Foy at Morlaas (Ill. 456–460). A Cluniac priory on the road and dedicated to the great saint of Conques, it naturally fell under precisely the same influences as the monuments beyond the Pyrenees. The restoration of the XIX century has unhappily reduced the magnificent portal (Ill. 456–460) to a pitiable state. What remains is, in-

Leprieur in Michel I, 1, 314; in an English Gospel of the XII century, illustrated *Burlington*, Pl. 24; and in the Perikopenbuch von St. Erentrud, Munich, Kgl. Hof- und Statsbibliothek, Clm 15903, c. p. 52; in a capital of Moissac, and in two Beatus manuscripts.

It was not, I think, as one might be tempted to suppose, from the sculptures placed under pendentives like Conques (Ill. 388, 389) and Santiago (Ill. 694, 695) that are derived those of the vaulting ribs of the Catedral Vieja of Salamanca (Ill. 736-739). The latter are much more probably inspired from northern France. As early as the end of the XI century, sculptures were placed flanking the vaulting shafts at Airvault (Ill. 898–900). At Bury these sculptures had already been moved to the base of the ribs. It was, however, especially in the Loire valley that the motive became popular; we find it at Cormery, at Crouzilles, at St.-Martin of Angers, in the porch of Loches, at La Trinité of Vendôme (Ill. 1516-1518). It was from this region that the motive found its way into Spain, to the porch of San Martín of Segóvia, to Salamanca (Ill. 736-739), to Ciudad Rodrigo (Ill. 873), to the Pórtico de la Gloria at Santiago (Ill. 837, 838).

The style of San Martín of Segóvia resembles that of the West in several particulars. The jamb sculptures (Ill. 755, 756) are extraordinarily close to those of Véreaux (Ill. 1479-1481) a monument which if not situated in Poitou is still well west of Burgundy.

deed, modern. A few fragments preserved in the local museum and casts under the rafters of the roof are all that can give an idea of the quality of what must have been one of the most interesting portals of southern Europe.

Light is thrown upon the original character of Morlaas by a comparison with the portal of Ste.-Marie at Oloron (Ill. 461). This monument has also suffered from a reconstruction almost as radical, but some bits of the ancient work have happily survived. Although the restorations undergone by both monuments make any close analysis of style impossible, there can be little doubt that the two are the work of the same artist. In both two minor tympana are grouped under a larger one. The grotesque figures in the two archivolts show the closest analogies. The peculiar ornament of rosette-like flowers is repeated in both works. So also is the moulding ornamented with a series of little round balls. The strings of the outer archivolt are identical in the two monuments. In both the figures are placed floating in space as it were, without the indication of any support beneath their feet.

A conspicuous element in the style of both portals is the evident Burgundian influence. The motive of twin portals with tympana grouped under a larger tympanum recalls Avallon. It is true that twin portals are also characteristic of Santiago; and it is certain that our sculptor knew the work of Mateo and his predecessors. The elders of Oloron are obvious derivatives of those of the Pórtico de la Gloria (Ill. 824–828); and the iconography of Morlaas with Christ and the evangelists has equally evident analogies with the Puerta Francigena. But the borrowings of our master from Burgundy are even more patent. The Flight into Egypt of the right-hand tympanum of Morlaas (Ill. 458) resembles vaguely the unforgettable rendering of the same theme at Bois-Ste.-Marie (Ill. 142). The adossed jamb figures at Morlaas are placed high up, in the Burgundian manner (which, however, was also copied in the Pórtico de la Gloria). The floating of the figures in space (to which attention has already been called), suggests the figures on the archivolt of Anzy-

le-Duc (Ill. 96). The movement of the angels in one of the capitals
to the left at Morlaas (Ill. 460) is distinctly Burgundian. There is
noticeable, likewise, the influence of the master of the southern porch
of St.-Sernin (Ill. 308–316) who also worked at Santiago. His are the
draperies, his the feet, his the movement of the apostles at Morlaas.
From Lombardy came the caryatids of the trumeau of Morlaas and
of the voussures with the elders. The Morlaas elders themselves, like
the figures of the outer voussures, all seated on a roll-moulding, are
perhaps later derivatives of the north portal at Toro (Ill. 734). We
are clearly in the last quarter of the XII century.

In the cloister of Oviedo are two curious reliefs (Ill. 869, 870), dating, perhaps, from about 1200, representing St. Peter and St. Paul.
This strange art, in which the vigorous archaic modelling of the draperies and bodies contrasts so strangely with the Gothically immobile
faces, reappears at Santillana del Mar, where in the cloister are, by
the same hand, a Virgin (Ill. 867), a Santa Juliana with devil and a
most impressive *Christ* (Ill. 868). A singular echo of the style of this
pilgrimage artist may be found in the distant Capitanata in a relief
at Rapolla, dated 1209.[1] The strange altar at Santillana (Ill. 861) is
of a different, though not unrelated style; and to the same atelier
belong the capitals of the cloister (Ill. 862–866). This group of sculptors is, perhaps, connected with Leire (Ill. 711–716) on the one hand,
and the Puerta de las Platerias (Ill. 674–691) on the other.

The crude sculptures of San Quirce (Ill. 717) may be considered
another off-shoot of the pilgrimage style. They are possibly distant
relatives of Leire (Ill. 711–716).

[1] Illustrated by Bertaux, *Ital. Mer.*, 517.

THE PORTICO DE LA GLORIA

WE have now arrived at the moment when there dawned in Spain
a third period of sculpture, unhappily of brief duration, but in some
respects even more brilliant than that which opened the XII century.
This golden age is ushered in by the sculptures of the Cámara Santa
of Oviedo (Ill. 811–819). In the dim light of a small chapel, the figures of supernatural apostles are adossed two by two against the
vaulting-shafts. An Egyptian solemnity invests these sculptures,
which, indeed, unite the fervour and imagination of Spain, the
restraint of France, the delicacy of Burgundy, the strength of Toulouse, with an exaltation that could only be mediaeval. In comparison even the Pórtico de la Gloria (Ill. 820–840) seems coarse and
cold. This, not that, is the supreme master-work.

Who was this superlatively gifted sculptor? I was at one time
tempted to believe that the Oviedo Cámara Santa was an early
work of Mateo. But the hypothesis, seductive as it is, can not be
held. Notwithstanding the many analogies, the difference in style
is too great. The Oviedo master is a comet which flashes with extraordinary brilliance across the horizon, then disappears. At a
period when the sculptors of northern France were listlessly repeat-
ing the time-worn gospel of Chartres; when Provence was sinking
into such senility as the tympanum of Maguelonne (Ill. 1384); when
Benedetto had not yet awakened Lombardy to new life; when his
own compatriots were patching together works out of stolen fragments with as little conscience as a modern architect and as little
coherence as a crazy quilt, this unknown artist created out of his
own genius a great and a new manner. In his work there breathes
the spirit rather than the detail of the destroyed jamb sculptures of
St.-Denis (Ill. 1445–1457); his draperies are analogous to those of

the Romanesque tomb now incorporated in the north transept portal of Reims; his beard conventions recall the XI-century crucifixes of S. Isidoro (Ill. 654, 703) and the Cutbrecht Gospels of Vienna;[1] he shows relationship to, perhaps even derivation from, the master of Carrión (Ill. 722–726). Yet when we have deduced from his manner all this and much else which cleverer eyes than mine will still discover, we have not plucked the heart of his mystery. A great artist is always incomprehensible. And this sculptor was great. Nothing in Toulouse, nothing in Languedoc, nothing in Spain (unless it be Santo Domingo de Silos), I almost wrote nothing in Europe, surpasses the apostles of Oviedo.

Mateo knew Oviedo, certainly. He knew much else besides. The Christ of the Puerta de las Platerias (Ill. 676), which must be part of the original doorway, since specifically mentioned in the *Guide*, exercised a profound influence upon Mateo as, indeed, upon much other work of the XII century. Mateo's lovely St. James (Ill. 830) is certainly derived from this model.

From Burgundy Mateo came by his jamb sculptures, raised above the columns; the great figure of the Deity in the centre of the tympanum, and the figure on the trumeau below; perhaps, too, the idea of a porch. From Lombardy — or was it peradventure Apulia? — came the portrait of the artist (Ill. 831), and the monsters under the columns (Ill. 832), the latter, perhaps, by the way of Provence. From Arles came, I suppose, the proportions of his jamb figures, which seem to approach this canon more closely than that of northern France.

The result of these influences, plus the genius of Mateo, was the first work of Gothic sculpture in Europe. Neither the Porte-Ste.-Anne of Paris, nor the jambs of Senlis (Ill. 1508) foreshadowed to such an extent the future development of the style. It is not too much to say that the work of Mateo stood to the XIII century in much the same relationship as that in which the early school of the pilgrimages stood to the XII century.

[1] Lat. 1224, fol. 17 b, illustrated by Zimmermann, 297.

Little of Mateo's life is known. We find him at work at Santiago in 1168; twenty years later the doors of the Pórtico de la Gloria (Ill. 820–840) were hung, so that the sculptures must have been essentially finished by this time. As late as 1217, however, he was still master-builder at Compostela.

The Pórtico de la Gloria is in quality less fine than the Cámara Santa (Ill. 811–819) of Oviedo. This or that detail has been surpassed by this or that master of northern France. But for the sum of the impressions it remains, perhaps, the most overwhelming monument of mediaeval sculpture.

Notwithstanding the casts which were made for the South Kensington Museum, the polychromy is still on the whole well preserved. This singularly increases the realism of the figures. In northern Europe the colouring of the statues has usually been destroyed; but one suspects that it was never as vivid and naturalistic as that which still remains on Mateo's work. These figures are, indeed, almost startling, they seem so to jump out at us; their effect may be compared to that produced by certain Florentine painters of the Quattrocento such as Castagno or Pollaiuolo. Their existence is realized with extraordinary facility. They anticipate the naturalism of Claus Sluter.

We have here not the symbolic and dogmatic art of the Gothic cathedrals of the North; it is much more a good-natured realism not without a streak of vulgarity; an art which would impress quickly the passing crowd and required no painstaking study for its appreciation. In all this it is fair to see the point of view of the average pilgrim with his interest in the extraordinary, his *bonhommerie*, and his, perhaps, not over-profound intellect.

The influence of the art of Mateo, as might be expected, was enormous. The sculptures of the cathedral of Orense (Ill. 852–859) have long been recognized as having been inspired by the Pórtico de la Gloria. Although they are assuredly far from equalling their original, they by no means deserve the aspersions which it has been fashionable to heap upon them. The western portal of San Vicente of Avila (Ill. 841–849) is one of the best works inspired by Mateo; in quality it is indeed little if at all below his level. It seems here as if the Mateo tradition had been purified by fresh drafts from Burgundy. The Annunciation (Ill. 841) of the south portal, as M. Bertaux recognized, is by the same hand. Ciudad Roderigo (Ill. 876–878), Toro (Ill. 886–889), the portal of the Colegio San Jeronimo at Santiago, may all be considered as derivatives of the Pórtico de la Gloria.[1] Miss King recognizes the same influence at S. Julián of Moraime. Even as late as 1404, the sculptor of the portal of S. Martín of Noya still repeated the types of Mateo.

But it was not only in Spain that the influence of Mateo was felt. His art, as little as that of his predecessors, found in the Pyrenees a barrier.

The sculptors of Bamberg sought inspiration from Mateo. It has been much discussed whether the apostles and prophets of the choir-screen are derived from Saxony, from Byzantine tradition, or from Toulouse. It is probable that the sculptor was acquainted not only with Saxony and the sculptures of St.-Etienne (Ill. 434–443) and Cahors (Ill. 422–429), but also with the jamb sculptures of Santiago (Ill. 820–840). His Isaiah[2] is reminiscent of the prophet to the left of the left-hand doorway at Santiago (Ill. 820). This Compostelan prophet seems, indeed, to have inspired the facial type of the school of Bamberg. The Bamberg sculptors were also influenced by the Daniel of Santiago (Ill. 829 b). The Hosea[3] of Bamberg is manifestly inspired by this model of which it reproduces even the curls. The Bamberg "smile" may as well be derived from Santiago direct, as via Reims.

Internal evidence, therefore, justifies the inference that the master of Bamberg had been to Compostela. Now there is external proof that he had been to Palestine. He has sculptured his own portrait in the tympanum of the Gnadetür. On the sleeve of his coat may clearly be seen a cross, indicating that he had made the pilgrimage to

[1] See Buschbeck, 48 f.
[2] Illustrated by Weese, 5. It is the prophet holding a saw, next to the *David*.
[3] Illustrated by Weese, 4.

the Holy Land. We are probably justified in assuming that, like so many others, he combined this journey with that to Santiago.

It was, however, in France that the work of Mateo proved most fecund. His St. James on the central trumeau of Santiago (Ill. 830) is the ancestor of the Beaux Dieux of Chartres and Amiens. The great porches of Chartres were, perhaps, inspired by Mateo's Pórtico de la Gloria, which, as originally built, must have produced a not dissimilar effect. It is certain that the masters of Chartres had studied Santiago. The head of the Queen of Sheba of the north portal of Chartres [1] reproduces exactly the head of the queen on the outer respond of the Pórtico de la Gloria (Ill. 839). The torso of a jamb sculpture from Notre-Dame of Paris, now in the Musée de Cluny,[2] reproduces, line for line and stroke for stroke, the corresponding portions of the Daniel of Santiago (Ill. 829). The elders now in the Musée Archéologique of Montpellier [3] (Ill. 1400–1402) and said, I know not on what authority, to come from St.-Guilhem-le-Désert, are evident copies of the voussure sculptures of the Pórtico de la Gloria (Ill. 824–828).

In Switzerland we find the Pórtico de la Gloria accurately copied in the cathedral of Lausanne; [4] the apostles of the Münster at Basle owe their draperies to the same original.[5] In England, as Mssrs. Prior and Gardner have recognized, the celebrated statues of York repeat the models of Mateo.[6]

The sculptors of Reims sought inspiration at Santiago. The statue of Daniel, on the left jamb of the Pórtico de la Gloria (Ill. 829, 829 b) determined the type which gives the school of Reims its peculiar and unforgettable character. It is the influence of archaic Santiago that lifts Reims above the classicism and monotony of the work at Amiens or the south portal of Chartres. Everywhere through the cathedral of Reims echoes and re-echoes the theme of the Daniel of Santiago, but varied and beautified. We recognize it in the angels

---

[1] Illustrated by Houvet, 41.
[2] Photograph by Stoedtner, No. 130058.
[3] 14 rue Eugène Lisbonne.
[4] Illustrated by Michel, II, 1, 196.
[5] Illustrated by Lindner, Taf. VIII.
[6] See Prior and Gardner, 214.

of the buttresses, in the angel of the Annunciation (829 a), almost
unaltered in the *Sourire*, embellished and transposed, but still unmistakable in the *Joseph*, in the *Anna*, in the *Queen of Sheba*, in the
Solomon, in the caryatid of the west façade, in the angels of the
Coronation.[1] The smile of Reims is indeed as old as archaic Greece
and as young as the Mona Lisa. It had lurked upon the lips of num-
berless Buddhas before it alighted on those of the angels of Monopoli (Ill. 158). It continued to fascinate the sculptors and ivory-
carvers of the XIV century.

It is, I think, admitted by competent critics that the sculptures of
Reims show German influence. It has not, however, so far as I am
aware, been remarked that the head of a prophet about the rose of
the south transept [2] reproduces the Jonah of the Bamberg choir-
screen.[3] The Reims figure, I think, must be a work of that sculptor
of the second atelier at Bamberg, who has been suspected on independent grounds of having been connected first with the earlier
atelier at Bamberg, then with Reims (where he shows himself especially familiar with the transepts) before being called to direct the
second Bamberg atelier. I detect, indeed, his hand at Reims also in
an angel of a buttress of the south façade.[4] The suspicion arises that it
may have been this master who fetched the smile of Mateo's Daniel
from Santiago and handed it on to the " Joseph master " of Reims.

However this may be, the debt of the sculptors of Reims to Santiago does not end with the smile. Other facial types appear to be
derived from the same original. More than this, the Reims sculptors
owe to Santiago one of their happiest innovations. At Chartres, at
Amiens, at Senlis, in all the older northern French portals, the jamb
figures stand in rigid rows, facing nearly or quite stark outwards.
Mateo had animated his (Ill. 829, 834); they turn as if to talk with
one another. Now this motive of Mateo's is reproduced at Reims.

---

[1] All these sculptures are reproduced by Vitry.
[2] Illustrated by Vitry, II, Pl. LVII.
[3] Illustrated by Weese, II, 4
[4] Illustrated by Vitry, II, Pl. LXVIII.

VI

ST.–GILLES

WE are fortunate in being able to commence our study of the Provençal school with a dated monument. The sculptured altar of St. Cannate and St. Antonin in the Cathédrale Ancienne at Marseille (Ill. 1283, 1284) seems to have escaped the attention of those who have written upon the controverted subject of southern French Romanesque. Yet this monument contains the solution of nearly all the difficulties, for it was erected in 1122.[1]

The style is singularly archaic in the draperies, singularly advanced in the facial types. The sagging folds in the middle of the skirt of St. Cannate are more finely executed, but essentially like those of one of the figures flanking the vaulting shafts of the church at Airvault (Ill. 899), a monument consecrated in 1100. The side folds also recall the same model. Indeed, it is probable that these draperies show that there was already an influence of the school of the West in Provence. The facial types on the other hand seem to foreshadow much later work. That of the Virgin is closely analogous to Gilbert's *Virgin* at Solsona (Ill. 552).

This Virgin of the Marseille altar seems, indeed, to have exerted a peculiar influence upon monuments of the fifth decade of the XII century. It apparently was the original from which was derived the Virgin of the south tympanum at Chartres. When we place these two sculptures beside each other, we perceive that the composition is the same in both. In both the Virgin is seated on a throne; in both she holds the Child square in the middle of her lap; in both the Child's feet hang stiffly down below the bottom of His draperies; in

[1] Caeteras SS. Cannati et Antonini Reliquias, clero prius populoque palam ostensas, decenti arcae inclusit Raymundus Massiliensis episcopus anno 1122 die Assumptae in coelo Virgini Mariae sacro, cujus quidem rei ex Archivis ecclesiae Massiliensis Henricus de Belzance sequens testimonium exhibet, etc. (*Acta Sanctorum*, 15 October VII, 1, 20.)

both the Virgin's feet emerge stiffly below hers; the left hand of the Virgin in both is held in the same position; the right hand of Christ was in both raised in blessing; the facial type of the Virgin is in both the same; the crown of the Virgin has in both the same form; the face of the Christ Child is in both the same; there is even a certain similarity in the draperies, although those of Marseille are obviously more archaic. It appears, therefore, that the Master of the Angels, when he sculptured the southern tympanum of Chartres, set the Virgin of Marseille under the canopy of Beaucaire and added a pair of Burgundian angels.

The advanced facial types of the Marseille arca recall the fact that the school of Provence was distinguished for the naturalism of its faces as early as the XI century, as is witnessed by the tomb of St. Isarne of 1048 (Ill. 1278).

In the portal of the cathedral of Maguelonne constructed in 1178 [1] (as recorded in verses by the celebrated troubadour Bernard de Treviis inscribed upon it) [2] are incorporated earlier fragments of sculpture. These consist of the crouching forms of St. Peter (Ill. 1287) and St. Paul (Ill. 1288), obviously fragments of a tympanum, and two consoles (Ill. 1285, 1286). It is a curious fact that the faces of the tympanum sculptures are repeated on the consoles. Evidently then the consoles also represent St. Peter and St. Paul.

The style of these figures at Maguelonne (Ill. 1285-1288) does not seem to be closely related to that of the Marseille altar (Ill. 1283, 1284). At Marseille we found advanced faces and archaic draperies; at Maguelonne the draperies seem more developed than the faces. Yet there are similarities between the two works. There is the same peculiar little spiral in the draperies on the right shoulder of the Marseille St. Cannate (Ill. 1283) and on the right shoulder of the Maguelonne *St. Paul* (Ill. 1288). The grooving of the draperies

[1] † AD PORTV̄ VITE: SITIENTES QVIQ̄ VENITE:
HAS INTRANDO FORES: VESTROS COMPONITE MORES:
HINC INTRANS ORA TVA SĒP(ER) CRIMI†NA PLORA:
QVICQD PECCATVR: LACRIMA(RVM) FONTE LAVATVR †
BD' III VIIS FECIT HOC † AÑO INC̄ D'. MCLXXVIII
[2] See Joubin.

about this shoulder of the Marseille St. Cannate (Ill. 1283) resembles the grooving in the skirts of the right thigh of the Maguelonne *St. Paul* (Ill. 1288). The facial types are not without affinity, although Marseille is finer. In both there is the same bald handling, the same love of broad surfaces, the same tendency towards conventionalization.

A closer parallel to the fragments of Maguelonne is to be found in the lunettes of Angoulême. This cathedral we shall see was begun in 1110 and finished about 1128. The composition of the lunettes (Ill. 936–940) with two crouching figures at the ends, and a third figure between them, is precisely the composition of the Maguelonne tympanum (Ill. 1287, 1288). Moreover, when we compare the draperies of the right thigh of the Maguelonne St. Paul (Ill. 1288) with those between the legs of the central figure in the Angoulême lunette (Ill. 938) we see that there is a similar division into strands ending in a curve which is like a Greek fret made very rapidly. Again, therefore, we feel the influence of the school of the West upon Provence.

This crouching attitude is very characteristic of sculptures of the first quarter of the XII century. We find it, for example, in the bronze doors of Rogerius, made for the mausoleum of Bohemond at Canosa, a dated monument of 1111–1118, in the figures just below Christ, variously explained as princes, or as personages of the Transfiguration.[1]

The tympanum of San Pablo al Campo of Barcelona, a church consecrated in 1125, has precisely the same composition which must have existed at Maguelonne. In the centre is Christ (Ill. 550); at the ends the two crouching figures of St. Peter and St. Paul. The similarity does not, however, extend to the style; the draperies of the Barcelona sculptures impress one as much more advanced than those of Maguelonne (Ill. 1285–1288).

The Maguelonne fragments also present points of contact with the ambulatory sculptures of St.-Sernin (Ill. 296–305) which date from

[1] This attitude is found as early as 980 in the figure of St. Paul in a miniature of the Benedictional of St. Aethelwold at Chatsworth, of the school of Winchester, illustrated by Warner and Wilson, *f.* 96.

about 1105. There is the same love of polished surfaces, the same
brutality of treatment, the same vigour. Maguelonne is, however,
patently later. The faces are more characterized, and indicated in
more detail; there is more movement — in this respect Maguelonne
is abreast of the tympanum of St.-Sernin (Ill. 308–317); — the
draperies are far more developed and more naturalistic.

From all this we conclude that the fragments of Maguelonne must
be considerably later than 1105 and somewhat earlier than 1125. We
may ascribe them to c. 1120 with confidence. They, without doubt,
belonged to the choir of the cathedral built by the bishop Galterius
(1110–1133).[1] In 1178, they were incorporated in the reconstruction
of the bishop Jean II de Montlaur (1159–1190).[2]

The next monument shows a most notable development. It is the
arca (Ill. 1289, 1290) of St.-Hilaire, first bishop of Carcasonne, now
preserved in the church of the town of the same name.

The form of this sarcophagus shows the evident copying of a Roman model; it is the earliest example in Provence of that classic influence which has been so widely remarked in the sculpture of the
school. I suspect that this may first have come in through the copying of an antique sarcophagus in an arca precisely like this one at
St.-Hilaire. Our sculptor without question owed much to his antique
original. He preserved, however, his own tradition. The draperies
indicated by angular grooves (Ill. 1289, 1290) are a development of
those we have already observed about the legs and in the girdle of
the *St. Paul* of Maguelonne (Ill. 1288). The violent movement came
from the same source. It is also certain that our sculptor held in his
hand a Byzantine ivory. His facial types are peculiar, and without
relation to others that I know in sculpture. The forehead is low, the
eye-brow deeply arched, the nose sharp, the eye of a peculiar pointed
oval type. Now precisely such faces are found in a Byzantine ivory
casket of the XI century in the Museo Kirchiano at Rome.[3]

---

[1] Galterius caput ecclesie Magalonensis ruinosum fulcivit (*cit.* Mortet, 90).
[2] Videns ecclesiam ruinam minari, . . . eccelesia vetus demolita est et nova ex majori parte
constructa (*ibid.*, 91).
[3] Illustrated by Graeven, II, 59.

The arca of St.-Hilaire is evidently much more advanced than the fragments of Maguelonne (Ill. 1285–1288). Since the latter we have seen must date from about 1120, St.-Hilaire may be ascribed to *c.* 1130.

The celebrated frieze at Beaucaire (Ill. 1292–1298) is related to the St.-Hilaire arca (Ill. 1289, 1290). The draperies in both cases are formed on the same system of angular grooving. There is the same tendency to cover the entire surface with these grooves. Beaucaire is the logical culmination of the method of design inaugurated at Maguelonne (Ill. 1285–1288). The relationship of Beaucaire and St.-Hilaire is, moreover, witnessed by a similarity of spirit; both works are vigorous and determined, full of movement and naturalism.

It is therefore entirely probable that the Beaucaire sculptor came out of the same atelier as the one of St.-Hilaire, or at least from one closely allied. His style was, however, deeply influenced by the work of the Flagellation Master at Santiago (Ill. 680). In fact, if we put the Christ at the Column of Beaucaire (Ill. 1297) beside the rendering of the same subject at Compostela (Ill. 680), we shall perceive how much the Beaucaire sculptor owes to this source. The two Christs are in fact strikingly alike. The right arm is held in the same position, there is the same too large head, the expression is the same, the features are of the same cast, the hair falls down the back in the same manner, the two loin-cloths are alike even to the knot in front. It is evident that the Beaucaire rendering is more naturalistic, more brutal. The hair and face are more realistic. The Santiago Christ is more refined, more restrained, more sensitive, more archaic.

It is probable that the Beaucaire Master took over not only this figure of Christ from the Puerta de las Platerias. Unfortunately both series of reliefs are fragmentary. In each probably was represented at length the story of the Passion,[1] but it so happens that Christ at the Column is the only subject which has been preserved in both.

---

[1] It is true that the missing scenes at Santiago are not mentioned in the Guide. They may well, nevertheless, have existed. The sculptured cycles were doubtless originally inspired by some miniature, like that of the cathedral of Auxerre.

When we see how exactly the Beaucaire Master has taken over this one figure, we can hardly doubt that the entire frieze of Beaucaire was little more than a transcription of the reliefs at Santiago. We are confirmed in this conjecture by observing that the cross which is seen in the hands of an executioner at Santiago (Ill. 680) is precisely like the cross which is carried by Christ at Beaucaire (Ill. 1297, 1289).

The tympanum of Beaucaire, of which the Virgin (the subject represented was the Adoration of the Magi) still survives (Ill. 1299) was certainly not by the master of the frieze. The long straight folds of the drapery, the attenuation, the finer quality, show a very different, and much superior, touch. These " organ-pipe " draperies must be derived from the Christ of the Puerta de las Platerias (Ill. 676). In fact, the master of the Beaucaire tympanum was clearly well acquainted with Compostela. His composition is evidently inspired by the eastern tympanum of the Puerta de las Platerias (Ill. 680). Here, in fact, we have the same subject similarly placed in a tympanum; the Virgin is seated precisely as at Beaucaire; the Child is seated in the same way on her left knee; her left hand touches His elbow in exactly the same manner; even the folds of drapery about her neck are the same. The tympanum of Beaucaire was a reproduction of the tympanum of Santiago, plus the draperies of the Santiago Christ, and plus certain other new features.

The latter, I think, were probably derived from a Byzantine ivory Madonna of the XI century of the well-known type of which there is an example in the Metropolitan Museum at New York.[1] Here we find draperies which might have given to the Beaucaire Virgin everything which the Santiago Christ did not supply. The general type is strikingly analogous to that of the Beaucaire Virgin. There is the same attenuation, the same thin hands, the Child's head is set on the body in the same jerky way, the Child's right hand is similarly extended, the Virgin's right hand is in the same position, her feet are similarly treated. The distinctive feature of the Beaucaire tympanum is the introduction of a canopy over the Virgin. It

---

[1] Illustrated in *Art in America*, 1922, X, 198.

was this which seems to have particularly struck contemporary sculptors, and was, as we have seen,[1] frequently reproduced. Now this motive of a canopy must certainly have come from Byzantine ivories, in which the motive is frequent. There may, in fact, very well have been just such a canopy over the New York Madonna, since the background of the figure, which once existed, has been broken away.

The much finer quality of the work in the tympanum of Beaucaire might make us suppose it later than the frieze. There is, however, proof that the two are contemporary. In the scene of the Maries buying spices the sculptor of the frieze has copied the draperies of the Master of the Tympanum. The skirts of these three figures (Ill. 1298) are evidently reproductions of those of the Virgin (Ill. 1299).

The date of Beaucaire may be determined from the circumstances that the frieze is later than St.-Hilaire (*c.* 1130) and, as we shall presently see, earlier than St.-Gilles which dates from about 1140. We shall therefore not risk falling into serious error if we assign it to *c.* 1135.

Several hands may be distinguished in the sculptures of the façade of St.-Gilles (Ill. 1302–1328).

By the first, whom I shall venture to designate as the Angoulême Master, is the *St. Thomas* (Ill. 1304), the podium reliefs representing the Sacrifice of Cain and Abel (Ill. 1325) and the Murder of Abel (Ill. 1324) and the relief under the columns representing David and Goliath (Ill. 1326). This sculptor also, I think, touched up some of the draperies of the *St. James the Less* (Ill. 1305) by the Third Master.

The Angoulême Master has usually been considered Toulousan for no better reason than that the legs of the *St. Thomas* (Ill. 1304) are crossed. There can, however, be little doubt that he really came from the West. If we compare the *St. Thomas* with the lunettes of

---

[1] See above, p. 245 f. The canopy was also copied in the tympana of the cathedral of Valence (Ill. 1189) and Notre-Dame-du-Port of Clermont-Ferrand (Ill. 1158).

the cathedral at Angoulême (Ill. 936–940), we shall at once perceive that the two works are characterized by the same movement, the same draperies, the same technical peculiarities. At St.-Gilles, however, the style is notably more advanced and exaggerated.

The relief of David and Goliath (Ill. 1326) may be compared with a capital representing the same subject at Notre-Dame-de-la-Couldre of Parthenay (Ill. 1045).

It is certain that this master, like the sculptors of Angoulême, fell under the strong influence of miniatures. The relief of the Sacrifice of Cain and Abel (Ill. 1325) for example, shows unmistakable indications of having been inspired by this source.[1] The ideas may well indeed have come to our sculptor from the X-century Bible of St.-Aubin of Angers.[2] The sculptors of Angoulême also fell under the spell of manuscripts. The resemblance between Angoulême and St.-Gilles is, however, much greater than can be accounted for by a common manuscript source. If we compare the apostle to the right of the lunette to the south of the portal at Angoulême (Ill. 938) with the Cain in the St.-Gilles Sacrifice (Ill. 1325), we shall be convinced that the St.-Gilles artist knew the work at Angoulême.

The second hand which may be distinguished at St.-Gilles is that of the sculptor Brunus. His signature may be read near the statue of St. Matthew (Ill. 1302).[3] The *St. Bartholomew* (Ill. 1303) which is the next statue to the south shows a style identical with that of the *St. Matthew* (Ill. 1302); it also, therefore, must be by the hand of Brunus. The four statues flanking the central portal — *St. Peter* (Ill. 1308, 1309), *St. John* (Ill. 1306, 1307), *St. Paul* (Ill. 1311) and *St. James the Less* (Ill. 1310) — are notably more advanced in style, but are also by the hand of Brunus. As this has been generally ad-

---

[1] See, for example, St. Gallen, Stiftsbibliothek, Cod. 902, illustrated by Merton, Pl. IL and L, No. 2; Perikopenbuch von St. Erentrud of Munich, Kgl. Hof- und Stadtsbibliothek, Clm. 15903, c. p. 52, illustrated by Swarzenski, No. 200; Bamberg Apocalypse, ed. Wöllflin; miniature of Christ before Pilate in Perikopenbuch Kaiser Heinrichs II, Reichenau school before 1014, illustrated by Leidinger, V, 18; or the draperies of a bed-cover in a miniature of an English manuscript of the XII century, Brit. Mus. MS. 37472, No. 1.

[2] Compare the Christ illustrated by Boinet, Pl. CLII. The manuscript is preserved in the Bibliothèque de la Ville at Angers, No. 4.

[3] BRVNVS ME FECIT.

mitted by the critics, and as the reader has the photographs under his eyes, it is unnecessary to weary him with a repetition of the reasoning which leads to the attribution.

These works show an extraordinary variation of style. If we should try to place them in chronological order, we should have to arrange the series: *St. Matthew* (Ill. 1302), *St. Bartholomew* (Ill. 1303), *St. James the Less* (Ill. 1310), *St. Peter* (Ill. 1308, 1309), *St. Paul* (Ill. 1311) and *St. John* (Ill. 1306, 1307).

Brunus worked not only at St.-Gilles. The sculptures of the portal of Romans (Ill. 1334, 1335) have been recognized to be by his hand. These are evidently the latest of the series.

We have, therefore, not a few works through which we can trace the growth of this artistic personality. In the *St. Matthew* (Ill. 1302) we find him gruff, coarse and heavy. The folds of the undergarment over the chest show the unmistakable influence of the school of the pilgrimage — compare for example the *David* of Santiago (Ill. 687). These folds are much modified in the *St. Bartholomew* (Ill. 1303); but in the later works they are no longer found. There are, however, even in the later works, numerous reminiscences of the pilgrimage school. The peculiar series of tight-clinging folds like metal rings, in which terminates the right sleeve of the *St. Bartholomew* of St.-Gilles (Ill. 1303), is precisely the same mannerism as that which is found in the right sleeve of the Christ at Santiago (Ill. 676). The lower skirts of the draperies of the *St. Bartholomew* (Ill. 1303) and especially of the St. John (Ill. 1307) at St.-Gilles are certainly derived from the skirts of the Christ at Santiago (Ill. 676). Only thence could have come the long parallel folds, the wavy bottom edge, the "organ-pipe" effect. The folds on the left leg of the St.-Gilles *St. Matthew* (Ill. 1302) are like those on the right leg of the Santiago *St. James* (Ill. 676). The peculiar ornament of the border of St. Peter's garment (Ill. 1308) must have been inspired by some border ornament like those of the Souillac *Isaiah* (Ill. 344) of the Moissac *Beatus Rogerus* (Ill. 379), or Virgin of the Adoration (Ill. 375). The face of the *St. Peter* (Ill. 1308) at St.-Gilles is distinctly reminiscent of the facial types of the

Betrayal Master of Santiago (Ill. 680) and Conques (Ill. 392–401).
The draperies of the upper part of the left sleeve of the St.-Gilles
St. Bartholomew (Ill. 1303) reproduce those of the lower part of
the left sleeve of the angel facing to the right in the St.-Sernin
ambulatory (Ill. 300). We may conclude that Brunus knew pilgrimage sculpture before he executed any of the works which have come
down to us.

Other features of his early style show different influences. The
wattled socks of the *St. Matthew* are a motive we have already found
at Cluny (Ill. 7); but in Brunus' version it has become strangely
clumsy and heavy. In his later work the motive is transferred to the
sleeves of the *St. Paul* at St.-Gilles (Ill. 1311), and to those of the two
figures of the south jamb at Romans (Ill. 1335). The edge of the over-
mantle of the *St. Bartholomew* (Ill. 1303) falling across the left knee,
is like the edge of the over-garment of the St. Paul of Maguelonne
(Ill. 1288). The papery edges of the draperies of the *St. Matthew*
(Ill. 1302) and the *St. Bartholomew* (Ill. 1303) seem to be derived
from those of the Angoulême Master's *St. Thomas* (Ill. 1304). So
also are the incised drapery folds below the scroll of the *St. Bartholomew* (Ill. 1303). The curious convention of indicating the drapery
folds on the right leg of the *St. Matthew* (Ill. 1302) consisting of a
curved groove ending in a little round hole is peculiar. In the later
work of Brunus it recurs in the *St. James* (Ill. 1310) and the *St. John*
(Ill. 1306, 1307). We have seen that this mannerism was copied by
the St.-Martin master at Volterra (Ill. 194–196). A similar peculiarity is found in the work of the Charlieu Master at Donzy (Ill.
112–114).

The type of drapery which Brunus took over, as we have seen,
from the Christ of Santiago, and applied somewhat timidly in the
skirts of his *St. Matthew* (Ill. 1302) grew upon him in his later works.
As his style advances, this type of drapery is gradually, but consistently, developed. At Romans (Ill. 1334, 1335) it entirely predomi-
nates. The change in the draperies is accompanied by a corresponding development in the character of the sculptures. The fussy,

awkward and angular manner of the *St. Matthew* (Ill. 1302) has become at Romans (Ill. 1334, 1335) suave, dignified and classic. The heavy and stocky proportions have become slim and graceful. Certainly, if we did not have the intermediate statues, we should hardly suspect that the *St. Matthew* (Ill. 1302) of St.-Gilles and the right jamb of Romans (Ill. 1335) were the work of the same artist.

This change in the style of Brunus was no doubt in part due to his own growing maturity, but even more I suspect to the influence of other artists with whom he came in contact. It is, for example, certain that he took, directly or indirectly, ideas from the Beaucaire tympanum. This lovely work was indeed copied at St.-Gilles. In the ruins of the choir may be still seen a fragment of relief (Ill. 1329) which obviously once formed part of an Adoration of the Magi, which was the subject of the Beaucaire tympanum. The lower part of the Virgin's legs and the torso of a kneeling king only survive. The king kneels to the left of the Virgin, and is of smaller stature, precisely as in the Virgin of Fontfroide (Ill. 1301), which, we have seen, reproduces the composition of the Beaucaire tympanum. Moreover, when we place the St.-Gilles fragment beside the Virgin of Beaucaire (Ill. 1299), the relationship is patent. The draperies are of the same "organ-pipe" type. The spread-apart knees are held in precisely the same position; the bottom fringe of the draperies is the same, the sagging folds between the legs identical. At St.-Gilles the proportions are less slender, and the over-skirt, which at Beaucaire sags between the legs, is carried horizontally across.[1]

Now the grave and noble style of the Beaucaire tympanum could not have left unaffected a much less sensitive artist than Brunus. And in fact its influence becomes unmistakable in the jamb figures of St.-Gilles (Ill. 1302, 1303, 1306–1311). The folds of the over-skirt of the *St. Peter* (Ill. 1309) have in the middle "organ-pipe" a groove separated from two rounded-over folds by sharp edges, and ending at the bottom in a curve something like the figure "3." Now

---

[1] Other Adorations belonging to this cycle may be found in the Baptistry of Parma, the cathedral of Verona, the Goldene Pforte of Freiberg i. Sa. and St. Paul in Lavanthal.

there are folds of precisely this character in the Beaucaire Virgin in the draperies following down the centre of each leg (Ill. 1299). The sharply pointed sagging folds several times repeated at the bottom of the skirts of the *St. Peter* (Ill. 1308, 1309) are like those between the legs of the Beaucaire Virgin (Ill. 1299). But it was not only technical tricks that Brunus learned from this masterpiece. His increasing use of "organ-pipe" draperies, the greater emphasis of the vertical line, the poise and dignity of his later figures must be due to this inspiration.

The third hand which may be recognized in the portal of St.-Gilles is to be found in the *St. James the Less* to the north of the central portal (Ill. 1305) and in the four unnamed apostles of the southern half of the façade (Ill. 1312–1315). The *St. James the Less* (Ill. 1305) seems to have been touched up by the Angoulême Master, the two apostles to the extreme right by Brunus (Ill. 1314). The style of the Third Master was clearly much controlled by Brunus, more perhaps, however, in the broad lines of the composition than in the details, although the latter, too, have been imitated — for example, the right sleeve of the first apostle south of the central portal (Ill. 1312) ends in the same series of little circles which Brunus had taken over from Santiago in his St. Bartholomew (Ill. 1303). The head of the apostle to the south of the central portal (Ill. 1313) is a notable achievement. It foreshadows to a singular degree the style of the XIII century.[1] It appears to have been inspired by the head of Brunus' St. Paul (Ill. 1311), and in turn to have been the inspiration of certain of the apostles of St.-Etienne of Toulouse (Ill. 437) and of the jamb sculptures of Senlis (Ill. 1509). Perhaps a conscious purpose to imitate the manner of the Midi determined our master to cross, so badly and ineffectually, the legs of one of his apostles (Ill. 1312). Behind all this forced mannerism, however, the true nature of the artist emerges here and there unmistakably into sight. He is, in fact, Burgundian. The heavy spiral on the right of the chest of the apostle to the

[1] See for example the head of the St. Jude of the south portal of Chartres illustrated by Houvet, 37.

extreme south (Ill. 1314) is a south Burgundian mannerism — we find similar draperies in the work of Guillaume Martin at Vienne (Ill. 1218). But our artist, while he may have seen the work in south Burgundy, still comes from farther to the north. The bit of drapery which falls over the right shoulder of the second apostle south of the portal at St.-Gilles (Ill. 1312) is exactly like the drapery on the zig-zag edge of the over-garment about the legs of the angel to the right of the aureole in the Autun tympanum (Ill. 81). The draperies about the right shin of the same apostle at St.-Gilles (Ill. 1312) are precisely like those about the shin of the St. Michael of the Autun tympanum (Ill. 81). The bunch of drapery to the right of the knee of the first apostle at St.-Gilles (Ill. 1312) is like that to the left of the feet of the St. Michael (Ill. 81) in the Autun tympanum. There can be no question that our master knew Autun well.

The closest analogies which he shows, however, are with the tympanum of the *Majestas Domini* of St.-Bénigne of Dijon (Ill. 134, 135). It is evident that his system of draperies is precisely the system of this commonplace and uninteresting artist of Burgundy. In both there are ornamented borders. In both there are the same characterless, banal folds. The draperies of the left leg of the angel to the right of the aureole at Dijon (Ill. 135) repeat those of the left leg of the first apostle at St.-Gilles (Ill. 1312). Both works are characterized by the same spineless inanity, the same stupidity.

I suspect that the classic character of the architecture of the façade of St.-Gilles may be due to the influence of Burgundian motives imported by the Third Master, as well as to the direct copying of Roman ruins. The fluted pilasters, so striking at St.-Gilles, had long before been acclimated in Burgundy. The Greek frets of St.-Gilles (Ill. 1321, 1325) recall the equally classic ones of La Charité (Ill. 118). It is certain that the composition of the central tympanum of St.-Gilles repeated a Burgundian motive.

The hand of the Third Master of St.-Gilles reappears in the series of reliefs now divided between St.-Guilhem-le-Désert (Ill. 1399) and the University of Montpellier (Ill. 1397, 1398).

The fourth hand which may be distinguished at St.-Gilles is that of the master who was at least in part responsible for the frieze, and whom I venture to designate by the term "St.-Gilles Master."

The frieze (Ill. 1315–1322) is surely not all the work of one hand. We have already remarked that the scene of the Betrayal (Ill. 1319, 1320) seems to show, at least in part, the hand of the Master of the Bari Throne.[1] The hand of the Third Master seems to me to be traceable in certain draperies in the first scene of the Money-Changers (Ill. 1316), and in the entire figure, second from the right of this scene (Ill. 1316), also in the head of Christ in the scene of the Denial (Ill. 1316). There are doubtless retouches here and there by various ones of the sculptors who worked upon other portions of the church. The end portions of the frieze over the two side portals, as we shall see, are of a different period. With this exception, however, the frieze as a whole has a distinct and unified character, and in it the personality of one artist is clearly felt.

The most striking fact about the frieze is that the composition is copied, episode for episode, from the frieze of Beaucaire (Ill. 1292–1298). If, for example, we compare the two scenes of the Denial (Ill. 1293 and Ill. 1316), we shall perceive that in both Christ is placed to the right; then comes Peter, with the cock in front of him, then other disciples. At St.-Gilles the number of these has been increased, and the composition is more complicated. The scene of the Washing of the Feet is also analogous in the two works (Ill. 1292, 1293, and Ill. 1318). St. Peter is seated to the right; his right foot is held by the kneeling Christ over a tub of water; to the left is a column, on the top of which hangs a towel. The two Last Suppers (Ill. 1292, 1294, 1295 and Ill. 1318) follow as nearly as it is possible to tell in the present mutilated condition of the St.-Gilles version, the same composition. In both there is an apostle seated at either end of the table; in both the right-hand apostle cuts in the middle a loaf of bread held in his left hand. Christ is in the centre, St. John at his right leans against his bosom; Judas is the second apostle to the

[1] See above, p. 61.

right, and the Saviour gives him the sop. The table furnishings are the same, even the cloth is indicated by a similar convention.[1] Then follows in both series the scene of Judas receiving the price of his treason (Ill. 1295, 1318, 1319) — he kneels before the high priest.[2] The group of spectators is the same with a shorter figure placed directly in front of a taller one (at Beaucaire the panel with the spectators has been by error placed in the resetting to the right, instead of to the left of the central group). The composition is similar in both works, but as usual St.–Gilles is more expanded, more elaborate, amplified. The next scene in both series is the Betrayal (Ill. 1295 and Ill. 1319, 1320). In each case an executioner stands to the right; then comes the group of Judas embracing Christ, the Saviour to the left, a little taller, Judas' left hand upon His right shoulder. Behind is a group of executioners; the Peter and Malchus at the extreme left of the St.–Gilles composition perhaps once existed also at Beaucaire, but if so, have been lost. Again we note that St.–Gilles is more diffuse, more complicated. The two scenes of Christ before Pilate (Ill. 1296 and Ill. 1321) are as similar. In each case Pilate is seated to the right; he is in precisely the same posture; even the draperies of the upper part of his tunic fall in the same folds. The minister at his left in the Beaucaire version is omitted at St.–Gilles — this is one of the very few instances in which a figure of the Beaucaire rendering is eliminated at St.–Gilles. To Pilate's right stands another minister in both versions; even the peculiar face seen in profile is alike in the two reliefs. Then follows an executioner dragging Christ by the hands; behind at St.–Gilles is another executioner who is lacking at Beaucaire. In the two scenes of the Flagellation (Ill. 1297 and Ill. 1322) the column is represented in both versions in precisely the same way; Christ in the same attitude is to the left of it; His hands crossed and tied in front are represented in exactly the same way even to the leather thongs which tie them. At Beaucaire the exe-

---

[1] The Last Supper of St.–Gilles was imitated at Nantua (Ill. 1214 a), Vizille (Ill. 1185) and S. Giovanni Fuorcivitas of Pistoia (Ill. 199).

[2] Comte de Lasteyrie, 108, seems to have entirely overlooked this scene. He tried with evident error to interpret the panels of the Money-Changers as a representation of this subject.

cutioners which surely once existed have disappeared. The final scene of the Carrying of the Cross was quite as similar at Beaucaire (Ill. 1297, 1298) and St.-Gilles (Ill. 1321). Christ carries the cross of the same form and size held in the same diagonal position; He is followed by executioners, destroyed at St.-Gilles, but who doubtless once carried, as they still do at Beaucaire, nails and hammers.

There is therefore no doubt of the close relationship of the two friezes. It is equally certain that the St.-Gilles version is later than that of Beaucaire. We have seen that throughout it is an expansion, an elaboration of the simpler original. We have only to compare the draperies of the two Pilates (Ill. 1296 and Ill. 1322) or of the two Christs at the Column (Ill. 1297 and Ill. 1322) to perceive that St.-Gilles is fussier, more elaborate, more naturalistic.

Now while the St.-Gilles Master has taken over from Beaucaire quite slavishly his composition, certain draperies like those of his Pilate (Ill. 1296 and Ill. 1322) and even facial types like that of the executioner at Pilate's left (Ill. 1296 and Ill. 1322), it is nevertheless evident that important elements of his style can not be accounted for solely on the basis of the Beaucaire frieze. He fell under other influences as well.

Since the St.-Gilles Master had certainly been at Beaucaire, we are not surprised that he should have studied the tympanum as well as the frieze. In fact, he takes over in the skirts of the executioner to the left of Christ at the Column (Ill. 1322) the peculiar "organ-pipe" draperies which we have seen are characteristic of the Virgin of Beaucaire (Ill. 1299). The most distinctive feature of these draperies, it will be recalled, is a strand following down the front of each leg, with a groove separated from two rounded-over folds by sharp edges, and ending at the bottom in a curve something like a figure "3." Now exactly these draperies occur in the skirts of the executioner at St.-Gilles, and also the sagging folds between the legs which are likewise characteristic of the Virgin of Beaucaire. It is clear, therefore, that the St.-Gilles Master acquired these

draperies directly from Beaucaire, and not from Brunus, although
we have seen the latter also borrowed them in his *St. Peter*
(Ill. 1309).

It seems also certain that the St.-Gilles Master fell under the influence of an ivory-carving — probably a Byzantine work of the XI
century, or some occidental imitation of such. His work shows close
analogies with a Byzantine ivory casket of the XI century in the
Museo Kirchiano at Rome.[1] In both there are the same stocky figures in violent motion with over-large heads and short skirts. The
clumsy animals are almost as uncouth as those which the St.-Gilles
Master perpetrated in the scene of the Money-Changers (Ill. 1317).
Two ivory panels in the Metropolitan Museum of New York [2] also
resemble the St.-Gilles frieze. These represent the labour of Adam
and Eve; they are Byzantine since they have Greek inscriptions, and
are assigned to the XI century. Again we have short heavy-headed
figures, full of energetic motion, and with facial types and draperies
strikingly like those of the frieze. The sleeves have the same wattling, the leggings the horizontal striping which occurs in some of the
St.-Gilles figures. The garments have a border of little dots, like the
lower border of the garment of the executioner dragging Christ before
Pilate at St.-Gilles (Ill. 1321). The frieze even shows analogies with
ivory-carvings of an earlier time. The proportions of the figures and
the facial types should be compared with a Byzantine ivory of the
VI century in the British Museum.[3] The spiral leggings, which are a
marked peculiarity of the style of the St.-Gilles Master (they are
found, for example, in the executioner to the left of Christ in the
Carrying of the Cross, Ill. 1321) occur in the Grado throne, an
Alexandrine work of the VI century, which was much copied at the
end of the XI and in the early XII century.[4] It was undoubtedly
from some ivory, if not this one, that the St.-Gilles Master came by

[1] Illustrated by Graeven, II, 57–61. The casket was presented to a Byzantine emperor and
has a Greek inscription; it may, however, have been made in the provinces.

[2] Accession numbers 17. 190. 138 and 17. 190. 139.

[3] Illustrated by Graeven, I, 24, 25.

[4] Illustrated by Venturi, II, 626 and by Maclagen, Plate II, II.

the motive, which is not common.[1] A German pyxis of the IX century in the British Museum [2] also presents points of contact with the frieze.

To the other influences which the St.-Gilles Master underwent must certainly be added that of antique sarcophagi. So much has already been said upon this subject that it is useless to insist upon it further. The sarcophagus which resembles his work more closely than any other which I know is that of Tarragona.[3] It should be remarked, however, that many of the details which the St.-Gilles Master appears to have taken from classical sculpture might easily have come to him through the medium of Byzantine ivories.

It is a striking fact that the composition inaugurated in the frieze of Beaucaire was echoed not only at St.-Gilles. At Modena the same cycle of scenes is repeated in the reliefs of the pulpit, episode for episode. The Modena version is the finest, the most elaborated and the latest of the three. It must be, as M. Mâle has recognized, a derivative, not a prototype of Beaucaire, and executed under strong Provençal influence. Like the apostles of the Milan pulpit of 1186, these reliefs bear witness to the wave of Provençal artistic ideas that swept over northern Italy in the last quarter of the XII century.

In France the Beaucaire frieze was as industriously copied. A very literal version seems to have existed at Savigny.[4] The procession of the executioners reappears in a capital of L'Ile-Bouchard (Ill. 1105). The capitals of Issoire (Ill. 1214) owe something to this source. The Last Supper of Nantua (Ill. 1214 a) is derived from that of St.-Gilles (Ill. 1318). The arches representing the temple in the two panels of St.-Gilles showing the Money-Changers (Ill. 1316) are repeated in the wooden doors of St. Marien im Kapitol of Cologne.[5]

Mr. Alan Priest[6] has made the very interesting suggestion that the

[1] It occurs on the cover of the Oviedo Arca Santa of 1075 (Ill. 660) and in a miniature of the Missal of Robert of Canterbury at Rouen, illustrated by Westwood, Pl. 40.

[2] Illustrated by Dalton, Pl. XXIII, 43.

[3] Illustrated by Puig, I, 83.

[4] Illustrated by Thiollier, Pl. XXVII.

[5] Illustrated by Dehio und von Bezold, XII, 13.

[6] See his forthcoming article in the first number of *Art Studies*.

St.-Gilles Master may have worked upon the cathedral of Chartres. In fact, he is unquestionably right in holding that in addition to the four principal hands recognized by Prof. Vöge in the west façade, and since his time universally accepted — the hands of the head master, the Etampes Master, the St.-Denis Master and the Master of the Angels, there must also be recognized a fifth hand. To this sculptor are to be attributed the two lintels of the southern portal [1] except the left-hand figure in the upper zone which is by a St.-Denis-esque master. In the Grammar this fifth artist is evidently co-operating with a St.-Denis-esque master; his touch is especially unmistakable in the heads of the two children. In the lintel he was, as we have already seen,[2] copying detail by detail the frieze of Montmorillon and the lintel of La Charité. He was, moreover, working under the supervision of the head master, who even seems to have touched up with his own hand the draperies in various places.

Now when we divest the fifth master at Chartres from the superficial characteristics obviously borrowed from Montmorillon, from La Charité, from the head master, from the St.-Denis and Madonna Masters, we have left, as Mr. Priest saw, the personality of the St.-Gilles Master. In fact, if the reader will put M. Houvet's excellent reproductions of Chartres beside our reproductions of the frieze of St.-Gilles (Ill. 1315–1322), he will observe:

(1) The sheep at Chartres show the same wooden and lifeless drawing as the animals in the scene of the Money-Changers at St.-Gilles. The horn of the ram to the left of the group of animals at Chartres curls completely around the ear and ends in a point below the lower lobe. Now the horn of the ram, the second animal from the right in the group of animals at St.-Gilles, curls around in precisely this same way. The eyes of the two rams are executed in exactly the same fashion in the two works. So are the nostrils and the mouth. It is true that the sheep of Chartres are very conventionalized, much less naturalistic than those of St.-Gilles. This may be due partly to a

[1] Houvet, 51, 52, 53, 54, 55, 56, 57, 58.
[2] See above, p. 125 f.

conscious purpose on the part of the sculptor to adapt them to the
more dignified and monumental style of the head master of Chartres, partly to the study he must have made of the sheep of Montmorillon (they have been destroyed, but we can judge of their style
from the fragment that remains, Ill. 1072 a, and from the sheep
of Parthenay, Ill. 1054, to which they must have been very similar).
If the animals in the scene of the Money-Changers at St.-Gilles,
those by the Master of the Bari Throne below the frieze at St.-Gilles,
and the sheep at Chartres be all placed together, we shall at once
feel that the animals of Chartres and of the Money-Changers belong
in one group, those below the frieze in another.

(2) It is characteristic of both the Chartres lintels and the St.-
Gilles frieze that the heads are too big for the bodies. At Chartres,
the St.-Denis Master occasionally runs into this fault, but in general
it is found only in the sculptures which we attribute to the St.-Gilles
Master. This mistake is typical of the drawing of the St.-Gilles
frieze — see, for example, the Washing of the Feet.

(3) The heads are badly put on the bodies in the two works. Compare, for example, the Simeon of Chartres with the Christ of the
Washing of the Feet at St.-Gilles.

(4) The same facial types are found in the two works. The head of
the Gabriel in the Chartres Annunciation is the face of the apostle
next to the right-hand end of the table in the St.-Gilles Last Supper.
The face of the seated figure in the Money-Changers of St.-Gilles is
very like the face of the Simeon in the Chartres Presentation. The
face of Joseph in the scene of the Presentation at Chartres is the face
of Christ in the Betrayal of St.-Gilles. The face of the child with
curly hair in the Grammar of Chartres is like the face of the fourth
figure from the left in the Betrayal of St.-Gilles, and also, most unexpectedly, like the face of an executioner in the capital of Christ
Taken at Brive (Ill. 355). The face of the third figure from the left
in the Chartres Presentation is like that of the figure on the right-
hand angle of the St.-Gilles Betrayal. Undoubtedly the Chartres
faces show greater repose, less characterization, less naturalism than

those of St.-Gilles. The change must be ascribed to the influence of the head master. Still the St.-Gilles master's innate love of naturalism every now and then shows through. The shepherds of Chartres are as realistic, as finely characterized as any of the figures at St.-Gilles. I should hardly know where to find a more dramatic representation of what Shakespeare would have called a natural.

(5) In both series of reliefs the drawing of the eye is precisely the same. The opening of the lids is of almond shape, sharply pointed at both ends; a double line indicates the upper lid, the pupil is represented by a round bored hole. It is the boring-out of the pupil which is especially characteristic. At Chartres this convention is rarely found except in the works of the St.-Gilles Master.

(6) A peculiar hair convention at St.-Gilles consists in drawing an incised spiral upon a rounded bump. This, for example, is found in the Peter of the Betrayal at St.-Gilles and in the executioner which is the next figure but one to him to the right. Now this convention is repeated at Chartres. We find it in the third figure from the left in the Presentation; and in the child to the right in the Grammar.

(7) This sculptor was clearly fond of copying other people's compositions. At St.-Gilles he reproduces the frieze of Beaucaire, at Chartres that of Montmorillon.

(8) The peculiar drapery folds of the skirts of the executioner to the left of Christ at the column at St.-Gilles which we have already seen the St.-Gilles Master took over from the tympanum at Beaucaire,[1] reappear at Chartres, in the skirts of the two shepherds, especially the one playing a flute to the right.

(9) The wattling of the draperies of the sleeve, both on the forearm and on the upper arm is a constant mannerism in both series of reliefs.

(10) The convention of representing the end of the sleeve by a series of circles like metal rings, which Brunus had fetched from Santiago[2] was taken over by the St.-Gilles Master in his frieze at St.-Gilles. We find it, for example, in the figure to the right of the pair

[1] See above, p. 282.   [2] See above, p. 275.

at the extreme left of the first relief of the Money-Changers, and on the right sleeve of the executioner behind Christ in the Christ before Pilate, and in other places as well. Now this same convention is typical of the work of the St.-Gilles Master at Chartres, being found for example, in the right sleeve of the third figure from the left in the Presentation, and in the right-hand shepherd.

(11) Perforated borders are characteristic of the style of both series of reliefs. Compare, for example, that of the skirts of the executioner to the right of Christ at the Column of St.-Gilles with that of the over-garment of the third figure from the left in the Presentation of Chartres.

(12) The most striking similarity of all is the spiral leggings. This mannerism we have seen came to the St.-Gilles frieze from ivories, and is introduced several times — in the executioner behind Christ in the Carrying of the Cross, in the executioner behind Christ in the Christ before Pilate and in the merchant to the right of Christ in the second relief of the Money-Changers. Now this extremely rare[1] motive reappears at Chartres in the Joseph of the Nativity.

(13) The short skirts of the shepherds at Chartres vividly recall the costumes of the frieze at St.-Gilles.

The conclusions to be drawn from these analogies will doubtless give rise to difference of opinion. I do not conceal my own suspicion that the St.-Gilles Master of Chartres had actually worked upon the frieze of St.-Gilles, widely divergent as the two styles appear to be. We have already found ample proofs that Romanesque sculptors travelled far, and underwent extraordinary changes of manner.

Whether the same sculptor wandered from St.-Gilles to Chartres is, however, an academic question which students of the future may be left to argue. What becomes certain in the light of Mr. Priest's observations is that the master of the southern lintel at Chartres is very closely related to the master of the frieze of St.-Gilles. It is also

---

[1] I know it elsewhere in Romanesque sculpture only at St.-Ursin of Bourges (Ill. 1263) and in a capital of Santo Domingo de Silos (Byne phot.).

clear, that of the two, St.-Gilles is the older. The central frieze of St.-Gilles shows no trace of the influence of the head master of Chartres. Were the influence from Chartres to St.-Gilles, it is inconceivable that only technical mannerisms of the Fifth Master, but none of the great innovations of the chief sculptor, should have been taken over.

The striking resemblances between the adossed statues of St.-Gilles and Arles, on the one hand, and St.-Denis and Chartres on the other, have been much discussed. We may now, I think, safely say that Chartres certainly did not influence the earlier work at St.-Gilles. It is more likely that knowledge of Provençal motives was brought to Chartres by the master of the southern lintel. We have seen that the Virgin of the southern tympanum at Chartres is derived from Marseille and Beaucaire. That there was influence of St.-Gilles upon Chartres is entirely probable. It may also be that St.-Denis influenced directly or indirectly St.-Gilles. The jamb sculptures of Chartres seem to proceed directly from St.-Denis, and those of St.-Gilles directly from Lombardy and Santiago; but that the two were connected by innumerable cross-currents will not be doubted by any one familiar with the multiplicity of artistic waves radiating in all directions from every mediaeval atelier of importance.

Before leaving the St.-Gilles Master, a word should be said of his relationship with Lombardy and Apulia. The spiral curls, which we have mentioned as peculiar to his style, were in all probability brought to him by the Master of the Bari Throne, of whose work we have seen, they are characteristic.[1] He might, however, have come by them as well from Byzantine ivories, for the motive is of ancient Eastern origin. The "snail curls" of Oriental Buddhas are perhaps not unconnected. Both are possibly descendants of archaic Greek works, like the Harmodios. However this may be, spiral curls already appear in the same form in which the St.-Gilles Master uses them in a Coptic relief of St.-Menas from Thekla.[2] They also found their way into the Grado throne, which is believed to be an Alexandrine

[1] See above, p. 61. [2] Illustrated by Kaufmann, 65.

work of the VI century.[1] We have seen that the Grado throne shows more than one point of contract with the St.-Gilles frieze.

These same curls are found in North Italian sculpture. They occur, for example, in the left-hand saint above in a relief of S. Marco of Venice.[2] They are also found in a relief representing Hercules and the Nemaean Lion at Borgo S. Donnino.[3] The style of this relief comes indeed very close to that of the St.-Gilles Master. The head is obviously related to that of the third figure from the left in the Chartres Presentation. Benedetto, who worked later at Borgo, shows the strong influence of St.-Gilles. This relief, however, seems to belong to an earlier atelier. It seems very Byzantine in character. It is not probable that the Borgo Hercules was influenced either by St.-Gilles or Chartres. There is far more likelihood that either it, or other works of the school to which it belonged, exerted an influence upon the St.-Gilles Master.[4]

The fifth hand which may be distinguished at St.-Gilles is that of the Master of the Bari Throne. We have already discussed his work at St.-Gilles.[5] I have nothing to add at this point beyond what has already been said, except that his exquisite heads in profile in relief (Ill. 1316) seem to have relationship to one of similar character on the arca of St.-Hilaire (Ill. 1289).

In addition to the five distinct hands which we have distinguished at St.-Gilles, a separate group should be made of the two tympana of the side portals (Ill. 1385, 1386), the frieze of these portals (Ill. 1387-1391) and the two angels at either end of the façade (Ill. 1392–1396). These are all certainly additions made to the original façade a considerable time after the rest of the work had been completed;[6]

---

[1] Illustrated by Maclagen.   [2] Illustrated by Ongania, Pl. 279.
[3] Illustrated by Venturi III, 331.
[4] Similar spiral curls are found in the Daniel of the Pórtico de la Gloria (Ill. 829 b).
[5] See above, p. 59 f.
[6] The original scheme for the façade of St.-Gilles seems to have contemplated a single portal like that of Arles (Ill. 1366). This was subsequently enlarged by the addition of two side portals. The iconography of the frieze was pieced out by adding to the north the much expanded scene of the Entry into Jerusalem; to the south the story of the three Maries. The scene of the Feast in the House of Simon, out of its logical position, proves the change in the iconographic program.

yet the style is so similar to that of the earlier work that the break
might easily escape casual inspection. The apparent coherence is
probably in part due to conscious imitation of the earlier work; but
also, I fancy, to the fact that at least one of the old masters was recalled to add the side portals. The southern angel, in fact, seems to
be by the same hand as the apostle south of the central portal — we
can easily convince ourselves by comparing the two heads (Ill. 1395
and Ill. 1313). The draperies of the northern angel (Ill. 1392) are not
unlike those of the second statue south of the central portal (Ill.
1312). The draperies of the Virgin in the tympanum of the Adoration (Ill. 1386) are very close to those of the first statue south of the
central portal (Ill. 1312). If we suppose that the Third Master was
called back to make the additions to the original façade, we can explain facts which would otherwise be puzzling: why the draperies of
the earlier frieze are reproduced in the later work with entire success
(for as we have seen the Third Master co-operated with the St.-
Gilles Master in the production of the original frieze, and hence
would, of course, be thoroughly in touch with all the details of the
technique) whereas the draperies of Brunus are imitated with dili-
gence, but never really caught (compare the angel, Ill. 1396, with
Brunus' St. Bartholomew, Ill. 1303); how the sculptor of the later
work knew the model, the frieze of Beaucaire, from which the St.-
Gilles Master had taken the composition of his frieze, and was able
to continue to copy the same original in the new scenes which he
added in the southern lintel (compare Ill. 1298 with Ill. 1391).

It is clear that the Third Master had come in contact with new influences after he worked upon the earlier portions of his frieze, and
before he undertook the later. The imitation of La Charité is not
evident in his earlier sculptures, but is prominent in his later work.
It is not surprising that a Burgundian should have re-visited his
native land in the thirty years which appear to have separated the
two periods of building at St.-Gilles. The peculiar ornament consisting of three perforated dots [1] which we find on the socks of the first

[1] The motive of three dots is as old as archaic Greece and diffused from Persia to Ireland.

Magus at La Charité (Ill. 118) reappears on the garment of the
Church in the St.-Gilles tympanum of the Crucifixion (Ill. 1385).
The facial types of the angels of St.-Gilles (Ill. 1393, 1395) are
strongly reminiscent of those of the angels of La Charité (Ill. 117).

It is also clear that the Third Master was influenced by Chartres
after he had completed the first part of his frieze, for many Chartres-
esque mannerisms are found in the later part, while such are notably
absent in all the earlier work at St.-Gilles. Thus the angel of the St.-
Gilles Adoration (Ill. 1386) reproduces one of the angels of the northern tympanum of Chartres. The rhythm of the Entry into Jerusalem
(Ill. 1388) is distinctly Chartres-esque, and is very different from the
jerky rhythm of the earlier portions of the frieze (Ill. 1315–1322).
The fine parallel folds of the later draperies, contrasting with the less
rhythmical folds of the earlier work, show unquestionably the influence of Chartres. The folds of the sleeve of the third figure from
the left of the Entry into Jerusalem (Ill. 1388) reproduce exactly a
familiar mannerism of the head master of Chartres.[1]

Finally, the draperies of the later work at St.-Gilles clearly show,
as has already been remarked, the influence of the tomb of St.-
Junien (Ill. 450–452).[2]

It may well be that two or even more artists were employed upon
the enlargement of the original façade; but although the style does
not seem entirely coherent, I am unable to differentiate with any
clarity the hands. I shall only remark that the tympanum of the
Crucifixion (Ill. 1385) seems very inferior in quality to that of the
Adoration (Ill. 1386). We can discuss the date of the later work at
St.-Gilles more intelligently after we have studied the question of
the date of the earlier atelier.

The church of St.-Gilles was begun in 1116, as is recorded in an
inscription on a buttress of the south exterior wall of the nave.[3] The

[1] All these similarities with La Charité and Chartres were first brought to my attention by
Mr. Priest.
[2] See above, p. 156.
[3] [ANN]O DNI MCXVI HOC TEPLV
[SANCTI AE]GIDII AEDIFICARI CEPIT
. . . PL FRII. IN OCTAB. PASCHE

construction doubtless began with the rib-vaulted choir. It may well have been some years before the west façade was attacked. The foundation wall of this was, however, laid before 1142, since an epitaph of this date is inscribed upon it.[1] Indeed, I think more may be inferred from this inscription. It seems unlikely that any one should be buried in this spot while the façade was still in process of construction. It is not too much to conclude that the façade was finished before 1142.

Let us now compare this documentary evidence with what we may deduce from the style of the sculptures.

It was certainly an egregious error to ascribe the frieze to the end of the XII century. From what has been said above it is evident that the frieze of the central portion of the façade is contemporary with the great statues below.

The superior limit for the date of the St.-Gilles frieze is determined by several sculptures which must be later. One of the most interesting of these is the pulpit at Cagliari in Sardinia (Ill. 186–188). This remarkable monument, which passed as a work of Fra Guglielmo, the assistant of Niccola Pisano and as executed in 1260, now appears to be instead a signed work of that Guglielmo Tedesco or da Innspruch who in 1174 began with Bonnano the construction of the cathedral of Pisa.[2] Not only that, but the pulpit is dated 1158–1162. It was made for the cathedral of Pisa, but was removed when Giovanni Pisano constructed his pulpit in 1302–1310. It was then carried by ship to Cagliari. It has unfortunately been split up into two ambos, and otherwise mutilated, but the sculptures still remain. Now these are evidently under the influence of the school of Provence.[3] Guglielmo Tedesco had certainly seen the St.-Gilles frieze, for he repro-

[1] † HIC SEPVLTVS
EST CAVSITVS
ANN DNI M: C: XLII
ORATE PRO EO

[2] See the important study by Scanno, 277 f. Prof. Vöge first called my attention to the importance of the Cagliari pulpit.

[3] Labande, 82, cites a document which shows that in 1156 monks of Avignon went to Pisa and Carrara for marble with which to build the cloister of St.-Ruf. There were evidently many ways in which artistic ideas might be exchanged between Tuscany and Provence.

duces the arcades which stand for the temple in the St.-Gilles scenes of the Money-Changers (Ill. 1317) in his relief representing the Presentation (Ill. 187). But he had seen not only St.-Gilles. His "organ-pipe" draperies are of a type more advanced than any achieved by Brunus; he must have known a work as late as the cloister of St.-Trophîme at Arles, probably that cloister itself. Therefore the early portions of the cloister at Arles are anterior to 1158, and the façade of St.-Gilles is considerably anterior.

Guglielmo da Innspruch was not the only sculptor who went to Provence in search of ideas. Guillaume Martin of Vienne also made the journey. In the church of St.-André-le-Bas he sculptured a capital representing Samson and the Lion (Ill. 1219). Now in the face of the Samson he reproduces, stroke for stroke, the face of the youth to the extreme right in the first St.-Gilles relief of the Money-Changers (Ill. 1316). Happily, the sculptor not only signed his name to his work at St.-André-le-Bas, but added the date 1152. Therefore the St.-Gilles frieze is anterior to 1152.

We may even draw a more radical inference from the work of Guillaume Martin at St.-André-le-Bas of Vienne. On another capital he has sculptured the story of Job. Now the face of Job (Ill. 1218) reproduces, line for line and wrinkle for wrinkle, the face of the patriarch to the right in the frieze of the Arles façade (Ill. 1370). Therefore the façade of Arles is anterior to 1152. Now the Arles façade is much more advanced than St.-Gilles. It is more developed than the cloister (Ill. 1344–1348), and the cloister in turn is more developed than the latest work of Brunus at Romans (Ill. 1334, 1335). Ten years is the least we can allow for such progress as took place between the façade of St.-Gilles and that of Arles. This brings us to the conclusion that the façade of St.-Gilles is anterior to 1142. Our deductions from style entirely confirm the documentary evidence.

The lintels of S. Salvatore of Lucca (Ill. 225) and S. Giovanni Fuorcivitas of Pistoia (Ill. 199) show strong Provençal influence. They are indeed closely related to the lintel at Nantua (Ill. 1214 a).

Now S. Giovanni Fuorcivitas is dated 1162. Therefore Nantua is earlier than 1162. The façade of St.-Trophîme at Arles is earlier than Nantua, and St.-Gilles is earlier than Arles. We are forced to conclude that the frieze of St.-Gilles can hardly be later than 1140.

Another train of reasoning brings us to the same result. The façade of Chartres was begun very shortly before 1145. We have seen that Chartres is later than the frieze of St.-Gilles. Therefore the frieze must be earlier than 1145.

Again, the master of the Bari Throne worked at Bari in 1098. Let us suppose that at this time he was as young as possible, let us say twenty. He could hardly have been older than seventy when he worked upon the St.-Gilles frieze. That would prove that St.-Gilles was executed not more than fifty years later than 1098 or before 1148.

We may therefore feel confident that the façade of St.-Gilles was erected before 1142.

An inferior limit of date is obviously furnished by the inscription of 1116. The sculptures were not executed before the church was begun.

We therefore conclude that the façade was erected between 1116 and 1142. Is it possible to determine more accurately the date between these uncomfortably broad limits?

The facts that the Master of the Bari Throne, who was already active in 1098 worked upon the façade; and that the Angoulême Master shows points of contact with the lunette sculptures of Angoulême which must have been executed c. 1115, might be taken as indications that the façade dates from the earlier, rather than the later part of the period in question. Neither is, however, a proof; the Bari Master might still have been working as late as 1148, and the Angoulême Master might have kept a retarded style.

There are other considerations which force us to place the façade of St.-Gilles in the later part of the period in question, in the years immediately preceding 1142.

First of all there is a documentary hint. It is natural to suppose that the reconstruction of the church was begun at the east end. I seem to find an indication that such was indeed the case at St.-Gilles.

The description in the Pilgrims' Guide, written probably in the 1120's, does not mention the church, as it does in the case of nearly all the other important centres of pilgrimage — Périgueux, Saintes, St.-Sernin of Toulouse, Santiago. The explanation doubtless is, that at that period there was not much church to mention. Otherwise the guide would surely have praised it, for the desire and intention to "puff" everything at St.-Gilles is unmistakable. It is not inferring too much to conclude that at this period the façade had not yet been constructed.

On the other hand, the choir may have been finished. The style of the existing remains accords perfectly with the date 1116–1129. Moreover, the Guide describes at length the golden altar; this, therefore, was already in place. It is probable, that as at Santiago, the altar was made upon completion of the new choir.

We therefore infer from the documents that the façade of St.-Gilles was not begun before 1130.

The internal evidence of style leads to the same conclusion. It is clear that the source of much at St.-Gilles lies beyond the Alps. The Master of the Bari Throne doubtless brought with him knowledge of Apulian and Lombard buildings which was turned to full account in the design of St.-Gilles. Thus the jamb figures of the St.-Gilles portal (Ill. 1302–1314) are clearly derived from Guglielmo's work at Cremona (1107–1117); the figures are similarly placed in the inner jambs; the resemblance of type, even of the faces, is striking; Brunus in his *St. Peter* (Ill. 1308) has even taken over the accentuated cords of the hands so characteristic of Guglielmo. Yet Brunus' figures with their conscious and elaborate draperies, their developed style, are obviously of a later generation. Twenty years is the least we can place between the two. Similarly the lions, monsters and caryatids under the columns and statues of St.-Gilles are evident derivatives from Lombard prototypes, but more elaborate and advanced than any we find in the work of either Guglielmo or Nicolò. They can not be earlier than the late 30's. Again the idea of a frieze is Lombard, and was first introduced by Guglielmo at Modena. At St.-Gilles it was taken over, via Beaucaire (Ill. 1292–1298), but how advanced this frieze of St.-Gilles is, compared with the Lombard! The idea of seeking inspiration in ancient Roman remains may also very probably have come to St.-Gilles from Italy. Guglielmo had copied antique models at Modena, and the rinceaux at St.-Gilles are almost precisely like those of the Pisa façade. Here again one feels, however, that Brunus carried much farther the principles of his predecessors.

Another road leads us to the same result. We have seen that Brunus worked also at Romans. Now the church at Romans was not begun until 1133.[1] The nave must have been in construction in the late 30's, for one of the capitals (Ill. 1338) is by a sculptor of the North, of the Montmorillon-La Charité group. The façade must be slightly later, say of the early 40's. Now the close relationship in style between these sculptures (Ill. 1334, 1335) and Brunus' latest work at St.-Gilles (Ill. 1306–1311) forces the conclusion that the latter can not be very much earlier.

Even more conclusive is the evidence of style afforded by the Third Master. We have seen that he knew and copied the tympanum of Autun (Ill. 80, 81); therefore he worked after 1132. More than that he shows close relationship with the sculptor of the tympanum of the *Majestas Domini* of St.-Bénigne of Dijon (Ill. 315). Now we have seen that this tympanum is later than 1137.

All this leads us to conclude that the west façade of St.-Gilles was erected in the years immediately preceding 1142. The variation of style displayed by the works of Brunus justifies the conclusion that the construction lasted some years — it may possibly have been begun as early as 1135.

When the date of St.-Gilles has been determined, the remaining monuments of Provence quickly fall into place. If we put beside each other Brunus' work at Romans (Ill. 1334, 1335), the *St.-Trophîme* from the cloister at Arles (Ill. 1345, 1346) and the adossed sculptures of the Arles façade (Ill. 1371, 1373), we shall perceive a close relationship, and a steady development, especially in the "organ-pipe"

[1] Giraud, 193.

draperies. Romans (Ill. 1334, 1335) is clearly the earliest; then the cloister of Arles; and the façade of Arles is latest. Now it is possible to date the façade of Arles very precisely. We have seen that it was copied in 1152 by Guillaume Martin at St.-André-le-Bas of Vienne. It was therefore completed by this time. It could not, however, have been erected much before, for ten years is the least we can allow for the evolution we have indicated, and which began in 1142 or thereabouts. Now the conclusion we have drawn from the style that the façade was completed in 1152 corresponds with the documentary evidence. For we know that in this very year the body of St.-Trophîme was translated from the Aliscamps into the church, which in consequence changed its title from St.-Etienne to St.-Trophîme. Without doubt the translation took place when the new façade had been finished. We may therefore consider the façade of Arles as a dated monument of 1152.

We have remarked that the earliest part of the cloister, the north gallery and especially the west end of the north gallery, seem a little earlier than the façade. That the north gallery is anterior to 1151 is indicated by an epitaph of that date in the wall.[1]

The sculptures of St.-Trophîme are evidently direct derivatives of St.-Gilles. Undoubtedly, however, they were also influenced from other directions as well. Certain draperies surely came from Chartres. The face of the Christ in the *Majestas Domini* of the tympanum (Ill. 1372) recalls somewhat vaguely the face of the Christ in the tympanum of Moissac (Ill. 341). The scene of the Temptation (Ill. 1367), the corded hands and feet (Ill. 1371) and the supporting figure below the trumeau (Ill. 1366) make us think of the art of Guglielmo; the superb nude reclining figure of the south podium (Ill. 1368) recalls the *Eve* of Autun; the three patriarchs with souls in their bosoms (Ill. 1370) could only have been derived from Byzantine icon-

[1] VI. IDVS OCT
OBIIT PONCIVS DE
BABICO CAPVT SCOLE ET
CANONICVS REGVLARIS
SCI TROPHIMI ANNO
DNI MCLI

ography; the Three Maries of the cloister (Ill. 1344) are possibly derived from lost reliefs of Beaucaire, and foreshadow Armentía (Ill.
761) and Estella (Ill. 785); the Ascension of the cloister (Ill. 1353),
like the entire design of this part of the structure, is probably derived
from Santo Domingo de Silos (Ill. 672); and the gored caps in the
Stoning of St. Stephen of the façade (Ill. 1374) come from Toulouse
(Ill. 310, 312).

In the east gallery of the cloisters, the style of the sculptures
changes. It is evident that construction proceeded slowly, and that
this gallery, especially its southern end, is notably later than the
north gallery. By an entirely different hand are the *Gamaliel* (Ill.
1362), the figure adossed to the next pier to the north (Ill. 1358),
several capitals and the holy-water basin (Ill. 1363).[1]

The limit *ante quem* for the eastern gallery is supplied by an epitaph of 1181 in the wall.[2] This documentary evidence is confirmed
by a study of the style. The folds of the draperies of the "Gamaliel
Master," especially those of the supporting figure of the holy-water
basin, are much like those of the consoles which are the only surviving remains of the once splendid portal of Ste.-Marthe of Taras-
con (Ill. 1404 a, 1404 b). Only it is evident that the folds of Arles are
less developed, slightly earlier. Now the portal of Ste.-Marthe was
part of the church begun in 1187 and finished in 1197.[3] The sculptures of the cloister at St.-Trophîme are therefore earlier than 1187;
we may assign them to *c.* 1180, which agrees with the documentary
evidence of the epitaph, showing that they were completed before
1181.

[1] The strongly Nicolò-esque character of the supporting figure should be compared with the
holy-water basin at Romans and with the lions in the court-yard of Fenway Court.

[2] III IDVS SEPTĒBRIS OBIIT . . . etc.
ANNO DN̄I MCLXXX PRIMO

[3] Inscription east of portal:
VIGĪTI: NOVIES: SEPTĒ: CŪ: MILLE: RE
LAPSIS: AÑO: POSTREMO: NOBIS: PA
TET: OSPITA: XPE MILLE DUCĒTIS
TRĀSACTIS MINVS AT TRIBVS: AN
NIS UMBERTUS: PRESUL: ROSTAG
NO: PRESULE: SECUM: IN PRIMA:
IUNII: CONSECRAT: ECCLESIAM:

The sculptured frieze of the cathedral of Nîmes (Ill. 1378–1383) is clearly a derivative of the frieze at St.-Gilles (Ill. 1315–1322), but one which in brutal energy, in realism and in vigour of modelling surpasses its original. It must date from about 1150.

The powerful lions of Aix-en-Provence (Ill. 1331) show the same vigour and massiveness; they doubtless date from about the same period. It is believed that they once formed the support of a throne, which indeed, may very well have been the case. The coarse and rather uninteresting work in the cloister of Aix (Ill. 1406–1408) seems midway between the cloister of Notre-Dame-des-Doms of Avignon (Ill. 1342, 1343) and the last work in the cloister of St.-Trophîme (Ill. 1359–1365); it may be ascribed to *c.* 1165.

The sculptures now [1] flanking the portal in the cloister of Montmajour (Ill. 1332, 1333) are related to the work of the Third Master at St.-Gilles, but are evidently later, as the draperies are more developed. They were perhaps executed about 1145.

Let us return to the later work at St.-Gilles. We have already remarked that this shows the influences of La Charité (Ill. 115–122), Chartres and St.-Junien (Ill. 450–452) which are not traceable in the original façade. [2] Since St.-Junien is not earlier than 1150, the later work at St.-Gilles must certainly fall within the second half of the XII century.

One of the peculiarities of the later work at St.-Gilles is the perforated ornament on the garment of the Church (Ill. 1385). The earliest example of this system of decoration with which I am acquainted is the halo of the Moon in the Santo Domingo de Silos Deposition (Ill. 669). Perforation is here used with the utmost restraint and timidity; and so it continued to be used throughout the first half of the XII century. At St.-Jouin-de-Marne (1132) the garment of the St. Peter is decorated with a pattern formed of three perforated dots arranged to form a triangle (Ill. 949), and the same motive reappears in a fragment of a lectern in the museum of Marseille (Ill. 1410). It is

---

[1] They are not in their original position.
[2] See above, p. 292.

perhaps the translation into stone of a motive which was already old in Irish manuscripts [1] and which still survives in Asia Minor rugs of the XVI century. At La Charité (Ill. 115–118) about 1140, perforated decoration was carried to a point hitherto unequalled in sculpture. But at La Charité the motive is used with much greater moderation than in the Church (Ill. 1385) of St.-Gilles. Such exuberance is surely a mark of the last quarter of the XII century, and recalls the works of Benedetto. The Church in the Parma Deposition of 1178 has for example a garment very like that of the Church at St.-Gilles. The relationship of our artist with Benedetto is still further suggested by the figure to the extreme left in the tympanum of the Crucifixion, which has a face of strongly Antelami-esque character, and by the position of the Synagogue [2] at St.-Gilles, rigidly tipped as Benedetto so often drew his figures.

Other mannerisms of the tympanum, however, suggest works nearer home. The face of the Sun (Ill. 1385) is very like the face of the *Gamaliel* of the St.-Trophîme cloister (Ill. 1362). The draperies at the bottom also have the same stupid character as those of the "Gamaliel Master." The draperies on the left thigh of the southern angel at St.-Gilles (Ill. 1394) have an unmistakable resemblance to those of the "Gamaliel Master" even while reproducing most assiduously Beaucaire (Ill. 1299). The draperies of the northern angel, despite Brunus-esque digs, have also obviously a late character (Ill. 1392).

The composition of the southern tympanum (Ill. 1386) was certainly very directly inspired by Beaucaire (Ill. 1299) where, as we have seen,[3] the same subject was represented in the tympanum in the same manner. The Crucifixion tympanum on the other hand appears to have been imitated from Die (Ill. 1230) and Champagne (Ill. 1186). It seems that passing years had no power to eradicate the St.-

---

[1] See, for example, the Book of Kells, fol. 28 b, illustrated by Zimmermann, III, Taf. 173.

[2] The Church and the Synagogue seem to have been introduced into the iconographic formula of the sculptors in stone about the eighth decade of the XII century. The earliest example of their appearance which I know is the tympanum of St.-Bénigne of Dijon (Ill. 134), a monument not earlier than 1170.

[3] See above, pp. 277, 278.

Gilles habit of taking over other people's compositions. The movement of the St.-Gilles angels [1] (Ill. 1392–1396), the posture of the
Virgin in the Adoration (Ill. 1386), the insipidity of the draperies of
the prophet in this tympanum (Ill. 1386) and the general flabbiness
of modelling throughout show close relationship between the later
work at St.-Gilles and the tympanum of Maguelonne (Ill. 1384).
The latter we have seen is a dated monument of 1178.[2]

Finally, we notice that the peculiar ornament on the neck-band of
the third apostle to the left of Christ in the scene of the Magdalen
Anointing Christ's Feet (Ill. 1390) is like the neck-bands of the
apostles from St.-Benoît of the Musée des Antiquaires de l'Ouest at
Poitiers (Ill. 1133).[3] There are many reasons for believing that the
latter can not be earlier than 1170.

So we are confirmed in our conclusion that the later work at St.-
Gilles dates from about 1180. But it is time to turn to earlier and
more vital works.

[1] The composition of the southern angel at St.-Gilles recalls an ivory book-cover in the
Stadtsbibliothek at Leipzig, a work of the Ada group of the IX century, representing St.
Michael (illustrated by Goldschmidt, I, No. 11 a).

[2] See above, p. 268.

[3] Mr. Priest calls my attention to the fact that this ornament seems like the simplification
of one used by the Etampes Master at Chartres.

VII

ANGOULEME

In the West of France, sculpture developed later than in Burgundy, Lombardy or Spain. The school of the XI century which has left us such astonishing creations at Hildesheim, at Arles-sur-Tech (Ill. 518), at Regensburg (Ill. 1279–1282), at Santo Domingo de Silos (Ill. 666–673), at Oviedo (Ill. 656–660), at Sahagún (Ill. 770), at Charlieu (Ill. 4) and at Cluny (Ill. 5–9), did not flourish on the windswept Atlantic sea-board. When, however, we reflect how close this region lies to the Ile-de-France, where sculpture worthy of the name did not appear at all until the fourth decade of the XII century, the wonder perhaps is not that the XI century carving of the West was crude, but that figure sculpture existed at all.

The church of Airvault, begun between 1093 and 1096 [1] and consecrated in 1100,[2] possesses sculptures adossed to the wall flanking the vaulting capitals (Ill. 898–900), and also sculptured capitals. We have here a dated and admitted work of the end of the XI century.

The striking fact in regard to the sculptures of Airvault, aside from their crudity, is the similarity in the folds of certain draperies to those in the south portal of St.-Sernin of Toulouse (Ill. 308–318). Now St.-Sernin of Toulouse is later than Airvault, but it is difficult to admit that the advanced school of the pilgrimage could have been influenced by the retarded work in the West. The explanation I believe is this: The ateliers of Toulouse and Santiago were closely interrelated, and we find the same sculptors travelling back and forth from one to the other. Now while no work anterior to the XII century has come down to us at Santiago, it is certain that an atelier of sculpture must have existed there much before, and probably from the beginning of the reconstruction of the cathedral in 1078. It is not

---

[1] Robouchon, 6. [2] *Cong. Arch.*, 1910, LXXVII, 119.

unreasonable to suppose that the work at Airvault may have been influenced by the XI-century atelier of Santiago.

In addition to the sculptures which actually form part of the building, Airvault contains a sculptured tomb (Ill. 903) and a sculptured altar-frontal (Ill. 964). The tomb is that of the abbot Pierre who built the church and died in 1110. It may consequently be considered a dated monument. The altar-frontal is of very similar style, but since it is, perhaps, a little more advanced, it may be assigned to about 1115.

All the work at Airvault is characterized by that strong Lombard influence which we shall find is one of the marked and unexplained peculiarities of the school of the West. The architecture of the church is adorned with arched corbel-tables; the capital of Adam and Eve (Ill. 901) distinctly recalls the manner of Guglielmo; the supporting figures under the tomb of the abbot Pierre (Ill. 903) are obviously of Lombard derivation.

The two reliefs of Ste.-Radegonde of Poitiers (Ill. 907, 908) are of better quality. One feels distinctly in them, although in strangely weakened form, the inspiration which emanated from Cluny. They are degenerates, but after all of the race of the older portal at Charlieu (Ill. 4) or of the Virgin at Sahagún (Ill. 770), as the animals of one of the capitals of the ambulatory (Ill. 911) are an echo of the much finer ones of the nave of St.-Martin-d'Ainay at Lyon. The Ste.-Radegonde reliefs obviously are not now in their original position, but were embedded at a comparatively recent epoch in the narthex below the tower. It unfortunately seems impossible to determine where they were placed. Their style, however, justifies the conclusion that they belonged to the church built between 1083 and 1099. They are, in fact, by the same hand as the Daniel capital of the ambulatory (Ill. 909) which is admitted to be of 1083–1099.

When we turn from Ste.-Radegonde to the sculptures of the lunettes of the cathedral of Angoulême (Ill. 936–940), we recognize between the two a close relationship. There are the same draperies cut in the same rope-like forms, and falling in the same characteristic wave-patterns along the lower edges. Angoulême appears slightly more advanced; the execution is better, and there is more move-ment. Seven or eight or at most ten years might easily account for this development. It is therefore with considerable astonishment that we find current archaeological opinion ascribes the façade of Angoulême to the second half of the XII century. And when we compare the primitive style of these sculptures with that of monu-ments with which they are supposed to be contemporary, such as, for example, the west portal of Chartres or the transept portals of Bourges, our astonishment deepens into amazement.

We naturally turn with haste to the reasoning on which this dating is based. We are told, first of all, what alas is only too true, that the cathedral of Angoulême lost all character in the XIX century resto-ration. To study its archaeology we are therefore advised to go not to the building itself, but to the manuscript study of Michon who saw the church before it was reconstructed. Now Michon thought that the western bay was *earlier* than the rest of the church; we are asked to accept this as a proof that it and the façade are a half century *later!*

Nor do I find the other arguments for the late dating of Angou-lême more convincing. The lunette sculptures of Angoulême (Ill. 936–940), we are told, are by the same atelier (*sic*) as the sculptures of St.-Amand-de-Boixe (Ill. 941–945). These last are thought to be dated 1170.

Now it is true that St.-Amand-de-Boixe was consecrated in 1170. But there was an earlier consecration in 1125. The monument as it stands corresponds perfectly with the documents. Begun at the eastern end, as was the custom (the choir was rebuilt in the XIV century), the transepts with the sculptures and the east bay of the nave were finished in 1125. Then work was interrupted, ap-parently for a number of years. Subsequently the construction of the nave was resumed and completed in 1170. Nothing could be clearer.

Since, however, the fact that the western part of the nave is later seems to have escaped attention, it will be well to note down some of the proofs that such is the case:

(1) The capitals of the nave, broad-leaved and crocketed, are of a strikingly different, and obviously later type from those of the transepts. They must be separated by an interval of at least twenty-five years.

(2) There is an equally striking difference of style between the west portal, Ill. 1135 (that is to say the little of it that is ancient), and the decoration of the west façade of the north transept (Ill. 944, 945).

(3) The design of the church was completely changed when work was resumed after it had been interrupted at the east bay of the nave.

(4) The groin vaults of the side aisles in the east bay of the nave are replaced by barrel vaults in the western bays.

(5) The ornamental frieze on the north exterior wall, begun in the east bay, is discontinued in the western bays.

(6) The side-aisle window in the east bay is placed higher than in the western bays.

(7) The string-course of the abacus of this window is brusquely interrupted where the two constructions adjoin.

(8) In the barrel vault of the nave is visible a break in the masonry between the easternmost and western bays of the nave.

(9) This break continues in the masonry of the easternmost piers of the nave on both sides.

(10) The arcade arch of the east bay of the nave is narrower and higher than those of the western bays.

(11) The high dado separating nave and side aisles in the eastern bay is discontinued in the western bays.

(12) The abacus string-course of the eastern bays is brusquely interrupted at the point of junction, and a new string-course begun a metre further down.

(13) On the south side of the nave the design of the upper string-course is changed at the point of junction.

(14) The capitals of the side-aisle responds are placed at a lower level in the eastern bay than in the western bays.

(15) Blind arches, decorating the side-aisle wall, non-existent in the eastern bay, are introduced into the western bays.

It seems therefore evident that it is a grave error to consider the sculptures of St.-Amand-de-Boixe as dated monuments of 1170. They are indeed dated, but they belong to the church consecrated in 1125.

There is consequently no reason for assigning the façade of Angoulême to the second half of the XII century. The documents inform us categorically that the cathedral was begun by the bishop Girard, who was elected in 1101; built by him (he died in 1136) and consecrated in 1128.[1] It follows that the façade sculptures were executed between 1101 and 1128.

There is, indeed, even more conclusive documentary evidence upon the subject. In the spandrel between the two great engaged arches which on the southern side of the façade rise from the ground to the top-most gallery is inscribed a monogram. M. de Mély [2] has read this; it is the name Itius. Now there is in the cathedral of Angoulême an epitaph of Iteus Archembaldi who died in 1125, *canonicus huius matricis aecclesiae in qua multa bona operatus est*. A contemporary chronicle is a little more explicit in regard to the good works of Itier Archembauld. He furnished half the funds for the construction of the walls of the new cathedral.[3] We begin to understand why his monogram was placed upon the façade. It was because it had been built, at least in part, at his expense. Since Itier Archembauld died in 1125, and his monogram is placed in the upper part of the façade, it is clear that the façade up to this level, or nearly so, must have been erected from funds given by him before 1125.

[1] A document of 1128 signed by the bishop of Angoulême, Girard, is dated *tertio die post dedicationem*. The author of the article in the *Congrès Archéologique*, 1912, LXXIX, 61, tried to explain this away by supposing that it was a quotation from the calendar of the diocese; he believed it to mean the third day after the day on which the anniversary of the dedication is celebrated. That also this interpretation is impossible has already been shown by M. de la Martinère. (See *Bulletin Monumental*, 1920, 173). There is no doubt that the cathedral of Angoulême was consecrated in 1128.

[2] 294.   [3] *Bulletin Monumental*, 1920, 274-275.

Comparison of the style of Angoulême with numerous other dated monuments leads us to the same conclusion. The abbey of Fontevrault was consecrated in 1119. Parts of earlier buildings were incorporated, and additions were subsequently made, but it is clear that the nave which has come down to us belonged to the building consecrated by Callixtus II. Now the style of the capitals of this nave (Ill. 923) is obviously contemporary with that of the sculptures of Angoulême.[1]

The style of the façade of Angoulême is also obviously contemporary with that of the east end of St.-Eutrope of Saintes (Ill. 918). But the construction of the choir of St.-Eutrope was doubtless undertaken when the crypt was finished in 1096, and the church was completed, or virtually so, when visited by the author of the Pilgrims' Guide about 1129. Again we are led to the conclusion that Angoulême must be of the first third of the XII century.

We know that in general Romanesque sculptures were executed before being placed in position in the building, and we know that they were often prepared at the very beginning of the works that they might be ready when the masons had need of them. Mediaeval buildings were constructed sometimes in vertical, sometimes in horizontal sections. At least the façade of Angoulême was constructed horizontally. The sculptures are of three distinct styles: the lunettes are the oldest, then the sculptures in the arches above and finally those of the top-most story. If we compare the latter, the angel of St. Matthew (Ill. 929), for example, with the tympanum of St. Michel d'Entraigues (Ill. 1006), dated 1137, we shall perceive that the cathedral sculptures are distinctly earlier. The façade of Angoulême must therefore have been completed by 1128 or at least very shortly after.

Everything would therefore indicate the lunette sculptures were executed about 1110 or soon after. They have much such movement as is characteristic of the tympanum of the south portal of St.-Sernin

---

[1] Nothing but an inveterate habit of post-dating everything can account for the ascription of this nave to the second quarter of the XII century (*Cong. Arch.*, 1910, LXXVII, 50).

(Ill. 308–318). Closer analogies are, however, to be found with the sculpture of Lombardy. The draperies are those characteristic of Guglielmo.[1] The same folds with the same wave pattern at the bottom are found, for example, in the angel of the Cremona Expulsion, a work executed between 1107 and 1117. These draperies are originally derived from manuscripts. They are found in miniatures of the German school of the X century,[2] in bibles of Angers,[3] and Amiens[4] of the same period, and in an English manuscript of the XII century.[5] It is not entirely clear whether these manuscript draperies were first translated into stone by Guglielmo and copied from him by the master of Angoulême, or whether the reverse was the case. I incline, however, to think the latter and to suppose that Guglielmo, especially in his later works, was influenced by Angoulême. The draperies in question are found more consistently and persistently at Angoulême than at Cremona; at Modena they hardly occur.

The conjecture may indeed be risked that Guglielmo and the master of Augoulême came into personal contact with each other. At any rate, it is certain that the Angoulême work was strongly influenced by Italian models. Like Guglielmo, the Angoulême master keeps both feet of his figures firmly planted on the ground, even when the figures are in motion; like Guglielmo, he uses two parallel lines to indicate the modelling of his draperies. The ornamental decoration at Angoulême is strongly Lombardic. The rinceau beneath the lunette might have been sculptured for a church of the Parmigiano c. 1110; the interlaces of animals and foliage over the lunettes are equally north Italian. Most striking of all is the frieze to the right of the central portal beneath the lunette. We have

---

[1] The wide diffusion of the art of Guglielmo throughout Europe is becoming increasingly evident. Dehio, 176, has remarked that the portal of Andlau in Alsace is inspired by Nonantola.

[2] See, for example, the Perikopenbuch Kaiser Heinrichs II, Reichenau school, before 1014, illustrated by Leidinger, V, 18 or the Bamberger Apocalypse, ed. Wölfflin.

[3] Bible of St.-Aubin of Angers, Angers, Bibl. de la Ville, No. 4, ed. Boinet, Pl. CLII.

[4] Illustrated by Haseloff in Michel, I, 2, 748.

[5] British Museum MS. 37472, No. 1.

already seen[1] how closely this is connected with ultramontane monuments.

The crouching attitude of the lunette figures at Angoulême is probably derived from manuscripts. We find parallel drawing in the elders of the Codex Aureus of St. Emmeran of Ratisbonne,[2] a manuscript which dates from 870, and in the sacramentary of Marmoutiers[3] of c. 850.

The motive of placing three figures crouched or in motion in a tympanum or lunette enjoyed a certain popularity in the first third of the XII century, before the more elaborate compositions inaugurated at Cluny came into vogue. This is the type of the tympanum at San Pablo del Campo (Ill. 550) of Barcelona, a church consecrated in 1125. It appears also to have been the type of the ancient tympanum of Maguelonne (Ill. 1287, 1288), which as we have seen[4] must date from c. 1120.

In the local museum at Angoulême is preserved a relief by the same hand that executed the lunette sculptures of the cathedral. This, too, seems to have come from a lunette. I am tempted to conjecture that it may have formed part of the central tympanum, destroyed in the XVIII century, and now replaced by a modern pastiche. The museum fragment is of importance because unrestored. It therefore affords an opportunity for obtaining a more exact conception of the style and quality of our master.

The first atelier at Angoulême seems to have influenced later sculptors of distant regions, more apparently than the later work of the upper zones of the façade. We have already seen that the Angoulême Master of St.-Gilles derived his art from this source.[5] He worked at St.-Gilles in the fourth decade of the XII century, or twenty years after the Angoulême lunettes had been executed.

Another interesting derivative of the lunettes of Angoulême is the relief representing St. Paul and St. John at the cathedral of Zamora

[1] See above, p. 63.
[2] Munich, Kgl. Bibl. lat. 140,000, illustrated by Boinet, Pl. CXVI.
[3] Preserved at Autun, Bibl. de la Ville, No. 19bis, ed. Boinet, Pl. XLIII.
[4] Above, p. 270.   [5] See above, p. 273, 274.

(Ill. 740). The relationship to Angoulême is evident. The posture of the St. John must have been inspired by the apostle to the left of the northernmost lunette at Angoulême (Ill. 936); the facial type of the St. John seems studied from the central apostle of the same lunette; the hair convention of the St. John is the hair convention of the apostle to the left in the Angoulême lunette; the folds of the draperies of the upper part of the under-garment of the St. John reproduce the corresponding ones of the apostle to the right in the Angoulême lunette; the face of the St. Paul is the face of the apostle to the right of the lunette north of the central portal at Angoulême; the vertically falling folds of the outer mantle of both the Zamora figures is evidently derived from those of the Angoulême lunettes; the draperies of the thigh of the St. Paul (Ill. 740) are like those of the thigh of the central figure in the northern lunette at Angoulême (Ill. 936). It is therefore certain that the Zamora sculptor had seen and studied the lunettes of Angoulême.

It was not only Angoulême that he observed on his journey to the North. The swirl of drapery to the right of St. John can only be derived from Burgundy. His second tympanum of Zamora (Ill. 741), representing the Virgin enthroned under a canopy between angels, is obviously copied from the southern tympanum of Chartres. The Child, however, is not placed in the frontal position, but on the left knee as at Beaucaire (Ill. 1299).

I suspect that the same sculptor may be responsible for the figures under the vaulting ribs of the Catedral Vieja of Salamanca (Ill. 736–739). The draperies, it is true, are different; but the face of the figure trampling a dragon at Salamanca (Ill. 736) is the face of the Virgin at Zamora (Ill. 741), and the face of the crouching figure at Salamanca (Ill. 739) is the face of the St. Paul of Zamora (Ill. 740). Moreover, the draperies for all their apparent dissimilarities have many points of contact. If the identification of these hands be admitted, we may infer that our master also brought from the West of France, possibly from Cormery, the idea of placing sculptures below the vaulting ribs.

It is known that the cathedral of Zamora was built by the bishop Esteban (1150–1168) and was consecrated in 1174.[1] Since our sculptor shows knowledge of no monuments in the North later than the southern tympanum of Chartres which was probably finished by 1150, he might have worked at Zamora at any time between 1150 and 1174. That his activity is to be assigned to the earlier rather than to the later part of this period is indicated by the fact that the sculptures are placed upon the façade of the south transept, which would presumably have been one of the parts of the building erected rather early, and also by the finely archaic vigour and delicacy of his style. The sculptures of the Catedral Vieja of Salamanca must surely date from about 1150. Señor Lampérez discards the consecration date of 1160, but thinks that the cathedral was begun before 1130, and that the choir and transepts were finished by 1150.[2]

Another derivative of the first Angoulême atelier somewhat nearer home is the portal of the refectory of St.-Aubin of Angers (Ill. 965–972). We have here the work of an excellent sculptor who imitated, about 1130, the manner of the earlier work at Angoulême, but shows no traces of having been influenced by the poorer sculptures of the upper stories.

The relationship of the Angoulême lunettes to the frescos of Catalonia is a puzzling one. The analogies in the working of the draperies are obvious, and closer than can be accounted for by common derivation from Othonian miniatures. Catalan fresco painters were evidently in close touch with work in France; one of them indeed executed the frescos at Vicq,[3] which, too, are related to the Angoulême lunettes. The question of the date of the Catalan frescos is still unsolved. The churches of Sant Climent de Tahull and Santa Maria de Tahull were consecrated in 1123; I can see no reason to doubt that their frescos are of this time. On the other

---

[1] 1150. X. sed. Stefanus. Eccl. Cathedr. aedif. et dedicatur 15 IX. 1174. †I. 1168 (Gams).

[2] 527 f.

[3] A comparison between the frescos at Vicq and those of Catalonia was first suggested to me by Mr. Cook; Mr. Melville Webber has pointed out that the Vicq frescos are especially close to Santa Maria de Bohi. There are illustrations of all these frescos in *Les Pintures Murals Catalanes* published by the *Institut d'Estudis Catalans*.

hand, the frescos from Mur, now in the Boston Museum, are later, perhaps *c.* 1150; they are related to St.-Gilles and Chartres (as Mr. Cook has recognized), as well as to Angoulême.

When we pass from the sculptures of the lunettes at Angoulême (Ill. 936–940) to the reliefs of the upper stories (Ill. 929–935), we are at once conscious of a change of style. All of the sculptures included under the great arcades and in the arches flanking the central window seem to form an homogeneous group, which is distinguishable from the lunettes. Yet the two are only very slightly separated. Whether this difference is to be explained by supposing that the upper sculptures are later, or the work of a different master, it is difficult to determine in the present restored condition of the edifice. The photographs made before the restoration are unfortunately not sufficiently clear to be of much assistance. As nearly as it is possible to judge, the differences of manner are sufficient to justify the inference that the upper sculptures are both later and by another hand.

There can in any case be no doubt that the top-most sculptures (Ill. 929–930) are by a different master, although still closely related. The figures are often elongated; the draperies are finer and more clinging; the execution more skilful. The subject of this remarkable composition is not, I think, the Last Judgment. The angel blowing a trumpet indicates that as little here as does the similar figure in the Puerta de las Platerias at Santiago from which it is perhaps copied.[1] The subject is the apocalyptical vision, precisely as in the sculptures in the gable of the cathedral at Modena.

---

[1] It is true that the Pilgrims' Guide speaks of the angels at Santiago (Ill. 675–677) as *cornua singula tenentes, Judicii diem pronuntiantes*. But the composition obviously does not and never did represent the Last Judgment. Angels blowing trumpets without connection with the Last Judgment abound in mediaeval iconography; to cite the first examples that come to mind, they are found in a miniature of the Utrecht Psalter, fol. 36 b; in a miniature of the Benedictional of St. Aethelwold at Chatsworth, a work of the school of Winchester of *c.* 980, illustrated by Wilson and Warner, fol. 20; in the Exultet roll of Bari; in the capital representing the Journey to Emmaus from Moûtier-St.-Jean (Ill. 65) now in the Fogg Museum; in the tympanum of Neuilly-en-Donjon (Ill. 93); on the façade of St.-Jouin-de-Marne (Ill. 946); in a fresco of S. Pietro di Civate, illustrated by Toesca, 110; in one of the sculptures under the vaulting ribs of the Catedral Vieja of Salamanca (Ill. 737). The motive is probably reminiscent of a Last Judgment, which is all that the text in the Guide means to imply.

We have, indeed, here another proof of the relationship between Angoulême and the Emelian cathedral.

The master of the upper sculptures remains under the influence of miniatures — at least I take it that the busts in medallions are derived from manuscripts rather than from other sources, although it is impossible to be certain in the case of a motive so widely diffused.[1] It is, however, reasonable to suppose that German miniatures of the X century continued to be the source of inspiration for the sculptors of the West.

Especially notable are the angels sculptured at Angoulême on the voussure of the central arch over the Christ (Ill. 929). The motive, characteristic of the school of the West, is here found in its fully developed form.

Turning now to the sculptures of St.-Amand-de-Boixe (Ill. 941–945), we perceive that the work is indeed strikingly analogous to Angoulême (Ill. 929–940). There are the same lunettes with three figures, with the same friezes and ornamental patterns. But is current archaeology correct in calling them the work of the same masters? Notwithstanding the bad preservation of the reliefs of St.-

---

[1] Heads in medallions are found: in an ivory box of the IV century in the museum at Brescia, illustrated by Graeven, II, 11–15; in frescos of the late IV or early V century at S. Paolo f. l. m. at Rome (mostly destroyed); in the *Christ* of the triumphal arch of the same church of about the middle of the V century; in the Christ of uncertain date incorporated in the apse mosaic of S. Giovanni in Laterano at Rome; in the mosaic of S. Pier Crisologo of Ravenna, of the VI century; in the mosaics of the early VIII century at S. Demetrius of Salonica; in the V century mosaic of the basilica of Fausta at S. Ambrogio of Milan; in the mosaics of S. Vitale at Ravenna of the VI century; in innumerable coins; in mosaic in the façade of the chapel of S. Zeno at S. Prassede at Rome (817–824); in a fresco at Bawit in Egypt, illustrated by Grüneisen, Pl. XLII; in a Byzantine ivory triptych of the X (?) century at the Vatican; in a Byzantine enamel box of the same collection; in innumerable other enamels; in two Byzantine ivory caskets of the X century in the Metropolitan Museum of New York; in an ivory triptych of the Bibliothèque Nationale at Paris, illustrated by Schlumberger, *Ep. Byz.*, I, 17; in an ivory diptych of the X century (*ibid.*, 53); in a triptych of the X century of the Louvre (*ibid.*, 64); in a mosaic of the XI century at St. Luke of Phokis (*ibid.*, 165, 341); in an ivory casket of the X or XI century at Lyon (*ibid.*, 281); in a destroyed icon of the XI century (*ibid.*, 353); in a mosaic of 1040 at Kief (*ibid.*, 373); in the XII century mosaics at Cefalù, the Cappella Palatina of Palermo, the Martorana of Palermo, Monreale; in an early Italian ivory of the XII century in the Barberini library at Rome, illustrated by Graeven, II, 56; in a plaster relief of S. Ambrogio, in the church of S. Ambrogio at Milan; in stone sculpture in Armenia, in the church at Achthamar of the early X century, illustrated by Strzygowski, *Arm.*, 291 f.; in the destroyed portal of Cluny; and in German ivories and miniatures of the X century — *e.g.*, those of the Bibliothèque Nationale of Paris, illustrated by Goldschmidt, I, No. 38.

Amand, and the restoration at Angoulême, I have little hesitation in replying in the negative. St.-Amand is the work of an inferior. copyist. He has taken his conception from Angoulême, but his execution is entirely different. His lunette figures are weak and timid compared with their originals. They have not the movement, the vigour, the daring, nor the decorative quality of the Angoulême lunettes. The technical details are different. The St.-Amand artist introduces a beaded ornament in his halos and on the robes of his ecclesiastics, which is not found at Angoulême. His draperies are of another type. They seem, indeed, inspired by the master of the upper row of reliefs at Angoulême. This point is important. Since St.-Amand was consecrated in 1125, we are confirmed in our dating of even the latest work of the Angoulême façade to within the third decade of the XII century.

St.-Jouin-de-Marne (Ill. 946–950) was begun in 1095; in 1130 [1] the church was consecrated. The western bays of the nave seem to be the latest part of the construction; we may assume that the façade dates from the years immediately preceding 1130. The style of the sculptures seems, in fact, a little more advanced than that of the latest work at Angoulême.[2] The draperies are more clinging, less schematized, more naturalistic. The heads of the St. Peter (Ill. 950) and of the St. John (Ill. 949) are finer than any of the heads at Angoulême (Ill. 929–940). In the upper figure to the left of the window (Ill. 947) and the Delilah (Ill. 948) appear those trailing sleeves [3] which were to become characteristic of the school of the West in the fourth decade of the century. These are barely foreshadowed in the angel of St. Matthew (Ill. 929) at Angoulême. The heads of the two apostles (Ill. 949, 950) below the Annunciation have already a Chartrain quality.

[1] Altare princeps Ecclesiae S. Ioħis Euang. anno 1130 denuo consecratu fuit ab Epo cujus nomen reticetur, in honorem sanctorum Jouini, Martini atque Sebastiani (*Chartularium Monasterii S. Jovini de Marnis*, Paris, Bibliothèque Nationale, Fond Latin, No. 5449, fol. 5).

[2] Yet according to the *Cong. Arch.*, 1903, LXX, 71, these are "des bas-reliefs plus anciens" "appliqués dans le plein des murs."

[3] They are also characteristic of Far Eastern art from a very early period. Compare, *e.g.*, the gilt bronze image owned by the Imperial Household, and anterior to 781, exhibited in the Kyoto Exposition. It is illustrated in the catalogue.

St.-Jouin-de-Marne (Ill. 946–950) was a pilgrimage church. Although apparently not directly on the road, the rich relics it contained must have induced many to detour on their way to Santiago or Rome. On the upper gable is sculptured a procession of pilgrims — the same subject that was later repeated in the pilgrimage church of Borgo S. Donnino in Lombardy. The façade of St.-Jouin-de-Marne shows the characteristics of pilgrimage art in the many foreign influences it reflects. The strongest of these is that of Lombardy. The division into three parts by shafts; the ending of these shafts inconsequentially; the setting-in of random bits of sculpture in high relief; the arched corbel-tables; the grotesques of the capitals; the cross in the gable; many of the anthemia and rinceaux, are evidently inspired by models in Italy, and more especially in the neighbourhood of Pavia. The sculpture, on the other hand, shows rather French and Spanish influences. The Annunciation (Ill. 948) recalls the master of the Creation of Adam at Santiago (Ill. 686); the two statues below (Ill. 949, 950) seem to be reminiscent of the Puerta de las Platerias (Ill. 674–691), of Cluny (Ill. 5–10) and of Charlieu (Ill. 4); the Luxury possibly recalls Moissac (Ill. 371).

It is worthy of remark that the school of the West is by no means so exclusively under the influence of Toulouse as has generally been assumed. That wind, however, did unquestionably blow. The peculiar stomach folds in the draperies, so characteristic of later work in the West, are found in the cloister of Moissac (Ill. 273). This particular resemblance, however, may possibly be due to derivation from a common original. Precisely such stomach folds are found in a manuscript life of Ste. Radegonde, illuminated about 1050 and now preserved in the Bibliothèque Municipale of Poitiers[1] and also in Spanish ivories (Ill. 664).

In addition to St.-Michel-d'Entraigues, which is a dated and admitted monument of 1137 (Ill. 1006), there remain two more works of sculpture in the West, the date of which may be considered to be accurately determined by documentary sources.

[1] MS. 250 fol. 40, illustrated in the Bulletin de la S. F. R. M. P., 1914.

The little church at Chadennac (Ill. 1034–1040) offers the lover of
XII-century art an unexpected delight. These sculptures, lost in the
country and mentioned only cursorily in out-of-the-way books dealing with the antiquities of the region, are a masterpiece of the first
rank. Their quality is even finer than that of Chartres. They lack,
it is true, the repose and monumental grandeur of the work at Parthenay; their merits are rather delicacy and finesse. This sculptor
was the Pisanello of Romanesque art. Like the Italian he delights in
the world — the pomp of extravagant costume, the beauty of lithe
and graceful limbs. Like Pisanello, too, he takes particular joy in animals. Indeed, I suspect that the slender hounds, so characteristic of
the Veronese artist's work, and which came to him from French miniatures, may be the lineal descendants of the no less lovely ones
sculptured on the portal of Chadennac.[1]

The date of this important monument — 1140 — is happily determined by an inscription,[2] which if not of great antiquity, doubtless still preserves an authentic tradition. Several heads are absolutely Chartrain in style, as, for example, the restored male portrait
in the cornice over the central portal. One of the heads in the voussures (Ill. 1035) is very close to those of Gilbert at Toulouse (Ill.
434–436).

The portal of Blazimont (Ill. 1041–1044) is another work by the
sculptor of Chadennac. The arch of the door-way at Blazimont is
pointed; the attenuation of certain figures is more extreme; the style
a little more mannered; but on the whole the two works are very
much alike. The draperies, the animals, the drawing, numerous
technical peculiarities are the same. The angel on the column at
Chadennac (Ill. 1039) is the sister of the angels in the inner voussures at Blazimont (Ill. 1043). Like Chadennac, Blazimont is a pure
and beautiful example of the quasi-Burgundian art of the West.
There are, it is true, details of this portal at which criticism must
cavil; but in its entirety it is a master-work. Here, indeed, is the per-

[1] The Chadennac hounds are, perhaps in turn, derived from those of the Utrecht Psalter,
f. 23, 24 b, 33.
[2] Dangibeaud, 26.

fection of manner. Charm of line and grace of contour unite with delicacy of execution.

The derivation of this art from the tympanum of Autun — 1132 — (Ill. 80, 81) is obvious. So is its relationship with St.-Michel — 1137 — (Ill. 1006) in which we perceive the same tendencies. If Blazimont is purer, more Burgundian, that is doubtless because its sculptor came in more direct touch with the fountain-head. Blazimont was probably executed about 1145.

A confirmation of this dating may be derived from an English manuscript of 1119–1146.[1] The angels here have the same elongated and crossed legs as in our sculptures. The two works must be nearly contemporary; but one has the impression that in this case the miniature is not the original but the copy. If this feeling be correct, we must place Blazimont before 1146.[2]

The angel on the outer voussure of the portal at Varaize (Ill. 1002) comes exceedingly close to the style of the Chadennac Master, but the inner voussures are of an entirely different manner.

The sculptures at Moreaux (Ill. 1065–1068) are even less known than those of Chadennac. Indeed, when I visited the ruins of this chapel in 1921, the reliefs had entirely disappeared underneath a luxuriant growth of ivy. Since some of the vines were several inches thick, it was evident that the sculptures had not been seen by human eyes since Longuemar copied the inscriptions more than half a century ago.

These inscriptions, which may still be read, imply that the chapel was erected by Grimoard and Guillaume Adelelme, bishops of Poitiers, and Arnaud, arch-deacon.[3] Now Guillaume Adelelme was

---

[1] Reproduced by Haseloff in Michel, II, 1, p. 312.

[2] This type of angel became typical of English manuscripts of a late period — see the calendar of c. 1200 illustrated in the Burlington Catalogue, Pl. 34; the Psalter of St. Mary's of Winchester, c. 1220–1240 (ibid., Pl. 37); the Psalter of St. Swithun's Priory, Winchester, British Museum, Cotton MS., Nero, C. IV, f. 39; the late XII century Life of St. Guthlac of Croyland, Brit. Mus. Harley Roll Y. 6, ed. British Museum Reproductions from Illuminated Manuscripts, Series I, viii.

[3] Inscription of central portal:
VT FVIT INTROITVS TEMPLI SC̄I SALOMONIS:
† SIC EST ISTIVS IN MEDIO BOVIS ATQ: LEONIS:

elected bishop of Poitiers in 1128; he died in 1140, and was succeeded by Grimoard, who died two years later, in 1142. Since both bishops are mentioned in the inscriptions, the chapel must have been begun before 1140, and finished after, but before 1142. It is, therefore, a very precisely dated monument of 1140.

Two other monuments should perhaps be considered of determined date, although the documentary evidence in regard to them is circumstantial rather than explicit. The church of St.-Vivien was given by the bishop of Bazas to the priory of La Réole in 1144;[1] since the style of the existing sculptures (Ill. 1085, 1086) is precisely that of this date, we are justified in concluding that the donation occasioned a reconstruction of the church. Similar considerations lead me to place both friezes of Selles-sur-Cher (Ill. 1074–1082) in 1145.[2]

In fact one of the flanking statues stands on a lion, the other on a bull. Left of the portal:
DS MISEREATVR GRIMOARDI
PICTAVENSIS EPI ET ARNAVDI
ARCHIDIACONI PAT NR.
Right of the portal:
DS MISEREATVR GVILMI ADALELMI PICTAVENSIS EPI ET ARNAVDI ARCHI-
DIACONI PAT NR.
[1] Archives de la Gironde, V, 151.
[2] See what has been said above, p. 24 f.

VIII

LATER MONUMENTS OF THE WEST

WE have now passed in review, at least so far as known to me, the monuments of sculpture in the school of the West, the date of which can be determined by documentary evidence. The list is meagre, especially in view of the large number of undocumented monuments extant; yet by rare good fortune the dates are distributed over the first forty years of the XII century with sufficient frequency to determine the development of sculpture in this critical period. After the formation of the Gothic style at St.-Denis (Ill. 1437–1457) in 1140, the course of art runs smooth. The documents, therefore, help us out precisely at the point where we have most need of them.

Several undated monuments are still of importance for comprehending the evolution of sculpture in the West.

Among these, one of the best known is certainly Notre-Dame-la-Grande of Poitiers (Ill. 951–962). Because of its analogy with Angoulême (Ill. 929–940), which as we have seen has been much post-dated, archaeologists have generally considered this façade as of c. 1180. That would make it about contemporary with Senlis (Ill. 1505–1513) and the Pórtico de la Gloria at Santiago (Ill. 820–840). It is only necessary to compare Notre-Dame-la-Grande (Ill. 951–962) with these two monuments to be convinced of the extravagance of the theory.

The façade of Notre-Dame-la-Grande (Ill. 951–962) is certainly more unified than that of Angoulême (Ill. 929–940); it is, however, possible to trace in the sculptures the work of three different hands. To the first belong all the reliefs to the left of the central portal (Ill. 956–959), also the Joseph (Ill. 962) and the wrestlers (Ill. 962) to the right. By the second are the Visitation (Ill. 960) and the Nativity (Ill. 961); and by the third the apostles (Ill. 952–955) above. It is evident that the first two masters worked contemporaneously; if the third came after them, it must have been by a comparatively short interval of time, since his style hardly seems essentially more advanced.

Comparison with Angoulême (Ill. 929–940) gives the impression that the façade of Notre-Dame (Ill. 951–962) was begun later. At Poitiers the design is more coherent; the pointed arches introduced in the side lunettes have no counterpart at Angoulême. The lunette sculptures of Angoulême (Ill. 936–940) are obviously more primitive than any of the work at Notre-Dame-la-Grande. But if the Pictave façade was begun later, it may well have been finished about the same time. In fact the sculptures seem contemporary with the later work at Angoulême (1128) and St.-Amand-de-Boixe (Ill. 941–945) —1125. The rudimentary Jesse Tree (Ill. 959) must have been executed before this motive received its definitive form at St.-Denis. We may, therefore, assign Notre-Dame-la-Grande to c. 1130. The trailing sleeves of the figure to the right of the Visitation need not disquiet us in this dating. We have seen that such sleeves are also found at St.-Jouin-de-Marne (Ill. 946–950) which was completed in 1130.

The iconography of these sculptures is interesting. Beginning in the spandrel above the northern great arch to the left we have represented the Temptation. The inscription is now in part illegible, but can be reconstituted with the help of the copy of Lecointre, published by Longuemar:[1]

ADA: EVA CRIMEN FERT HOMINI PRIMORDIA LUCTUS

Then follows the figure of Nebuchadnezzar; the inscription NABVCODNOSOR REX is still well preserved.

We have next four prophets, the two at the ends holding scrolls, the two in the centre, books. The first is Daniel; on his scroll can still be read: CV VENERIT SCS SCORVM CES(*sabit unctio vestra*). The second holds a book; he is Moses and he once was

[1] 213.

supplied with the inscription: PROPHETAM DABIT VOBIS DE
FRATRIBUS VESTRIS ET NON ESTIMA. The third was
Jeremiah; he once was supplied with the inscription: POST HAEC
IN TERRIS VISUS EST ET CUM HOMINIBUS CONVER-
SATUS EST. The fourth was Isaiah; on his scroll was inscribed:
EGREDIETUR VIRGA DE RADICE JESSE, ET FLOS DE
RADICE EJUS ASCENDET.

The next scene is the Annunciation; then Jesse, with a tree growing from his head, on the top of which perches the dove of the Holy
Spirit; last the Nativity.

It is generally admitted that this peculiar order of scenes was inspired by a miracle play. That may be, although I do not know any
text with which the sculptures correspond.

It has been held in particular that the four prophets holding scrolls
or books with inscriptions are derived from a miracle play, and that
the proof of this is to be found in the quotations selected for the
scrolls.

Now it is true that these quotations are peculiar. That of Daniel
does not correspond precisely with any text in the scriptures, but is
taken from a pseudo-Augustine sermon. This sermon,[1] which enjoyed universal popularity in the Middle Ages, to the point that it
waś incorporated as a regular part of the liturgy, was written in the
form of a dialogue. The theme is the confutation of the Jews from
the mouths of their own prophets. Character after character is in-
terrogated, and answers. First Isaiah comes forward. *Dic*, says the
writer, *Ysaia, testimonium Christo.* Isaiah replies with the text:
*Ecce inquit virgo in utero concipiet et pariet filium et vocabitur nomen
ejus Hemanuhel.*[2] Then comes Jeremiah. *Dic et tu, Jheremia, testimonium Christo. Hic est, inquit, Deus noster et non estimabitur alius
absque illo qui invènit omnem viam scientie et dedit eam Jacob puero
suo et Israel dilecto suo. Post hec in terris visus est et cum hominibus
conversatus est.*[3] Next is Daniel: *Dic, sancte Danihel, dic de Christo*

---

[1] Published by Migne, *Pat. Lat.*, XLII, 1123.
[2] Isai., vii, 14.   [3] Bar., iii, 36, 37.

quod nosti. Cum venerit, inquit, Sanctus Sanctorum, cessabit unctio (vestra).[1] *Dic et Moyses . . . testimonium Christo. Prophetam, inquit, vobis suscitabit Deus de fratribus vestris; omnis anima que non audivit prophetam illum, exterminabitur de populo suo.*[2] *Accedat autem David sanctus. Adorabunt inquit eum omnes reges terre, omnes gentes servient illi.*[3] *Dic et tu Abacuch propheta testimonium de Christo. Domine, inquit, audivi auditum tuum et timui; consideravi opera tua et expavi.*[4] Then comes Simeon: *Nunc dimittis, Domine, servum tuum in pace, quia viderunt oculi mei salutare tuum.*[5] Zacharias and Elizabeth testify: *Tu puer propheta Altissimi vocaberis, preibis ante faciem Domini parare viam ejus.*[6] Then is mentioned the scene of the Visitation; Elizabeth adds: *Unde mihi hoc ut veniat mater Domini* etc.[7] John the Baptist is also introduced. Then comes Virgil: *Jam nova progenies celo dimittitur alto.*[8] The next witness is Nebuchadnezzar: *Dic, Nabuchodonosor, quid in fornace vidisti quando tres viros justos injuste illuc miseras, dic, dic quid tibi fuerit revelatum. — Nomine inquit tres viros misimus in fornace ligatos.— Et aiunt ei, Vere rex.— Ecce inquit video quattuor viros solutos deambulantes in medio ignis et corruptio nulla est in eis et aspectus quarti similis Filio Dei.*[9] Last comes the Sibyl with the verses made celebrated by St. Augustine:

> *Judicii signum tellus sudore madescet;*
> *E celo rex adveniet per secla futurus,* etc.

This sermon, already half dramatic, incorporated in the ritual of the Church, seems to have developed into a miracle play. The various parts were presumably first read by different members of the clergy; then costumes came to be assumed, and finally the sermon was re-written in dramatic form, the dialogue being put into rhyme.

Now whether the iconography of Notre-Dame-la-Grande is inspired by a lost prose version of the drama of the prophets, or di-

---

[1] Cf. Dan., ix, 24.   [2] Deut., xviii, 15.
[3] Ps., lxxi, 11.   [4] Hab., iii, 1; cf. Eccle., vii. 14.
[5] Luc., ii, 29.   [6] Luc., i. 76.
[7] Luc., i, 43.   [8] Ecloga, IV, 7.
[9] Dan., iii, 92.

rectly by the sermon is a very open question. There is no proof that the play entered into the composition. That it did has simply been assumed by writers anxious to make their point. The question is perhaps at bottom an academic one. The sermon slipped into the drama by imperceptible degrees. The conceptions of the sermon were so striking that they impressed themselves indelibly upon the XII century, and found expression in different forms.

That the iconography of Notre-Dame-la-Grande goes back directly or indirectly to the sermon is certain. In no other way can be explained the juxtaposition of Nebuchadnezzar and the prophets. The sermon also explains the association of the scene of the Visitation with these other subjects. Moreover, the scrolls of the prophets are quotations not from the scriptures, as we have observed, but from the sermon. Only Isaiah is given a verse which is taken from his prophecy, and not quoted in the sermon. The prophets selected at Notre-Dame are among those that appear in the sermon — Moses, Daniel, Jeremiah, Isaiah.

It has been claimed that the motive of prophets holding scrolls was first introduced at St.-Denis; this is said to have been a translation into stone of the drama of the prophets, and from there the motive spread over Europe.

In point of fact the motive of prophets holding scrolls goes back to the earliest times of Christian art. We find them, for example, in the Codice Sinopense, an Asia Minor manuscript of the VI century.[1] Here scenes from the Testaments are flanked on both sides by a prophet holding a scroll on which is inscribed a sentence from his prophecy. In the Codice Purpureo of Rossano, a contemporary monument, scenes from the New Testament have placed below them four prophets with similar scrolls. Prophets similarly flanking scenes from the Gospels are also found in the Greek St. Matthew of the VI–VII centuries.[2] In the Occident we find the motive in the Utrecht Psalter.[3] In the XI century the motive appears in the destroyed

[1] Bib. Nat. Supp. gr. 1286.
[2] Illustrated by Omont, Pl. XVI, XVII, XVIII, XIX.
[3] Folio 6 b.

mosaics of Capua,[1] in the frescos of S. Angelo in Formis, and in the mosaics [2] of Daphni.[3]

The texts selected for the scrolls of the prophets do not seem to have been rigidly fixed. There appears to have been considerable variety and freedom of choice at all times. From the beginning of the XII century we begin to feel the influence of the pseudo-Augustine sermon in the texts selected, and in the prophets represented. Thus at Cremona, in Lombardy, in the jambs sculptured by Guglielmo (1107–1117) we have represented the four prophets Daniel, Jeremiah, Isaiah and Ezekiel. All except Ezekiel are among those mentioned in the sermon; and the scrolls of the first three are quotations not from the scriptures, but from the sermon.[4] In Nicolò's work at Ferrara (1135) are the same four prophets, with the same inscriptions, obviously taken over from Cremona.[5] But at the cathedral of Verona in 1139 Nicolò has given a different selection of prophets. David, Jeremiah, Isaiah, Daniel and Habakkuk are the same as appear in the sermon; with the exception of David their scrolls are either quotations from the sermon, or the texts cited in it; but to these have been added Malachi, Haggai, Zechariah, Micah and Joel, who do not appear in the sermon.[6] In a cupola of S. Marco at Venice, which is one of the earliest mosaics of the church, and probably executed not

---

[1] Bertaux, *Ital. Mér.*, I, 187.

[2] Scrolls were given not only to prophets. The seated consul holds a scroll with inscription in the Probianus-Diptychon of the Berlin Staatsbibliothek (illustrated by Pelka, 58). A personage, identified as St. Mark by Mr. Maclagen, carries a scroll in an ivory-carving from the throne of Grado now in the Museo Archeologico of Milan, a Coptic work of the VI century, but this piece is perhaps a later restoration (illustrated by Maclagen, Pl. III, xii); scrolls are carried by St. Mark and St. John in a miniature of the Gudohinus Gospel at Autun (No. 3), which is earlier than 750. St. Matthew carries a scroll in a miniature of the *Codex Aureus* of Stockholm, fol. 9 b; the motive is also found in a South Anglo-Saxon Gospel of the IX century, illustrated by Zimmermann, 314 (Rome, Vat. Barb. Lat. 570); and in the Landisfarne Gospels of the British Museum (Cotton MS. Nero D. IV, fol. 209 b, illustrated by Zimmermann, 226). Christ is represented carrying a scroll with inscription in a Byzantine ivory of the X century in the museum of Berlin, illustrated by Schlumberger, II, 460. A book-cover of the Cluny Museum, at Paris, by the Echternach master, a work of the end of the X century, represents St. Paul carrying a scroll with the inscription: *Gratia dei sum id quod sum.* It is the same inscription which is repeated on the scroll of the *St. Paul* of the façade of St.-Gilles (Ill. 1311).

[3] Millet, 83.

[4] See my *Lombard Architecture*, II, 386–387.

[5] *Ibid.*, II, 419, 420.   [6] *Lombard Architecture*, III, 476.

long after the mosaic decoration was commenced in 1070, are represented a series of prophets with scrolls. Solomon, Malachi, Zechariah, Haggai, Sophonias, Jonah, Abdias are not included in the cycle
of the sermon; David is, but his scroll is not the text cited in the sermon; however, Habakkuk, Daniel, Jeremiah, and Isaiah have
scrolls which are either quotations from the sermon, or repetitions
of the texts there cited.[1] In the east window of the cathedral of
Piacenza is sculptured the Annunciation and the two prophets
Balaam and Isaiah. Isaiah bears a scroll with the text cited in the
sermon; Balaam does not appear in the sermon, but was introduced
into the mysteries at an early date — first apparently in the Mystery
of Adam, which is in certain ways more primitive than that of Rouen.
It is therefore not impossible that we have here some influence of the
drama. In the apse arch of S. Clemente at Rome, in a mosaic of
1108, is represented Jeremiah with a scroll on which is inscribed the
text quoted by the sermon. Isaiah with the text quoted by the sermon is represented at Moissac (Ill. 361). The same prophet is found
at Conques (Ill. 391) and Notre-Dame-du-Port of Clermont-Ferrand
(Ill. 1162) balancing St. John the Baptist. The coupling of these two
characters must certainly be ascribed to the influence of the sermon.
At Ancona Jeremiah has the text cited by the sermon, and Habakkuk
a quotation from the sermon. In the pulpit of S. Leonardo at Arcetri
(Ill. 226) Moses has the text cited by the sermon, and Daniel a quotation from the sermon.[2] At Orense Daniel has a scroll with a
quotation from the sermon (Ill. 855). At S. Pellegrino at Bomiaco in
the Abruzzi are frescos of 1263; Daniel holds a scroll with a quotation
from the sermon.[3] Three scenes from Duccio's Siena reredos are
flanked by prophets holding scrolls. The Isaiah of the Berlin Nativity still has the same text cited by the sermon. At S. Marco of Venice,
a mosaic by Pasterini dating from 1634 still shows Jeremiah carrying
a scroll with the text cited in the sermon.

We may conclude that the motive of prophets holding scrolls with

[1] Saccardo in Ongania, 305.　　　　　[2] Durand, 26.
[3] Bertaux, *Ital. Mér.*, 291.

a quotation from their prophecies is an exceedingly old one, which may be traced back as far as the VI century. These scrolls at first contained texts from their prophecies; but about the end of the XI century preference came often to be given to the texts cited in the pseudo-Augustine sermon, and even quotations from the sermon came to be substituted for the scriptures.

It is not true that the scrolls of Guglielmo's prophets at Cremona are copied from those of Notre-Dame-la-Grande. We have only to compare the scrolls of the two Jeremiahs to perceive that the two are derived from a common original, the sermon, and that neither is copied from the other. The scroll at Poitiers was: *Post haec in terris visus est et cum hominibus conversatus est . . .* ; that at Cremona is: *hic est inquit deus noster et non estimabitur alius absque illo qui invenit omnem viam scientie et dedit eam Iacob puero suo et Israel dilecto suo.* We should, indeed, hardly suspect that the two were related, did we not possess the key in the common source.

Although the scrolls are derived independently from a common original, there is still no doubt that the first hand which we have distinguished in the sculptures of Notre-Dame-la-Grande shows points of stylistic contact with the work of Guglielmo. One of Guglielmo's marked peculiarities is the habit of representing his figures in full face, but showing the feet in profile. Now the sculptures at Notre-Dame-la-Grande of Poitiers show this same mannerism, for example, in the handmaiden to the right of the Visitation (Ill. 960). The Joseph of Notre-Dame is remarkably similar to the *Elijah* of Guglielmo at Modena.[1] The Poitiers Temptation (Ill. 957) is not without resemblances to Guglielmo's rendering of the same theme at Modena and Cremona. Moreover, the arched corbel-tables of the façade of Notre-Dame-la-Grande and much of the decoration are strongly reminiscent of Lombardic models. Our artist seems to have known Souillac also; his wrestlers (Ill. 962) are a weak echo of those on the sculptured column (Ill. 350), and recall the similar

[1] This figure should be compared with a Byzantine ivory casket of the IX century, in the Museo Kirchiano at Rome, illustrated by Graeven, II, 58.

motive sculptured on the portal of the cathedral of Trani in Apulia (Ill. 206).

The Visitation (Ill. 960) of the second sculptor is close to the Temptation of Christ in the Puerta de las Platerias (Ill. 678). The embroidered borders of the draperies are indicated by perforations — the earliest completely developed example I know of a feature later so popular, and which is only foreshadowed at St.-Jouin-de-Marne (Ill. 949).

The composition of the *Majestas Domini* in the upper gable (Ill. 951) looks as if it might have been inspired by a seal.[1]

The portal at La Lande de Fronzac (Ill. 916, 917) seems to have been inspired by an ivory casket like the one of 1005 preserved in the cathedral of Pamplona.[2] The eyes are executed according to the same convention;[3] the draperies are similarly rendered, there are the same stiff skirts, the same stocky figures, the same relief in two planes, the same angularity of drawing. Most striking of all, the decorative interlace of the guilloche of the box is reproduced on the inner archivolt of the portal.

The style is crude and barbarous, but perhaps not as primitive as it appears. The sleeves of the principal figure already tend to trail, a characteristic which we have seen appear at Angoulême only in the 20's.[4] However, our doorway can hardly be as late as that.

A striking feature of La Lande de Fronzac is the proto-voussure sculptures,[5] forming an evident link between the Burgundian type, such as we have it in the portal of Cluny or at Calvenzano and the developed motive as we have seen it at Angoulême (Ill. 929) in 1128. La Lande de Fronzac evidently falls at an early stage of this evolu-

---

[1] I owe this suggestion to Mr. Berenson.

[2] This analogy was called to my attention by Mr. Breck.

[3] See the Mas photograph, no. C 15164.

[4] This motive was especially popular in France from 1120–1150, but was certainly known at an earlier date. Since, as we have already remarked (see above, p. 315), it is common in Far Eastern art, it is indeed probably of very ancient origin. It is found in the ivory box of Pamplona of 1005; in the sculptures of 1060 from the Mauritzkirche, now in the Westfälischen Landesmuseum at Münster; and in the pier sculptures of the Moissac cloisters of 1100 (Ill. 269).

[5] Proto-voussure sculptures are also found at Grossenlinden.

tion. Moreover, the iconography, taken from the first chapter of the Apocalypse, is unusual. We should hardly find this particular subject after the stock Burgundian themes had been elaborated. I am therefore inclined to believe that this portal dates from the first decade of the XII century.

We are confirmed in this dating by observing that the style of the sculptures at La Lande de Fronzac seems analogous to that of one of the capitals (Ill. 913) of St.-Hilaire-le-Grand of Poitiers. The facial types are very similar, and so are the short stocky skirts. This capital assuredly belongs to the works executed when the wooden roof of the church was replaced by a vault; a document of 1130 mentions that this alteration had been made within the memory of those until recently living, hence at the end of the XI century.[1] Contemporary capitals at St.-Hilaire (Ill. 915) are of a different style, and indeed recall rather the monuments of the Velay. In fact, close connections existed between the collegiate church of St.-Hilaire and Le Puy, where the canons had retired when forced into exile in the IX century.

An unexpected connection of the master of the tympanum of La Lande de Fronzac (Ill. 917) is with a capital at Anzy-le-Duc in Burgundy (Ill. 17). This capital falls as completely out of the Burgundian tradition, as it is obviously closely related to the style of the tympanum at La Lande de Fronzac. It must be the work of a sculptor of the West who wandered to Burgundy, and unless I mistake, of the very master of the Lande de Fronzac tympanum. From this relationship we can draw another confirmation of our dating of the Lande de Fronzac sculptures. On the nave of Anzy-le-Duc there worked also a Burgundian master who executed a peculiar capital (Ill. 21). Now this same hand reappears at St.-Parize-le-Châtel (Ill. 25), a monument which is dated 1113.

The influence of Moorish ivories upon Romanesque sculpture is not an isolated phenomenon which occurs only at La Lande de Fronzac. The same source of inspiration lies at the base of much of

[1] Mortet, 142.

the decorative ornament of the school of the West of the XII century. A common origin in Moorish ivories explains analogies between works of sculpture widely separated geographically. Thus the two pulpits by Nicodemo in the Abruzzi, one at Moscufo, dated 1159 (Ill. 180), and the other, an extraordinarily exact duplicate, at Cugnoli, dated 1166,[1] are not really influenced by the school of the West, but the resemblance to this work is due to the fact that they are copied from originals similar to those imitated in the West. The analogy of the facial types at La Lande de Fronzac (Ill. 917) with those of the "Tomba de Rotari" at Monte S. Angelo (Ill. 197, 198) might be explained in the same way; but at Monte S. Angelo the draperies have a distinctly Western character which gives reason to believe that we have here direct influence.

The façade of Ste.-Marie-des-Dames at Saintes (Ill. 974–976) dates from two distinct periods. The upper story is analogous in style to the western portal of St.-Amand-de-Boixe (Ill. 1135); it must therefore have been erected in the second half of the XII century. The lower story is obviously more archaic. It seems like a direct development from La Lande de Fronzac with the influence of Moorish ivories still predominating in the ornament. However, if this church owed much to Spain, it also gave much. We have here one of the earliest examples of voussure sculptures (Ill. 974) as well as of rows of figures placed parallel to the radii of the portal (Ill. 975, 976). The latter motive was taken over by the Spanish sculptors at Toro (Ill. 734), in both churches at Carrión de los Condes (Ill. 773), at Sepúlveda (Ill. 802), at Soria (Ill. 795) and in the Pórtico de la Gloria at Santiago (Ill. 824–828). This interchange of influences between Saintes and Spain is easily explained by the position of the former on the road of St. James.

In the luxuriant barbarity of its decoration, as well as in individual motives, the portal of Ste.-Marie-des-Dames (Ill. 974–976) resem-

---

[1] Illustrated by Poggi, 74.
Nicodemo worked also at S. Maria in Valle Porclaneta in collaboration with Roberto. See Bertaux, *Ital. Mér.*, 562.

bles S. Michele of Pavia. Its wildness suggests a date within the first quarter of the XII century; it will be recalled that at Angoulême refinement and delicacy had begun to supplant the earlier more savage manner before 1128. The voussures of Angoulême are distinctly more developed than those of Ste.-Marie. It is therefore probable that the portal of Ste.-Marie dates from not later than 1125.

The church of Aulnay (Ill. 979–986) is situated some distance from the village, and on the pilgrimage road. We may, indeed, recognize in the architecture and sculpture a pilgrimage character, not only in the extraordinary sumptuousness of the decoration, but in the influences to and from Spain. The inspiration of Moorish ivories is still patent in the facial types of the transept portal (Ill. 979) and in the ornament, even in the elephants sculptured on one of the capitals. Pilgrimage character is also evident in the building in other foreign influences: the arched corbel-tables and much of the ornament is Lombard; and the sculpture, especially of the façade, shows Burgundian tendencies.

It is evident that the portal of the transept (Ill. 979) is earlier than the façade (Ill. 983–986). The transept doorway (Ill. 979) is indeed the *nec plus ultra* of the line of development we have been following out. More exquisite drollery than that of the outer voussures has rarely been attained. Grotesque art can go no farther.

A comparison of the transept portal of Aulnay (Ill. 979) with that of Ste.-Marie-des-Dames (Ill. 974–976) shows how greatly superior was the Aulnay sculptor. He has suppressed the numerous small members, the confusion of detail which make the work of his predecessor restless and confusing. He has made his orders all rectangular, his voussure sculptures all of the radiating type. In short, there is in his work a sense of order, of subordination of the details to the whole, which is characteristic of the second rather than the first quarter of the XII century. In detail his figures are better executed and more advanced in character than those of Saintes. Although far from being as fine as the later work at Angoulême, they may none the less be contemporary; the master of Aulnay was essentially a dec-

orator rather than a figure-carver. His portal may be assigned to
c. 1130.

The western portal of Loches (Ill. 1111–1119) is clearly related to
the transept portal of Aulnay. It is, perhaps, the work of a sculptor
trained in the Saintonge school of the 30's who a score of years later
still repeated a formula by that time entirely *démodé*. In the outer
voussure (Ill. 1116), however, he shows himself conscious of the new
movements — the figures here are quite Chartrain in character. The
fragments of sculpture enwalled above the portal are certainly not in
the position for which they were carved; probably as in Spain they
were sculptured some time before the church was actually built, and
when the construction came to be carried out they were not set up as
originally intended. At all events four of the figures (Ill. 1115, 1117)
are adossed on colonnettes, which must have been intended to stand
free. The position of the Virgin holding the Child in the frontal position recalls Chartres; but the subject, — the Adoration of the Magi,
— the canopy over St. Joseph (Ill. 1113) and the folds of the drapery
which covers the bed of the Magi (Ill. 1114) must be derived from
Beaucaire (Ill. 1299).

A more interesting sculptor executed, doubtless somewhat earlier,
two consoles in the church (Ill. 1108–1110). The same hand reappears in the capitals of L'Ile-Bouchard (Ill. 1100–1107) and in the
zodiac of Aubeterre (Ill. 1098, 1099). Among the Romanesque sculptors of France known to me, there is none so strongly Guglielmo-
esque in character. This artist must assuredly have been formed
in Lombardy. He uses Guglielmo's faces, Guglielmo's draperies,
Guglielmo's proportions, Guglielmo's beards, and most striking of all
his spirit is Guglielmo's. But although he imitates so assiduously the
manner of the early years of the XII century, our artist obviously
worked at a later time. This is evident not only from the character
of the architecture at Loches and at L'Ile-Bouchard, but also in certain details of his style. His garments have the ornamented borders
which hardly came into general use before 1135; the composition of
his capital with the Last Supper at L'Ile-Bouchard (Ill. 1104) is like

that of the capital of the same subject at Issoire (Ill. 1214), with the table forming a skirt cutting the bell of the capital into two parts; his Visitation at L'Ile-Bouchard (Ill. 1101) recalls the composition of Nicolò at Ferrara; the architecture of his gates of Paradise (Ill. 1106) at L'Ile-Bouchard is advanced in style. The activity of our master must be placed in the 40's and 50's. A comparison of his style, with that of the Chadennac master (Ill. 1034–1040) who worked contemporaneously in the same region, is eloquent proof of the freedom and individuality of Romanesque sculptors.

Returning to Aulnay, we notice that the pointed window above the transept portal, with the superb psychomachia sculptured upon the voussures (Ill. 980), seems to be contemporary with the portal, or nearly so, but is of a very different style.

A different and later art, on the other hand, appears in the western façade (Ill. 983–986). Burgundian influence is evident in the flat folds of the draperies, in the elongated proportions, in the sweeping contours. Calligraphic line is indeed here, as frequently in the Burgundy-izing work in the West, carried to a sugary extreme which the wiser artists in the land of its origin were clever enough to avoid. In Burgundy I know of nothing quite so obviously graceful as the Foolish Virgins of Aulnay (Ill. 985). The spirit of this work has evidently much in common with Chadennac (Ill. 1034–1040) — 1140 — with which it must be about contemporary.

The same hand which executed the western portal at Aulnay (Ill. 983–986) reappears at Argenton-Château (Ill. 987–996). Fenioux (Ill. 997–998) is also so closely related that I am inclined to think the three monuments all the work of the same sculptor. The portal at St.-Pompain (Ill. 1058) signed by Guillaume (GIEGLELM) is also close to this group, but I think Guillaume is an imitator, not to be identified with the finer sculptor of Aulnay and Argenton-Château.

The west façade of Aulnay was imitated at Pont-l'Abbé-d'Arnoult (Ill. 1003–1005). Not only was the composition of the tympanum of the side lunette representing the Crucifixion of St. Peter (Ill. 1005) repeated in a form that is singularly reminiscent of Aulnay

(Ill. 983), but the arrangement of the subjects, and the general scheme of the two central portals is very much alike (Ill. 984 and Ill. 1004).

Two distinct hands may be distinguished in the sculptures of Notre-Dame-de-la-Couldre of Parthenay. To the one belong the sculptures still in place on the ruins of the façade of the church (Ill. 1047–1052); to the other the two capitals now enwalled in the gate of the neighbouring school (Ill. 1045, 1046) and the six reliefs now divided between the Louvre (Ill. 1053–1057) and the collection of Mrs. Gardner. The distinction of style is so sharp that it is natural to suppose that it corresponds with a difference in date; yet there can be no great interval of time between the two groups.

The reliefs from the Louvre and at Mrs. Gardner's can only be a small part of the sculptures which once existed on the upper part of the façade. This must have been, indeed, one of the most lavishly decorated monuments in France. And what is singular is that the simple and rather commonplace lower part of the façade which still survives gives no hint of the splendour of the destroyed upper portions.

These facts can, I think, be best explained by reference to the historical events of the time. It is in fact known that in 1135 a church of Parthenay, which is traditionally identified as Notre-Dame-de-la-Couldre, was the scene of a celebrated event. St. Bernard at the portal completely and almost miraculously converted the stubborn and recalcitrant duke of Aquitaine, Guillaume IX. We may suppose that the lower part of the façade had been finished just before this dramatic scene; and that the upper part was added immediately afterwards to commemorate the occurrence, and possibly at the expense of the duke.

However this may be, it is certain that the later sculptures must have been executed about 1140. The style is exceedingly close to that of Chadenac (Ill. 1034–1040); so close, in fact, that I almost suspect that they may be by the very hand of that artist. If so, they are earlier, for they distinctly fall away from Blazimont (Ill. 1041-

1044). At any event, the head of Mrs. Gardner's elder with the goatee beard is very like the head of the Gilbertian prophet at Chadennac (Ill. 1035); the draperies on the upper part of the body of the Louvre elder with the bag-pipe (Ill. 1057) are precisely like those of the corresponding portions of the Virtue at Blazimont (Ill. 1042); the naturalistic sheep of the Louvre relief (Ill. 1054) make us think of the animals of Chadennac (Ill. 1036–1040) and Blazimont (Ill. 1041–1044); the fluttering draperies of the Parthenay elders (Ill. 1057) recall those of the angel on the column at Chadennac (Ill. 1039).

Whether or not this identification of hands be accepted, it is certain that the later work is exceedingly close to Chadennac, and not much later than Chadennac, and Chadennac is a dated monument of 1140.

Furthermore the second atelier at Parthenay is very closely connected with the later work on the Moissac porch. If we compare the Abraham of the Parthenay capital (Ill. 1046) with the Simeon of the Moissac Presentation (Ill. 372), we shall be convinced of the very close relationship between the two. The eyes, the shape of the head, the beard, the draperies are all similar. We feel that the Parthenay work can not be very much later. Now the adjustment work on the Moissac porch we have seen is probably not later than 1130. This, again, would lead us to place the Parthenay sculptures in the fourth decade of the XII century.

On the other hand, the Parthenay elders show obvious relationship with those of Chartres. The vase held by Mrs. Gardner's left-hand elder [1] is of exactly the same form as the vases held by the two elders in the lowest voussures at Chartres.[2] The Parthenay elder holds the end of his long trailing sleeve to veil his hand, precisely as does the elder to the right at Chartres. The similarity in the folds of the two sleeves is unmistakable.[3] On the other hand, it is certain that the Parthenay elder is not copied from Chartres. The Parthe-

---

[1] Photographs of Mrs. Gardner's elders may be obtained from Thomas E. Marr and Son, 180 Tremont Street, Boston, Mass.

[2] Illustrated by Houvet, 50.

[3] This comparison was first suggested to me by Mr. C. S. Niver.

nay work shows no trace of the Chartrain draperies and other mannerisms; the resemblance between the two figures is only general.
The head master of Chartres was inspired by these originals, but he
did not slavishly reproduce them. The Parthenay work is obviously
more archaic, more primitive. Since Chartres was begun before 1145,
and Parthenay is earlier, we are brought again to the date 1140 for
Parthenay.

The shape and size of the relief of the Shepherds (Ill. 1053) shows
that it must originally have formed part of a frieze, such as still
exists, although no longer in its original position, in the not very distant church of Montmorillon (Ill. 1072 a, 1073). Such friezes were in
fashion about 1140; we have seen that they were introduced at Beaucaire (Ill. 1292–1298), St.-Gilles (Ill. 1315–1322), St.-Trophîme of
Arles (Ill. 1375, 1377), Dax (Ill. 327–332), Selles-sur-Cher (Ill.
1078–1082), St.-Paul-de-Varax (Ill. 86–90), Carrión de los Condes
(Ill. 722–726), Moarves (Ill. 729), Nîmes (Ill. 1378, 1379), Ripoll
(Ill. 560). Friezes are also found at Modena and Cremona in Italy
and St. Jacob of Regensburg in Germany. Like the Montmorillon
frieze (Ill. 1072 a, 1073), that of Parthenay doubtless represented a
cycle of scenes dealing with the story of the nativity of Christ. Mrs.
Gardner's rider is shown by its height and shape to have belonged to
this frieze. The subject of the relief has been called the Entry into
Jerusalem, but this identification is doubtful. The Entry into Jerusalem could hardly have formed part of the same cycle of reliefs with
the Shepherds. It is much more likely that we should have had some
scene connected with the Nativity. Moreover, the figure seated
upon the female animal — whether it is a horse or donkey is not entirely clear — is crowned; Christ is never represented crowned in the
Entry into Jerusalem. It is far more probable that the relief is a
fragment from the scene of the Journey of the Magi; the broken
object which the king carried in his left hand was possibly a gift, although this naturalistic sculptor may have represented there a tree,
like the one he has put in front of the animal's head. The fatigue of
the animal after the long journey is admirably rendered.

The work at Foussais (Ill. 1061–1063) is interesting, not only because of its own intrinsic qualities, but because the northern lunette (Ill. 1061) is signed by a certain . . . RAVDVS AVDEBERTVS (= Giraud Audebert) of St.-Jean-d'Angély. This sculptor seems to have been called in to supply the plastic decoration for the two lunettes, representing the Feast in the House of Simon, the *Noli me Tangere* and the Deposition. The central portal with radiating voussures (Ill. 1062) is by a coarser hand. The analogies of Giraud Audebert's work (Ill. 1061–1063) with Chartres are striking. The aedicule separating the two reliefs in the south lunette is precisely similar to the aedicules over the capitals and above the statues at Chartres. The folds of the table-cloth and of the draperies below it are like those of the figures in the central tympanum at Chartres, although somewhat coarser. The horizontal banding on the dresses, on the other hand, seems derived from the tympanum of Autun (Ill. 80, 81). Something in the disjointedness of the anatomy, the wattling of the sleeves and certain draperies seems to foreshadow the later work at La Daurade of Toulouse (Ill. 474–479). The "ribbed" draperies are like those of St.-Antonin (Ill. 359).

A much more unexpected analogy is with the capitals from St.-Pons (Ill. 1265, 1266) now in the Fogg Museum. Not only is the composition of the two representations of the Feast in the House of Simon strangely similar, but the figure to the left in the Foussais relief (Ill. 1061) has the same hair convention as the three figures in the St.-Pons Journey to Emmaus; the head has the same top-heavy proportions. The draperies of the body of the figure to the extreme right in the St.-Pons Journey to Emmaus are formed by parallel bands, separated by raised rolls bounded by sharply incised lines. The same peculiar convention occurs at Foussais, in the figure to the extreme right of the Feast at the House of Simon. It is, indeed, characteristic both of Foussais, and of one of the sculptors of St.-Pons. The skirts of the figure to the extreme right in the St.-Pons Journey to Emmaus are exactly the same as those of the Moon in the Foussais Crucifixion (Ill. 1061).

The explanation of these similarities may give rise to difference of opinion. We have seen that similar marked analogies, combined with strong differences, occur not infrequently between widely separated monuments of Romanesque sculpture. It is my hypothesis that Romanesque sculptors underwent swift changes of style as they fell under successive influences, or worked with different colleagues; and that the analogies are due to identity of hand. I should not dare to say that the points of resemblance between Foussais and St.-Pons are numerous enough, or striking enough, to prove that the Fogg capital is by Giraud Audebert. I confess, however, to a suspicion that such may have been the case. What is certain is that the St.-Pons capital representing the Feast in the House of Simon (Ill. 1266) belongs neither to the school of Arles, as Prof. Vöge would have it, nor to that of Toulouse, as M. André Michel claimed, but to that of the West. In view of the geographical position of St.-Pons the fact is strange.

We have already remarked that the St.-Pons capitals are not all by the same sculptor. In the capital of the Journey to Emmaus (Ill. 1265) we have unmixed the hand which I am tempted to identify with that of Giraud Audebert. The capital representing the Feast in the House of Simon is suaver in style, although the scene in the kitchen (Ill. 1266) still retains many technical tricks of the first sculptor, and the composition of the feast repeats, as we have remarked, that of Foussais. I think we have here probably the Giraud-Audebert-esque artist working in collaboration with another sculptor, who worked alone in the capital now in the Boston Museum (Ill. 1267). This second hand has a strangely Gothic character — his facial types and draperies recall the south portal of Chartres. Possibly he finished, long after, a capital which had been blocked out by the Giraud-Audebert-esque sculptor. The manner of this second master shows that he also came from the West. His style, in fact, is close to that of the master who executed the apostles from St.-Benoît now in the Poitiers museum. If, for example, we compare the folds between the legs of Christ in the Fogg Museum capital representing

Christ in the house of Mary and Martha with those between the legs of the apostle to the right in the Poitiers fragment shown in Ill. 1133, we notice a certain similarity. The folds across the chest of the seated male figure in the capital of the Boston Museum are made with the same modification of the Giraud Audebert mannerism which we find in the apostle in the middle of the same fragment at Poitiers (Ill. 1133). The spirit of the draperies is similar in the two works. The Giraud-Audebert-esque sculptor had already introduced draperies of similar broad character in the Christ of his Crucifixion at Foussais (Ill. 1061).

A third hand may be distinguished in the Fogg capital representing the *Majestas Domini* and twelve apostles (Ill. 1270), and in the two capitals now in the University of Montpellier (Ill. 1268, 1269). This master makes use of draperies of the Giraud Audebert type; his faces are executed with extraordinary delicacy; he seems to fall between the two hands we have already distinguished.

How to account for the co-operation of these widely different hands upon the same capitals I hardly know. The old theory, to which I myself have subscribed, that the St.-Pons capitals are the work of an atelier the activity of which continued during a considerable period, with a gradual development of style, leaves the close inter-relationship of the sculptors unaccounted for. On the other hand I now find it hard to believe that men so divergent in style should have worked at the same time. In any event probably none of the work of this second atelier is earlier than the sack of the monastery in 1170.[1]

If Giraud Audebert worked at St.-Pons in 1170, it is not absolutely impossible that he might have executed his Foussais sculptures before Chartres was begun in 1145. It is difficult to suppose that he could have known the sculpture of Chartres, and picked up from it only insignificant details.

The portal at Cognac (Ill. 1096) has certain heads which recall vividly the style of Giraud Audebert. In other particulars, however,

[1] Sahuc, 13.

the manner is notably different from his. The poppy eyes of some figures recall the sculptor of Selles-sur-Cher (Ill. 1074–1081).

While it is evident that the head master of Chartres was chiefly formed at St.-Denis, it is also clear that he owes much to the West. Numerous anticipations of his style in this region have already been remarked. His voussure sculptures surely come from the West directly, and probably from the Chadennac (Ill. 1034–1040) master, rather than via St.-Denis (Ill. 1437–1457). His elders, we have seen,. his facial types, his gravity, are inspired by Parthenay (Ill. 1045–1057). From Montmorillon (Ill. 1072 a, 1073), one of the finest monuments in the West, came, not only as we have already seen[1] the composition of the lintels of the southern portal at Chartres, but much of the head master's drapery. Moreover, the mixture of Burgundian and Spanish-Aquitanian mannerisms, so noticeable in the style of the head master, is a characteristic of this school. Only here could the sculptors of Chartres have found that blending of grace and dignity, of delicacy and strength, which they carried to such perfection.

A confirmation of the debt of the sculptor of Chartres to the West is afforded by the arched corbel-tables which he introduces so unexpectedly in the right-hand tympanum. The arched corbel-table is notoriously a Lombard motive, and nothing could be more surprising than to find it here. Are we to suppose that the master of Chartres had studied Guglielmo's frieze at Modena? It is not probable. In fact, we have seen that the school of the West fell strongly under Lombard influence, and among the motives taken over was precisely the arched corbel-table. Now the arched corbel-tables of Chartres are not of purely Lombardic, but of Western, type (compare the portal of Montbron).

It seems to be a curious fact that the influence of Chartres, which spread so rapidly over the Ile-de-France, and reached remote regions of Spain, never deeply affected the art of the West. I do not know in that region a single instance of jamb sculptures, nor (except Cham-

[1] See above, p. 125 f.

pniers) of a tympanum with the Apocalyptic vision [1] anterior to the introduction of the Gothic style in the west façade of the cathedral of Angers (Ill. 1501–1503).

When the influence of Chartres does appear in the West the style was already in full decadence.[2] This is the case at Civray where

[1] The tympanum at Civray is modern.
The portal of Rochester in England shows interesting relationship with the school of the West. The jamb sculptures seem to have been set in at a later date; the tympanum reproduces the composition of Cluny, but the style comes closer to Angoulême or Notre-Dame-la-Grande of Poitiers. Owing to the erroneous dating of the latter to *c.* 1180 the tympanum at Rochester has been assigned to 1178 (Prior and Gardner, 198); but it would be astonishing if it is really so late.

[2] No region of Europe is as rich in monuments of Romanesque sculpture as the west of France. The limits of the reader's already I fear sorely over-tried patience forbid that I should here undertake a separate study of each one. Besides, the illustrations in the atlas will give a far better idea of their beauty and interest than I could hope to convey by description. I shall therefore content myself with a chronological table of those of which I have not already spoken.

The *terminus ante quem* for this group of monuments is the year 1166, when the cathedral of Poitiers was begun, and introduced the Plantagenet Gothic style into the region. The dating of the sculpture can be confirmed by a study of the architecture. This, unfortunately, has never been systematically undertaken, yet I note with satisfaction that the few dates assigned by the Congrès Archéologique (*passim*) on the basis of the architecture, correspond in general with those at which I have arrived solely through the study of the sculpture.

Here then are the dates which seem to me probable:

c. 1115. St.-Symphorien, portal (Ill. 919); upper sculptures, *c.* 1135 (Ill. 1007).
c. 1120. St.-Maixent. Relief of a saint with crozier under an arch, now in Musée des Antiquaires de l'Ouest, Poitiers.
c. 1120. Parthenay-le-Vieux (Ill. 924, 925).
c. 1120. Ste.-Croix of Bordeaux (Ill. 920–921).
c. 1125. Châteauneuf-sur-Charente, portal (Ill. 973) — compare Fontaine d'Ozillac. Ill. 978 —; upper sculptures, *c.* 1135 (Ill. 1008–1010).
c. 1130. Fontaines d'Ozillac (Ill. 977, 978).
c. 1130. Maillezais (Ill. 963).
c. 1130. Castelvieil (Ill. 926–928).
c. 1135. Pérignac (Ill. 1018–1024).
c. 1135. Echillais.
c. 1135. Melle, St.-Hilaire (Ill. 1011).
c. 1135. Corme Royal (Ill. 1012–1017).
c. 1140. Matha (Ill. 1031–1033).
c. 1140. Montmorillon, Octagone (Ill. 1030).
c. 1140. Ruffec (Ill. 1025–1029).
c. 1140. Melle, St.-Pierre (Ill. 1090, 1091).
c. 1140. Thouars, St.-Médard, sculptures restored (Ill. 1059, 1060).
c. 1140. Trois Palis (Ill. 1064).
c. 1145. St.-Aubin of Angers, cloister (Ill. 1069, 1070).
c. 1150. Surgères (Ill. 1092, 1093).
c. 1150. Poitiers, St.-Hilaire-de-la-Celle, tombeau de St. Hilaire (Ill. 1134).
c. 1150. La Villedieu (Ill. 1120, 1121).
c. 1150. St.-Saturnin (Ill. 1071, 1072).

adossed statues flanking the shafts of the façade (Ill. 1122, 1123, 1125) are introduced. This is a development of the motive in the nave of Airvault (Ill. 898–900) which had opened the cycle of sculpture in the West; it had once before been tried on a façade at Chalais (Ill. 1087).

c. 1160.   Gensac-la-Pallue (Ill. 1094, 1095).
c. 1165.   Civray (Ill. 1122–1131).
c. 1170.   Vouvant (Ill. 1136).
c. 1175.   Crouzilles (Ill. 1137).

LIST OF BOOKS REFERRED TO

ABBATE, Enrico. *Guida dell' Abruzzo.* Roma, Club Alpino Italiano, Sezione di Roma, 1903. 2 vols. 120.

Album des monuments et de l'art ancien du midi de la France. Toulouse, 1897. 4to.

ALLMER, A. et TERREBASSE, Alfred de. *Inscriptions antiques et du moyen âge de Vienne en Dauphiné.* Vienne, Girard, 1875. 7 vols. 8vo.

ANONYMOUS. *Description de la basilique Saint-Remi à Reims à l'usage des visiteurs.* Reims, Monce, s. d.

Latin Psalter in the University Library of Utrecht. London, Spencer, Sawyer, Bird and Co., s. d., Folio.

AUBENAS, J.-A. *Histoire de Fréjus.* Fréjus, Leydet, 1881. 8vo.

AUBERT, Marcel. *L'église abbatiale de Selles-sur-Cher.* (Bulletin Monumental, 1913, LXXVII, 387.)

AZNAR, F. y R. *España, detallés arquitectonicos de sus principales monumentos.* Madrid, Fuencarral, 1902. 4to.

BAILLET, Dom Louis. *Les Miniatures du "Scivias" de sainte Hildegarde.* (Fondation Piot, 1911, XIX, 49.)

BALUZE, Etienne (Stephanus Baluzius). *Miscellaneorum libri septem.* Parisiis, Muguet, 1700. 3 vols. 120.

BARRET, P. *Le tympan de l'ancienne église romane d'Issy.* (Bulletin Monumental, 1902, LXVI, 296.)

BAUER, Adolf und STRZYGOWSKI, Josef. *Eine Alexandrinische Weltchronik.* (Denkschriften des kaiserlichen Akademie der Wissenschaften. Philosophisch-Historische Klasse, L, 1904, II, 1.)

BAUM, Julius. *Romanische Baukunst in Frankreich.* Stuttgart, Hoffmann, 1910. 4to. English edition under title: *Romanesque architecture in France.* London, Heinemann, 1912. 4to.

BAYET, Charles. *Recherches pour servir à l'histoire de la peinture et de la sculpture chrétiennes en Orient avant la querelle des Iconoclastes.* Paris, Thorin, 1879. 8vo.

BÉDIER, Joseph. *Les légendes épiques.* Paris, Champion, 1913. 4 vols. 8vo.

BEDIN, P. *Saint Bertrand, évêque de Comminges.* Toulouse, Privat, 1912. 120.

BÉGULE, Lucien. *L'église Saint-Maurice, ancienne cathédrale de Vienne.* Paris, Laurens, 1914. 4to.

BERCHEM, Max van; STRZYGOWSKI, Josef. *Amida.* Heidelberg, Carl Winter, 1910. 4to.

BERNOUILLI, Rudolf. *Die romanische Portalarchitektur in der Provence.* Strassburg, Heitz, 1906. 4to.

BERTAUX, Emile. *Exposicion retrospectiva de arte.* Zaragoza, La Editorial, 1908. 4to.

L'art dans l'Italie méridionale. Paris, Fontemoing, 1904. 4to.

L'émail de Saint-Nicolas de Bari. (Fondation Piot, 1899, VI, 61.)

BERTONI, Giulio. *Atlante storico-artistico del duomo di Modena.* Modena, Orlandini, 1912. 8vo.

BILSON, John. *Les origines de l'architecture gothique*. (Revue de l'art chrétien, 1901, XLIV, 365, 463; 1902, XLV, 213.)

BOINET, Amédée. *La miniature carolingienne*. Paris, Picard, 1913. Folio.

BOND, E. A. and THOMPSON, E. M. *The Palaeographical Society facsimiles of manuscripts and insciptions*. London, 1873–1894. 4 vols. Folio.

BONNAY, Louis. *Description des découvertes archéologiques faites à l'église Saint-Martin de Brive*. (Bulletin de la Société Scientifique, Historique et Archéologique de la Corrèze, 1878, I, 233.)

BOUILLART, Dom Jacques. *Histoire de l'abbaye royale de Saint Germain des Prez*. Paris, Dupuis, 1724. Folio.

BOUILLET, A. *L'église et le trésor de Conques*. Rodez, Carrère, 1914. 120.

BOUILLET, A. et SERVIERES, L. *Sainte Foy vierge et martyre*. Rodez, Carrère, 1900. 4to.

BOYER, Victor. *La cité de Carcassonne*. Paris, Chamerot, 1884. 120.

BRECK, Joseph. *Spanish ivories in the Morgan Collection*. (American Journal of Archaeology, 1920, XXIV, 217.)

BRÉHIER, Louis. *L'art chrétien*. Paris, Renouard, 1918. 4to.

Les miniatures des homélies du moine Jacques et le théâtre religieux à Byzance. (Monuments Piot, 1920, XXIV, 101.)

Les origines de l'art roman. (Revue de l'art ancien et moderne, 1920, XXXVIII, 129, 231, 263.)

BROCHE, Lucien. *La date de la chapelle de l'évêché de Laon*. Caen, Delesques, 1903, 8vo. (Extrait du Bulletin monumental, 1902.)

L'église de Presles. Caen, Delesques, 1905. 8yo. (Extrait du Bulletin monumental, 1904.)

BRUEL, Alexandre. *Receuil des chartes de l'abbaye de Cluny par August Bernard*. Paris, Imprimerie Nationale, 1876–1903. 6 vols. 4to. (Documents inédits sur l'histoire de France.)

BRUTAILS, Jean-Auguste. *Les vielles églises de la Gironde*. Bordeaux, Feret et Fils, 1912. 4to.

Notes sobre l'art religiós en el Rosselló. Barcelona, Tip. l'Avenç, 1901. 8vo.

BUBERL, Paul. *Die illuminierten Handschriften in Steiermark*. 1 Teil. Leipzig, Hiersemann, 1911. Folio.

Bullarium sacri ordinis Cluniacensis. Lugduni, Antonii Jullieron, 1680. Folio.

Burlington Fine Arts Club, London. *Exhibition of illuminated manuscripts*. London, Burlington Fine Arts Club, 1908. Folio.

BUSCHBEK, Ernst H. *Der Pórtico de la Gloria*. Berlin, Bard, 1919. 8vo.

CAMERA, Matteo. *Memorie storico-diplomatiche dell' antica città e ducato di Amalfi*. Salerno, Tipografico Nazionale, 1876–1881. 2 vols. 8vo.

Catalogue du Musée de la Commission des Antiquités du Département de la Côte-d'Or. Dijon, Lamarche, 1894. Folio.

CHALVET DE ROCHEMONTEIX, Ad. de. *Les églises romanes de la haute Auvergne*. Paris, Picard, 1902. 4to.

CHARLES-ROUX, J. *Fréjus*. Paris, Blond, 1909. 120.

Saint-Gilles. Paris, Lemerre, 1910. 4to.

CHENEVARD, A. *L'ancien Bourbonnais, histoire, monumens, mœurs*. Par Achille Allier continué par A. Michel et L. Batissier . . . sous la direction d'A. Chenavard. Moulins, Desrosiers, 1838. 3 vols. Folio.

CHÉREST. *Les documents écrits ne constatent-ils pas l'introduction du style ogival à l'église de Vézelay dès la première moitié du XII siècle?* (Congrès Scientifique de France, 1858, XV, 2, 191.)

CHIFFLET. *Histoire de l'abbaye royale de la ville de Tournus.* Dijon, 1664. 4to.

CHOMTON, Abbé L. *Histoire de l'église Saint-Bénigne de Dijon.* Dijon, Jobard, 1900. Folio.

CLEMEN, Paul. *Die romanische Monumentalmalerei in den Rheinlanden.* Düsseldorf, Schwann, 1916. 4to.

CLERMONT-GANNEAU, Charles. *Horus et Saint Georges.* (Revue archéologique, 1876, XXXVI, 196, 372.)

Codice diplomatico barese. Bari, Vecchi, 1897–1914. 8 vols. 4to.

CONGRÉS ARCHÉOLOGIQUE DE FRANCE. Paris, Picard, 1833 seq. 82 vols. 8vo.

CREUTZ, M. *Die Anfänge des monumentalen Stiles in Norddeutschland.* Köln, Dumont-Schauberg, 1910. 8vo.

CROZES, Hippolyte. *Travaux de restauration et d'achèvement de la cathédrale de Sainte-Cécile d'Albi.* Paris, Victor Didron, 1861. Pamphlet.

DALTON, O. M. *Catalogue of the ivory carvings of the British Museum.* London, Longmans, 1919. 4to.

DANGIBEAUD, Charles. *L'école de sculpture romane saintongeaise.* Paris, Imprimerie Nationale, 1910. 8vo. (Extrait du Bulletin archéologique, 1910.)

DEBENGA, Alvaro. *Los marfiles de San Millán de la Cogolla.* (Arte Español, 1916, V, 243, 296, 328.)

DÉCHELETTE, Joseph. *Guide des monuments d'Autun.* Paris, Picard, 1909. 8vo.

DEHIO, Georg. *Geschichte der deutschen Kunst.* Berlin und Leipzig, de Gruyter, 1921. 2 vols. 4to.

DEHIO, Georg und von BEZOLD, Gust. *Die Denkmäler der deutschen Bildhauerkunst.* Berlin, Wasmuth, s. d. 3 vols. Folio.

DELISLE, Léopold. *Vie de Gauzlin, par André de Fleury.* Orléans, Jacob, 1853. 8vo. (Extrait du tome II des Mémoires de la Société Archéologique de l'Orléanais.)

DELORT, J. *Notice sur l'église de Saint-Pierre-des-Cuisines.* (Mémoires de la Société Archéologique du Midi de la France, 2me série, XII, 1880–1882, 200.)

DEMAY, Germain. *Le costume au moyen âge d'après les sceaux.* Paris, Dumoulin, 1880. 8vo.

DEVIC, Dom Cl., et VAISETTE, Dom J. *Histoire générale de Languedoc.* Ed. Dulaurier, Mabille et Barry. Toulouse, Privat, 1852–1892. 15 vols. 4to.

DIBELIUS, Franz. *Die Bernwardstür zu Hildesheim.* Strassburg, Heitz, 1907. 8vo.

DIDRON. *Manuel d'iconographie chrétienne grecque et latine.* Paris, Imprimerie Royale, 1845. 8vo.

DIEHL, Charles. *Les mosaïques byzantines de Saint-Luc.* (Monuments Piot, 1896, III, 231.)

Manuel d'art byzantin. Paris, Picard, 1910. 8vo.

DIEHL, Charles et le TOURNEAU, M. *Les mosaïques de Saint-Démétrius de Salonique.* (Fondation Piot, 1910, XVIII, 225.)

DIEHL, Charles, le TOURNEAU, M., SALADIN, H. *Les monuments chrétiens de Salonique.* Paris, Leroux, 1918. 2 vols. Folio.

DIEULAFOY, Marcel. *La statuaire polychrome en Espagne.* Paris, Hachette, 1908. Folio.

Dorez, Léon. *Les manuscrits à peintures de la bibliothèque de Lord Leicester à Holkham Hall, Norfolk.* Paris, Leroux, 1908. Folio.

Döring, Oskar. *Der romanische Grabstein in Altenplathow.* (Zeitschrift für christliche Kunst, 1907.)

Duchesne, L., *Saint Jacques en Galice.* Toulouse, Privat, 1900. 8vo.

Dufourcet, J.-Eugène. *Les voies romaines et les chemins de Saint-Jacques dans l'ancienne Novempopulanie.* (Congrès Archéologique de France, 1888, LV, 241.)

Durand, Georges. *Eglises romanes des Voges.* Paris, Champion, 1913. 4to.

Durand, Julien. *Monuments figurés du moyen âge executés d'après des textes liturgiques.* Caen, Delesques, 1889. 8vo. (Extrait du Bulletin monumental, 1888, LIV, 521.)

Ebersolt, Jean. *Mission archéologique de Constantinople.* Paris, Leroux, 1921. 8vo.

Egidi, Pietro. *I capitelli romanici di Nazaret.* (Dedalo, 1921, I, 761.)

Escalona, Romualdo. *Historia del real monasterio de Sahagún.* Madrid, I barra, 1782. 4to.

Escher, Konrad. *Die Miniaturen in den Basler Bibliotheken, Museen und Archiven.* Basel, Spittlers, 1917. Folio.

Espitalier, l'Abbé H. *Les évêques de Fréjus.* Draguignan, 1894. Pamphlet.

Fage, René. *L'église de Luhersac (Corrèze).* (Bulletin monumental, 1912, LXXVI, 38.)

Fatigati, D., Enrique Serrano. *Escultura romanica en España.* Madrid, Sales, 1900. 4to. (Boletín de la Sociedad Española de Excursiones, 1900, VIII, 181.)

Esculturas de los siglos IX al XIII. (Boletín de la Sociedad Española de Excursiones, IX, 1901, 35, 59.)

Portadas artísticas de monumentos españoles. Madrid, Hauser y Menet, (1907). 4to.

Portadas del período románico y del de transición al ojival. (Boletín de la Sociedad Española de Excursiones, 1906, XIV, 6.)

Fayolle, Marquis de. *La basilique Saint-Front de Périgueux.* (Bulletin monumental, 1920, LXIX, 197.)

Felibien, Dom Michel. *Histoire de l'abbaye royale de St.-Denis en France.* Paris, Leonard, 1706. Folio.

Férotin, D. Marius. *Histoire de l'abbaye de Silos.* Paris, Leroux, 1897. 8vo.
Recueil des chartes de l'abbaye de Silos. Paris, Leroux, 1897. 8vo.

Ferrari, Filippo. *Santa Maria Maggiore di Guardiagrele.* Guardiagrele, Palmerio, 1905. 4to.

Fett, Harry. *Billedhuggerkunsten i Norge under Sverreaetten.* Kristiania, Cammermeyer, 1908. 4to.

Fita, F. *Le codex de Saint-Jacques-de-Compostelle.* Paris, Maisonneuve et Cie., 1882. 8vo.

Fita, P. Fidel y Fernández-Guerra, D. Aureliano. *Recuedos de un viage á Santiago de Galicia.* Madrid, Lezcano, 1880. 4to.

Fleury, Edouard. *Antiquités et monuments du département de l'Aisne.* Paris, Claye, 1877–1882. 4 vols. Folio.

Fleury, Gabriel. *Etude sur les portails imagés du XIIe siècle.* Mamers, Fleury et Dangin, 1904. 4to.

FOGOLARI, Gino. *Cividale del Friuli.* Bergamo, Istituto Italiano d'arti Grafiche, 1906. 8vo. Italia Artistica, No. 23.

FOLNESICS, Hans. *Die illuminierten Handschriften in Dalmatien.* Liepzig, Hiersemann, 1917. Folio.

Die illuminierten Handschriften im Oesterreichischen Küstenlande in Istrien und der Stadt Triest. Leipzig, Hiersemann, 1917. Folio.

FONCIN, Pierre. *Guide à la Cité de Carcassonne.* Toulouse, Privat, 1902. 12o.

FONT, François. *Histoire de l'abbaye royale de Saint-Michel de Cuxa.* Perpignan, Comet, 1881. 12o.

FONTENAY, Harold de et CHARMASSE, Anatole de. *Autun et ses monuments.* Autun, Dejussieu, 1880. 12o.

FOROT, Victor. *Catalogue raisonné des richesses monumentales et artistiques du département de la Corrèze.* Paris, Schemit, 1913. 8vo.

FROTHINGHAM, A. L. *A new Mithraic relief from Syria.* (American journal of archaeology, 1918, XXII, 54.)

FURMANKIEWICZ, Casimira. *La porte de bronze de la cathédrale de Gniezno.* (Gazette des beaux-arts, 1921, 361.)

GABELENTZ, Hans von der. *Mittelalterliche Plastik in Venedig.* Leipzig, Hiersemann. 1903. 8vo.

GALL, Ernst. *Die Apostelreliefs im Mailander Dom.* (Monatshefte für Kunstwissenschaft, 1921, XIV, 1.)

GARCÍA DE PRUNEDA, Salvador. *Cuatro iglesias románicas en la ria de Camariñas.* (Boletín de la Sociedad Española de Excursiones, 1907, XV, 156.)

GAUTHEY, J. Christophe. *Mosaïques dans les ruines de l'église prieurale de Ganagobie.* (Revue de l'art chrétien, 1898, XLI, 310.)

GEORGE, J., et GUÉRIN-BOUTAUD, Al. *Annexe de l'interprétation du monogramme de la cathédrale.* (Bulletin mensuel de la Société Archéologique et Historique de la Charente, Série VIII, No. 92, Mars, 1920, 6.)

GEROLA, Giuseppe. *An old representation of Theodoric.* (Burlington magazine, 1918, XXXII, 146.)

GIRARDIN. *Histoire de la ville et de l'église de Fréjus.* Paris, Delaulne, s. d. 12o.

GIRAUD. *Essai historique sur l'abbaye de S. Barnard et sur la ville de Romans.* Lyon, Perrin, 1856. 8vo.

GOLDSCHMIDT, Adolph. *Der Albanipsalter in Hildesheim.* Berlin, Siemens, 1895. 8vo.

Die Elfenbeinskulpturen aus der Zeit der Karolingischen und Sächsischen Kaiser. Berlin, Cassirer, 1914. 2 vols. Folio. Denkmäler der deutschen Kunst.

Die Stilentwickelung der romanischen Skulptur in Sachsen. (Jahrbuch der königlich preussischen Kunstsammlungen, 1900, XXI, 225.)

GÓMEZ-MORENO, Manuel. *Iglesias mozárabes.* Madrid, Centro de Estudios Históricos, 1919. 2 vols. 4to.

San Pedro de la Nave. (Boletín del Centro Excursionista de Zamora, Agosto-Diciembre de 1911, Año II, Número 9.)

Santa Marta de Tera. (Boletín de la Sociedad Española de Excursiones, 1908, XVI, 81.)

GRAEVEN, Hans. *Frühchristliche und mittelalterliche Elfenbeinwerke in photographischer Nachbildung.* Serie I. *Aus Sammlungen in England.* Serie II.

Aus Sammlungen in Italien. Göttingen, Archäologische Institut, 1898. 2 vols. 12o.

Die Vorlage des Utrechtpsalters. (Repertorium für Kunstwissenschaft, 1898, XXI, 28.)

GRASSET, M. *La Société Archéologique de Montpellier, ses travaux et ses collections.* Montpellier, Martel, 1882. 8vo.

GRÜNEISEN, W. de. *Les caracteristiques de l'art copte.* Florence, Alinari, 1922. 4to. *Sainte-Marie Antique.* Rome, Bretschneider, 1911. Folio.

HAMANN, Richard. *Deutsche und französische Kunst im Mittelalter.* Marburg, Kunstgeschichtliches Seminar, 1922. 4to.

HELBIG, Jules. *La sculpture et les arts plastiques au pays de Liège et sur les bords de la Meuse.* Bruges, Desclée, de Brouwer et Cie., 1890. 4to.

HERBERT, J. A. *Illuminated manuscripts.* London, Methuen, 1911. 8vo.

HOMBURGER, Otto. *Die Anfänge des Malschule von Winchester im X. Jahrhundert.* Leipzig, Weicher, 1912. 8vo.

HOUVET, Etienne. *Cathédrale de Chartres.* Chartres, Durand, (1920). 6 vols. 4to.

IVEKOVÍC, Cirillo M. *Dalmatiens Architektur und Plastik.* Wien, Schroll, 1910. 5 vols. Folio.

[JAMES, M. R.] *Catalogue of the manuscripts and early printed books of the library of J. Pierpont Morgan.* London. Privately printed for the Chiswick Press, 1906. Folio.

Descriptive catalogue of the Latin manuscripts in the John Rylands Library at Manchester. Manchester, University Press, 1921. 2 vols. 4to.

JARA, Alfonso. *Impresiones de una visita á Segóvia.* (Boletín de la Sociedad Española de Excursiones, 1900, VIII, 49.)

JEFFERY, George. *A brief description of the Holy Sepulchre Jerusalem.* Cambridge, University Press, 1919. 8vo.

JOUBIN, André. *Quelques aspects archéologiques du Languedoc méditerranéen.* (Revue archéologique, 1920, 269; 1921, 37.)

(JUÉNIN.) *Nouvelle histoire de l'abbaye . . . de Saint Filibert et de la ville de Tournus.* Dijon, Fay, 1733. 4to.

KARLINGER, Hans von. *Die hochromanische Wandmalerei in Regensburg.* München, Schmidt, 1920. 4to.

KAUFMANN, Karl Maria. *Die Menasstadt und das Nationalheiligtum der altchristlichen Aegypter.* Leipzig, Hiersemann, 1910. Folio.

KONDAKOFF, N. *Histoire de l'art byzantin, considéré principalement dans les miniatures.* Traduction de M. Trawinski. Paris, Ronam, 1886. 2 vols. 4to.

KOWALCZYK, Georg. *Denkmäler der Kunst in Dalmatien.* Berlin, Verlag für Kunstwissenschaft, 1910. 2 vols. Folio.

KURTH, G. *Renier de Huy, auteur véritable des fonts baptismaux de Saint-Barthélemy de Liège et le prétendu Lambert Patras.* (Académie Royale de Belgique, Bulletins, 1903, 519.)

LABANDE, L.-H. *L'église Notre-Dame-des-Doms d'Avignon des origines au XIIIe siècle.* Paris, Imprimerie Nationale, 1907. (Extrait du Bulletin archéologique, 1906.)

LACROIX, J. *Espalion.* Esquisses et souvenirs. (Bulletin de la Solidarité Aveyronnaise, 1914, VIII, 78.)

LAHONDÈS, Jules de. *Les monuments de Toulouse.* Histoire, archéologie, beaux-arts. Toulouse, Privat, 1920. 4to.

LAMPÉREZ, y Romea, Vicente. *Historia de la arquitectura cristiana española en la edad media.* Madrid, Blass, 1909. 2 vols. 4to.

LASTEYRIE, Charles de. *L'abbaye de S. Martial de Limoges.* Paris, Picard, 1901. 8vo.

LASTEYRIE, Robert de. *Etude archéologique sur l'église St.-Pierre d'Aulnay.* Gazette archéologique, 1886, XI, 277.)

Etudes sur la sculpture française au moyen âge. (Fondation Piot, 1902, VIII, 1.)

L'architecture religieuse en France à l'époque romane. Paris, Picard, 1912. 4to.

L'église Saint-Martin de Tours. Paris, Imprimerie Nationale, 1891. 4to. (Extrait des Mémoires de l'Académie des Inscriptions et Belles-Lettres, XXXIV, 1ère partie.)

LAURENT, Marcel. *Les ivoires prégothiques conservés en Belgique.* Bruxelles, Vromant, 1912. 8vo.

LAURIN, Abbé L. *Notice sur l'antique abbaye de St.-Victor de Marseille.* Marseilles, Aschero-Vial, 1915. 120.

LAVERGNE, Adrien. *Les chemins de Saint-Jacques en Gascogne.* Bordeaux, Chollet, 1887. (Extrait de la Revue de Gascogne.)

LEFEBVRE DES NOËTTES. *La tapisserie de Bayeux datée par le harnachement des chevaux et l'équipement des cavaliers.* (Bulletin monumental, 1912, LXVI, 213.)

Nouvelles remarques sur la date probable de la tapisserie de Bayeux. (Bulletin monumental, 1914, LXXVIII, 129.)

LEFÉVRE-PONTALIS, Eugène. *Deux statues du XII siécle au musée de Bourges.* (Bulletin monumental, 1913, LXXVII, 140.)

L'architecture religieuse dans l'ancien diocèse de Soissons au XIe et au XII siècle. Paris, Plon, 1894. 2 vols. Folio.

L'église de la Celle-Bruère. (Bulletin monumental, 1910, LXXIV, 272.)

Les campagnes de construction de Notre-Dame d'Etampes. (Bulletin monumental, 1909, LXXIII, 5.)

LEGUINA, D., Enrique de. *Encuadernaciones romano-bizantinas.* (Boletín de la Sociedad Española de Excursiones, 1895, II, 246.)

Esmaltes españoles. Madrid, Fé, 1909. 160.

LEIDINGER, Georg. *Miniaturen aus Handschriften der kgl. Hof- und Staatsbibliothek in München.* München, Riehn und Tietze, s. d. 5 vols. Folio.

LEMAIRE, R. *Les origines du style gothique en Brabant.* Bruxelles, Vromant, 1906. 8vo.

LENOIR, Alexandre. *Monumens des arts libéraux, mécaniques et industriels de la France.* Paris, Techener, 1840. Folio.

Musée des monumens français. Paris, Guilleminet, 1800–1821. 8 vols. 8vo.

LEVÉ, A. *Antériorité de la tapisserie de Bayeux sur la chanson de Roland.* (Bulletin monumental, 1913, LXXVII, 1913, 129.)

LIGTENBERG, Dr. Raphael. *Die romanische Steinplastik in den nördlichen Niederlanden.* Haag, Nijhoff, 1918. 4to.

LINDNER, Dr. Arthur. *Die Basler Galluspforte und andere romanische Bildwerke der Schweiz.* Strassburg, Heitz, 1899. 8vo.

LOCQUIN, Jean. *Nevers et Moulins.* Paris, Laurens, 1913. 4to. (Les villes d'art célèbres.)

LONGUEMAR, M. de. *Epigraphie du haut Poitou*. (Mémoires de la Société des Antiquaires de l'Ouest, 1863, XXVIII, 43.)

LORAIN, M. P. *Essai historique sur l'abbaye de Cluny*. Dijon, Popelain, 1839. 8vo.

LUCOT, M. le Chanoine. *L'église de Binson et sainte Posenne*. Châlons-sur-Marne, Thouille, 1882. 120.

MABILLON, Jean. *Annales ordinis Sancti Benedicti*. Lucae, Venturini, 1740. 6 vols. Folio.

MACLAGEN, Eric. *An early Christian ivory relief of the miracle of Cana*. (Burlington magazine, 1921, XXXVIII, 178.)

MÂLE, Emile. *La part de Suger dans la création de l'iconographie du moyen âge*. (Revue de l'art ancien et moderne, 1914, XXXV, 91, 161, 253, 339.)

L'art allemand et l'art français. Paris, Colin, 1917. 120. Replies by German scholars in Monatshefte für Kunstwissenschaft, X Jahrgang, 1917, 127.

L'art du moyen âge et les pèlerinages. Les routes d'Italie. (Revue de Paris, 15 Octobre, 1919.) Les routes de France et d'Espagne. (Revue de Paris, 15 Février, 1920.)

Le portail de Senlis et son influence. (Revue de l'art ancien et moderne, 1911, 161.)

Les chapiteaux romans du musée de Toulouse. (Revue archéologique, Troisième Série, 1892, XX, 2, 28, 176.)

Les influences du drame liturgique sur la sculpture romane. (Revue de l'art, 1907, II, 81.)

MANERBA, D. Pasquale. *Memorie sulla origine della città di Foggia e sua maggior chieca*. Napoli, Morelli, 1798. 8vo.

MARIGNAN, A. *La décoration monumentale des églises de la France septentrionle du XIIᵉ au XIIIᵉ siècle*. Paris, Leroux, 1911. 120.

Le portail occidental de Notre-Dame de Chartres. (Le moyen âge, 1898, 2e série, II, 341.)

L'école de sculpture en Provence du XII au XIII siècle. (Moyen âge, 1899, 2e série, III, 1.)

MARRIER, Dom Martin et CHESNE, André du. *Bibliotheca Cluniacensis*. Paris, 1614.

MARTÈNE, Edmund, et DURAND, Ursin. *Thesaurus novus anecdotarum*. Lutetiae Parisiorum, Sumptibus bibliopolarum Parisiensium, 1727. 3 vols. Folio.

MARTIN, Camille. *L'art roman en France*. L'architecture et la décoration. Paris, Eggimann, s. d. 3 vols. Folio.

MAYEUX, Albert. *Saint-Jean-le-Vieux à Perpignan*. (Bulletin monumental, 1913, LXXVII, 73.)

MAYEUR, P. *Le portail occidental de Ste.-Marie d'Oloron*. (Revue de l'art chrétien, 1909, LIX, 23.)

L'église de l'ancien prieuré clunisien de Charlieu. (Revue de l'art chrétien, 1909, LII, 33.)

McDOUGALL, Dorothy. The choir capitals of St.-Pierre-en-Haute, Chauvigny (Poitou). (Burlington magazine, 1920, XXXVI, 11.)

MÈGE, Alexandre du. *Description du musée des antiques de Toulouse*. Toulouse, Douladoure, 1835. 8vo.

Le cloître de la Daurade. (Mémoires de la Société Archéologique du Midi de la France, 1834–1835, II, 241.)

Notice des monuments antiques et des objets de sculpture moderne conservé dans le musée de Toulouse. Toulouse, Douladore, 1828. 120.

MÉLIDA, José Ramón. *La iglesia de San Juan de Rabanera en Soria* (Boletín de la Sociedad Española de Excursiones, 1910, XVIII, 2.)

MÉLY, F. de. *La renaissance et ses origines françaises.* (Revue de l'art ancien et moderne, 1906, 62.)

Les primitifs français et leurs signatures. Les sculpteurs. Paris, l'Ami des Monuments et des Arts, 1908. 8vo. (Extrait de l'Ami des monuments et des arts.)

Nos vieilles cathédrales et leurs maîtres d'oeuvre. (Revue archéologique, 1920. 290; 1921, 77.)

MERTON, Adolf. *Die Buchmalerei in St. Gallen.* Leipzig, Hiersemann, 1912. Folio.

MICHEL, André. *Histoire de l'art.* Paris, Colin, 1905–1913. 10 vols. 8vo.

Les accroissements du département des sculptures au Musée du Louvre. (Gazette des beaux-arts, 1917, LIX, 49.)

Les sculptures de l'ancienne façade de Notre-Dame-de-la-Couldre à Parthenay. (Monuments Piot, 1918, XXII, 179.)

MICHEL, Edmond. *Monuments religieux, civils et militaires du Gâtinais.* Paris, Champion, 1897. 2 vols. 4to.

Millénaire de Cluny. Mâcon, Protat, 1910. 2 vols. 8vo. (Annales de l'Académie de Mâcon. 3me Série, tome XV, 1e et 2e partie.)

MILLET, Gabriel. *Le monastère de Daphni.* Paris, Leroux, 1899. Folio.

Mosaïques de Daphni. (Fondation Piot, 1895, II, 197.)

Recherches sur l'iconographie de l'évangile aux XIV, XV et XVI siècles. Paris, Fontemoing, 1916. 8vo.

MITCHELL, H. P. *Some enamels of the school of Godefroid de Claire.* (Burlington magazine, 1919, XXXIV, 85; 1920, XXXV, 34, 92, 217; 1920, XXXVI, 18, 128.)

MOLINIER, Emile. *Histoire générale des arts appliqués à l'industrie.* Paris, Levy, 1896f. 6 vols. Folio.

MONACA, Andrea della. *Memoria historica dell' antichità della città di Brindisi.* (The title page is lacking in the copy in the library at Brindisi.)

MONTEVERDI, Angelo. *Il duomo di Cremona.* Milano, Bonomi, 1911. 120. L'Italia Monumentale, No. 18.

MONUMENTOS *arquitectonicos de España, publicados de rl. orden.* Madrid, Imprenta nacional, 1877 seq. 35 cuadernos. Great Folio.

MORELLET, BARAT, BUSSIERE. *Le Nivernois, album historique et pittoresque.* Nevers, Bussiere, 1838. 2 vols. Folio.

MORTET, Victor. *Recueil de textes relatifs à l'histoire de l'architecture et à la condition des architectes en France, au moyen âge.* Paris, Picard, 1911. 120.

MÜLBE, W. H. von der. *Die Darstellung des jüngsten Gerichtes an den romanischen und gotischen Kirchenportalen Frankreichs.* Leipzig, Klinkhardt und Biermann, 1911. 8vo.

Museo español de antigüedades. Madrid, Fortanet, 1872f. 11 vols. Folio.

Nella terra di Bari. Ricordi de arte medioevale. Trani, Vecchi, 1898. 4to.

NICOLAS, Abbé C. *Construction et réparations de l'église de Saint-Gilles.* (Mémoires de l'Académie de Nîmes, VII série, 1900, XXIII, 95.)

NODIER, Ch., TAYLOR, J., et de CAILLEUX, Alph. *Voyages pittoresques et roman-tiques dans l'ancienne France.* Paris, Didot, 1825. 7 vols. Folio.

Notice des tableaux, statues, bustes, bas-reliefs et antiquités composant le musée de Toulouse. (Toulouse, 1818.) 120.

OMONT, H. *Le mystère d'Emmaus.* Paris, 1913. (Extrait de la Bibliothèque de l'Ecole des Chartes, LXXIV, 1913.)

Peintures de l'évangile de saint Matthieu. (Fondation Piot, VII, 1900, 175.)

Peintures d'un évangelaire syriaque du XIIe ou XIIIe siècle. (Fondation Piot, 1911, XIX, 201.)

PACE, Biagio. *Escursioni in Asia Minore.* Monumenti medievali de Adalia e Conia. (Rassegna d'Arte, 1920, XX, 102.)

PAGENSTECHER, Rudolf. *Apulien.* Leipzig, Seemann 1914. 120. Berühmte Kunst-städten, No. 65.

PELKA, Otto. *Elfenbein.* Berlin, Schmidt, 1920. 120.

PERDRIZET, P. et CHESNAY, L. *La métropole de Serrès.* (Fondation Piot, 1903, X, 123.)

PERKINS, Thomas. *The cathedral church of Saint Albans.* London, Bell, 1903. 120.

PHILIPPE, André. *L'église de la Charité-sur-Loire.* (Bulletin monumental, 1905, LXIX, 469.)

PIJOAN, Joseph. *Les miniatures de l'octateuch a les biblies romaiques catalanes.* (Institut d'Estudis Catalans, Annuari, Any 4, 475.)

The Mozarabic churches of the ninth and tenth centuries in Spain. (Burlington magazine, 1922, LX, 214.)

PILLION, Louise. *Deux vies d'évêques sculptés à la cathédrale de Rouen.* (Gazette des Beaux Arts, 1903, 441; 1904, 149.)

Les soubassements des portails latéraux de la cathédrale de Rouen. (Revue de l'art ancien et moderne, 1905, 81, 199.)

PINARD, M. *Monographie de l'église Notre-Dame de Corbeil.* (Revue archéologique, 1845, II, 165, 643.)

PLANCHER, Fr. Urbain. *Histoire générale et particulière de Bourgogne.* Dijon, Antoine de Fay, 1739. 4 vols. Folio.

PLAT, Abbé Gabriel. *Notes pour servir à l'histoire monumentale de la Trinité de Vendôme.* Vendôme, Vilette, 1907. 8vo. (Extrait du Bulletin de la Société Archéologique du Vendomois.)

POGGI, Giovanni. *Arte medioevale negli Abruzzi.* Roma, Itala Ars, 1914. Folio.

POLENTINOS, Conde de. *Excursión á Santillana y San Vicente de la Barquera.* (Bole-tín de la Sociedad Española de Excursiones, XVI, 1908, 68.)

PORÉE, Charles. *L'abbaye de Vézelay.* Paris, Laurens, s. d. 120.

PORTER, A. Kingsley. *La sculpture du XIIe Siècle en Bourgogne.* Paris, Gazette des beaux-arts, 1921. 4to. (Extrait de la Gazette des beaux-arts, 1920, 5e Période, II, 73.)

Les débuts de la sculpture romane. (Gazette des beaux-arts, 1919, LXI, 47.)

Lombard architecture. New Haven, Yale University Press, 1916. 3 vols. 8vo and atlas in Folio.

Pilgrimage sculpture. (American journal of archaeology, 1922, XXVI, 1.)

Romanesque capitals. (Fogg Museum Notes, 1922, I, 2, 23.)

The development of sculpture in Lombardy in the XII century. (American journal of archaeology, 1915, XIX, 137.)

The sculpture of the West. Boston, Marshall Jones, 1921. Pamphlet.

Two romanesque sculptures in France by Italian masters. (American journal of archaeology, 1920, XXIV, 121.)

POUSSIN, Abbé. *Monographie de l'abbaye et de l'église de St.-Remi de Reims.* Reims, Lemoine-Canart, 1857. 120.

POUZET. *Notes sur les chapiteaux de l'abbaye de Cluny.* Paris, Champion, 1912. 4to. (Extrait de la Revue de l'art chrétien, 1912.)

PRIOR, Edward S., and GARDNER, Arthur. *An account of mediaeval figure-sculpture in England.* Cambridge, University Press, 1912. 8vo.

PUIG y Cadafalch, FALGUERA, Antoni de, GODAY y Casals, J. *L'arquitectura romànica a Catalunya.* Barcelona, Institut d'Estudis Catalans, 1909. 3 vols. 8vo.

QUICHERAT, J. *Histoire de la costume en France.* Paris, Hachette, 1875. 8vo.

Rapport de la commission chargée de l'examen des travaux à exécuter pour la restauration et l'assainissement de l'église St.-Etienne de Nevers. Bulletin de la Société Nivernaise des Sciences, Lettres et Arts, 1854, I, 109.)

RÉVOIL, Henry. *Architecture romane du midi de la France.* Paris, Morel, 1874. 3 vols. Folio.

RIEHL, Berthold. *Geschichte der Stein- und Holzplastik in Ober-Bayern.* (Abhandlungen der historischen Klasse der königlich Bayerischen Akademie der Wissenschaften, 1906, LXXVI, 1.)

RIU y Cabanas, Ramón. *Efigie de Nuestra Señora del claustro en la catedral de Solsona.* (Boletín de la Sociedad Española de Excursiones, 1895, III, 94.)

RIVOIRA, G. T. *Architettura musulmana.* Milano, Hoepli, 1914. 4to.

RIZZO, G. E., e TOESCA, Pietro. *Storia dell' arte classica e italiana.* Torino, Unione Tipografico-Editrice Torinese, in course of publication.

ROBLOT-DELOUDRE, Louise. *St.-Loup-de-Naud.* (Fondation Piot, 1913, XXI, 111.)

ROCHIAS, Abbé G. *Les chapiteaux de l'église de Saint-Nectaire.* (Bulletin monumental, 1909, LXXIII, 213.)

RODRIGO, Juan Pedro. *Recuerdo del monasterio de Santo Domingo de Silos.* Madrid, San Francisco de Sales, 1916. 120.

ROHAULT de Fleury. *La sainte Vierge.* Paris, Poussielque, 1878. 2 vols. 4to.

ROOSVAL, Johnny. *Die Steinmeister Gottlands.* Stockholm, Fritz, 1918. Folio.

ROSCHACH, Ernest. *Catalogue des antiquités et des objets d'art.* Musée de Toulouse. Toulouse, Viguier, 1865. 8vo.

ROULIN, Dom Eugène. *L'ancien trésor de l'abbaye de Silos.* Paris, Leroux, 1901. 4to.

Les cloîtres de l'abbaye de Silos. (Revue de l'art chrétien, 1909, LIX, 75, 166, 359; 1910, LX, 1.)

Les églises de l'abbaye de Silos. (Revue de l'art chrétien, 1908, LVIII, 289, 371.)

Oeuvres de sculpture de l'abbaye de Silos. (Revue de l'art chrétien, 1909, LIX, 1.)

Orfèvierie et emaillerie mobilier liturgique d'Espagne. (Revue de l'art chrétien, 1903, XLVI, 19, 201, 292.)

ROUX, Abbé J. *La basilique St.-Front de Périgueux.* Périgueux, Cassard, 1920. 4to.

RUPIN, Ernest. *L'abbaye et les cloîtres de Moissac.* Paris, Picard, 1897. 4to.

L'oeuvre de Limoges. Paris, Picard, 1890. 4to.

Rupp, Fritz. *Inkrustationstil der romanischen Baukunst zu Florenz*. Strassburg, Heitz, 1912. 8vo.

Sacs, J. *El Beda de Girona*. (Vell i Nou, Any V, 287, 329, 345, 386, 408.)

Sahuc, J. *L'art roman à Saint-Pons-de-Thomières*. Montpellier, Société Anonyme de l'Imprimerie Générale du Midi, 1908. 4to.

Santeramo, S. *Il simbolismo della cattedrale di Barletta*. Barletta, Dellisanti, 1917. 8vo.

Sauerlandt, Max. *Deutsche Plastik des Mittelalters*. Leipzig, Karl Robert Lange-wiesche Verlag, s. d.

Scanno, Dionigi. *Storia dell' arte in Sardegna dal XI al XIV secolo*. Cagliari-Sassari, Montorsi, 1907. 4to.

Schlumberger, Gustave. *Bas-relief du campo Angaran à Venise représentant un empereur byzantin du X siècle*. (Byzantinische Zeitschrift, 1893, II, 192.)
Deux bas-reliefs Byzantins de stéatite. (Fondation Piot, 1902, IX, 229.)
L'epopée byzantine. Paris, Hachette, 1896–1905. 3 vols. 8vo.
L'ivoire Barberini. (Fondation Piot, 1900, VII, 79.)
Un ivoire chrétien inédit, Musée du Louvre. (Fondation Piot, 1894, 165.)

Schmarsow, August. *Kompositionsgesetze in der Kunst des Mittelalters*. Leipzig, Teubner, 1920. 2 vols. 8vo and atlas in folio.

Schubring, Paul. *Bischofsstühle und Ambonen in Apulien*. (Zeitschrift für christliche Kunst, 1900, XIII, 193.)

Schulz, Guillermo. *Miniaturas de la biblia de Avila*. (Boletín de la Sociedad Española de Excursiones, 1897, V, 100.)

Schulz, Heinrich Wilhelm. *Denkmäler der Kunst des Mittelalters in Unteritalien*. Dresden, Schulz, 1860. 4 vols. 4to and atlas in folio.

Semper, H. *Ivoires du musée national de Buda-Pesth*. (Revue de l'art chrétien, 1897, XL, 389, 477.)

Sentenach, N. *Crucifijos románicos españoles*. (Boletín de la Sociedad Española de Excursiones, 1903, XI, 245.)
Miniaturas notables del Museo Arqueológico Nacional. (Boletín de la Sociedad Española de Excursiones, 1907, XV, 215.)
Relieves en marfil del arca de San Millán de la Cogolla. (Boletín de la Sociedad Española de Excursiones, 1908, XVI, 4.)

Sepet, Marius. *Les prophètes du Christ, étude sur les origines du théâtre au moyen âge*. (Bibliothèque de l'Ecole des Chartes, 1867, XXVIII, 1, 210; 1868, XXIX, 105, 261.) Published separately, Paris Didier, 1878. 8vo.

Stettiner, Richard. *Die illustrierten Prudentiushandschriften*. Berlin, Preuss, 1895. 8vo.

Strzygowski, Josef. *Catalogue général des antiques égyptiennes du musée du Caire*. Koptische Kunst. Vienne, Holzhausen, 1904. 4to.
Der Bilderkreis des griechischen Physiologus. Leipzig, Teubner, 1899. 8vo.
Der Dom zu Aachen und seiner Entstellung. Leipzig, Heinrichs, 1904. 8vo.
Der koptische Reiterheilige und der hl. Georg. (Zeitschrift für Aegyptische Sprache und Altertumskunde, 1902, XX, 49.)
Die altbyzantinische Plastik der Blütezeit. (Byzantinische Zeitschrift, 1892, I, 575.)
Die Baukunst der Armenier und Europa. Wien, Schroll, 1918. 2 vols. 4to.
Hellenistiche und koptische Kunst in Alexandria. Wien, Mechitharist, 1902. 8vo.

The origin of Christian art. (Burlington magazine, 1911, XX, 146.)

SWARENSKI, Georg. *Die Salzburger Malerei.* Leipzig, Hiersemann, 1913. 2 vols. 4to.

TERRET, Victor. *La sculpture bourguignonne.* Paris, L'Art Catholique, 1914.

TESTI, Laudedeo. *Le baptistère de Parme.* Florence, Sansoni, 1916. 4to.

TEXIER, Abbé. *Histoire de la peinture sur verre en Limousin.* Paris, Didron, 1847. 120.

THIOLLIER, F. *L'art roman à Charlieu et en Brionnais.* Montbrison, Brassart, 1892. Folio.

Vestiges de l'art roman en Lyonnais. (Bulletin archéologique du Comité des Travaux Historiques et Scientifiques, 1892, 396.)

THOMAS, Abbé Jules. *Les vitraux de Notre-Dame de Dijon.* Dijon, Jobard, 1898, 120.

THOREL, Oct. *L'equipement d'un pèlerin picard à St. Jacques de Compostelle.* Amiens. Yvert et Tellier, 1909. 8vo.

TIKKANEN, J. J. *Die Psalterillustration im Mittelalter.* (Acta Societatis Scientiarum Fennicae, Helsingforsicae, 1903. 4to. Tomus XXXI.)

TOBLER, Titus et MOLINIER, Augustus. *Itinera Hierosolymitana.* Genevae, Fick, 1879. 2 vols. 8vo.

TOURNEAU, M. le. *Les mosaïques de Sainte-Sophie de Salonique.* (Fondation Piot, 1909, XVI, 39.)

TRÉNEFF, D. K. *Miniatures du ménologe grec du XIe siècle de la Bibliothèque Synodale à Moscou.* Moscou, 1911. Folio.

TRUTAT, M. *Ancien hotel-de-ville de Saint-Antonin.* (Bulletin archéologique de la Société Archéologique de Tarn-et-Garonne, 1876, IV, 158.)

URLICHS, Carolus Ludovicus. *Codex urbis Romae topographicus.* Wirceburgi, Stahelianis, 1871. 120.

VENTURI, Adolfo. *Storia dell' arte italiana.* Milano, Hoepli, 1901f. 7 vols. 8vo.

VIGIL, Don Ciriaco Miguel. *Asturias monumental, epigráfica y diplomatica.* Oviedo, Hospicio Provincial, 1887. 4to.

VIOLLET-LE-DUC, Eugène Emmanuel. *Dictionaire raisonné de l'architecture française du XIe au XVIe Siècle.* Paris, Morel, 1867. 10 vols. 8vo.

VIREY, Jean. *Les dates de construction de Saint-Pholibert de Tournus.* (Bulletin monumental, 1903, LXVII, 515.)

VITRY, Paul. *La cathédrale de Reims.* Paris, Librairie Centrale des Beaux Arts, 1920. 2 vols. Folio.

Une tête de Christ du XII siècle. (Fondation Piot, 1908, XVI, 137.)

VITRY, Paul et BRIÈRE, Gaston. *Documents de sculpture française du moyen âge.* Paris, Longuet, 1904. Folio.

L'église abbatiale de Saint-Denis et ses tombeaux. Paris, Longuet, 1908. 160.

VIVES, Antonio. *Arqueta arabe de Palencia.* (Boletín de la Sociedad Española de Excursiones, 1894, I, 34.)

VÖGE, Wilhelm. *Der provençalische Einfluss in Italien und das Datum der Arler Porticus.* (Repertorium für Kunstwissenschaft, 1902, XXV, 409.)

WACKERNAGEL, Martin. *Die Plastik des XI und XII Jahrhunderts in Apulien.* Leipzig, Hiersemann, 1911. 4to.

Die Anfänge des monumentalen Stiles im Mittelalter. Strassburg, Heitz, 1894. 8vo.

Ueber die Bamberger Domsculpturen. (Repertorium für Kunstwissenschaft, 1899, XXII, 94 ; 1901, XXIV, 195, 255.)

WARNER, Sir George. *Gospels of Matilda, Countess of Tuscany, 1055–1115.* Privately printed for the Roxburghe Club, 1917. Folio.

WARNER, George Frederic and WILSON, Henry Austin. *The Benedictional of St. Aethelwold.* Oxford. Privately printed for the Roxburghe Club, 1910. Folio.

WEBER, Paul. *Geistliches Schauspiel und kirchliche Kunst.* Stuttgart, von Ebner und Seubert, 1894. 8vo.

WEESE, Artur. *Die Bamberger Domskulpturen.* Strassburg, Heitz, 1914. 2 vols. 8vo.

WEISE, G. *Studien über Denkmäler romanischer Plastik am Oberrhein.* (Monatshefte für Kunstwissenschaft, 1920, XIII, 1.)

WESTWOOD, J. O. *Fac-similes of the miniatures and ornaments of Anglo-Saxon and Irish manuscripts.* London, Quaritch, 1868. Folio.

WILPERT, Joseph. *Die römischen Mosaiken und Malereien der kirchlichen Bauten von IV bis XIII Jahrhundert.* Freiburg im Breisgau, Herder, 1916. 4 vols. Folio.

WÖLFFLIN, Heinrich. *Die Bamberger Apokalypse.* München, Königlich Akademie der Wissenschaften, 1918. 4to.

ZIMMERMANN, E. Heinrich. *Vorkarolingische Miniaturen.* Berlin, Deutsches Verein für Kunstwissenschaft, 1916. 8vo and 4 vols. Folio.

ZIMMERMANN, Max Georg. *Oberitalische Plastik.* Leipzig, Liebeskind, 1897. 4to.

ADDRESSES OF PHOTOGRAPHERS

ALINARI, Fratelli. Amministrazione, Via Nazionale 8, Florence, Italy. Stores, Via Strozzi, Florence; Via Condotti al Corso Umberto I, Rome; 3 Via Calabritto, Naples. The largest collection of any of the Italian commercial houses. Well arranged catalogues.

ALONSO, R. Palencia. A small collection of the city and province of Palencia.

ANDERSON, D. 7a Via Salaria, Rome. A large collection of exceptionally high quality. Catalogues.

ANTONELLI-MATTEUCCI, Cav. Liborio, Via Piccinni, 24, Bari. Collection of Apulian monuments made for the Museo Provinciale of Bari.

Les Archives Photographiques d'Art et d'Histoire. 1 bis Rue de Valois, Paris. A consolidation of the old collections of the Commission des Monuments Histoiques, Service Photographique et Cinématographique des Beaux-Arts, Neurdein, F. Martin Sabon etc., constituting almost a monopoly of photographs of French monuments.

ARMONI, Piazza del Duomo, Orvieto.

BAYLAC, L. R., 21 rue Bouquières, Toulouse.

BENVENUTI, Cesare, Piazza Superiore S. Francesco, Assisi.

BROGI, Via Tornabuoni, Florence. A collection of importance. Catalogue.

BYNE, Arthur, Monte Esquinza 6, Madrid. An exceedingly well-selected collection of Spanish architecture and industrial arts.

CARBONI, Cav., Direttore del Gabinetto Fotografico del Ministero della Pubblica Istruzione, Via in Miranda, 7, Rome. Italian government photographs.

GIRAUDON, 9 rue des Beaux-Arts, Paris. Photographs of exceptionally high quality.

GOMBAU, Venancio, Calle de Prior, 18, Salamanca, Spain.

KENNEDY, Prof. Clarence, Department of Art, Smith College, Northampton, Mass. Photographs of the highest quality. Catalogue.

KUNSTHISTORISCHES SEMINAR, Marburg (Lahn).

LASSALLE, C., rue de l'Etoile 32, Toulouse.

LOMBARDI, Via di Città, Siena, Italy. Catalogue.

MARSAL, M., sucesores de, Rambla de Castelar, 36, Tarragona.

MAS, Roselló 277, Barcelona. A remarkably well selected and complete collection of subjects in Catalonia and Spain.

MILLET, Prof. Gabriel, 34 rue Hallé, Paris. XIVe. The collection of the Ecole des Hautes-Etudes consists chiefly of Byzantine subjects.

MOSCIONI, Via Condotti 76, Rome. Collection includes many unusual subjects. The catalogue is unfortunately of little use.

POPPI, Pietro, 19 Via d'Azeglio, Bologna.

REMY-GORGET, Près de la Gare, Dijon.

ROIG, J., successor to Laurent y Lacoste, Carrera de San Jerónimo, 53, Madrid.

SILVESTRE, rue de Bonnele, 2, Lyon.

SOMMER, G., e Figlio, Piazza Vittoria, Naples. Catalogue.

STOEDTNER, Dr. Franz, Universitätstrasse 3b, Berlin N. W. 7. A large and admirably selected collection. Catalogue.

TARABELLI, Via Torquato Tasso, Bergamo. Catalogue.

TILLI, G., Via Mazzini, Perugia.

WINOCIO, Calle San Marcelo, Léon.

INDEX

INDEX

The light italic figures refer to illustrations; the light Roman figures refer to the text of Volume I. Specially important references in the text are printed in heavy type.

ROMANESQUE SCULPTURE

OF THE PILGRIMAGE ROADS

VOLUME II

BURGUNDY

ILLUSTRATIONS

ILLUSTRATIONS

(1–150)

BURGUNDY

20. ANZY-LE-DUC, (Saône-et-Loire). Capital of nave. St. Michael. L. W. P. phot.

21. ANZY-LE-DUC, (Saône-et-Loire). Capital of nave. B.-A. phot.

22. ANZY-LE-DUC, (Saône-et-Loire). Capital of nave. The Rivers of Paradise. B.-A. phot.

23. ANZY-LE-DUC, (Saône-et-Loire). Capital of nave. The Damned. L. W. P. phot.

24. ANZY-LE-DUC, (Saône-et-Loire). Northern corbel of western portal. The Ass with a Book; supporting figure. L. B. W. phot.

25. ST.-PARIZE-LE-CHÂTEL, (Nièvre). Capital of crypt. The Owl; Sciapodes. A. K. P. phot.

26. ST.-PARIZE-LE-CHÂTEL, (Nièvre). Capital of crypt. The Siren, unknown subject, *l'Ane qui joue*. A. K. P. phot.

27. CLUNY, (Saône-et-Loire). Musée Ochier. Fragment. Combat of Knights; Samson and the Lion. A. K. P. phot.

28. VÉZELAY, (Yonne). Capital of nave, north side, ninth pier. The Temptation. "Ainay Master." F. M. S. phot.

29. VÉZELAY, (Yonne). Ancient capital, now in second story of narthex. St. George and the Dragon. "Ainay Master." L. W. P. phot.

30. VÉZELAY, (Yonne). Capital of nave, south side, second pier. "Cluny Master." F. M. S. phot.

31. VÉZELAY, (Yonne). Capital of nave, south side, fifth pier. The Winds. "Cluny Master." F. M. S. phot.

32. VÉZELAY, (Yonne). Capital of nave, south side, third pier. St. Eustace. "Cluny Master." F. M. S. phot.

33. VÉZELAY, (Yonne). Capital of nave, south side, sixth pier. Daniel and the Lions. "Cluny Master(?)." F. M. S. phot.

34. VÉZELAY, (Yonne). Capital of nave, north side, fourth pier. David and Goliath. "Vézelay Master No. 1." F. M. S. phot.

34 a. VÉZELAY, (Yonne). Capital of nave, south side, second pier. Wrath, Luxury. "Vézelay Master No. 1." F. M. S. phot.

35. VÉZELAY, (Yonne). Capital of nave, south side, fourth pier. The Death of Cain. "Vézelay Master No. 2." F. M. S. phot.

36. VÉZELAY, (Yonne). Capital of narthex, south side, second pier. St. Peter and St. Paul resuscitate the dead Youth. "Vézelay Master No. 2." F. M. S. phot.

37. VÉZELAY, (Yonne). Capital of gallery, narthex. The stolen Blessing. "Vézelay Master No. 2." F. M. S. phot.

38. VÉZELAY, (Yonne). Capital of narthex, north side, second pier. Nathan reproaches David. "Vézelay Master No. 2." F. M. S. phot.

39. VÉZELAY, (Yonne). Capital of nave, north side, sixth pier. The golden Calf. "Vézelay Master No. 3." F. M. S. phot.

40. VÉZELAY, (Yonne). Capital of nave, south side, fourth pier. A Prophet brings to the Mill of St. Paul the Grain for the Eucharistic Bread. "Vézelay Master No. 3." F. M. S. phot.

41. VÉZELAY, (Yonne). Capital of nave, north side, first pier. St. Mary Magdalen(?). "Androche Master." F. M. S. phot.

42. VÉZELAY, (Yonne). Capital of nave, north side, eighth pier, now in narthex. St. Anthony assailed by Daemons. "Bifora Master." F. M. S. phot.

43. VÉZELAY, (Yonne). Capital of narthex. The Sacrifice of Bread in the Ancient Law. "Bifora Master." F. M. S. phot.

44. VÉZELAY, (Yonne). Capital of nave, north side, third pier. Judith. "Bathsheba Master." F. M. S. phot.

45. VÉZELAY, (Yonne). Capital of gallery of narthex. Tobias anoints his Father's Eyes. "Tobias Master." F. M. S. phot.

46. VÉZELAY, (Yonne). Capital of narthex, north side, second pier. Samson and the Lion. "Master of the Tympanum." F. M. S. phot.

47. VÉZELAY, (Yonne). Central western portal. Zodiac; Pentecost; St. John, St. James, St. John the Baptist, St. Peter, St. Paul. N. D. phot.

48. VÉZELAY, (Yonne). Western portal, tympanum, northern portion. Zodiac; Pentecost. F. M. S. phot. from cast.

48 a. VÉZELAY, (Yonne). Central portal, tympanum, central portion. Detail of the Pentecost, St. John the Baptist. Giraudon phot. from cast.

49. VÉZELAY, (Yonne). Central portal, tympanum, southern half. Zodiac, Pentecost. F. M. S. phot. from cast.

50. VÉZELAY, (Yonne). Northern portal, tympanum. Journey to Emmaus, *Noli me tangere.* Ascension. B.-A. phot.

51. VÉZELAY, (Yonne). Tympanum of southern portal. Adoration of Magi, Annunciation, Visitation, Shepherds, Nativity. N. D. phot.

52. SAULIEU, (Côte-d'Or), St.-Androche. Capital of nave. Judas hangs himself. B.-A. phot.

53. SAULIEU, (Côte-d'Or), St.-Androche. Capital of nave. The Temptation. B.-A. phot.

54. SAULIEU, (Côte-d'Or), St.-Androche. Capital of nave. Flight into Egypt. B.-A. phot.

55. SAULIEU, (Côte-d'Or), St.-Androche. Capital of nave. *Noli me tangere.* B.-A. phot.

56. SAULIEU, (Côte-d'Or), St.-Androche. Capital of nave. Balaam. B.-A. phot.

57. SAULIEU, (Côte-d'Or), St.-Androche. Capital of nave. Centaur. B.-A. phot.

58. SAULIEU, (Côte-d'Or), St.-Androche. Capital of nave. B.-A. phot.

59. SAULIEU, (Côte-d'Or), St.-Androche. Capital of nave. B.-A. phot.

60. SAULIEU, (Côte-d'Or), St.-Androche. Capital of nave. B.-A. phot.

61. SAULIEU, (Côte-d'Or), St.-Androche. Capital of nave. B.-A. phot.

62. MOÛTIER-ST.-JEAN, (Côte-d'Or). Capital now in Fogg Museum, Cambridge, Mass. Elizabeth and a Youth. Fogg Museum phot.

63. MOUTIER-ST.-JEAN, (Côte-d'Or). Capital now in Fogg Museum, Cambridge, Mass. The Annunciation to Zacharias. Fogg Museum phot.

64. Moûtier-St.-Jean, (Côte-d'Or). Capital now in Fogg Museum, Cambridge, Mass. The Temple(?). Fogg Museum phot.

65. Moûtier-St.-Jean, (Côte-d'Or). Capital now in Fogg Museum, Cambridge, Mass. The Journey to Emmaus. Fogg Museum phot.

66. Moûtier-St.-Jean, (Côte-d'Or). Capital now in Fogg Museum, Cambridge, Mass. Offerings of Cain and Abel. Fogg Museum phot.

67. Autun, (Saône-et-Loire), Cathédrale. Capital. B.-A. phot.

68. Autun, (Saône-et-Loire), Cathédrale. Capital of nave. Samson. Stoedtner phot.

69. Autun, (Saône-et-Loire), Cathédrale. Capital of nave. St. Vincent. Stoedtner phot.

70. Autun, (Saône-et-Loire), Cathédrale. Capital of nave. Christ washing the Feet of St. Peter. B.-A. phot.

71. Autun, (Saône-et-Loire), Cathédrale. Capital now in museum. The Flight into Egypt. B.-A. phot.

72. Autun, (Saône-et-Loire), Cathédrale. Capital now in museum. Adoration of the Magi. B.-A. phot.

73. Autun, (Saône-et-Loire), Cathédrale. Capital of nave. Flight of Simon Magus. B.-A. phot.

74. Autun, (Saône-et-Loire), Cathédrale. Modern copy of a capital of transept. The Duke, Hugh II, offers the new Cathedral to St. Lazare. A. K. P. phot.

75. Autun, (Saône-et-Loire), Cathédrale. Capital of nave, south side, fifth pier. Fall of Simon Magus. A. K. P. phot.

76. Autun, (Saône-et-Loire), Cathédrale. Capital of nave. Body of St. Vincent guarded by Crows. B.-A. phot.

77. Autun, (Saône-et-Loire), Cathédrale. Capital of nave. The Stoning of St. Stephen. B.-A. phot.

78. Autun, (Saône-et-Loire), Cathédrale. Capital of nave. *Noli me tangere.* B.-A. phot.

79. Autun, (Saône-et-Loire), Cathédrale. Capital of nave. St. Peter liberated by the Angel. A. K. P. phot.

80. Autun, (Saône-et-Loire), Cathédrale. Tympanum of western portal. The Last Judgment. Signed "Gislebertus." A. K. P. phot.

81. Autun, (Saône-et-Loire), Cathédrale. Tympanum of western portal. Detail of the Last Judgment. Signed "Gislebertus." Giraudon phot. from cast.

82. Gargilesse, (Indre). Capital of nave. Dance of Salome. L. W. P. phot.

83. Gargilesse, (Indre). Capital of nave. The Visitation. L. W. P. phot.

84. Perrecey-les-Forges, (Saône-et-Loire). Tympanum of western portal. *Majestas Domini.* A. K. P. phot.

85. Perrecey-les-Forges, (Saône-et-Loire). Lintel of western portal. The Kiss of Judas; Christ is taken; Peter cuts off the ear of Malchus. L. W. P. phot.

86. St.-Paul-de-Varax, (Ain). Western façade, northern lunette. The Fall of Simon Magus (?). L. W. P. phot.

87. St.-Paul-de-Varax, (Ain). Western façade, second lunette from north. Adoration of Magi; Simon and Nero (?), St. Peter resuscitates the dead Man(?). L. W. P. phot.

88. St.-Paul-de-Varax, (Ain). Tympanum of western portal. The Ascension. B.-A. phot.

89. St.-Paul-de-Varax, (Ain). Lunette south of central portal. Tortures of the Damned. L. W. P. phot.

90. St.-Paul-de-Varax, (Ain). Western façade, southern lunette. The Souls of the Damned are driven to Hell. L. W. P. phot.

91. St.-Paul-de-Varax, (Ain). Tympanum of southern portal. St. Anthony and the Faun. L. W. P. phot.

92. Macon, (Saône-et-Loire), St.-Vincent. Tympanum of western portal. The Last Judgment. Silvestre phot.

93. Neuilly-en-Donjon, (Allier). Tympanum of western portal. Adoration of Magi; Temptation; Last Supper. L. W. P. phot.

94. Neuilly-en-Donjon, (Allier). Western portal, tympanum, detail. Adoration of Magi; Temptation; Last Supper. L. W. P. phot.

95. Anzy-le-Duc, (Saône-et-Loire). Portal of priory. Adoration of Magi; Temptation; Shame of Adam and Eve; Hell. L. W. P. phot.

96. Anzy-le-Duc, (Saône-et-Loire). Western portal. Elders, Ascension. L. W. P. phot.

97. Anzy-le-Duc, (Saône-et-Loire). Tympanum of western portal, detail. An Angel. L. W. P. phot.

98. Anzy-le-Duc, (Saône-et-Loire). Tympanum from western portal of priory, now in Musée Eucharistique, Paray-le-Monial. *Majestas Domini*, Virgin and Saints. L. W. P. phot.

99. Anzy-le-Duc, (Saône-et-Loire). Tympanum from western portal of priory, now in Musée Eucharistique, Paray-le-Monial. Detail of *Majestas Domini*. L. W. P. phot.

100. St.-Révérien, (Nièvre). Western portal, southern archivolt. A Cherub. A. K. P. phot.

101. St.-Révérien, (Nièvre). Western portal, northern archivolt. A Cherub. A. K. P. phot.

102. St.-Révérien, (Nièvre). Capital of ambulatory. Journey of the Magi. L. W. P. phot.

103. St.-Révérien, (Nièvre). Capital of ambulatory. Jacob's Dream. L. W. P. phot.

104. Montceaux-l'Etoile, (Saône-et-Loire). Western portal, tympanum. The Ascension. L. W. P. phot.

105. Montceaux-l'Etoile, (Saône-et-Loire). Western portal, detail of tympanum. Virgin, six Apostles and Enoch from the Ascension. L. W. P. phot.

106. St.-Amour, (Saône-et-Loire). Relief now in interior of church, south wall. *Majestas Domini*. L. W. P. phot.

107. Fleury-la-Montagne, (Saône-et-Loire). Tympanum of western portal. The Ascension, the Adoration. B.-A. phot.

108. Charlieu, (Saône-et-Loire), Abbaye. Tympanum and lintel of outer portal. *Majestas Domini*, Virgin, two Angels and twelve Apostles. A. K. P. phot.

109. Charlieu, (Saône-et-Loire), Abbaye. Outer portal, detail of tympanum. The Virgin, an Angel, and six Apostles. A. K. P. phot.

110. Charlieu, (Saône-et-Loire), Abbaye. Outer portal, western window. The Transfiguration, the Holy Spirit, Christ, Moses, Isaiah, St. John, St. St. James, Peter; the Last Supper; Sacrifice according to the Old Testament. A. K. P. phot.

111. St.-Julien-de-Jonzy, (Saône-et-Loire). Tympanum of western portal. *Majestas Domini*, the Last Supper. L. W. P. phot.

112. Donzy, (Nièvre), Notre-Dame-du-Pré. Western portal, detail of tympanum. An Angel. L. W. P. phot.

113. Donzy, (Nièvre), Notre-Dame-du-Pré. Western portal, detail of tympanum. The Virgin. L. W. P. phot.

114. Donzy, (Nièvre), Notre-Dame-du-Pré. Western portal, detail of tympanum. A Prophet. L. W. P. phot.

115. La Charité-sur-Loire, (Nièvre). Tympanum of southern portal now in church, detail. A Prophet and an Apostle. L. W. P. phot.

116. La Charité-sur-Loire, (Nièvre). Tympanum of southern portal, now inside church, detail. *Majestas Domini*. L. W. P. phot.

117. La Charité-sur-Loire, (Nièvre). Tympanum of southern portal, now inside church, detail. A Prophet, two Apostles. L. W. P. phot.

118. La Charité-sur-Loire, (Nièvre). Lintel of southern portal now inside church. The Adoration of the Magi. L. W. P. phot.

119. La Charité-sur-Loire, (Nièvre). Lintel of southern portal, now inside church. Presentation in the Temple. L. W. P. phot.

120. La Charité-sur-Loire, (Nièvre). Western façade, tympanum of northern portal, now in house. *Majestas Domini*. L. W. P. phot.

121. La Charité-sur-Loire, (Nièvre). Western façade, lintel of northern portal, now in house, detail. Annunciation, Visitation, Nativity. L. W. P. phot.

122. La Charité-sur-Loire, (Nièvre). Western façade, lintel of northern portal now in house, detail. Nativity, Shepherds. L. W. P. phot.

123. La Charité-sur-Loire, (Nièvre). Central tower, exterior. Four Apostles. B.-A. phot.

124. Souvigny, (Allier). Sculptures in west wall. Christ, two Apostles, a Saint and a Bishop. Silvestre phot.

125. Souvigny, (Allier). Sculptures in west wall. Christ, two Apostles, a Saint. Stoedtner phot.

126. Nevers, (Nièvre), St.-Sauveur. Capitals now in the Musée de la Porte du Croux. A Monkey playing the Violin; *l'Ane qui joue*. L. W. P. phot.

127. Nevers, (Nièvre), St.-Sauveur. Capitals now in the Musée de la Porte du Croux. The Licorne and the Aspic. A. K. P. phot.

128. NEVERS, (Nièvre), St.-Sauveur. Capital now in the Musée de la Porte du Croux. A. K. P. phot.

129. NEVERS, (Nièvre), St.-Sauveur. Capital now in the Musée de la Porte du Croux. Ethiopian. A. K. P. phot.

130. NEVERS, (Nièvre), St.-Sauveur. Capital now in the Musée de la Porte du Croux. The Basilisk. A. K. P. phot.

131. NEVERS, (Nièvre), St.-Sauveur. Capitals now in the Musée de la Porte du Croux. The Dromedary; the Salamander. L. W. P. phot.

132. NEVERS, (Nièvre), St.-Sauveur. Capital now in the Musée de la Porte du Croux. St. Peter and St. John heal the Cripple before the Temple Beautiful. L. W. P. phot.

133. NEVERS, (Nièvre), St.-Sauveur. Tympanum, now in the Musée de la Porte du Croux. Christ gives the Keys to St. Peter. L. W. P. phot.

134. DIJON, (Côte-d'Or), St.-Bénigne. Tympanum from abbey, now in Musée Archéologique. *Majestas Domini*. A. K. P. phot.

135. DIJON, (Côte-d'Or), St.-Bénigne. Tympanum from abbey, now in Musée Archéologique. *Majestas Domini*. A. K. P. phot.

136. DIJON, (Côte-d'Or), St.-Bénigne. Tympanum from abbey, now in Musée Archéologique. Last Supper. A. K. P. phot.

137. AVALLON, (Yonne), St.-Lazare. Western façade, central portal, northern voussures. Angels, Elders, Zodiac. F. M. S. phot.

138. AVALLON, (Yonne), St.-Lazare. Western façade, central portal, southern voussures. Angels, Elders, Zodiac. F. M. S. phot.

139. AVALLON, (Yonne), St.-Lazare. Western façade, central portal, southern jamb. A. K. P. phot.

140. AVALLON, (Yonne), St.-Lazare. Western façade, southern portal, tympanum. Adoration of Magi, Journey of Magi, Magi before Herod. F. M. S. phot.

141. AVALLON, (Yonne), St.-Lazare. Southern portal, base of southern jamb. F. M. S. phot.

142. BOIS-STE.-MARIE, (Saône-et-Loire). Southern portal, tympanum. The Flight into Egypt. A. K. P. phot.

143. SEMUR-EN-BRIONNAIS, (Saône-et-Loire). Tympanum of western portal. *Majestas Domini*; St. Hilaire before the Council; Death of the pseudo-pope Leo. L. W. P. phot.

144. DIJON, (Côte-d'Or), St.-Bénigne. Western portal, according to Plancher's engraving. *Majestas Domini*, Magi, Shepherds, Nativity, St. Bénigne.

145. DIJON, (Côte-d'Or), St.-Bénigne. Head of statue addossed to trumeau of western portal, now in Musée Archéologique. St. Bénigne. A. K. P. phot.

146. STE.-MAGNANCE, (Yonne). Tomb of the saint. Ste. Magnance. L. W. P. phot.

147. AUTUN, (Saône-et-Loire), Cathédrale. St. Mary Magdalen, from tomb of St. Lazare, now at St.-Pierre (Musée Lapidaire). By *Martinus monachus*. A. K. P. phot.

148. AUTUN, (Saône-et-Loire), Cathédrale. St. Martha from the tomb of St. Lazare, now at St.-Pierre (Musée Lapidaire). By *Martinus monachus.* A. K. P. phot.

149. AUTUN, (Saône-et-Loire), Cathédrale. St. Andrew from the tomb of St. Lazare, now at St.-Pierre (Musée Lapidaire). By *Martinus monachus.* A. K. P. phot.

150. ROUGEMONT, (Yonne). Western portal. Flagellation, Maries at Tomb, Limbo, Presentation, Massacre of Innocents, Flight, Annunciation, Visitation, Nativity, Shepherds, Adoration; Virgin, St. Peter, Aaron. L. W. P. phot.

1. CHARLIEU, (Loire), Abbaye. Relief now in cloister. Daniel in the Lions' Den
   B.-A. phot.

2. CHÂTEAUNEUF, (Saône-et-Loire). Southern portal. Twelve Apostles. A.K.P. phot.

3. Mont-St.-Vincent, (Saône-et-Loire). Western portal, tympanum. *Majestas Domini*, St. Peter, St. Paul. L. W. P. phot.

4. CHARLIEU, (Loire). Tympanum of western portal. *Majestas Domini*, Apostles.
A. K. P. phot.

5. CLUNY, (Saône-et-Loire). Capital from ambulatory of abbey, now in Musée
    Ochier. The Rivers of Paradise. A. K. P. phot.

6. CLUNY, (Saône-et-Loire). Capital from ambulatory of abbey, now in Musée Ochier. Grammar. A. K. P. phot.

7. CLUNY, (Saône-et-Loire). Capital from ambulatory of abbey, now in Musée Ochier. The Third Tone of Plain Song. A. K. P. phot.

8. CLUNY, (Saône-et-Loire). Capital from ambulatory of abbey, now in Musée
Ochier. The Seventh Tone of Plain Song. Giraudon phot.

9. CLUNY, (Saône-et-Loire). Capital from ambulatory of abbey, now in Musée Ochier. The Arts of Metal Work and Miniature Painting. A. K. P. phot.

10. CLUNY, (Saône-et-Loire). Capital from abbey, now in Musée Ochier. The Sacrifice of Abraham. A. K. P. phot.

11. CHARLIEU, (Loire), Abbaye. Relief from refectory, now in cloister. The Annunciation, Joseph, a Prophet. B.-A. phot.

12. AVENAS, (Rhône). Altar, west front. *Majestas Domini*, Apostles. L. W. P. phot.

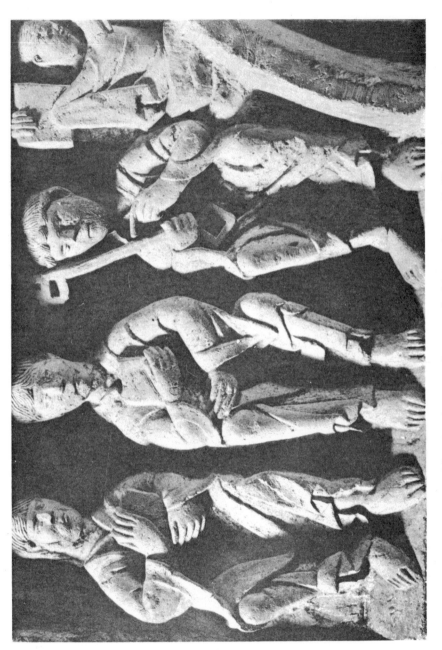

13.   AVENAS, (Rhône). Altar, west front, detail. *Majestas Domini.* L. W. P. phot.

14. AVENAS, (Rhône). Altar, west front, detail. St. Matthew, St. John, St. Simon. L. W. P. phot.

15. AVENAS, (Rhône). Altar, north face. Annunciation, Presentation. L. W. P. phot.

16. AVENAS, (Rhône). Altar, south face. Louis the Pious offers the church to St. Vincent. L. W. P. phot.

17. ANZY-LE-DUC, (Saône-et-Loire). Capital of nave. B.-A. phot.

18. ANZY-LE-DUC, (Saône-et-Loire). Capital of nave. Samson and the Lion.
L. W. P. phot.

19. Anzy-le-Duc, (Saône-et-Loire). Capital of nave. L. W. P. phot.
20. Anzy-le-Duc, (Saône-et-Loire). Capital of nave. St. Michael. L. W. P. phot.

21. ANZY-LE-DUC, (Saône-et-Loire). Capital of nave. B.-A. phot.

22. ANZY-LE-DUC, (Saône-et-Loire). Capital of nave. The Rivers of Paradise.
B.-A. phot.

23. ANZY-LE-DUC, (Saône-et-Loire). Capital of nave. The Damned. L. W. P. phot.

24. ANZY-LE-DUC, (Saône-et-Loire). Northern corbel of western portal. The Ass with a Book; supporting figure. L. B. W. phot.

25. St.-Parize-le-Châtel, (Nièvre). Capital of crypt. The Owl; Sciapodes.
A. K. P. phot.

26. St.-Parize-le-Châtel, (Nièvre). Capital of crypt. The Siren, unknown subject, *l'Âne qui joue*. A. K. P. phot.

27. CLUNY, (Saône-et-Loire). Musée Ochier. Fragment. Combat of Knights; Samson and the Lion. A. K. P. phot.

28. VÉZELAY, (Yonne). Capital of nave, north side, ninth pier. The Temptation.
"Ainay Master." F. M. S. phot.

29. VÉZELAY, (Yonne). Ancient capital, now in second story of narthex. St. George and the Dragon. "Ainay Master." L. W. P. phot.

30. VÉZELAY, (Yonne). Capital of nave, south side, second pier. "Cluny Master."
     F. M. S. phot.

31. VÉZELAY, (Yonne). Capital of nave, south side, fifth pier. The Winds. "Cluny Master." F. M. S. phot.

32. Vézelay, (Yonne). Capital of nave, south side, third pier. St. Eustace. "Cluny Master." F. M. S. phot.

33. Vézelay, (Yonne). Capital of nave, south side, sixth pier. Daniel and the Lions. "Cluny Master(?)." F. M. S. phot.

34. VÉZELAY, (Yonne). Capital of nave, north side, fourth pier. David and Goliath. "Vézelay Master No. 1." F. M. S. phot.

34 a. Vézelay, (Yonne). Capital of nave, south side, second pier. Wrath, Luxury. "Vézelay Master No. 1." F. M. S. phot.

35. VÉZELAY, (Yonne). Capital of nave, south side, fourth pier. The Death of
Cain. "Vézelay Master No. 2." F. M. S. phot.

36. Vézelay, (Yonne). Capital of narthex, south side, second pier. St. Peter and St. Paul resuscitate the dead Youth. "Vézelay Master No. 2." F. M. S. phot.

37. Vézelay, (Yonne). Capital of gallery, narthex. The stolen Blessing. "Vézelay Master No. 2," F. M. S. phot.

38. Vézelay, (Yonne). Capital of narthex, north side, second pier. Nathan reproaches David. "Vézelay Master No. 2." F. M. S. phot.

39. VÉZELAY, (Yonne). Capital of nave, north side, sixth pier. The golden Calf. "Vézelay Master No. 3." F. M. S. phot.

40. Vézelay, (Yonne). Capital of nave, south side, fourth pier. A Prophet brings
to the Mill of St. Paul the Grain for the Eucharistic Bread. "Vézelay Master No. 3." F. M. S. phot.

41. VÉZELAY, (Yonne). Capital of nave, north side, first pier. St. Mary Magda-
len(?). "Androche Master." F. M. S. phot.

42. Vézelay, (Yonne). Capital of nave, north side, eighth pier, now in narthex. St. Anthony assailed by Daemons. "Bifora Master." F. M. S. phot.

43. VÉZELAY, (Yonne). Capital of narthex. The Sacrifice of Bread in the Ancient Law. "Bifora Master." F. M. S. phot.

44. Vézelay, (Yonne). Capital of nave, north side, third pier. Judith. "Bath-sheba Master." F. M. S. phot.

45. VÉZELAY, (Yonne). Capital of gallery of narthex. Tobias anoints his Father's Eyes. "Tobias Master." F. M. S. phot.

46. Vézelay, (Yonne). Capital of narthex, north side, second pier. Samson and the Lion. "Master of the Tympanum." F. M. S. phot.

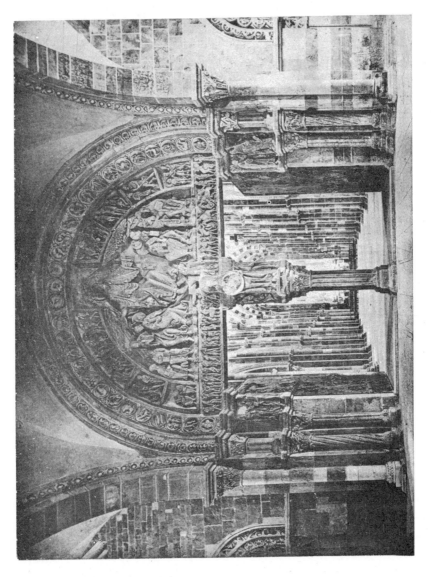

47. Vézelay, (Yonne). Central western portal. Zodiac; Pentecost; St. John, St. James, St. John the Baptist, St. Peter, St. Paul. N. D. phot.

48. Vézelay, (Yonne). Western portal, tympanum, northern portion. Zodiac; Pentecost. F. M. S. phot. from cast.

48 a. Vézelay, (Yonne). Central portal, tympanum, central portion. Detail of the Pentecost, St. John the Baptist. Giraudon phot. from cast.

49. Vézelay, (Yonne). Central portal, tympanum, southern half. Zodiac, Pentecost. F. M. S. phot. from cast.

50. Vézelay. (Yonne). Northern portal, tympanum. Journey to Emmaus, *Noli me tangere*. Ascension. B.-A. phot.

51. VÉZELAY, (Yonne). Tympanum of southern portal. Adoration of Magi, Annunciation, Visitation, Shepherds, Nativity. N. D. phot.

52. SAULIEU, (Côte-d'Or), St.-Androche. Capital of nave. Judas hangs himself.
B.-A. phot.

53. SAULIEU, (Côte-d'Or), St.-Androche. Capital of nave. The Temptation.
B.-A. phot.

54. SAULIEU, (Côte-d'Or), St.-Androche. Capital of nave. Flight into Egypt. B.-A. phot.

55. SAULIEU, (Côte-d'Or), St.-Androche. Capital of nave. *Noli me tangere*. B.-A. phot.

56. SAULIEU, (Côte-d'Or), St.-Androche. Capital of nave. Balaam. B.-A. phot.

57. SAULIEU, (Côte-d'Or), St.-Androche. Capital of nave. Centaur. B.-A. phot.

58. SAULIEU, (Côte-d'Or), St.-Androche. Capital of nave. B.-A. phot.

59. SAULIEU, (Côte-d'Or), St.-Androche. Capital of nave. B.-A. phot.

60. SAULIEU, (Côte-d'Or), St.-Androche. Capital of nave. B.-A. phot.
61. SAULIEU, (Côte-d'Or), St.-Androche. Capital of nave. B.-A. phot.

62. Moûtier-St.-Jean, (Côte-d'Or). Capital now in Fogg Museum, Cambridge, Mass. Elizabeth and a Youth. Fogg Museum phot.

63. MOUTIER-ST.-JEAN, (Côte-d'Or). Capital now in Fogg Museum, Cambridge, Mass. The Annunciation to Zacharias. Fogg Museum phot.

64. MOÛTIER-ST.-JEAN, (Côte-d'Or). Capital now in Fogg Museum, Cambridge, Mass. The Temple(?). Fogg Museum phot.

65. MOÛTIER-ST.-JEAN, (Côte-d'Or). Capital now in Fogg Museum, Cambridge, Mass. The Journey to Emmaus. Fogg Museum phot.

66. Moûtier-St.-Jean, (Côte-d'Or). Capital now in Fogg Museum, Cambridge, Mass. Offerings of Cain and Abel. Fogg Museum phot.

67. AUTUN, (Saône-et-Loire), Cathédrale. Capital. B.-A. phot.

68. AUTUN, (Saône-et-Loire), Cathédrale. Capital of nave. Samson. Stoedtner
    phot.

69. AUTUN, (Saône-et-Loire), Cathédrale. Capital of nave. St. Vincent. Stoedt-
    ner phot.

70. AUTUN, (Saône-et-Loire), Cathédrale. Capital of nave. Christ washing the Feet of St. Peter. B.-A. phot.

71. AUTUN, (Saône-et-Loire), Cathédrale. Capital now in museum. The Flight into Egypt. B.-A. phot.

72. AUTUN, (Saône-et-Loire), Cathédrale. Capital now in museum. Adoration of the Magi. B.-A. phot.

73. AUTUN, (Saône-et-Loire), Cathédrale. Capital of nave. Flight of Simon
Magus. B.-A. phot.

74. AUTUN, (Saône-et-Loire), Cathédrale. Modern copy of a capital of transept. The Duke, Hugh II, offers the new Cathedral to St. Lazare. A. K. P. phot.

75. AUTUN, (Saône-et-Loire), Cathédrale. Capital of nave, south side, fifth pier. Fall of Simon Magus. A. K. P. phot.

76. AUTUN, (Saône-et-Loire), Cathédrale. Capital of nave. Body of St. Vincent
guarded by Crows. B.-A. phot.

77. Autun, (Saône-et-Loire), Cathédrale. Capital of nave. The Stoning of St. Stephen. B.-A. phot.

78. Autun, (Saône-et-Loire), Cathédrale. Capital of nave. *Noli me tangere.*
    B.-A. phot.

79. AUTUN, (Saône-et-Loire), Cathédrale. Capital of nave. St. Peter liberated by
the Angel. A. K. P. phot.

80. AUTUN, (Saône-et-Loire), Cathédrale. Tympanum of western portal. The Last Judgment. Signed "Gislebertus." A. K. P. phot.

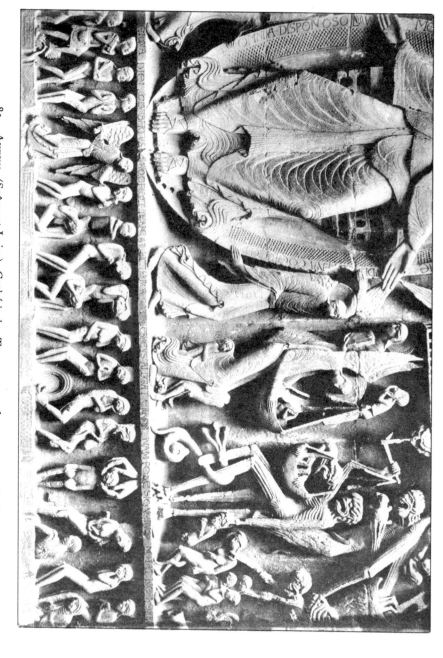

81. AUTUN, (Saône-et-Loire), Cathédrale. Tympanum of western portal. Detail of the Last Judgment. Signed "Gislebertus." Giraudon phot. from cast.

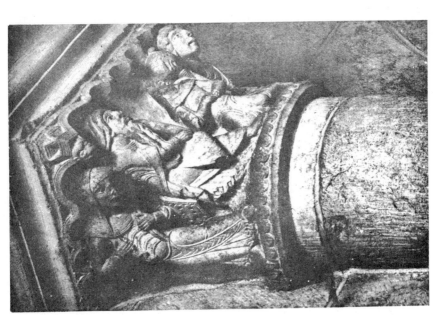

82. GARGILESSE, (Indre). Capital of nave. Dance of Salome. L. W. P. phot.
83. GARGILESSE, (Indre). Capital of nave. The Visitation. L. W. P. phot.

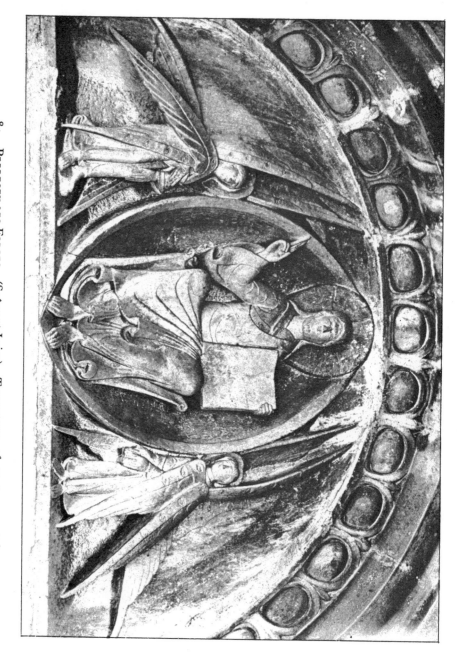

84. Perrecey-les-Forges, (Saône-et-Loire). Tympanum of western portal. *Majestas Domini*. A. K. P. phot.

85. PERRECEY-LES-FORGES, (Saône-et-Loire). Lintel of western portal. The Kiss of Judas; Christ is taken; Peter cuts off the ear of Malchus. L. W. P. phot.

86. St.-Paul-de-Varax, (Ain). Western façade, northern lunette. The Fall of
Simon Magus (?). L. W. P. phot.

87. St.-Paul-de-Varax, (Ain). Western façade, second lunette from north. Adoration of Magi; Simon and Nero (?), St. Peter resuscitates the dead Man(?). L. W. P. phot.

88. St.-Paul-de-Varax, (Ain). Tympanum of western portal. The Ascension. B.-A. phot.

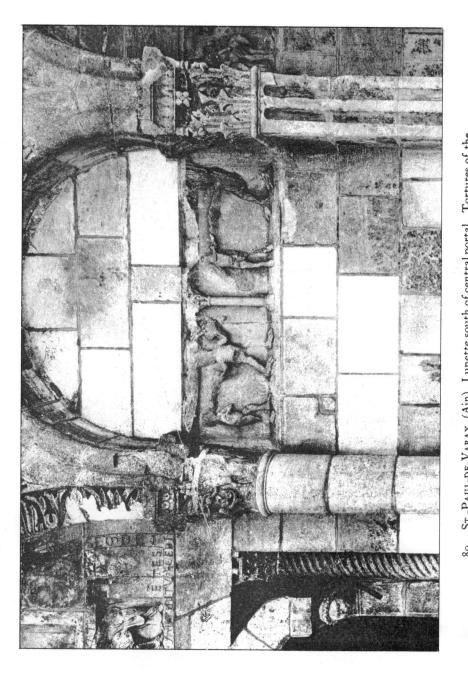

89.   St.-Paul-de-Varax, (Ain). Lunette south of central portal. Tortures of the Damned. L. W. P. phot.

90. St.-Paul-de-Varax, (Ain). Western façade, southern lunette. The Souls of the Damned are driven to Hell. L. W. P. phot.

91. St.-Paul-de-Varax, (Ain). Tympanum of southern portal. St. Anthony and the Faun. L. W. P. phot.

92. MACON, (Saône-et-Loire), St.-Vincent. Tympanum of western portal. The Last Judgment. Silvestre phot.

93. Neuilly-en-Donjon, (Allier). Tympanum of western portal. Adoration of Magi; Temptation; Last Supper. L. W. P. phot.

94. NEUILLY-EN-DONJON, (Allier). Western portal, tympanum, detail. Adoration
of Magi; Temptation; Last Supper. L. W. P. phot.

95. Anzy-le-Duc, (Saône-et-Loire). Portal of priory. Adoration of Magi; Temptation; Shame of Adam and Eve; Hell. L. W. P. phot.

96.   ANZY-LE-DUC, (Saône-et-Loire). Western portal. Elders, Ascension. L. W. P. phot.

97. ANZY-LE-DUC, (Saône-et-Loire). Tympanum of western portal, detail. An Angel. L. W. P. phot.

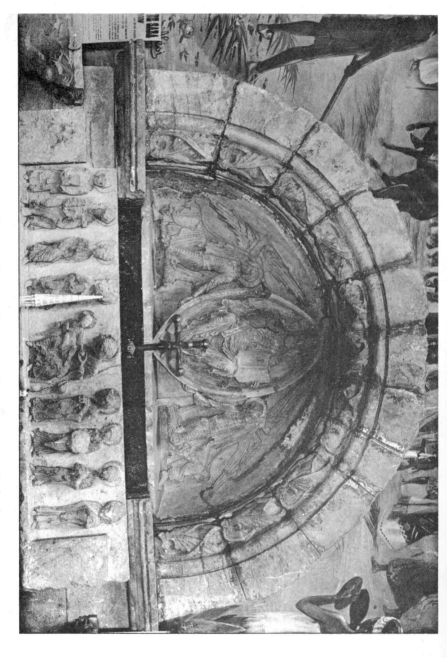

98. ANZY-LE-DUC, (Saône-et-Loire). Tympanum from western portal of priory, now in Musée Eucharistique, Paray-le-Monial. *Majestas Domini*, Virgin and Saints. L. W. P. phot.

99. ANZY-LE-DUC, (Saône-et-Loire). Tympanum from western portal of priory, now in Musée Eucharistique, Paray-le-Monial. Detail of *Majestas Domini*. L. W. P. phot.

100. St.-Révérien, (Nièvre). Western portal, southern archivolt. A Cherub. A. K. P. phot.

101. ST.-RÉVÉRIEN, (Nièvre). Western portal, northern archivolt. A Cherub.
A. K. P. phot.

102. St.-Révérien, (Nièvre). Capital of ambulatory. Journey of the Magi. L. W. P. phot.

103. St.-Révérien, (Nièvre). Capital of ambulatory. Jacob's Dream. L. W. P. phot.

104. Montceaux-l'Étoile, (Saône-et-Loire). Western portal, tympanum. The Ascension. L. W. P. phot.

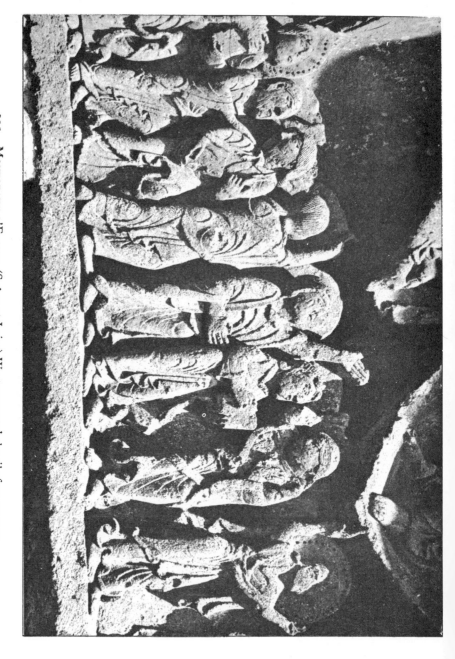

105. Montceaux-l'Etoile, (Saône-et-Loire). Western portal, detail of tympanum. Virgin, six Apostles and Enoch from the Ascension. L. W. P. phot.

106. ST.-AMOUR, (Saône-et-Loire). Relief now in interior of church, south wall. *Majestas Domini.* L. W. P. phot.

107. Fleury-la-Montagne, (Saône-et-Loire). Tympanum of western portal. The Ascension, the Adoration. B.-A. phot.

108. CHARLIEU, (Saône-et-Loire), Abbaye. Tympanum and lintel of outer portal.
Majestas Domini, Virgin, two Angels and twelve Apostles. A. K. P. phot.

109. CHARLIEU, (Saône-et-Loire), Abbaye. Outer portal, detail of tympanum. The Virgin, an Angel, and six Apostles. A. K. P. phot.

110. Charlieu, (Saône-et-Loire), Abbaye. Outer portal, western window. The
Transfiguration, the Holy Spirit, Christ, Moses, Isaiah, St. John, St.
St. James, Peter; the Last Supper; Sacrifice according to the Old Testa-
ment. A. K. P. phot.

111. St.-Julien-de-Jonzy, (Saône-et-Loire). Tympanum of western portal. Majestas Domini, the Last Supper. L. W. P. phot.

112. DONZY, (Nièvre), Notre-Dame-du-Pré. Western portal, detail of tympanum.
An Angel. L. W. P. phot.

113. DONZY, (Nièvre), Notre-Dame-du-Pré. Western portal, detail of tympanum. The Virgin. L. W. P. phot.

114. Donzy, (Nièvre), Notre-Dame-du-Pré. Western portal, detail of tympanum.
A Prophet. L. W. P. phot.

115. LA CHARITÉ-SUR-LOIRE, (Nièvre). Tympanum of southern portal now in
church, detail. A Prophet and an Apostle. L. W. P. phot.

116. La Charité-sur-Loire, (Nièvre). Tympanum of southern portal, now inside church, detail. *Majestas Domini*. L. W. P. phot.

117. La Charité-sur-Loire, (Nièvre). Tympanum of southern portal, now inside church, detail. A Prophet, two Apostles. L. W. P. phot.

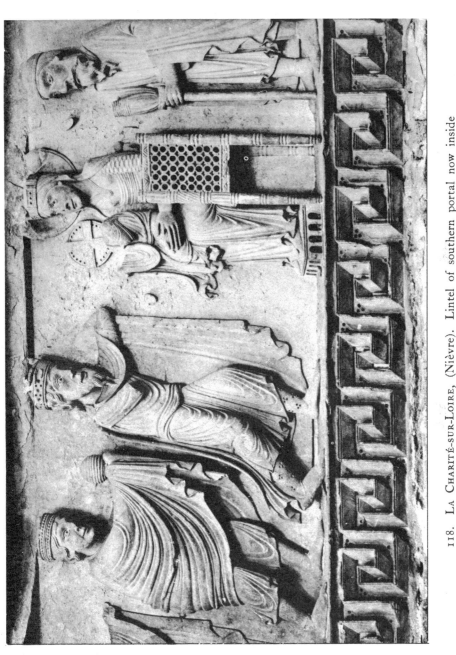

118. LA CHARITÉ-SUR-LOIRE, (Nièvre). Lintel of southern portal now inside
church. The Adoration of the Magi. L. W. P. phot.

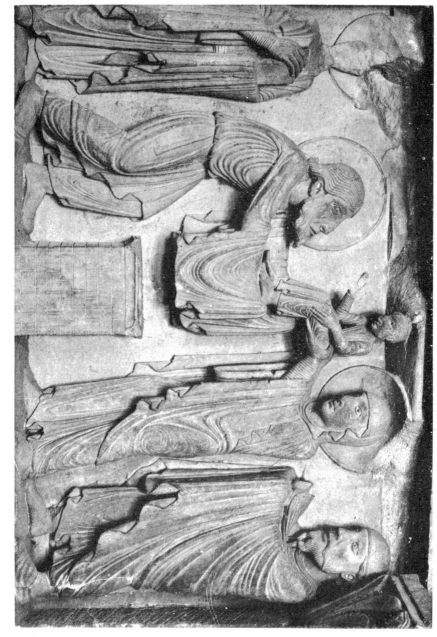

119. La Charté-sur-Loire, (Nièvre). Lintel of southern portal, now inside church. Presentation in the Temple. L. W. P. phot.

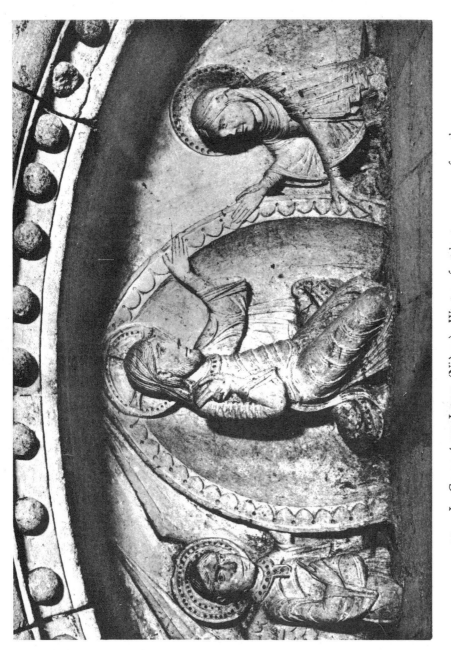

120. La Charité-sur-Loire, (Nièvre). Western façade, tympanum of northern portal, now in house. *Majestas Domini.* L. W. P. phot.

121.   LA CHARITÉ-SUR-LOIRE, (Nièvre). Western façade, lintel of northern portal,
now in house, detail. Annunciation, Visitation, Nativity. L. W. P. phot.

122. LA CHARITÉ-SUR-LOIRE, (Nièvre). Western façade, lintel of northern portal now in house, detail. Nativity, Shepherds. L. W. P. phot.

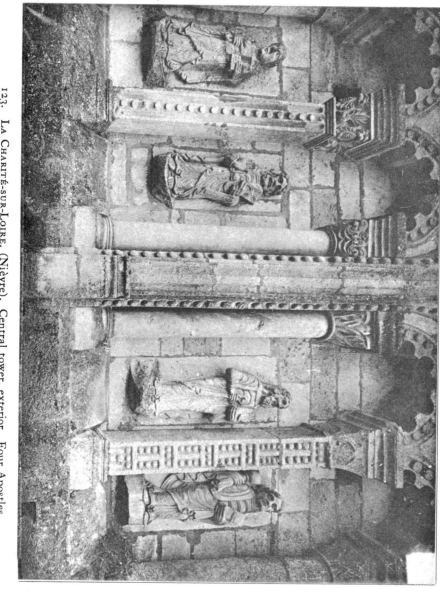

123. La Charité-sur-Loire, (Nièvre). Central tower, exterior. Four Apostles. B.-A. phot.

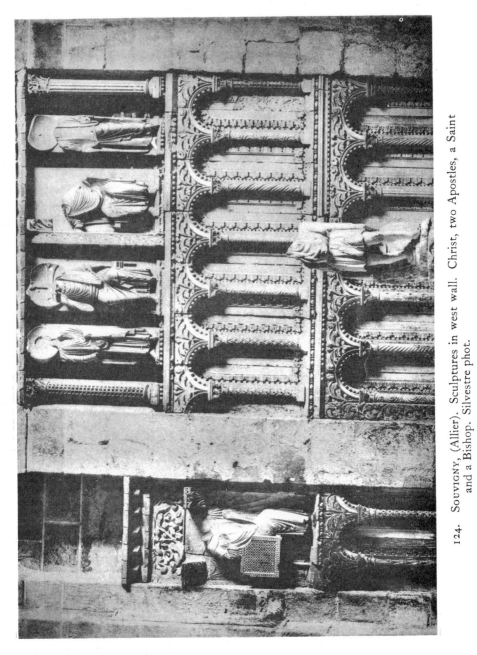

124. SOUVIGNY, (Allier). Sculptures in west wall. Christ, two Apostles, a Saint and a Bishop. Silvestre phot.

125. SOUVIGNY, (Allier). Sculptures in west wall. Christ, two Apostles, a Saint. Stoedtner phot.

126. NEVERS, (Nièvre), St.-Sauveur. Capitals now in the Musée de la Porte du Croux. A Monkey playing the Violin; *l'Âne qui joue.* L. W. P. phot.

127. NEVERS, (Nièvre), St.-Sauveur. Capitals now in the Musée de la Porte du
　　　Croux. The Licorne and the Aspic. A. K. P. phot.
128. NEVERS, (Nièvre), St.-Sauveur. Capital now in the Musée de la Porte du
　　　Croux. A. K. P. phot.

129.   NEVERS, (Nièvre), St.-Sauveur. Capital now in the Musée de la Porte du
        Croux. Ethiopian. A. K. P. phot.

130.   NEVERS, (Nièvre), St.-Sauveur. Capital now in the Musée de la Porte du
        Croux. The Basilisk. A. K. P. phot.

131. NEVERS, (Nièvre), St.-Sauveur. Capitals now in the Musée de la Porte du Croux. The Dromedary; the Salamander. L. W. P. phot.

132. Nevers, (Nièvre), St.-Sauveur. Capital now in the Musée de la Porte du Croux. St. Peter and St. John heal the Cripple before the Temple Beautiful. L. W. P. phot.

133. NEVERS, (Nièvre), St.-Sauveur. Tympanum, now in the Musée de la Porte du Croux. Christ gives the Keys to St. Peter. L. W. P. phot.

134. Dijon, (Côte-d'Or), St.-Bénigne. Tympanum from abbey, now in Musée Archéologique. *Majestas Domini.* A. K. P. phot.

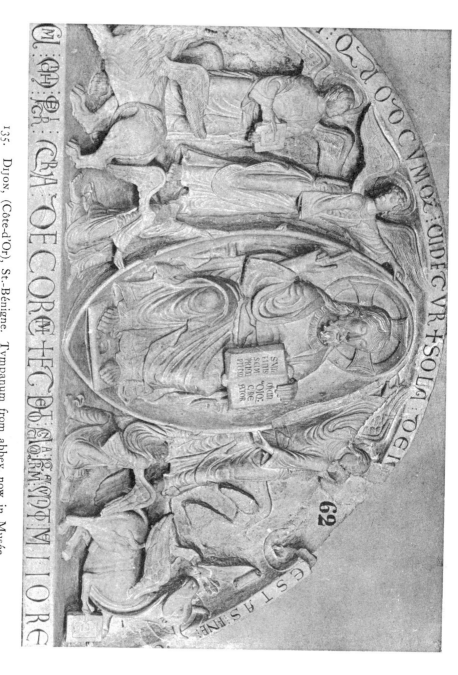

135. Dijon, (Côte-d'Or), St.-Bénigne. Tympanum from abbey, now in Musée Archéologique. *Majestas Domini.* A. K. P. phot.

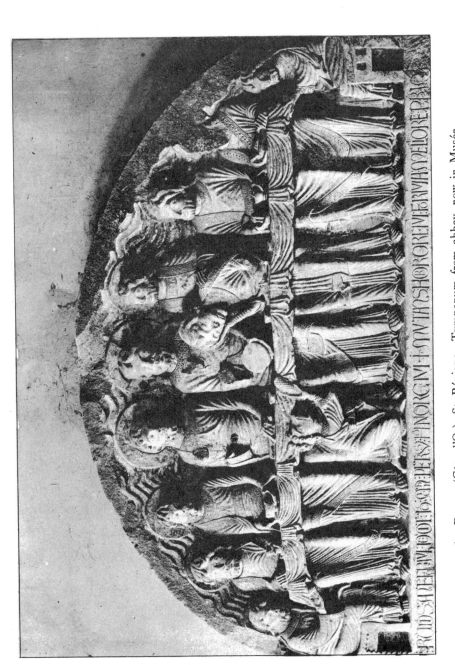

136.   DIJON, (Côte-d'Or), St.-Bénigne. Tympanum from abbey, now in Musée
Archéologique. Last Supper. A. K. P. phot.

137. AVALLON, (Yonne), St.-Lazare. Western façade, central portal, northern voussures. Angels, Elders, Zodiac. F. M. S. phot.

138. AVALLON, (Yonne), St.-Lazare. Western façade, central portal, southern voussures. Angels, Elders, Zodiac. F. M. S. phot.

139. AVALLON, (Yonne), St.-Lazare. Western façade, central portal, southern jamb. A. K. P. phot.

140. AVALLON, (Yonne), St.-Lazare. Western façade, southern portal, tympanum.
      Adoration of Magi, Journey of Magi, Magi before Herod. F. M. S. phot.

141. Avallon, (Yonne), St.-Lazare. Southern portal, base of southern jamb. F. M. S. phot.

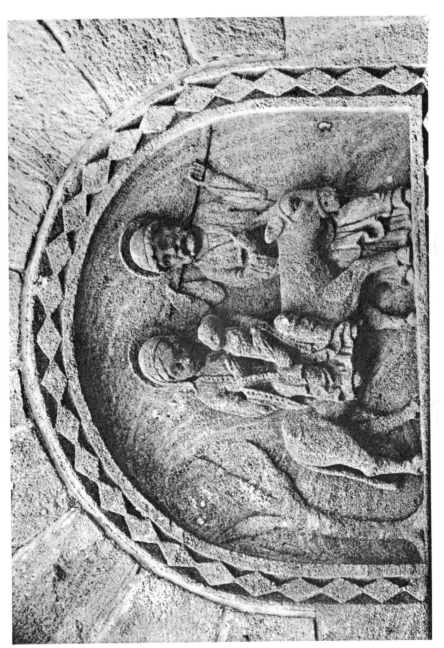

142. Bois-Ste.-Marie, (Saône-et-Loire). Southern portal, tympanum. The Flight into Egypt. A. K. P. phot.

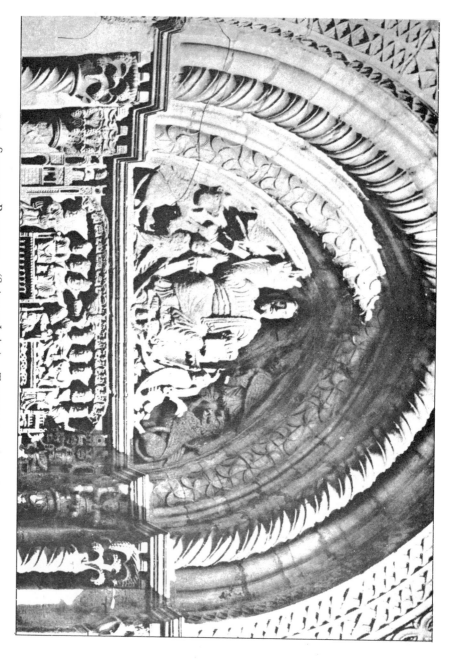

143. SEMUR-EN-BRIONNAIS, (Saône-et-Loire). Tympanum of western portal. *Majestas Domini*; St. Hilaire before the Council; Death of the pseudo-pope Leo. L. W. P. phot.

Portail principal de l'Eglise S.t Benigne de Dijon par ou l'on entre du porche ou vestibule distant de l'anciene l'eglise du costé d'occident

144. DIJON, (Côte-d'Or), St.-Bénigne. Western portal, according to Plancher's engraving. *Majestas Domini*, Magi, Shepherds, Nativity, St. Bénigne.

145. Dijon, (Côte-d'Or), St.-Bénigne. Head of statue addossed to trumeau of western portal, now in Musée Archéologique. St. Bénigne. A. K. P. phot.

146. STE.-MAGNANCE, (Yonne). Tomb of the saint. Ste. Magnance. L. W. P. phot.

147. Autun, (Saône-et-Loire), Cathédrale. St. Mary Magdalen, from tomb of
St. Lazare, now at St.-Pierre (Musée Lapidaire). By *Martinus monachus*.
A. K. P. phot.

148. AUTUN, (Saône-et-Loire), Cathédrale. St. Martha from the tomb of St. Lazare, now at St.-Pierre (Musée Lapidaire). By *Martinus monachus.* A. K. P. phot.

149. AUTUN, (Saône-et-Loire), Cathédrale. St. Andrew from the tomb of St. Lazare, now at St.-Pierre (Musée Lapidaire). By *Martinus monachus.* A. K. P. phot.

150. Rougemont, (Yonne). Western portal. Flagellation, Maries at Tomb, Limbo, Presentation, Massacre of Innocents, Flight, Annunciation, Visitation, Nativity, Shepherds, Adoration; Virgin, St. Peter, Aaron. L. W. P. phot.

ROMANESQUE SCULPTURE

OF THE PILGRIMAGE ROADS

VOLUME III

TUSCANY AND APULIA

ILLUSTRATIONS

ILLUSTRATIONS

(151–261)

TUSCANY AND APULIA

173. TROIA, (Foggia), Cattedrale. Western portal, lintel. Christ, the Virgin, St. Peter, and the four Evangelists. L. W. P. phot.

174. MILAN, S. Ambrogio. Detail of pulpit. The Last Supper. Alinari phot.

175. MILAN, S. Ambrogio. Detail of pulpit. Alinari phot.

176. BARLETTA, (Bari), Collegiata. West façade, southern portal. Samson with Lion; grotesque subjects. A. K. P. phot.

177. BARLETTA, (Bari), Collegiata. West façade, northern portal. Gabriel. 1153. A. K. P. phot.

178. BRINDISI, (Lecce), S. Lucia. Crypt. Annunciation. L. W. P. phot.

179. CONVERSANO, (Bari), Cattedrale. Tympanum of western portal. Virgin and Angels. 1159–1174. A. K. P. phot.

180. MOSCUFO, (Chieti), S. Maria del Lago. Pulpit. Evangelists, St. John, Samson, Man fighting Bear, Deacon with Chalice. Signed by Nicodemus. 1159. Moscioni phot.

181. PISA, Camposanto. Fragment. *Majestas Domini.* Signed by Buonamico. A. K. P. phot.

182. PISA, Camposanto. Fragments of a pulpit. David; St. Paúl (?); Evangelists. L. W. P. phot.

183. PISA, Camposanto. Fragment of a pulpit. A. K. P. phot.

184. PISA, Camposanto. Fragment of a pulpit. The Evangelists. L. W. P. phot.

185. PISA, Camposanto. Fragment of a pulpit. A. K. P. phot.

186. CAGLIARI, (Sardinia), Cattedrale. Ambo. Annunciation, Visitation, Nativity, Maries at Tomb, Evangelists. Fragments from pulpit of Pisa, by Guglielmo da Innspruch, 1158–1162. Alinari phot.

187. CAGLIARI, (Sardinia), Cattedrale. Ambo. Transfiguration, Baptism, Presentation, St. Paul. Fragments from pulpit of Pisa, by Guglielmo da Innspruch. 1158–1162. Alinari phot.

188. CAGLIARI, (Sardinia), Cattedrale. Lion from pulpit of Pisa. By Guglielmo da Innspruch, 1158–1162. Alinari phot.

189. PISA, Duomo. Exterior of choir, south side. David. L. W. P. phot.

190. PISTOIA, (Firenze), S. Bartolommeo in Pantano. Lintel of portal. Giving the Keys, Apostles and Angels. 1167. Alinari phot.

191. PISTOIA, (Firenze), S. Andrea. Capitals and lintel of portal. Magi before Herod; Adoration; Annunciation to Zacharias; Annunciation. Lintel signed by Gruamonte and Adeodato; capitals by Enrico. Alinari phot.

192. PISTOIA, (Firenze), S. Andrea. Northern impost of portal. Annunciation to Zacharias; the Visitation. By Enrico. Alinari phot.

193. PISTOIA, (Firenze), S. Andrea. Southern impost of portal. The Annunciation. Signed by Enrico. Alinari phot.

194. VOLTERRA, (Pisa), Duomo. Pulpit, detail. The Last Supper. Lombardi phot.

195. VOLTERRA, (Pisa), Duomo. Pulpit, detail. The Sacrifice of Abraham. Lombardi phot.

196. VOLTERRA, (Pisa), Duomo. Pulpit. Visitation, Annunciation. Lombardi phot.

197. MONTE S. ANGELO, (Foggia), "Tomba di Rotari." Tympanum of western portal. Deposition, Maries at Tomb. L. W. P. phot.

198. MONTE S. ANGELO, (Foggia), "Tomba di Rotari." Lintel of western portal, detail. Christ haled to Execution. L. W. P. phot.

199. PISTOIA, (Firenze), S. Giovanni Fuorcivitas. Lintel of portal. The Last Supper. Alinari phot.

200. BARI, S. Niccola. Western portal, southern spandrel. An Angel. A. K. P. phot.

201. TRANI, (Bari), Ognisanti. Narthex. Gabriel of the Annunciation. L. W. P. phot.

202. TRANI, (Bari), Ognisanti. Narthex. Virgin of the Annunciation. L. W. P. phot.

203. TRANI, (Bari), Ognisanti. Narthex. Gabriel of the Annunciation. L. W. P. phot. from cast.

204. TRANI, (Bari), Cattedrale. Western portal, northern jamb. Jacob's Dream. L. W. P. phot.

205. TRANI, (Bari), Cattedrale. Western portal, northern jamb. Jacob's Dream; Jacob and the Angel.

206. TRANI, (Bari), Cattedrale.. Western portal, northern jamb. Jacob wrestles with the Angel. L. W. P. phot.

207. TRANI, (Bari), Cattedrale. Western portal, podium of northern column. L. W. P. phot.

208. TRANI, (Bari), Cattedrale. Western portal, southern jamb. A Prophet. L. W. P. phot.

209. TRANI, (Bari), Cattedrale. Western portal, southern jamb. A Prophet. L. W. P. phot.

210. TRANI, (Bari), Cattedrale. Western portal, southern jamb. Peasant warming his Socks by Fire. L. W. P. phot.

211. TRANI, (Bari), Cattedrale. Western portal, southern jamb. A Siren. L. W. P. phot.

212. TRANI, (Bari), Cattedrale. Western portal, podium of southern column. L. W. P. phot.

213. S. LEONARDO, (Foggia). Southern portal, upper zone. A liberated prisoner and St. Leonard. L. W. P. phot.

214. S. LEONARDO, (Foggia). Tympanum of southern portal. *Majestas Domini.* L. W. P. phot.

215. SAN LEONARDO, (Foggia). Northern portal, eastern capital. The Adoration of the Magi. L. W. P. phot.

216. SAN LEONARDO, (Foggia). Northern portal, western jamb. Balaam and St. Michael; a Centaur. L. W. P. phot.

217. PIANELLA, (Chieti), S. Michele. Detail of pulpit. St. Matthew. A. K. P. phot.

218. PIANELLA, (Chieti), S. Michele. Lintel of western portal. L. W. P. phot.

219. TORRE DE' PASSERI, (Teramo), S. Clemente di Casauria. Western portal. St. Clement, St. Phebus, St. Cornelius, the abbot Leonas; Translation of the Relics of St. Clement; four Prophets. 1176. Alinari phot.

220. TORRE DE' PASSERI, (Teramo), S. Clemente di Casauria. Tympanum of portal. St. Clement, St. Phebus, St. Cornelius, the abbot Leonas; Translation of the Relics of St. Clement. 1176. Alinari phot.

221. TORRE DE' PASSERI, (Teramo), S. Clemente di Casauria. Detail of ciborium. Moscioni phot.

222. S. CASCIANO, (Pisa). Archivolt of lateral portal. Alinari phot.

223. S. CASCIANO, (Pisa). Archivolt of western portal. Resurrection of Lazarus; Entry into Jerusalem. Signed by Biduino. 1180. Alinari phot.

224. LUCCA, S. Salvatore. Western portal, lintel. The Infant St. Nicolas stands upright in his Bath. Signed by Biduino. Alinari phot.

225. LUCCA, S. Salvatore. Southern portal, lintel. Dieudonné is transported by St. Nicolas from serving the pagan King to the House of his Parents. Alinari phot.

226. ARCETRI, (Firenze), S. Leonardo. Detail of pulpit. Adoration of the Magi; Jesse Tree. Alinari phot.

227. LUCCA, S. Giovanni. Western portal. The Virgin, two Angels and ten Apostles. Alinari phot.

228. PISTOIA, (Firenze), S. Pietro Maggiore. Lintel of portal. The Giving of the Keys; the Apostles. Alinari phot.

229. GROPPOLI, (Pistoia), Chapel of Villa Dalpina. Detail of pulpit. Flight into Egypt; Nativity. 1194. Alinari phot.

230. GROPPOLI, (Pistoia), Chapel of Villa Dalpina. St. Michael. Alinari phot.

231. MONTE S. ANGELO, (Foggia), S. Maria Maggiore. Tympanum of western portal. Madonna of the Adoration, Angels, Donors. 1198. L. W. P. phot.

232. BITONTO, (Bari), Cattedrale. Tympanum of western portal. Christ in Limbo, Annunciation, Visitation, Adoration, Presentation. 1200. Moscioni phot.

233. BITONTO, (Bari), Cattedrale. Western portal, tympanum. Christ in Limbo. 1200. A. K. P. phot. from cast.

234. PISTOIA, (Firenze), S. Bartolommeo in Pantano. Detail of pulpit. The Evangelists; Annunciation; Adoration of Magi. By Guido Bigarelli da Como. Alinari phot.

235. SPOLETO, (Perugia), Cattedrale. Supporting figure of western façade. A. K. P. phot.

236. SPOLETO, (Perugia), Cattedrale. Supporting figure of west façade. A. K. P. phot.

237. SPOLETO, Chiesa di Ponziano. Western façade, detail of rose-window. St. Matthew. L. W. P. phot.

238. SPOLETO, Cattedrale. Western façade, detail of rose-window. St. Matthew. A. K. P. phot.

239. SPOLETO, S. Pietro. Western façade, reliefs north of central portal. Death of the Just; Death of the Unjust; the Lion's Paw is caught in the Log; the Man escapes Harm by bowing humbly to the Lion. Anderson phot.

240. TRANI, (Bari), Cattedrale. Southern transept, exterior. St. Luke. L. W. P. phot. from cast.

241. TRANI, (Bari), Cattedrale. Southern transept, exterior. St. Luke. L. W. P. phot. from cast.

242. FOGGIA, Cattedrale. Statue in garden behind church. St. Paul. A. K. P. phot.

243. FOGGIA, Cattedrale. Statue in garden behind church. St. Matthew. A. K. P. phot.

244. BITONTO, (Bari), Cattedrale. Detail of pulpit. Signed by Niccolò, 1229. Antonelli-Matteuci phot.

245. BITONTO, (Bari), Cattedrale. Stair-rail of pulpit. Frederic II, Yolande, Henry and Conrad. Signed by Niccolò, 1229. Alinari phot.

246. BARGA, (Lucca). Pulpit. Adoration of Magi; Evangelists; Nativity; Visitation. Alinari phot.

247. LUCCA, Cattedrale. Western portal, tympanum. The Ascension. Alinari phot.

248. GENOVA, Cattedrale. Capella S. Giovanni, Arca. Baptism of Christ; Dance of Salome. Alinari phot.

249. VOLTERRA, (Pisa), Cattedrale. Deposition (in wood). Lombardi phot.

250. S. STEFANO DI MONOPOLI, (Bari). Tympanum of western portal. Christ, St. Stephen, St. George, donors. 1236. A. K. P. phot.

251. BARLETTA, (Bari), S. Andrea. Western portal, tympanum. Deësis. Heads of Evangelists in bases of columns. Signed by Simeon of Ragusa, *incola Tranensis*. A. K. P. phot.

252. BARLETTA, (Bari), S. Andea. Western portal, north jamb. Virgin, Expulsion, Temptation. Moscioni phot.

253. BENEVENTO, S. Sofia. Tympanum of portal. Christ, the Virgin(?), St. Theodore and a Donor. A. K. P. phot.

254. GENOVA, Cattedrale. Tympanum of western portal. *Majestas Domini;* Martyrdom of St. Lawrence. L. W. P. phot.

255. GENOVA, Cattedrale. Central western portal, northern spandrel. L. W. P. phot.

256. GENOVA, Cattedrale. Central western portal, southern spandrel. L. W. P. phot.

257. GENOVA, Cattedrale. Western portal, northern jamb. The Visitation. L. W. P. phot.

258. GENOVA, Cattedrale. Western façade, southern corner. St. John. L. W. P. phot.

259. RUTIGLIANO, (Bari). Northern portal, tympanum. The Madonna and an Angel. L. W. P. phot.

260. TERLIZZI, (Bari), Collegiata. Tympanum now in portal of Chiesa del Rosario. The Last Supper. Signed by Anseramo. 1276. L. W. P. phot. from a cast.

261. MONTE S. ANGELO, (Foggia), S. Michele. Western portal, tympanum. Madonna, St. Paul and Donor. Signed by Simeon *de hac* (**urbe**). 1305. L. W. P. phot.

151. BARI, S. Niccola. Capital of crypt. Alinari phot.

152. BARI, S. Niccola. Episcopal throne. 1098. Alinari phot.

153. BARI, S. Niccola. Episcopal throne. 1098. Moscioni phot.

154. Bari, S. Niccola. Episcopal throne detail. 1098. A. K. P. phot.

155. BARI, S. Niccola. Episcopal throne detail. 1098. Alinari phot. from cast.

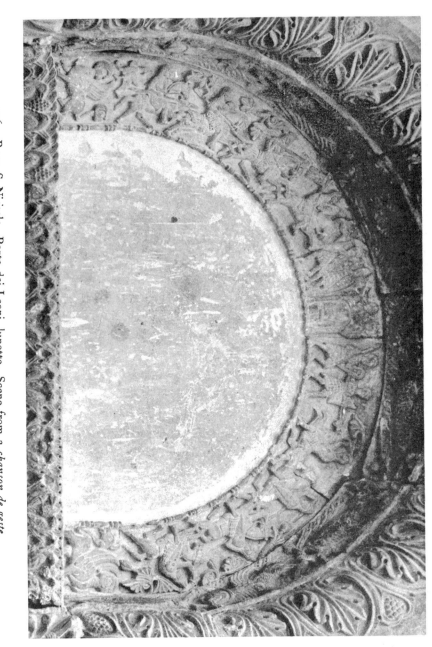

156. BARI, S. Niccola. Porta dei Leoni, lunette. Scene from a *chanson de geste*. L. W. P. phot.

157. MONOPOLI, (Bari), Cattedrale. Architrave in sacristy. Limbo; Maries at Tomb; Deposition. Moscioni phot.

158. Monopoli, (Bari), Cattedrale. Archivolt now in sacristy, detail. An Angel. Phot. Antonelli-Matteuci.

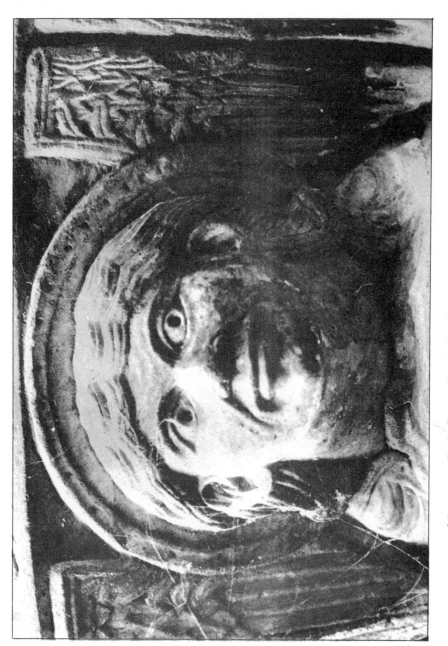

159. MONOPOLI, (Bari), Cattedrale. Archivolt now in sacristy, detail. An Angel.
Phot. Antonelli-Matteuci.

160. MONOPOLI, (Bari), Cattedrale. Archivolt now in sacristy, detail. An Angel.
Phot. Antonelli-Matteuci.

161. MONOPOLI, (Bari), Cattedrale. Archivolt now in sacristy, detail. Two Angels.
Phot. Antonelli-Matteuci.

162. Monopoli, (Bari), Cattedrale. Archivolt now in sacristy, detail. Two Angels. Phot. Antonelli-Matteuci.

163. RUTIGLIANO, (Bari). Lintel of western portal. Annunciation, Christ and Apostles. L. W. P. phot.

164. Rutigliano, (Bari). Relief over western portal. Annunciation. L. W. P. phot.

165. RUTIGLIANO, (Bari). Western portal, detail of lintel. Apostles. L. W. P. phot.

166. CAPUA, (Caserta), S. Marcello. South portal. Samson, Abraham and Angels, Sacrifice of Abraham. Alinari phot.

167.   VENOSA, (Potenza), S. Trinità. View from west end of southern side aisle.
       A. K. P. phot.

168. Venosa, (Potenza), S. Trinità. South side of nave from transept. L. W. P.
phot.

169. Venosa, (Potenza), S. Trinità. Southern portal. L. W. P. phot.

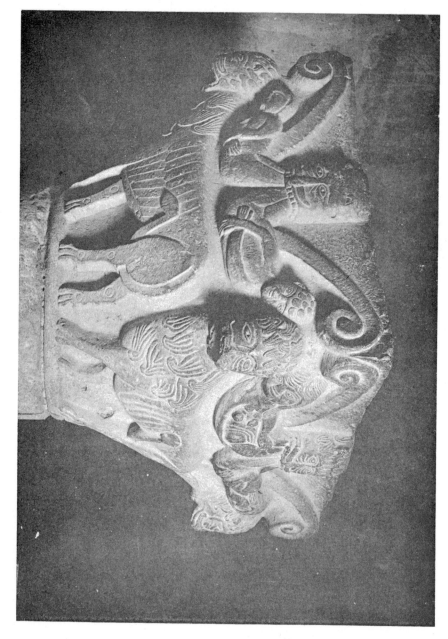

170. Venosa, (Potenza), S. Trinità. Capital now used as holy-water basin. Moscioni phot.

171. VENOSA, (POTENZA), S. Trinità. Lion. Moscioni phot.

172. TROIA, (Foggia), Cattedrale. South façade, tympanum of portal. Christ, the Aspic, the Basilisk, two Angels. L. W. P. phot.

173. TROIA, (Foggia), Cattedrale. Western portal, lintel. Christ, the Virgin, St. Peter, and the four Evangelists. L. W. P. phot.

174.   MILAN, S. Ambrogio.   Detail of pulpit.   The Last Supper.   Alinari phot.

175. MILAN, S. Ambrogio. Detail of pulpit. Alinari phot.

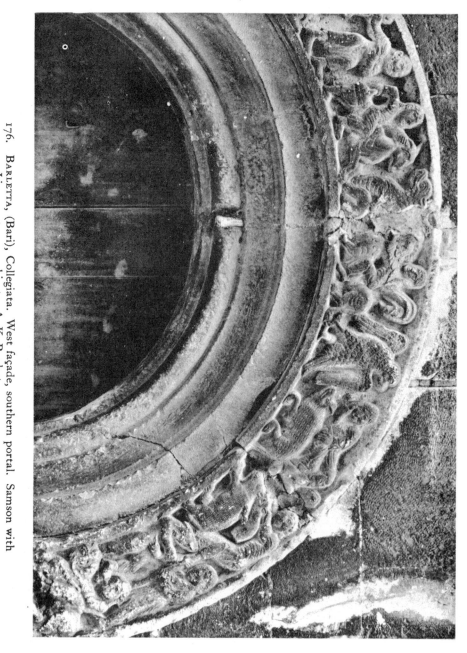

176. BARLETTA, (Bari), Collegiata. West façade, southern portal. Samson with Lion; grotesque subjects. A. K. P. phot.

177. BARLETTA, (Bari), Collegiata. West façade, northern portal. Gabriel. 1153. A. K. P. phot.

178. BRINDISI, (LECCE), S. Lucia. Crypt. Annunciation. L. W. P. phot.

179. CONVERSANO, (Bari), Cattedrale. Tympanum of western portal. Virgin and Angels. 1159–1174. A. K. P. phot.

180. Moscufo, (Chieti), S. Maria del Lago. Pulpit. Evangelists, St. John, Samson, Man fighting Bear, Deacon with Chalice. Signed by Nicodemus. 1159. Moscioni phot.

181. Pisa, Camposanto. Fragment. *Majestas Domini.* Signed by Buonamico.
A. K. P. phot.

182. PISA, Camposanto. Fragments of a pulpit. David; St. Paul (?); Evangelists.
L. W. P. phot.

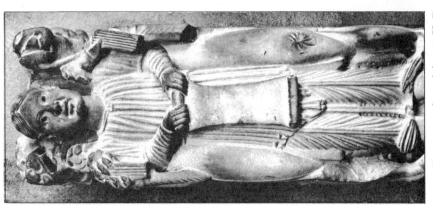

183. Pisa, Camposanto. Fragment of a pulpit. A. K. P. phot.
184. Pisa, Camposanto. Fragment of a pulpit. The Evangelists. L. W. P. phot.
185. Pisa, Camposanto. Fragment of a pulpit. A. K. P. phot.

186. CAGLIARI, (Sardinia), Cattedrale. Ambo. Annunciation, Visitation, Nativity, Maries at Tomb, Evangelists. Fragments from pulpit of Pisa, by
Guglielmo da Innspruch, 1158-1162. Alinari phot.

187. CAGLIARI, (Sardinia), Cattedrale. Ambo. Transfiguration, Baptism, Presentation, St. Paul. Fragments from pulpit of Pisa, by Guglielmo da Innspruch. 1158–1162. Alinari phot.

188. CAGLIARI, (Sardinia,), Cattedrale. Lion from pulpit of Pisa. By Guglielmo da Innspruch, 1158–1162. Alinari phot.

189. Pisa, Duomo. Exterior of choir, south side. David. L. W. P. phot.

190. Pisroia, (Firenze), S. Bartolommeo in Pantano. Lintel of portal. Giving the Keys, Apostles and Angels. 1167. Alinari phot.

191. PISTOIA, (Firenze), S. Andrea. Capitals and lintel of portal. Magi before Herod; Adoration; Annunciation to Zacharias; Annunciation. Lintel signed by Gruamonte and Adeodato; capitals by Enrico. Alinari phot.

192. PISTOIA, (Firenze), S. Andrea. Northern impost of portal. Annunciation to
Zacharias; the Visitation. By Enrico. Alinari phot.

193. PISTOIA, (Firenze), S. Andrea. Southern impost of portal. The Annunciation. Signed by Enrico. Alinari phot.

194. VOLTERRA, (Pisa), Duomo. Pulpit, detail. The Last Supper. Lombardi phot.

195. VOLTERRA, (Pisa), Duomo. Pulpit, detail. The Sacrifice of Abraham. Lombardi phot.

196. VOLTERRA, (Pisa), Duomo. Pulpit. Visitation, Annunciation. Lombardi phot.

197. Monte S. Angelo, (Foggia), "Tomba di Rotari." Tympanum of western portal. Deposition, Maries at Tomb. L. W. P. phot.

198. Monte S. Angelo, (Foggia), "Tomba di Rotari," Lintel of western portal, detail. Christ haled to Execution. L. W. P. phot.

199. PISTOIA, (Firenze), S. Giovanni Fuorcivitas. Lintel of portal. The Last Supper. Alinari phot.

200. BARI, S. Niccola. Western portal, southern spandrel. An Angel. A. K. P. phot.

201. TRANI, (Bari), Ognisanti. Narthex. Gabriel of the Annunciation. L. W. P. phot.

202. TRANI, (Bari), Ognisanti. Narthex. Virgin of the Annunciation. L. W. P. phot.

203. TRANI, (Bari), Ognisanti. Narthex. Gabriel of the Annunciation. L. W. P. phot. from cast.

204. TRANI, (Bari), Cattedrale. Western portal, northern jamb. Jacob's Dream.
L. W. P. phot.

205. TRANI, (Bari), Cattedrale. Western portal, northern jamb. Jacob's Dream; Jacob and the Angel.

206. TRANI, (Bari), Cattedrale.. Western portal, northern jamb. Jacob wrestles with the Angel. L. W. P. phot.

207. TRANI, (Bari), Cattedrale. Western portal, podium of northern column.
L. W. P. phot.

208. TRANI, (Bari), Cattedrale. Western portal, southern jamb. A Prophet.
L. W. P. phot.

209. TRANI, (Bari), Cattedrale. Western portal, southern jamb. A Prophet.
L. W. P. phot.

210. Trani, (Bari), Cattedrale. Western portal, southern jamb. Peasant warming his Socks by Fire. L. W. P. phot.

211. TRANI, (Bari), Cattedrale. Western portal, southern jamb. A Siren. L. W. P. phot.

212. TRANI, (Bari), Cattedrale. Western portal, podium of southern column.
L. W. P. phot.

213.　S. Leonardo, (Foggia).　Southern portal, upper zone.　A liberated prisoner
and St. Leonard. L. W. P. phot.

214. S. Leonardo, (Foggia). Tympanum of southern portal. *Majestas Domini.*
L. W. P. phot.

215. SAN LEONARDO, (Foggia). Northern portal, eastern capital. The Adoration of the Magi. L. W. P. phot.

216. SAN LEONARDO, (Foggia). Northern portal, western jamb. Balaam and St.
Michael; a Centaur. L. W. P. phot.

217. Pianella, (Chieti), S. Michele. Detail of pulpit. St. Matthew. A. K. P. phot.
218. Pianella, (Chieti), S. Michele. Lintel of western portal. L. W. P. phot.

219. Torre de' Passeri, (Teramo), S. Clemente di Casauria. Western portal.
St. Clement, St. Phebus, St. Cornelius, the abbot Leonas; Translation of
the Relics of St. Clement; four Prophets. 1176. Alinari phot.

220. TORRE DE' PASSERI, (Teramo), S. Clemente di Casauria. Tympanum of portal. St. Clement, St. Phebus, St. Cornelius, the abbot Leonas; Translation of the Relics of St. Clement. 1176. Alinari phot.

221. TORRE de' PASSERI, (Teramo), S. Clemente di Casauria. Detail of ciborium.
Moscioni phot.

222. S. Casciano, (Pisa). Archivolt of lateral portal. Alinari phot.

223. S. Casciano, (Pisa). Archivolt of western portal. Resurrection of Lazarus;
Entry into Jerusalem. Signed by Biduino. 1180. Alinari phot.

224. Lucca, S. Salvatore. Western portal, lintel. The Infant St. Nicolas stands upright in his Bath. Signed by Biduino. Alinari phot.

225. LUCCA, S. Salvatore. Southern portal, lintel. Dieudonné is transported by St. Nicolas from serving the pagan King to the House of his Parents. Alinari phot.

226. Arcetri, (Firenze), S. Leonardo. Detail of pulpit. Adoration of the Magi; Jesse Tree. Alinari phot.

227. Lucca, S. Giovanni. Western portal. The Virgin, two Angels and ten Apostles. Alinari phot.

228. Pistoia, (Firenze), S. Pietro Maggiore. Lintel of portal. The Giving of the Keys; the Apostles. Alinari phot.

229. GROPPOLI, (Pistoia), Chapel of Villa Dalpina. Detail of pulpit. Flight into Egypt; Nativity. 1194. Alinari phot.

230. GROPPOLI, (Pistoia), Chapel of Villa Dalpina. St. Michael. Alinari phot.

231. Monte S. Angelo, (Foggia), S. Maria Maggiore. Tympanum of western portal. Madonna of the Adoration, Angels, Donors. 1198. L. W. P. phot.

232. BITONTO, (Bari), Cattedrale. Tympanum of western portal. Christ in Limbo, Annunciation, Visitation, Adoration, Presentation. 1200. Moscioni phot.

233. BITONTO, (Bari), Cattedrale. Western portal, tympanum. Christ in Limbo.
1200. A. K. P. phot. from cast.

234. Pistoia, (Firenze), S. Bartolommeo in Pantano. Detail of pulpit. The
Evangelists; Annunciation; Adoration of Magi. By Guido Bigarelli da
Como. Alinari phot.

235. SPOLETO, (Perugia), Cattedrale. Supporting figure of western façade. A. K. P.
     phot.

236. SPOLETO, (Perugia), Cattedrale. Supporting figure of west façade. A. K. P.
     phot.

237. SPOLETO, Chiesa di Ponziano. Western façade, detail of rose-window. St.
       Matthew. L. W. P. phot.
238. SPOLETO, Cattedrale. Western façade, detail of rose-window. St. Matthew.
       A. K. P. phot.

239. SPOLETO, S. Pietro. Western façade, reliefs north of central portal. Death of the Just; Death of the Unjust; the Lion's Paw is caught in the Log; the Man escapes Harm by bowing humbly to the Lion. Anderson phot.

240. TRANI, (Bari), Cattedrale. Southern transept, exterior. St. Luke. L. W. P. phot. from cast.

241. Trani, (Bari), Cattedrale. Southern transept, exterior. St. Luke. L. W. P. phot. from cast.

242. FOGGIA, Cattedrale. Statue in garden behind church. St. Paul. A. K. P.
    phot.

243. FOGGIA, Cattedrale. Statue in garden behind church. St. Matthew. A. K. P.
    phot.

244. BITONTO, (Bari), Cattedrale. Detail of pulpit. Signed by Niccolò, 1229.
Antonelli-Matteuci phot.

245. BITONTO, (Bari), Cattedrale. Stair-rail of pulpit. Frederic II, Yolande, Henry and Conrad. Signed by Niccolò, 1229. Alinari phot.

246. BARGA, (LUCCA). Pulpit. Adoration of Magi; Evangelists; Nativity; Visitation. Alinari phot.

247. Lucca, Cattedrale. Western portal, tympanum. The Ascension. Alinari phot.

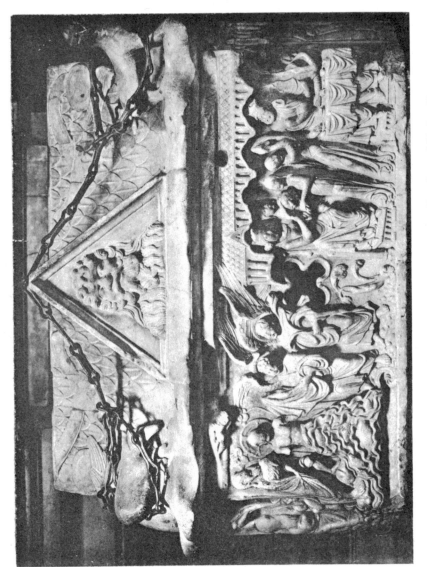

248. GENOVA, Cattedrale. Capella S. Giovanni, Arca. Baptism of Christ; Dance of Salome. Alinari phot.

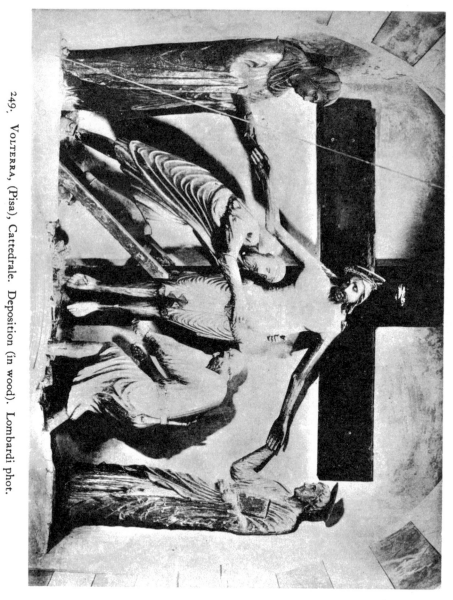

249, VOLTERRA, (Pisa), Cattedrale. Deposition (in wood). Lombardi phot.

250. S. Stefano di Monopoli, (Bari). Tympanum of western portal. Christ, St. Stephen, St. George, donors. 1236. A. K. P. phot.

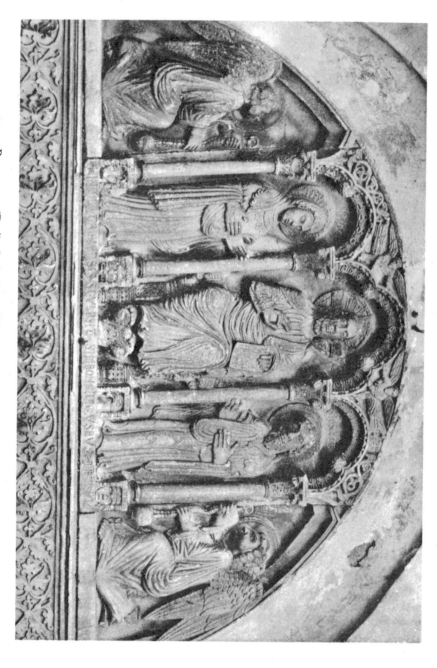

251. BARLETTA, (Bari), S. Andrea. Western portal, tympanum. Deësis. Heads of Evangelists in bases of columns. Signed by Simeon of Ragusa, *incola Tranensis*. A. K. P. phot.

252.   BARLETTA, (Bari), S. Andea. Western portal, north jamb. Virgin, Expulsion,
Temptation. Moscioni phot.

253. BENEVENTO, S. Sofia. Tympanum of portal. Christ, the Virgin(?), St. Theodore and a Donor. A. K. P. phot.

254. GENOVA, Cattedrale. Tympanum of western portal. *Majestas Domini*;
Martyrdom of St. Lawrence. L. W. P. phot.

255. GENOVA, Cattedrale. Central western portal, northern spandrel. L. W. P. phot.

256. GENOVA, Cattedrale. Central western portal, southern spandrel. L. W. P.
phot.

257. GENOVA, Cattedrale. Western portal, northern jamb. The Visitation.
L. W. P. phot.

258. Genova, Cattedrale. Western façade, southern corner. St. John. L. W. P. phot.

259. Rutigliano, (Bari). Northern portal, tympanum. The Madonna and an Angel. L. W. P. phot.

260. TERLIZZI, (Bari), Collegiata. Tympanum now in portal of Chiesa del Rosario. The Last Supper. Signed by Anseramo. 1276. L. W. P. phot. from a cast.

261. Monte S. Angelo, (Foggia), S. Michele. Western portal, tympanum. Madonna, St. Paul and Donor. Signed by Simeon *de hac (urbe)*. 1305. L. W. P. phot.